Reading Disabilities:
Diagnosis and Component Processes

NATO ASI Series

Advanced Science Institutes Series

A Series presenting the results of activities sponsored by the NATO Science Committee, which aims at the dissemination of advanced scientific and technological knowledge, with a view to strengthening links between scientific communities.

The Series is published by an international board of publishers in conjunction with the NATO Scientific Affairs Division

A Life Sciences	Plenum Publishing Corporation
B Physics	London and New York
C Mathematical	Kluwer Academic Publishers
and Physical Sciences	Dordrecht, Boston and London
D Behavioural and Social Sciences	
E Applied Sciences	
F Computer and Systems Sciences	Springer-Verlag
G Ecological Sciences	Berlin, Heidelberg, New York, London,
H Cell Biology	Paris and Tokyo
I Global Environmental Change	

NATO-PCO-DATA BASE

The electronic index to the NATO ASI Series provides full bibliographical references (with keywords and/or abstracts) to more than 30000 contributions from international scientists published in all sections of the NATO ASI Series.
Access to the NATO-PCO-DATA BASE is possible in two ways:

– via online FILE 128 (NATO-PCO-DATA BASE) hosted by ESRIN,
Via Galileo Galilei, I-00044 Frascati, Italy.

– via CD-ROM "NATO-PCO-DATA BASE" with user-friendly retrieval software in English, French and German (© WTV GmbH and DATAWARE Technologies Inc. 1989).

The CD-ROM can be ordered through any member of the Board of Publishers or through NATO-PCO, Overijse, Belgium.

Series D: Behavioural and Social Sciences - Vol. 74

Reading Disabilities: Diagnosis and Component Processes

edited by

R. Malatesha Joshi
College of Education,
Oklahoma State University,
Stillwater, Oklahoma, U.S.A.

and

Che Kan Leong
College of Education,
University of Saskatchewan,
Saskatoon, Saskatchewan, Canada

Kluwer Academic Publishers

Dordrecht / Boston / London

Published in cooperation with NATO Scientific Affairs Division

Proceedings of the NATO Advanced Study Institute on
Differential Diagnosis and Treatments of Reading and Writing Disorders
Château de Bonas, France
September 30 – October 11, 1991

Library of Congress Cataloging-in-Publication Data

```
Reading disabilities : diagnosis and component processes / edited by
R. Malatesha Joshi, Che Kan Leong.
      p.   cm. -- (NATO ASI series.  Series D, Behavioural and social
sciences ; no. 74)
   Papers based on the proceedings of the Advanced Study Institute
(ASI) sponsored by the NATO, held Oct. 1991 near Toulouse, France.
   Includes index.
   ISBN 0-7923-2302-5
   1. Reading disabilities--Congresses.  2. Learning disabled
children--Education--Congresses.  3. Dyslexic children--Education-
-Congresses.  4. Reading--Remedial teaching--Congresses.
5. Language and languages--Orthography and spelling--Congresses.
I. Joshi, R. Malatesha.  II. Leong, Che Kan.  III. Series.
LB1050.5.R382   1993
371.91'44--dc20                                              93-15556
```

ISBN 0-7923-2302-5   707957
                        R

Published by Kluwer Academic Publishers,
P.O. Box 17, 3300 AA Dordrecht, The Netherlands.

Kluwer Academic Publishers incorporates the publishing programmes of
D. Reidel, Martinus Nijhoff, Dr W. Junk and MTP Press.

Sold and distributed in the U.S.A. and Canada
by Kluwer Academic Publishers,
101 Philip Drive, Norwell, MA 02061, U.S.A.

In all other countries, sold and distributed
by Kluwer Academic Publishers Group,
P.O. Box 322, 3300 AH Dordrecht, The Netherlands.

Printed on acid-free paper

Printed in the Netherlands

CONTENTS

Contents

PREFACE

The present volume is based on the proceedings of the Advanced Study Institute (ASI) sponsored by the North Atlantic Treaty Organization (NATO). The Institute was conducted at the beautiful Chateau de Bonas, near Toulouse, France in October, 1991. A number of scholars from different countries participated in the two-week institute on differential diagnosis and treatments of reading and writing problems. The accepted papers for this volume are divided into three sections: (a) Differential diagnosis of reading disabilities; (b) Access to language-related component processes; and (c) Reading/spelling strategies. The other papers appear in a companion volume: Developmental and Acquired Dyslexia: Neuropsychological and Neurolinguistic Perspectives, also coedited by Joshi and Leong and published by Kluwer Academic Publishers.

Several people and organizations have helped us in this endeavor and their assistance is gratefully acknowledged. Our special thanks are due to: the Scientific Affairs Division of NATO for providing the major portion of the financial support; Dr. L. V. da Cunha of NATO and Dr. Tilo Kester and Mrs. Barbara Kester of the International Transfer of Science and Technology (ITST) for their help and support of the various aspects of the institute; Mr. Charles Stockman and the entire staff of the Chateau de Bonas for making our stay a pleasant one by helping us to run the Institute smoothly. We also wish to thank our reviewers and the following people for other assistance: Christi Martin, and Xi-wu Fang.

With the constraint of camera-ready publishing to conserve time and resources, the authors and the coeditors in their various editorial capacities have endeavored to keep the book to a high publication quality. We sincerely hope that readers of the different chapters will "read, mark, learn, and inwardly digest" the complex area of reading disabilities.

R. Malatesha Joshi, Oklahoma State University, U.S.A.
C. K. Leong, University of Saskatchewan, Canada
January, 1993

PART I DIFFERENTIAL DIAGNOSIS OF READING DISABILITIES - - EDITORS' INTRODUCTION

The aim of assessment and diagnosis should be the systematic, critical sampling of behavior and should move from the more molar assessing to the more fine-grained diagnosing for learning. From the early prescient work of Alfred Binet to current theory-based research and clinical studies, diagnosis should emphasize differential cognitive outcomes in a person-process approach within a developmental framework. This emphasis is important for a better understanding of the many-faceted field of learning disabilities (see, for example, Duane & Gray, 1991; Lyon, Gray, Kavanagh, & Krasnegor, 1993; Swanson & Keogh, 1990, Part 1, for details).

Within the above context and directly in the area of reading disabilities, **Stanovich** in this volume and elsewhere reminds us of the multidimensionality of reading disorders and argues forcefully from his and other research evidence for his phonological-core variable-difference model of reading and reading disabilities. This model provides for a strong explanation for unexpected reading failures (in relation to learning aptitude) in developmental dyslexics and other ("garden-variety") poor readers. There is converging evidence to show that children with developmental dyslexia exhibit relatively restricted "modular" (in the Fodorian sense) deficits in phonological processing; whereas "backward" or garden-variety poor readers have less modular, more generalized difficulties in other cognitive and linguistic domains including phonology. This phonological-core variable-difference conception differentiating subgroups of "retarded" and backward readers is supported empirically in a number of studies (see Special Series of Fletcher, 1992).

The explication by Stanovich and forceful argument of **Siegel** in this volume and other places have further alerted theoreticians, researchers and practitioners to the important issue of the role of intelligence measures in defining learning or reading disabilities. Siegel reemphasizes her position of the irrelevance of intelligence test scores in diagnosing reading disabilities. She shows from her studies that developmental dyslexics, as traditionally defined by IQ-reading performance discrepancies, and garden-variety poor readers with discrepant reading from chronological-age controls, perform similarly on a number of cognitive and linguistic tasks, although both groups lag behind normal readers. There is further, recent support from different samples of children for the existence of reading disabilities on a continuum (Fletcher, 1992, but see also Duane & Gray, 1991 for the biological determinants of dyslexia). Siegel also draws on the powerful Matthew effects of Stanovich of the reciprocal reading-intelligence connection to buttress her argument.

However, from the research and service delivery perspectives, **Leong** in this volume and elsewhere suggests that there may still be a place for general ability tests based on process-oriented components of ability, not so much product-oriented psychometric tests, as yardsticks for learning aptitude and that high IQ and low achieving children should all receive appropriate special education treatment (Fletcher, 1992; Swanson & Keogh, 1990). Leong further suggests a two-stage quantitative and qualitative approach to the assessment and diagnosis of children with reading disorders. He is in agreement with Stanovich, Siegel and others (see also Parts II & III of this volume) on the diagnostic efficacy of pseudoword reading, but would like to see a broader

1

R.M. Joshi and C.K. Leong (eds.), Reading Disabilities: Diagnosis and Component Processes, 1–2.
© 1993 *Kluwer Academic Publishers. Printed in the Netherlands.*

sampling of pseudowords and the inclusion of exception words and morphological and morphemic elements in lexical processing. This more comprehensive sampling aims at tapping lexical representation and should delineate more clearly component processes in diagnosis (see also Berninger & Hart, this volume).

As an alternative to IQ measures Stanovich endorses the use of listening comprehension tests as a general ability control to isolate modular deficits and to explain better "unexplained" or unexpected reading problems (see also Tunmer & Hoover in this volume). To this Siegel gives a summary equivocal answer. Leong takes up the challenge of the strong (Stanovich) argument and the lukewarm (Siegel) view regarding the role of listening comprehension tests in reading diagnosis. He reviews the psycholinguistic literature and empirical evidence on the analogous reading and "auding" (listening to text to gain knowledge) processes. From his research with the text-to-speech (DECtalk) computer system with readers, he proposes the rapprochement of simultaneous on-line reading and DECtalk auding for both written and oral language comprehension as efficacious in diagnosing and enhancing reading/listening comprehension.

Moving from conceptual and methodological issues, we are reminded by **Afflerbach** of the importance of constructing meaning from diagnostic reports and of extracting information useful to teachers, parents and students. From a different perspective, **Berninger and Hart** argue convincingly for individual profiles with "absolute", "relative" or combined absolute and relative criteria across developmental and reading and writing skills to complement group, quantitative data from complex statistical analyses. They emphasize the need to examine data from both individual and group analyses to understand better multiple etiologies of developmental processes contributing to academic achievement disorders and for greater clinical utility.

As enjoined by Binet many years ago "After the evil, the remedy", the authors in this Part and elsewhere all agree implicitly or explicitly that differential diagnosis should lead to more efficient and effective prognosis and treatment.

REFERENCES

Duane, D.D., & Gray, D.B. (Eds.). (1991). *The reading brain: The biological basis of dyslexia.* Parkton, MD: York Press.

Fletcher, J.M. (1992). The validity of distinguishing children with language and learning disabilities according to discrepancies with IQ: Introduction to the Special Series [Special Series]. *Journal of Learning Disabilities, 25,* 546-573; 618-648.

Lyon, G.R., Gray, D.B., Kavanagh, J.F., & Krasnegor, N.A. (Eds.). (1993). *Better understanding learning disabilities: New views from research and their implications for education and public policies.* Baltimore, MD: Paul H. Brookes.

Swanson, H.L., & Keogh, B. (Eds.). (1990). *Learning disabilities: Theoretical and research issues.* Hillsdale, NJ: Lawrence Erlbaum.

PROBLEMS IN THE DIFFERENTIAL DIAGNOSIS OF READING DISABILITIES

KEITH E. STANOVICH
Ontario Institute for Studies in Education
252 Bloor Street West
Toronto, Ontario
Canada M5S 1V6

ABSTRACT: Current definitions of reading disability and/or dyslexia all involve the assessment of a discrepancy between reading ability and measured intelligence. These discrepancy definitions carry the implicit assumption that the reading difficulties of the dyslexic stem from problems different from those characterizing the poor reader without IQ discrepancy. The phonological-core variable difference model is a framework for interpreting the evidence on the cognitive differentiability of poor readers of different types. The model and empirical data pertinent to it are discussed. Scientific and educational classification procedures that follow from the model are described. Problems with the use of intelligence test scores as aptitude benchmarks in the measurement of discrepancy are discussed. Finally, it is argued that procedures of discrepancy assessment, including those proposed here, are threatened by findings that the acquisition of literacy fosters the very cognitive skills assessed by aptitude measures.

During the 1960s and 1970s, several proposed definitions of reading disability had considerable influence on both research and service delivery debates. The definition of the World Federation of Neurology had many features that became canonical for many researchers and practitioners. Specific developmental dyslexia was characterized as, "A disorder manifested by difficulty in learning to read despite conventional instruction, adequate intelligence, and sociocultural opportunity. It is dependent upon fundamental cognitive abilities which are frequently of constitutional origin" (Critchley, 1970).

This particular definition highlighted the well-known "exclusionary criteria" that subsequently caused so much dispute in discussions of dyslexia (e.g., Applebee, 1971; Ceci, 1986; Doehring, 1978; Eisenberg, 1978; Rutter, 1978)--in particular it requires "adequate" intelligence to qualify for the dyslexia label. These exclusionary criteria were carried over into the definitions of learning disability employed in many different countries--for example, in the landmark Education for All Handicapped Children Act passed by the US Congress in 1975. Again, the exclusion of poor reading achievement due to mental retardation in that definition highlights the requirement of a mismatch between aptitude and achievement. The US National Joint Committee on Learning Disabilities responded to criticisms of the exclusionary criteria by emphasizing that the mere presence of other impairments or of environmental deprivation should not exclude children from the LD categorization (see also, Kavanagh & Truss, 1988).

Nevertheless, all of these professional and legal definitions highlight the same salient feature: The fact that a dyslexic child has an "unexpected" disability in the domain of reading,

3

R.M. Joshi and C.K. Leong (eds.), Reading Disabilities: Diagnosis and Component Processes, 3–31.
© 1993 *Kluwer Academic Publishers. Printed in the Netherlands.*

one not predicted by their general intellectual competence and socioeducational opportunities. Practically, this has meant a statistical assessment of the difference between their objectively measured reading ability and general intelligence (Frankenberger Fronzaglio, 1991; Frankenberger & Harper, 1987; Kavale, 1987; Kavale & Nye, 1981; Reynolds, 1985; Shepard, 1980). Typically, very little effort is expended in ascertaining whether adequate instruction has been provided or whether the child suffers from sociocultural disadvantage--in short, in ascertaining whether the disability is "intrinsic to the individual."   So much conceptual confusion has surrounded the more operational discrepancy criterion that researchers and practitioners have been reluctant to take on the potential additional complications of the other criteria. In short, despite repeated admonitions that the diagnosis of reading disability should be multidimensional (Johnson, 1988; McKinney, 1987; Senf, 1986; Tindal & Marston, 1986), in actual educational and clinical practice it is the assessment of a discrepancy between aptitude as measured by an individually administered intelligence test and reading achievement that is the key defining feature (Frankenberger & Fronzaglio, 1991). In identifying their samples, researchers have typically followed the lead of practitioners in this respect.

Dyslexia: Issues of Construct validity

The choice of IQ test performance as the baseline from which to measure achievement discrepancies was accepted by teachers, schools, professional organizations, and government agencies in the absence of much critical discussion or research evidence. Indeed, until quite recently, the researchers themselves seem not to have grappled very seriously with the question of why the benchmark should have been IQ. It is thus not surprising that the concept of intelligence is the genesis of so many of the conceptual paradoxes that plague the concept of dyslexia and that the use of IQ in the differential diagnosis of reading disability has been called into question (Aaron, 1991; Rispens, van Yeren, & van Duijn, 1991; Seidenberg, Bruck, Fornarolo, & Backman, 1986; Share, McGee, & Silva, 1989; Siegel, 1988, 1989; Stanovich, 1991a).

However, advocates of current practices might counter some of these criticisms by arguing that, despite conceptual difficulties, a strictly empirical orientation would support current procedures. That is, an advocate of the status quo might argue that all of the philosophical and conceptual criticisms are beside the point, because measuring discrepancy from IQ in the current manner distinguishes a group of children who, cognitively and behaviorally, are sufficiently distinct that the use of current procedures is justified on an empirical basis. Here we are getting to the heart of many recent research disputes.

The critical assumption that has fueled theoretical interest in the dyslexia concept from the beginning--and that has justified differential educational classification and treatment--has been that the degree of discrepancy from IQ is meaningful: That the reading difficulties of the dyslexic (I am here using the term dyslexic to signify a discrepancy-defined child) stem from problems different from those characterizing the poor reader without IQ discrepancy, the so-called "garden variety" poor reader (to use Gough & Tunmer's [1986] term); or, alternatively, if they stem from the same factors, that the degree of severity is so extreme for this dyslexic that it constitutes, in effect, a qualitative difference.

The operationalization of this assumption for purposes of empirical tests has been dominated by two different research designs. One is the reading-level match design, where an older group of dyslexic children is matched on reading level with a younger group of nondyslexic children and the cognitive profiles of the two groups are compared. The logic here is fairly straightforward. If the reading-related cognitive profiles of the two groups do not match, then it would seem that they are arriving at their similar reading levels via different routes. In contrast, if the reading subskill profiles of the two groups are identical, this would seem to undermine the rationale for the theoretical differentiation of dyslexic children. If dyslexic children are reading just like any other child who happens to be at their reading level, and are using the same cognitive skills to do so, they become much less interesting from a theoretical point of view.

The second major design--one pertinent not only to theoretical issues but also one quite relevant to the educational politics of reading disability--is to compare dyslexic children with children of the same age who are reading at the same level, but who are not labeled dyslexic and who of course have lower IQs. Adapting the terminology of Gough & Tunmer (1986), I have termed this design the "garden-variety control" design. Again, the inferences drawn are relatively straightforward. If the reading subskill profiles of the two groups do not match, then this is at least consistent with the assumption that they are arriving at their similar reading levels via different routes. In contrast, if the reading subskill profiles of the two groups are identical, this would certainly undermine the rationale for the differential educational treatment of dyslexic children and would again make dyslexic children considerably less interesting theoretically.

Before summarizing the current state of the evidence on the cognitive differentiability of dyslexic poor readers using these two designs, I will outline what patterns, given our current conceptions of dyslexia, our data should show, in the best of all possible worlds. I have summarized the idealized situation in a model that I have termed the phonological-core variable-difference framework (Stanovich, 1988a).

The Phonological-Core Variable-Difference Model

The model rests on a clear understanding of the assumption of specificity in definitions of dyslexia (Stanovich, 1986a). This assumption underlies all discussions of the concept of dyslexia, even if it is not explicitly stated. It is the idea that a child with this type of learning disability has a brain/cognitive deficit that is reasonably specific to the reading task. That is, the concept of dyslexia requires that the deficits displayed by such children not extend too far into other domains of cognitive functioning. If they did, this would depress the constellation of abilities we call intelligence and thus reduce the reading/intelligence discrepancy that is central to all current definitions.

In short, the key deficit in dyslexia must be a vertical faculty rather than a horizontal faculty--a domain-specific process rather than a process that operates across a wide variety of domains. For this, and other reasons, many investigators have located the proximal locus of dyslexia at the word recognition level (e.g., Bruck, 1988, 1990; Gough & Tunmer, 1986; Morrison, 1984, 1987; Perfetti, 1985; Siegel, 1985, 1988; Siegel & Faux, 1989; Stanovich, 1986b, 1988b) and have been searching for the locus of the flaw in the word recognition module.

Research in the last ten years has focused intensively on phonological processing abilities. It is now well established that dyslexic children display deficits in various aspects of phonological processing. They have difficulty making explicit reports about sound segments at the phoneme level, they display naming difficulties, their utilization of phonological codes in short-term memory is inefficient, their categorical perception of certain phonemes may be other than normal, and they may have speech production difficulties (Ackerman, Dykman, & Gardner, 1990; Bruck & Treiman, 1990; Cossu, Shankweiler, Liberman, Katz, & Tola, 1988; Hurford & Sanders, 1990; Kamhi & Catts, 1989; Liberman & Shankweiler, 1985; Lieberman, Meskill, Chatillon, & Schupack, 1985; Mann, 1986; Pennington, 1986; Pratt & Brady, 1988; Reed, 1989; Snowling, 1987; Taylor, Lean, & Schwartz, 1989; Wagner & Torgesen, 1987; Werker & Tees, 1987; Williams, 1984, 1986; Wolf, 1991). Importantly, there is increasing evidence that the linkage from phonological processing ability to reading skill is a causal one (Adams, 1990; Ball & Blachman, 1991; Blachman, 1989; Bradley & Bryant, 1985; Bryant, Bradley, Maclean, & Crossland, 1989; Cunningham, 1990; Lie, 1991; Lundberg,, Frost, & Petersen, 1988; Lundberg & Høien, 1989; Maclean, Bryant, & Bradley, 1987; Perfetti, Beck, Bell, & Hughes, 1987; Stanovich, 1986b, 1988b; Treiman & Baron, 1983; Wagner & Torgesen, 1987). Whether all of these phonologically related deficits are reflective of a single underlying processing problem and whether all of them can be considered causal or are instead correlates is a matter for future research, but some important progress is being made on this issue (e.g., Pennington, Van Orden, Smith, Green, & Haith, 1990).

In the phonological-core variable-difference model (Stanovich, 1988a), the term variable difference refers to the key performance contrasts between the garden-variety and the dyslexic poor reader *outside* of the phonological domain. Research has indicated that the cognitive status of the garden-variety poor reader appears to be well described by a developmental lag model. Cognitively, they are remarkably similar to younger children reading at the same level (Stanovich, Nathan, & Vala-Rossi, 1986; Stanovich, Nathan, & Zolman, 1988). A logical corollary of this pattern is that the garden-variety reader will have a wide variety of cognitive deficits when compared to chronological-age controls who are reading at normal levels. However, it is important to understand that the garden-variety poor reader does share the phonological problems of the dyslexic reader, and these deficits appear also to be a causal factor in their poor reading (Juel, 1988; Juel, Griffith, & Gough, 1986; Perfetti, 1985; Stanovich, 1986b). But for the garden-variety reader the deficits--relative to CA controls--extend into a variety of domains (see Ellis & Large, 1987) and some of these (e.g., vocabulary, language comprehension) may also be causally linked to reading comprehension. Such a pattern should not characterize the dyslexic, who should have a deficit localized in the phonological core.

The phonological-core variable-difference model assumes multidimensional continuity for reading ability in general and for all its related cognitive subskills. There is considerable evidence from a variety of different sources supporting such a continuity assumption (Ellis, 1985; Jorm, 1983; Olson, Kliegl, Davidson, & Foltz, 1985; Scarborough, 1984; Seidenberg, et al., 1985; Share, McGee, McKenzie, Williams, & Silva, 1987; Silva, McGee, Williams, 1985; Vogler, Baker, Decker, DeFries, & Huizinga, 1989). However, the fact that the distribution is a graded continuum does not necessarily render the concept of dyslexia scientifically useless, as some critics charge. Ellis (1985) has argued that the proper analogy for dyslexia is obesity. Everyone agrees that the latter condition is a very real health problem, despite the fact that it is operationally defined in a somewhat arbitrary way by choosing a criterion in a continuous distribution.

The framework of the phonological-core variable-difference model meshes nicely with the multidimensional continuum notion. Consider the following characterization: As we move in the multidimensional space of individual differences in cognitive subskills--from the dyslexic to the garden-variety poor reader--we will move from a processing deficit localized in the phonological core to the global deficits of the developmentally lagging garden-variety poor reader. Thus, the actual cognitive differences that are displayed will be variable depending upon the type of poor reader who is the focus of the investigation. The differences on one end of the continuum will consist of deficits located only in the phonological core (the dyslexic) and will increase in number as we run through the intermediate cases that are less and less likely to pass strict psychometric criteria for dyslexia. Eventually we will reach the part of the multidimensional space containing relatively "pure" garden-variety poor readers who will not qualify for the label dyslexic (by either regression or exclusionary criteria), will have a host of cognitive deficits, and will have the cognitively immature profile of a developmentally lagging individual.

This framework provides an explanation for why almost all processing investigations of dyslexia have uncovered phonological deficits, but also why some investigations have found deficits in many other areas as well (see Stanovich, 1986b)--a finding which is paradoxical if one takes the definition of dyslexia seriously. But this outcome can, with some additional assumptions, be explained by the phonological-core variable-difference model which posits that virtually all poor readers have a phonological deficit, but that other processing deficits emerge as one drifts in the multidimensional space from "pure" dyslexics toward garden-variety poor readers. Thus, the model's straightforward prediction is that those studies that revealed a more isolated deficit will be those that had more psychometrically select dyslexic readers. Or to state the model's prediction in another way: The reading/IQ discrepancy of the subject populations should be significantly greater in those studies displaying more specific deficits. Presumably, studies finding deficits extending beyond the phonological domain are in the "fuzzy" area of the multidimensional space and are picking up the increasing number of processing differences that extend beyond the phonological domain as one moves toward the garden-variety area of the space.

The phonological-core variable-difference model provides a parsimonious but realistic way of conceptualizing the idea of dyslexia. The model preserves at least some of the clinical insights of practitioners within the learning disabilities field who prefer traditional assumptions; yet its emphasis on continuity removes some of the more objectionable features of the term dyslexia--features which have actually stigmatized the term within some reading research subcommunities. Of course, the true test is the state of the empirical evidence on the model and it is to this that we now turn.

The Issue of Visual/Orthographic Deficits in Dyslexia

An important issue that must be dealt with is the validity of the simplifying assumption implicit in the phonological-core model: that the key deficits lie only in the phonological domain. Most certainly this assumption represents an oversimplification, because there is some evidence indicating that there may be utility in distinguishing a group of dyslexics who have severe problems in accessing the lexicon on a visual/orthographic basis. Suggestive evidence comes from the work on acquired reading disability that has revealed the existence of surface dyslexia (Patterson, Marshall, & Coltheart, 1985), a condition where the affected individual appears to have difficulty forming and/or accessing orthographic representations of words in memory. However, the interpretation of these cases has recently been somewhat clouded by claims that the performance patterns can be simulated by connectionist models without the dual-route architectures that in some sense define a separable concept of orthographic processing (Seidenberg & McClelland, 1989).

Nevertheless, further indirect evidence for an additional processing deficit--perhaps one in the visual/orthographic domain--comes from multivariate investigations indicating that efficient phonological processing is a necessary but not sufficient condition for attaining advanced levels of word recognition skill (Juel, Griffith, & Gough, 1986; Tunmer & Nesdale, 1985). If efficient phonological processing ability is a necessary but not sufficient condition for rapid reading acquisition this suggests that there must be at least one other sticking point for some children--let's call this factor X, so as to be at least temporarily noncommittal.

Two cautions are immediately in order here. First, there is a body of evidence indicating that the group of children with a factor X deficit must be numerically quite smaller than the group with phonological difficulties (Aaron, 1989a; Freebody & Byrne, 1988; Gough & Hillinger, 1980; Liberman, 1982; Liberman & Shankweiler, 1985; Pennington, 1986; Perfetti, 1985; Vellutino, 1979). One reason they must be very small in number is that they have not obscured the identification of phonological problems in samples that were not preselected for subtypes--a point to which we will return.

Secondly, if we identify factor X as problems in the visual/orthographic domain, these problems must be not at all similar to the "visual perception" problems popularized in the early history of the study of dyslexia--reversals and so forth (see Aman & Singh, 1983; Morrison, Giordani, & Nagy, 1977; Stanovich, 1986a; Vellutino, 1979). The actual problems in visual/orthographic processing must be much more subtle and localized than these older views suggested. However, there does exist some evidence from visual recognition experiments using nonverbal stimuli, brief presentations, and precise psychophysical procedures that does indicate subtle and localized visual processing problems (Lovegrove, Martin, & Slaghuis, 1986; Lovegrove & Slaghuis, 1989; Slaghuis & Lovegrove, 1985, 1987). However, most of these studies employ only chronological-age controls, and many of the reports appear in the psychophysical literature where it is not as customary to give a detailed description of the subject sample. Thus, the psychometric characteristics of the dyslexic sample are often sparsely reported and inadequate by the standards of accepted practice in the field of learning disabilities--a fact that has impeded the integration of these findings into mainstream theory.

But, most importantly, these experiments, as they stand, represent little more than demonstrations. They are the equivalent of the now classic paper by Liberman, Shankweiler, Fischer, and Carter (1974) showing the striking developmental trend on the phoneme tapping task that so excited experimental interest. But the Liberman et al. (1974) demonstration was just that--a demonstration. It was left to later work (a good deal of it by the Haskins group itself, of course) to determine the causal and correlative linkages of phonological skills to reading ability--a task that, dozens, if not hundreds of studies later, is still ongoing. The tough part always comes later--and is a much more arduous and drawn out procedure because we are a science that depends inordinately on converging evidence.

The reason why we are so dependent on converging evidence, rather than critical individual experiments is not hard to discern. Experiments in psychology are usually of fairly low diagnostically. That is, the data that support a given theory usually only rule out a small set of alternative explanations, leaving many additional theories as viable candidates. As a result, strong conclusions are usually only possible after data from a very large number of studies have been collected and compared. As Horace Judson (1979) notes in his book on the history of genetics and molecular biology, *The Eighth Day of Creation,* it took over 10 years of inconclusive experimentation for scientists to change their view about whether genes were made of protein or nucleic acid. We should not be surprised that it took over twice as long to arrive at whatever mild consensus we have on the role of phonological processes in reading. Such a time line suggests that we are in the very early stages indeed of our understanding of the visual processing differences suggested by the work of the Lovegrove group--a stage in which great caution is in order.

Consider a comparison of the state of the converging evidence *vis a vis* visual versus phonological-core deficit theories. The body of converging evidence in the area of phonological processing is basically of four types. Starting with the weakest evidence first: it has been shown that phonological awareness measured prior to reading instruction predicts early reading acquisition (e.g., Bradley & Bryant, 1985; Fox & Routh, 1975; Maclean, Bryant, & Bradley, 1987; Share, Jorm, Maclean, & Matthews, 1986; Williams, 1984). Additionally, there are some longitudinal studies where crosslagged correlational methods and/or structural equation modeling have been employed and have led to the conclusion that the development of phonological awareness leads to superior reading achievement, even when the link from reading to phonological awareness is partialed out (e.g., Perfetti, Beck, & Hughes, 1987; Torneus, 1984). A third class of evidence comes from studies employing the reading-level match designs (Bradley & Bryant, 1983; Olson et al., 1985). Finally, and of course most convincing, are the results of several studies where phonological skills were manipulated via training and resulted in significant experimental group advantages in reading, word recognition, and spelling (Ball & Blachman, 1991; Blachman, 1989; Bradley & Bryant, 1985; Cunningham, 1990; Lie, 1991; Lundberg, Frost, & Peterson, 1988; Treiman & Baron, 1983).

Thus, there are four classes of evidence that have suggested a causal role for phonological awareness in early reading acquisition: the early predictiveness of phonological awareness, cross-lagged longitudinal designs, reading-level match designs, and experimental studies where the skill has been manipulated via training. This increasing and converging body of evidence on phonological processing is what has so excited researchers studying individual differences in reading acquisition. There simply is not commensurately strong evidence on causal linkages involving visual processes.

It should be noted that there are certain arguments commonly made by visual deficit theorists that are not in dispute but that do need to be put in context. For example, the argument that visual deficits might coexist with phonological deficits is certainly not fallacious. However, the point then will be to determine whether the visual performance deficits reflect a mechanism that itself is a cause of reading disability. Thus, it will be easier to garner support for visual deficit theories if such deficits do not always co-occur with phonological or verbal problems. For example, it would be convincing to demonstrate that a group of pre-kindergarten children with better than average phonological awareness but *with* visual processing deficits developed into children with reading disabilities. This convincing evidence will not be obtainable if the two processing problems always co-occur.

Proponents of visual deficit theories often accuse investigators emphasizing phonological processing theories of ignoring the possibility of subtypes. I fully agree that we should continue the search for reliably obtainable subgroups of reading disabled children. However, I wish to point to an important asymmetry in the research literature that serves to explain some of the seeming disagreement among reading disabilities researchers on this issue. Most investigators would agree that the following generalization holds pretty well: Those investigators who champion the role of verbal or phonological factors in reading tend not to concern themselves with the subtype issue; whereas investigators supporting the visual deficit hypothesis tend to emphasize the issue of subtypes.

There may be many reasons for this correlation, but I believe that at least part of the reason resides in the fact that the subtypes argument is quite often put forth as an alternative hypothesis to explain null findings in the area of visual processing. The argument--which I have often heard, and it should be noted, do not disagree with--is that in heterogeneous groupings of reading disabled children, the visual processing problems of a small group of children with visual deficits will get swamped when the subgroup is combined with other groups of children with language and phonological deficits. This argument is correct and logical. But we must note a certain asymmetry here. Investigators examining the hypothesis that there is a phonolooical problem do not have a similar worry. That is, they are not concerned that the speech segmentation performance of the children with phonological problems will be statistically diluted by their being grouped together within a heterogeneous sample including children with visual problems. In short, phonological problems are so large in number that they can be detected even under the most disadvantageous sampling conditions.

This, of course, is *not* an argument against the idea of a visual subtype, but it does argue that there must be some restrictive quantitative boundaries on our estimates of this subtype. For example, years ago Bodor (1973) found many more dysphonetics than dyseidetics in her clinical sample and many other theorists have suggested that the visual subtype is considerably smaller than the language/phonological subtypes (Aaron, 1989a; Freebody & Byrne, 1988; Gough & Hillinger, 1980; Liberman, 1982; Liberman & Shankweiler, 1985; Pennington, 1986; Perfetti, 1985; Vellutino, 1979). But the place of numbers in these disputes is not irrelevant, because therein lies part of the reason for the controversy in the literature and why investigators in the various "camps" have had trouble reaching a rapprochement. The phonological deficit theorists often seem at first to admit that there is a small group of children with visual problems, but then easily slip in their writings into the assumption that they are entirely nonexistent. This understandably raises the ire of the visual deficit theorists. However, the latter are guilty of the same escalation by stealth. Their talk of a small subgroup of children with visual problems often graduates into an argument that large numbers of children are characterized by such a problem or that such children are "typical"-- language which teachers quite naturally translate to mean "most common". Thus, an underlying agreement grows into a full fledged controversy because both sides slip into defending their inflated claims.

We may, in fact, be at a critical juncture of choice in the dyslexia research community. The next major breakthrough in dyslexia research may well hinge on whether investigators with differing hypotheses can actually begin to work together--or at least cooperate in the sense of agreeing to help in external tests of their hypotheses by, for example, agreeing on a common methodology for the study of visual processing deficits that is easily portable to other laboratories. Otherwise, I see the potential for us to arrive at the same type of standoff that characterizes ESP research: Believers won't agree that their hypothesis is mistaken and skeptics won't agree that the believers' data have passed the requisite tests. Some may think that this analogy is forced, but I submit that the current climate of tightly intertwined investigators collecting around their own hypotheses and paradigms and publishing in journals that are largely read by themselves is approaching that stage already.

Empirical Tests of the Cognitive Differentiability of Dyslexic Children

Having outlined the basis for the major simplifying assumption of the phonological-core variable-difference model we will now survey the state of the evidence with a particular focus on the two research designs that I outlined previously--the reading level match and the garden-variety control design. In order to consider the pattern of results here we must make one final distinction. This distinction concerns what particular measure of reading that we wish to use to match the groups. A certain fuzziness on this point confused the literature on the reading-level match in the mid 1980s (see Stanovich et al., 1988). In particular, it must be specified whether the groups are to be matched on reading comprehension or on word recognition, because the use one of or the other of these two matches means that one is asking somewhat different questions.

I will turn first to reading comprehension match. The phonological-core model predicts that, when compared to reading level or garden variety controls, discrepancy defined dyslexic children should display a pattern that could be characterized as macrocompensation--tradeoffs among global processes that result in equivalent reading comprehension. The predicted pattern derives for the following reasons. First, the two groups will presumably be close in intelligence, IQ being a matching variable in most reading level studies. Of course, similar intelligence test scores at different ages mean different things in terms of the raw score or absolute level of performance on a given test or index of ability. Thus, when older dyslexics are matched with younger children progressing normally in reading, the former will have higher raw scores on the intelligence measure. It should then also be the case that the dyslexics will score higher on any cognitive task that is correlated with the raw score on the intelligence test, and of course there are a host of such tasks. This has implications for the expected outcome in a comprehension match design.

The argument goes as follows. The assumption of specificity dictates that dyslexics lag in a relatively modular, vertical faculty--probably phonological sensitivity--and, as a result, their reading progress also lags. But on any "horizontal faculty"--cognitive processes operating across a variety of domains like metacognitive awareness, problem solving, and higher-level language skills--the dyslexic should outperform the younger children (due to a higher mental age). However, when the reading test is a comprehension test, rather than a word recognition measure, the comprehension requirements of the test will implicate many of these higher-level processes. Thus, the psychometric constraints imposed by the matching in a comprehension level investigation dictate that a rigorously-defined sample of reading-disabled children should display performance inferior to the younger comprehension-matched children on phonological analysis and phonological coding skills, but should simultaneously display superior vocabulary, real-world knowledge, and/or strategic abilities (i.e., superior performance on other variables that should be correlated with the raw score on the IQ test). The similar overall level of comprehension ability in the two groups presumably obtains because the dyslexic children use these other skills and knowledge sources to compensate for seriously deficient phonological processing skills. The same pattern of macrocompensation should characterize comparisons of discrepancy-defined dyslexics and garden variety poor readers of the same age, for exactly the same reasons. In short, the interrelations of the processes that determine reading comprehension should be different when dyslexics are compared to either garden variety or comprehension-level equated younger children.

The actual evidence here is fairly clearcut in the case of the comprehension-level match; less so in the case of the garden variety control. Several studies have found the pattern of macro-compensation in comprehension-level designs (Bloom et al., 1980; Bruck, 1988; Fredman & Stevenson 1988; Seidenberg et al., 1985): poorer word recognition and phonological skills but superior "horizontal faculties" on the part of the dyslexics. The data here are fairly consistent. In the case of garden-variety comprehension match studies, there are data indicating macro-compensation (see Bloom et al., 1980; Ellis & Large, 1987; Jorm et al., 1986; Silva et al., 1985). However, there exist other contradictory data. The problems appear in studies that have employed word recognition matches and garden variety controls. A word recognition match study can serve as an indirect test of macro-compensation if a reading comprehension test is included in the study. Dyslexics, matched with garden-variety poor readers on word recognition skill should display superior reading comprehension. Siegel (1988) presents such a comparison from her extensive data-base on reading disabled and nondisabled children. In her data there is no indication of macro-compensation: Dyslexics and garden variety readers matched on word recognition skill perform similarly on a reading comprehension test.

Thus, we can summarize the evidence as follows. As regards macro-compensation, there is evidence that the pattern of abilities leading to a given level of comprehension is different for dyslexics when compared to younger children with similar levels of reading comprehension. However, although there is some supportive data, it has yet to be unequivocally established that the pattern of abilities leading to a given level of comprehension is different for dyslexics when compared to similarly aged poor readers without IQ discrepancy.

However, it is important to note that even if compensatory processing does characterize the comprehension patterns of dyslexic children, this does not necessarily guarantee the applicability of an analogous explanation of similar levels of decoding in a word recognition match. That is, it is perfectly possible that the comprehension ability of disabled readers is determined by compensatory processing (relative to younger comprehension controls), but that the operation of their word recognition modules is similar (in terms of regularity effects, orthographic processing, context effects, etc.) when compared to younger word recognition controls. Note that from the compensatory hypothesis it follows that the word recognition match controls for an older disabled group of readers will not completely overlap with the disabled group's comprehension controls,

We turn now to studies employing word level matches in order to study the organization of processes within the word recognition module itself. Here the phonological-core model predicts another tradeoff among relative strengths of processes--what we might call a micro-compensation, in order to differentiate it from the macro-compensation hypothesized to occur in the case of general reading comprehension. Specifically, for the majority of dyslexics with a phonological deficit, a word recognition match with a younger group of nondyslexic controls should reveal another patterns of ability tradeoffs: deficits in phonological sensitivity and in the phonological mechanisms that mediate lexical access, but superior orthographic processing and storage mechanisms. A similar pattern should hold when dyslexics are compared to a same-age garden-variety poor reader group.

Turning first to the results from word-level designs. Not too many years ago, this literature was a confusing mass of contradictions. However, Rack, Snowling, and Olson (1992) have recently completed a meta-analysis of these studies that explains some of the discrepancies in the literature.

It appears that dyslexic children, when matched with younger children on word recognition ability will display inferior phonological coding skills, particularly so in the case of pseudoword naming. This conclusion is based on data from dozens of subjects collected by numerous investigators from several different continents (Aaron, 1989b; Baddeley, Ellis, Miles, & Lewis, 1982; Bradley & Bryant, 1978; Bruck, 1990; Holligan & Johnston, 1988; Kochnower, Richardson, & DiBenedetto, 1983; Lundberg & Høien, 1989; Olson et al., 1985; Olson, Wise, Conners, Rack, & Fulker, 1989; Siegel & Faux, 1989; Siegel & Ryan, 1988; Snowling, 1980, 1981; Snowling, Stackhouse, & Rack, 1986). It is true that there are some exceptions to the pattern (Baddeley, Logie, & Ellis, 1988; Beech & Harding, 1984; Bruck, 1988; Treiman & Hirsh-Pasek, 1985; Vellutino & Scanlon, 1987), but most of these can be explained by a variety of factors that Rack, Snowling, and Olson (1992) discuss in their meta-analysis. For example, the nature of the words on the word recognition test must be carefully considered, as must the pseudowords used in the nonword naming test.

Additionally, some studies have demonstrated that dyslexic children perform relatively better on orthographic processing tasks than they do on phonological processing tasks when compared with younger nondyslexic readers matched on word recognition skill (Olson et al., 1985; Pennington et al., 1986; Siegel, in press). These studies give some hints at what the nature of the micro-compensation might be. Dyslexic readers, despite inferior phonological skills, appear to maintain word recognition levels equal to their younger nondyslexic controls because they have better orthographic representations in their lexicon and/or are better at accessing such representations (perhaps because they have had more print exposure, see Cunningham & Stanovich, 1990, 1991; Stanovich & West, 1989; Stanovich & Cunningham, 1992).

Thus, there is evidence for a different organization of cognitive skills within the word recognition module when dyslexics are compared to younger normals. However, when we turn our attention to studies employing garden-variety matches, where we would expect a similar type of micro-compensation--if that is, the concept of discrepancy-defined dyslexia has construct validity--we find something very puzzling indeed. The literature provides no strong support for a differential organization of cognitive subskills within the word recognition module among readers of different IQ levels. The results in the literature are, instead, quite inconsistent. Several studies have failed to find differences in tasks tapping word recognition subprocesses such as pseudoword naming, regular word naming, exception word naming, phonological choice tasks, and orthographic choice tasks (Fredman & Stevenson, 1988; Share et al., 1987a; Siegel, 1988). Additionally, Olson, Wise, Conners, and Rack (1990) have failed to find a correlation between degree of discrepancy within their sample of dyslexic twins and the degree of phonological deficit, a statistical test not quite equivalent to a garden-variety control design but troublesome nonetheless.

It is interesting to note that both Olson (Olson et al., 1985; Olson et al., 1990) and Siegel (1988; in press) have found a mismatch in processing abilities between dyslexics and younger word-level controls but no such mismatch between dyslexics and poor readers across the IQ range. Recall also that earlier, when discussing comprehension-level matches, it was also concluded that the evidence for macro-compensation was greater in studies employing younger comprehension-controls as opposed to garden-variety controls. Age thus appears to be a better predictor of the reorganization cognitive skills in reading than does IQ. Or, rather than age, one might say that it is reading failure which is a better predictor because, of course, reading failure is something that the dyslexics and the garden-variety poor readers also have in common. And here might be the key to the apparent puzzle (see Snowling, 1987).

Whether low phonological sensitivity is due to developmental lag, neurological insult, or whatever, the key fact is that the necessity of confronting the demands of the reading task upon entering school triggers the reorganization of skills we see in dyslexics and garden-variety poor readers when either are compared to younger matched controls. This interpretation--and the finding it seeks to explain: non-differentiability of dyslexia and garden-variety poor readers--is, however, a bit of a threat to the construct validity of IQ-based discrepancy measurement. This is because, when we look at the macro-level of comprehension processes we find a different organization of subskills among dyslexic and garden-variety poor readers, but when it comes to the critical locus of dyslexia-word recognition--the structure of processing looks remarkably similar. Looking across the now sizable literature one must conclude that it has often been surprisingly difficult to differentiate discrepancy-defined dyslexic readers from garden-variety poor readers on tasks that tap critical processing components of reading.

It is surprising because it is *intelligence* that is supposed to be the more encompassing construct. Consider, for example, the data published by Siegel (1988). It is *reading skill* and *not* IQ that separates subject groups more strongly on such variables as visual processing, phonological processing, ITPA performance, cloze performance, sentence correction tasks, short term memory tasks, working memory tasks, of course spelling, but also arithmetic performance, which tracks reading more closely than IQ. As a general cognitive probe, reading ability seems to be a more sensitive indicator than IQ test performance.

Additional Problems of Differentiability

Such findings are cause for some soul-searching. Indeed, the empirical picture is, if anything, even more incomplete than I have portrayed it here, for there is still inadequate data on several other foundational assumptions. For example, outside of the pioneering work of Lyon (1985), there is very little data on differential response to treatment. There are, for example, very little data indicating that discrepancy-defined dyslexics respond differently to various educational treatments than do garden-variety readers of the same age or than younger nondyslexic children reading at the same level (Pressley & Levin, 1987; van der Wissel, 1987; however, see Torgesen, Dahlem, & Greenstein, 1987). This is not a trivial gap in our knowledge. Differential treatment effects are, in large part, the *raison d'etre* of special education.

We are equally unenlightened on several other crucial issues. The data on differential prognosis for reading are contradictory. Rutter and Yule (1975) found differential growth curves for specifically disabled and garden-variety poor readers. The garden-variety poor readers displayed greater growth in reading but less growth in arithmetic ability than the specifically disabled children. However, this finding of differential reading growth rates has failed to replicate in some other studies (Bruck, 1988; Labuda & DeFries, 1989; McKinney, 1987; Share et al., 1987; van der Wissel & Zegers, 1985).

Until convincing data on these two issues are provided, the utility of the concept of dyslexia will continue to be challenged because the reading disabilities field will have no rebuttal to assertions that it is more educationally and clinically relevant to define reading disability without reference to IQ discrepancy (Seidenberg, Bruck, Fornarolo, & Backman, 1986; Siegel, 1988, 1989). No amount of clinical evidence, case studies, or anecdotal reports will substitute for the large-scale experimental demonstrations that, compared to groups of garden-variety poor readers, discrepancy-defined poor readers show differential response to treatment and prognosis--and for further evidence that the reading-related cognitive profiles of these two groups are reliably different.

The Role of Intelligence in Discrepancy Definitions

We are thus right back to the issue of why IQ scores should have been the benchmark from which to measure discrepancy in the first place. Indeed, it is surprising that for so long the concept of intelligence received so little discussion in the learning disabilities literature. Researchers and practitioners in the field seem not to have realized that it is a foundational concept for the very idea of dyslexia. As currently defined, IQ is a superordinate construct for the classification of a child as reading disabled. Without a clear conception of the construct of intelligence, the notion of a reading disability, as currently defined, dissolves into incoherence.

But problems with the IQ concept are numerous. Consider the fact that researchers, let alone practitioners, cannot agree on the type of IQ score that should be used in the measurement of discrepancy. For example, it has often been pointed out that changes in the characteristics of the IQ test being used will result in somewhat different subgroups of children being identified as discrepant and also alter the types of processing deficits that they will display in comparison studies (Bowers, Steffy, & Tate, 1988; Fletcher et al., 1989; Lindgren, DeRenzi, & Richman, 1985; Reed, 1970; Shankweiler, Crain, Brady, & Macaruso, 1992; Siegel & Heaven, 1986; Stanley, Smith, & Powys, 1982; Torgesen, 1985; Vellutino, 1978). Yet it is not hard to look in the research literature and find recommendations that are all over the map.

For example, a very common recommendation that one finds in the literature is that performance and/or nonverbal IQ tests be used to assess discrepancy (e.g., Beech & Harding, 1984; Perfetti, 1985; 1986; Siegel & Heaven, 1986; Stanovich, 1986a; Thomson, 1982), because verbally loaded measures are allegedly unfair to dyslexic children. In complete contrast, in an issue of *Learning Disabilities Research* devoted to the issue of measuring severe discrepancy, Hessler (1987) argues for the use of *verbally-loaded* tests because "Using a nonverbal test of intelligence because an individual has better nonverbal cognitive abilities than verbal cognitive abilities does not, of course, remove the importance of verbal processing and knowledge structures in academic achievement; it only obscures their importance and perhaps provides unrealistic expectations for an individual's academic achievement" (p. 46).

Of course, the use of full scale IQ scores results in some unprincipled amalgamation of the above two diametrically-opposed philosophies but is still sometimes recommended precisely *because* the field is so confused and so far from consensus on this issue (Harris & Sipay, 1985, p. 145). Finally, there is a sort of "either" strategy that is invoked by investigators who require only that performance or verbal IQ exceed 90 in dyslexic samples (e. g., Olson et al., 1985). As Torgesen (1986) has pointed out, the naturally occurring multidimensional continuum of abilities guarantees that such a criterion ends up creating more discrepancies with performance IQ.

Are there any implications in all of these differing practices beyond just the confusion created? Indeed, there are. First, there are implied value judgments in the measure used as a proxy for aptitude. Secondly, there are implications in just the research domain that was the focus of our earlier review: The empirical differentiation of dyslexic children from poor readers without aptitude/achievement discrepancy.   We shall take up each of these implications in turn.

Implied Value Judgments

It is rarely noted that the use of certain types of intelligence tests in the operationalization of dyslexia often conceals conceptions of "potential" that are questionable, if not downright illogical. Consider again some of the hidden assumptions behind the often-heard admonition that verbally-loaded intelligence tests are unfair to dyslexic children, and that performance IQ measures provide "fairer" measures of the reading potential of such children. Typical arguments are that "The instrument (WISC-R) is confounded and not a true measure of potential. The learning disability itself is reflected clearly in the IQ performance" (Birnbaum, 1990, p. 330) and that "Computing an IQ from items shown to be specifically associated with dyslexic difficulties may be an underestimate" (Thomson, 1982, p. 94). But it is not at all clear--even if one accepts the problematic notion of educational "potential"--that the spatial abilities, fluid intelligence, and problem-solving abilities tapped by most performance tests provide the best measures of the potential to comprehend verbal material. To the contrary, it would appear that verbally loaded measures would provide the best estimates of how much a dyslexic reader could get from written text if their deficient decoding skills were to be remediated.

As Hessler (1987) notes: "There are different types of intelligence, and they predict academic achievement differently .... In fact, the performance score accounts for so little academic achievement that there is reason to question its relevance for use as an ability measure to predict academic achievement. It is therefore a mistake to use any test of intelligence as an ability measure for predicting academic achievement in a severe discrepancy analysis simply because it is called a test of intelligence, without demonstrating some ability to predict academic achievement" (p. 45; see also, Lyon, 1987, pp. 78-79). Consistent with this interpretation, van der Wissel (1987) has demonstrated that the extent to which an IQ subtest separates dyslexic from garden-variety children is *inversely* related to how highly the subtest correlates with reading achievement. It is a paradoxical situation indeed when the indicators that best make this subgroup discrimination are those that do *not* relate to the criterion performance that drew professional attention in the first place: reading failure.

It goes largely unnoticed that when people make the "fairness" argument for the use of nonverbal tests they in fact jettison the notion of "potential", at least in its common meaning. They cannot mean the potential for verbal comprehension through print if the decoding deficits were remediated, since this is not what IQ tests--particularly the performance tests they are recommending--assess. What people who make the "verbal IQ scores are unfair to dyslexics" argument are asserting--implicitly--is that if we had a society that was not so organized around literacy, dyslexics would have the potential to do much better. True. But recognize that this is a *counterfactual* premise that contradicts more common usages, to the advantage of some and to the disadvantage of others. In fact, it could well be argued that it simply makes little sense to adopt linguistic usages of the term "potential" that require the assumption that literacy-based technological societies will be totally reconstructed.

We seem to find it difficult to use this crude cognitive probe--an IQ score--as a circumscribed behavioral index without loading social, and indeed metaphysical (Scheffler, 1985), baggage onto it. If these tests *are mere* predictors of school performance, then let us treat them as such. If we do, then performance IQ is manifestly not the predictor that we want to use, at least in the domain of reading prediction. An alternative conception of potential to apply in cases like dyslexia--where educational achievement in a particular domain is thwarted due to a circumscribed, modular dysfunction--was suggested previously: The degree of improvement in the particular educational domain that would result if the person's dysfunction were totally remediated.

Implications of Using Different IQ Measures

The choice of different aptitude measures also relates strongly to the possibility of isolating a modular dysfunction, perhaps in the phonological domain (Liberman & Shankweiler, 1985; Stanovich, 1988b), that might have some genetic specificity and neurological localizability. The point is this: Do we really want to look for a group of poor readers who are qualitatively differentiable in terms of etiology and neurophysiology? Officials at the National Institutes of Health in the United States who are funding several program projects on the neurological, genetic, and behavioral underpinnings of dyslexia certainly want to look for such a group (Gray & Kavanagh, 1985). Many in the learning disabilities field share their enthusiasm for the quest to isolate--behaviorally, genetically, and physiologically--a select group-of "different" poor readers.

Let us, for purposes of argument, accept this as a goal whether we believe in it or not. I want to argue that if we do, a somewhat startling conclusion results. The conclusion is that we must move away from measures of abstract intelligence as benchmarks for discrepancy and toward more educationally relevant indices.   In short, to get NIH's neurologically differentiable groups we need an aptitude benchmark of more educational relevance than IQ--than of nonverbal IQ in particular, contrary to some common recommendations.

However, it must be emphasized that the context for any such discussion must be the voluminous body of prior research on the cognitive correlates of individual differences in reading achievement. Our knowledge of the structure of human abilities in this domain puts severe constraints on the ability patterns that can be observed in studies of dyslexia. For example, an extremely large body of research has demonstrated that reading skill is linked to an incredibly wide range of verbal abilities. Vocabulary, syntactic knowledge, metalinguistic awareness, verbal short-term memory, phonological awareness, speech production, inferential comprehension, semantic memory, and verbal fluency form only a partial list (Baddeley, Logie, Nimmo-Smith, & Brereton, 1985; Byrne, 1981; Carr, 1981; Chall, 1983; Cunningham, Stanovich, & Wilson, 1990; Curtis, 1980; Evans & Carr, 1985; Frederiksen, 1980; Harris & Sipay, 1985; Jackson & McClelland, 1979; Just & Carpenter, 1987; Kamhi & Catts, 1989; Palmer et al., 1985; Perfetti, 1985; Rapala & Brady, 1990; Rayner & Pollatsek, 1989; Siegel & Ryan, 1988, 1989; Stanovich, 1985,1986a; Stanovich, Cunningham, & Feeman, 1984; Stanovich, Nathan, & Zolman, 1988; Vellutino, 1979; Vellutino & Scanlon, 1987).

In contrast, the nonverbal abilities linked to reading are much more circumscribed (Aman & Singh, 1983; Carr, 1981; Daneman & Tardiff, 1987; Hulme, 1988; Lovegrove & Slaghuis, 1989; Siegel & Ryan, 1989; Stanovich, 1986a; Vellutino, 1979; but see Carver, 1990, for an opposing view). Here, the abilities associated with reading are more likely to be distinct and domain specific (e.g., orthographic storage, processing of certain spatial frequencies). In the verbal domain, however, there are many more abilities that are related to reading and that are more likely to have more global influences (e.g., inferential comprehension, verbal STM, vocabulary), thereby affecting general verbal IQ.   Therefore, matching dyslexics and nondyslexics on performance IQ will necessarily lead to broad-based deficits on the verbal side. But even if there *are* visual/orthographic deficits linked to reading disability, the converse is not true. Because there are not as many reading-related nonverbal processes and because those that do exist will certainly be more circumscribed than something like vocabulary or verbal memory, verbal IQ matching will not necessarily result in dyslexic subjects with severely depressed performance lQs.

We will now travel across the continuum of potential aptitude candidates for discrepancy measurement with this research context and the goal of differentiating dyslexic children in mind. It immediately becomes apparent that the use of reading achievement discrepancies from performance IQ will make it extremely difficult to cognitively differentiate dyslexic children from other poor readers. Such performance-discrepancy dyslexics--because they are allowed to have depressed verbal components-will have a host of verbal deficits, some at levels higher than phonology, and they will not display the cognitive specificity required of the dyslexia concept. Torgesen (1986) has discussed how definitional practices that require only that verbal *or* performance scales be over some criterion value will have the same effect. The verbal scale is allowed to be considerably under that of the nondisabled control group, and it is not surprising that, subsequently, a broad range of verbal deficits are observed (see Vellutino, 1979). A behaviorally and neurologically differentiable core deficit will be virtually impossible to find, given such classification.

In contrast, discrepancies based on verbal aptitude measures would be likely to isolate a more circumscribed disability that may be more readily identifiable by neurophysiological and/or genetic methods. Such a procedure would preclude the possibility of deficits in broad-based verbal processes. It could potentially confine deficits exclusively to the phonological module. For example, Bowers, Steffy, and Tate (1988) demonstrated that if only performance IQ was controlled, dyslexic subjects were differentiated from nondyslexics on the basis of rapid naming, performance and on digit span and sentence memory. However, controlling for verbal IQ removed the association between reading disability and memory abilities. Importantly, an association with rapid naming remained. In short, verbal IQ control resulted in the isolation of a more circumscribed processing deficit.

Similarly, verbal IQ-based discrepancy measurement would be much more likely to demarcate a visual/orthographic deficit, if one exists (see Lovegrove & Slaghuis, 1989; Solman & May, 1990; Willows, 1991). Verbal-IQ matching in a comparison study would, of course, allow the performance IQ of the dyslexic group to fall below those of the control group. But since the number of nonverbal abilities linked to reading is much more circumscribed in the nonverbal than in the verbal domain, the groups would not become unmatched on a commensurately large number of abilities. Additionally, subtle, visually-based deficits would not be "adjusted away" by a procedure of performance-IQ matching. Thus, verbal-IQ control provides a greater opportunity for these visual/orthographic deficits--much harder to track than those in the phonological domain--to emerge in comparison studies.

In summary, by adopting verbal IQ as an aptitude measure we would be closer to a principled definition of potential in the reading domain: As the academic level that would result from instruction if the person's dysfunction were totally remediated. We would also be more likely to isolate a circumscribed deficit that would at least be more amenable to cognitive and neurological differentiation.

An Alternative Proposal

But, if we have come this far down the road of altering our treatment of IQ, why not go all the way? There are at least three major conceptual/logical/political problems with IQ to consider. One: IQ is not an educationally relevant benchmark for educational practitioners; Two: It does not--at least in the case of full scale or performance IQ--promise to demarcate a neurologically distinct group (a goal of many in the neuropsychology community and certainly of health-funding agencies in the US); and, lastly: It has driven a wedge between groups of investigators in the reading research community. The fact that the attendees of the conventions of the Orton Society and the International Reading Association are almost totally nonoverlapping is perfectly correlated with and partially explainable by the fact that one of these groups routinely uses the term dyslexia and the other finds the term mildly distasteful.

But now take heart, because I want to argue that there is a cognitive benchmark that, One: Is more educationally relevant than IQ; Two: Is more apt to identify a modular deficit amenable to neurological and genetic investigation; and Three: Is acceptable to a much wider segment of the reading, education community. It is in fact a proposal that has been around for quite some time, but has never gotten a proper hearing because studies and definitions of dyslexia have so strongly emphasized the measurement of intelligence.

Many educationally-oriented reading researchers have long suggested that measuring the discrepancy between reading ability and *listening comprehension* would be more educationally relevant and would seem to have been a more logical choice in the first place (see Aaron, 1989a, 1991; Carroll, 1977; Carver, 1981; Durrell, 1969; Gillet & Temple, 1986; Gough & Tunmer, 1986; Hood & Dubert, 1983; Royer, Kulhavy, Lee, & Peterson, 1986; Spring & French, 1990; Sticht & James, 1984). Certainly a discrepancy calculated in this way seems to have more face validity and educational relevance than the traditional procedure (Aaron, 1989a, 1991; Durrell & Hayes, 1969; Hoover & Gough, 1990; Spache, 1981). Children who understand written material less well than they would understand the same material if it were read to them appear to be in need of educational intervention. Presumably, their listening comprehension exceeds their reading comprehension because word recognition processes are inefficient and are a "bottleneck" that impedes comprehension (Gough & Tunmer, 1986; Perfetti, 1985; Perfetti & Lesgold, 1977). Listening comprehension correlates with reading comprehension much more highly than full scale or even verbal IQ. Children simultaneously low in reading and listening do not have an "unexplained" reading problem (Carroll, 1977; Hoover & Gough, 1990), and we must always remember that the idea of "unexplained" reading failure is the puzzle that enticed us into the idea of dyslexia in the first place.

As with verbal IQ but only more so, listening comprehension isolates a modular deficit, because in a comparison study dyslexic subjects would not become unmatched from nondyslexics on a host of reading-related verbal abilities. Additionally, even though the idea of visual deficits as an explanation of dyslexia is out of favor at the moment, this "layman's conception of dyslexia" (not totally without support in the literature, see Lovegrove & Slaghuis, 1989; Solman & May, 1990; Willows, 1991) would receive a fairer test if discrepancies from listening comprehension were the criteria for subject selection in research. Any potential visual deficits would not be "adjusted away" by performance-IQ matching. Thus, not only would we get a better to chance of demarcating the modular phonological deficits that are of great interest in current work on dyslexia (Liberman & Shankweiler, 1985; Stanovich,1988b), but more tenuous hypotheses in the visual domain would get a fairer hearing.

In short, a large reading discrepancy from listening comprehension has probably isolated--as well as we are ever going to get it--a modular decoding problem that then may or may not be amenable to genetic and neurological analysis in the manner of the ongoing NIH program projects.   It is indeed ironic that measuring discrepancies from listening comprehension--a procedure often suggested by those hostile to the dyslexia concept--may be just the procedure that allows those working from a neurological perspective to succeed in their quest.

There are, of course, several obstacles to implementing procedures of measuring reading disability with reference to discrepancies from listening comprehension. For example, while several individual measures of listening comprehension ability have been published (Carroll, 1972, 1977; CTB/McGraw-Hill, 1985; Durrell & Hayes, 1969; Spache, 1981), it may be the case that none have been standardized across the range of ages, nor attained the psychometric properties, to serve as an adequate measure from which to assess discrepancy (Johnson, 1988). Other complications may also arise, such as hearing problems or unfamiliarity with standard English.   However, many of these problems are no more severe for listening comprehension measures than they are for certain IQ tests. It is encouraging that work on listening comprehension as a diagnostic benchmark has recently been increasing in quantity, and some important progress is being made (see Aaron, 1989a, 1991; Carlisle, 1989; Hoover & Gough, 1990; Horowitz & Samuels, 1985; Royer, Sinatra, & Schumer, 1990; Spring & French, 1990).

Consider, though, how some of the other complications in this proposal illuminate the arguments previously outlined. From what type of material should we assess listening comprehension? One possibility is simply to employ oral presentations of text material (Hoover & Gough, 1990). This is often done in research investigations and is the method employed in most standardized measures of listening. Of course, such material will have the syntax, vocabulary, and language structures of text which, as is well known, differ somewhat from speech (Hayes, 1988; Hayes & Ahrens, 1988; Chafe & Danielewicz, 1987).   An alternative procedure would be to orally present more naturalistic nontextual language. Which method is preferable obviously depends upon the question being asked. But if our goal is to qualitatively distinguish reading disability, then the choice is orally presented *text*. Performance on this material will correlate more highly with reading comprehension and, most importantly, discrepancies will result more specifically from decoding problems.   In contrast, severe underachievement based on prediction from naturalistic language comprehension is more apt to implicate, in addition, more global difficulties with text structures that result from environmental causes such as lack of print exposure.

This comparison between the oral presentation of naturalistic speech and that of textual material is analogous in form to the choice between IQ measures that was discussed earlier. We want the measure that more closely operationalizes a more principled definition of potential: As the level of the skill that would result if the persons processing deficit were totally remediated.   And we want the measure that is more highly correlated with the criterion--reading--because such a measure will more cleanly isolate an unexpected, separable, modular failure in a more circumscribed cognitive domain--the critical intuition and assumption that has fueled interest in dyslexia from the time of Hinshelwood (1895, 1917) to the present.

Using listening comprehension as an aptitude benchmark also solves the perennially knotty problem of deciding what type of test to use as the *reading* test in a discrepancy analysis. When investigators use a word recognition test--because they believe that the key to reading disability lies somewhere in the word recognition module--they are often accused of ignoring the real educational context and real educational goal of reading which is comprehension. The proposal to use listening comprehension as the aptitude benchmark dissolves this problem for it would *allow* the use of a reading *comprehension* test as the achievement benchmark. Such a procedure simultaneously renders these criticisms ineffectual but at the same time it would end up isolating word recognition problems pretty exclusively. Of course, such a procedure would leave open the possibility that any subtle problems in dealing with visually presented text (caused by the absence of intonation, stress or whatever) would also be revealed. This, however, is not an entirely bad outcome.

Investigators advocating the use of a word recognition test exclusively are often accused of prejudging the issue of the causes of reading difficulties and, on the surface, it seems as if they are (the critics ignore the fact that this practice is motivated by the outcome of voluminous research). By using a reading comprehension test the bulk of the identified discrepancies would represent phonologically based word recognition problems, for the reasons I have outlined above. Yet investigators could not be accused of prejudging the issue by employing a word recognition test. It would be subsequent testing that would reveal the word recognition problem which would *result* from classification using other procedures, not by an *a priori* restriction to identification based on word recognition tests. This procedure might be more convincing to those in the reading education community who still doubt that reading disability has, as its main source, problems in word recognition.

Now an important caveat is in order. In light of the arguments I have been making, it is important to state that educational practitioners may well want to demarcate children high in nonverbal abilities and simultaneously low in both listening and reading ability and to give them special attention (this is a policy/political issue). But such children should not be considered dyslexic. They do not have a domain-specific difficulty in the area of reading if their general listening skills are also depressed. They may well present an important educational problem worth identifying and dealing with, but it is simply perverse to call them *reading* disabled.

Matthew Effects and Discrepancy Measurement

There remains, however, a further obstacle to measuring reading disability by reference to aptitude/achievement discrepancy--irrespective of the indicator used for the aptitude benchmark. Let us again consider the recommendation against the use of verbally loaded tests for discrepancy measurement. This admonition stems from the either tacit or explicit assumption that the reading difficulties themselves may lead to depressed performance on such measures. One reason that this may occur is because of so-called "Matthew effects" associated with reading: Situations where reading itself develops other related cognitive abilities (see Stanovich, 1986b, Walberg & Tsai, 1983). But the recognition of such phenomena perniciously undermines the whole notion of discrepancy measurement by weakening the distinction between aptitude and achievement. It serves to remind us that the logic of the learning disabilities field has implicitly given all of the causal power to IQ. That is, it is reading that is considered discrepant from IQ rather than IQ that is discrepant from reading. However, this is a vast oversimplification, because there are potent effects running in both directions.

Much evidence has now accumulated to indicate that reading itself is a moderately powerful determinant of vocabulary growth, verbal intelligence, and general comprehension ability (Hayes, 1988; Hayes & Ahrens, 1988; Juel, 1988; Nichols, Inglis, Lawson, & MacKay, 1988; Share, McGee, & Silva, 1989; Share & Silva, 1987; Stanovich, 1986b; Stanovich & West, 1989; van den Bos, 1989). These Matthew effects (reciprocal causation effects involving reading and other cognitive skills) highlight a further problematic aspect of discrepancy-based classification. The possibility of Matthew effects prevents us from ignoring the possibility that poor listening comprehension or verbal intelligence could be the *result* of poor reading.

Thus, Matthew effects are interrelated in some very complicated ways with the conceptual logic of discrepancy-based disability definitions. It appears, then, that any discrepancy-based conceptualization is going to require considerable refinement based on how Matthew effects alter the course of development, bringing education-related cognitive skills more into congruence with age. Thus, conceptually justified discrepancy-based classification--even from listening comprehension--will be maddeningly tricky to carry out in a principled fashion.

Conclusion: Is Discrepancy Measurement Worth the Effort?

Let us now recapitulate and summarize the argument so that we can see where we have been and where we are at. The history of the concept of dyslexia has followed a confused "cart before the horse" path in part because too many practitioners and researchers accepted at face value claims that IQ tests were measures of special "unlocked potential" in particular groups of children with low reading achievement. We have seen that in the area of reading disability the notion of unlocked potential was misconceived, because it was defined in a way that did not relate to the critical prediction in this domain: The prediction of how much growth in reading comprehension ability would be expected if the decoding deficit that was the proximal cause of the disability were to be totally remediated.

An alternative proposal for measuring aptitude/achievement discrepancies with reference to listening comprehension ability was explored and found to be superior to that of IQ assessment. Nevertheless, it was argued that complications stemming from the increasing difficulty of differentiating aptitude from achievement as a child gets older will plague all definitional efforts based on the discrepancy notion. Problems such as these have led to Linda Siegel's (1988, 1989) suggestion that reading disability be defined solely on the basis of decoding deficits, without reference to discrepancies from aptitude measures. Whether or not her proposal is adopted, the learning disabilities field is simply going to have to face up to the implications of current research findings, namely that: 1) Defining dyslexia by reference to discrepancies from IQ is an untenable procedure, 2) Much more basic psychometric work needs to be done in order to develop a principled method of discrepancy measurement from listening comprehension or some other verbal aptitude indicator, 3) If the field is unwilling to do the spade work necessary to carry out #2, or deems the potential benefit not worth the effort, then the only logical alternative is to adopt Siegel's proposal to define reading disability solely in terms of decoding deficiencies, without reference to aptitude discrepancy.

The research situation I have reviewed here highlights the challenge facing advocates of the dyslexic concept: Produce the data that indicates different cognitive processing in dyslexic and garden-variety poor readers reading at the same level, the data indicating that these two groups of poor readers have a differential educational prognosis, and the data indicating that they respond differently to certain educational treatments.

REFERENCES

Aaron, P G. (1989a). *Dyslexia and hyperlexia.* Dordrecht, The Netherlands: Kluwer.

Aaron, P G. (1989b). Qualitative and quantitative differences among dyslexic, normal, and nondyslexic poor readers. *Reading and Writing: An Interdisciplinary Journal, 1,* 291-308.

Aaron, P G. (1991). Can reading disabilities be diagnosed without using intelligence tests? *Journal of Learning Disabilities, 24,* 178-186.

Ackerman, R T., Dykman, R. A., & Gardner, M. Y. (1990). ADD students with and without dyslexia differ in sensitivity to rhyme and alliteration. *Journal of Learning Disabilities, 23,* 279-283.

Adams, M. J. (1990). *Beginning to read: Thinking and learning about print.* Cambridge, MA: MIT Press.

Aman, M., & Singh, N. (1983). Specific reading disorders: Concepts of etiology reconsidered. In K. Gadow & 1. Bialer (Eds.), *Advances in Teaming and behavioral disabilities* (Vol. 2, pp. 1-47). Greenwich, CT: JAI Press.

Applebee, A. N. (1971). Research in reading retardation: Two critical problems. *Journal of Child Psychology & Psychiatry, 12,* 91-113.

Baddeley, A. D., Ellis, N. C., Miles, T. R., & Lewis, V. J. (1982). Developmental and acquired dyslexia: A comparison. *Cognition, 11,* 185-199.

Baddeley, A. D., Logie, R. H., & Ellis, N. C. (1988). Characteristics of developmental dyslexia. *Cognition, 30,* 198-227.

Baddeley, A., Logie, R., Nimmo-Smith, I., & Brereton, N. (1985). Components of fluent reading. *Journal of Memory and Language 24,* 119-131.

Ball, E. W., & Blachman, B. A. (1991). Does phoneme segmentation training in kindergarten make a difference in early word recognition and developmental spelling. *Reading Research Quarterly, 26,* 49-66.

Baron, J. (1985). *Rationality and intelligence,* Cambridge: Cambridge University Press.

Beech, J., & Harding, L. (1984). Phonemic processing and the pool reader from a developmental lag viewpoint. *Reading Research Quarterly, 19,* 357-366.

Birnbaum, R. (1990). IQ and the definition of LD. *Journal of Learning Disabilities, 23,* 330.

Blachman, B. (1989). Phonological awareness and word recognition: Assessment and intervention. In A. G. Kamhi & H. W. Catts (Eds.), *Reading disabilities: A developmental language perspective* (pp. 133-158). Boston: College-Hill Press.

Bloom, A., Wagner, M., Reskin, L., & Bergman, A. (1980). A comparison of intellectually delayed and primary reading disabled children on measures of intelligence and achievement. *Journal of Clinical Psychology, 36,* 788-790.

Bodor, E. (1973). Developmental dyslexia: A diagnostic approach based on three atypical reading-spelling patterns. *Developmental Medicine and Child Neurology., 15,* 375-389.

Bowers, P, Steffy, R., & Tate, E. (1988). Comparison of the effects of IQ control methods on memory and naming speed predictors of reading disability. *Reading Research Quarterly. 23,* 304-319.

Bradley, L., & Bryant,, P E. (1978). Difficulties in auditory organization as a possible cause of reading backwardness. *Nature, 271,* 746-747.

Bradley, L., & Bryant, P E. (1985). *Rhyme and reason in reading and spelling.* Ann Arbor: University of Michigan Press.

Bruck, M. (1988). The word recognition and spelling of dyslexic children. *Reading Research Quarterly, 23.* 51-69.

Bruck, M. (1990). Word-recognition skills of adults with childhood diagnoses of dyslexia. *Developmental Psychology, 26.* 439-454.

Bruck, M., & Treiman, R. (1990). Phonological awareness and spelling in normal children and dyslexics: The case of initial consonant clusters. *Journal of Experimental Child Psychology, 50,* 156-178.

Bryant, P E., Bradley, L., Maclean, M., & Crossland, D. (1989). Nursery rhymes, phonological skills and reading. *Journal of Child Language 16,* 407-428.

Bryant, P E., & Goswami, U. (1986). Strengths and weaknesses of the reading level design: A comment on Backman, Mamen, and Ferguson. *Psychological Bulletin, 100*, 101-103.

Byrne, B. (1981). Deficient syntactic control in poor readers: Is a weak phonetic memory code responsible? *Applied Psycholinguistics, 2*, 201-212.

Carlisle, J. F. (1989). The use of the sentence verification technique in diagnostic assessment of listening and reading comprehension. *Learning Disabilities Research, 5*, 33-44.

Carr, T. H. (1981). Building theories of reading ability: On the relation between individual differences in cognitive skills and reading comprehension. *Cognition, 9*, 73-114.

Carroll, J. B. (1972). Defining language comprehension: Some speculations. In J. B. T. Carroll & R. Freedle (Eds.), *Language, comprehension, and the acquisition of knowledge* (pp. 1-29). Washington, DC: W. H. Winston & Sons.

Carroll, J. B. (1977). Developmental parameters of reading comprehension. In J. T. Guthrie (Ed.), *Cognition, curriculum, and comprehension* (pp. 1-15). Newark, DE: IRA.

Carver, R. P (1981). *Reading comprehension and rauding theory.* Springfield, IL: Charles C. Thomas.

Carver, R. P (1990). Intelligence and reading ability in grades 2-12. *Intelligence, 14*, 449-455.

Ceci, S. J. (1986). *Handbook of cognitive, social, and neuropsychological aspects of learning disabilities* (Vol. 1). Hillsdale, NJ: Erlbaum.

Chafe, W., & Danielewicz, J. (1987). Properties of spoken and written language. In R. Horowitz, & S. J. Samuels (Eds.), *Comprehending oral and written language (pp. 83-113).* New York: Academic Press.

Chall, J. S. (1983). *Stages of reading development.* New York: McGraw-Hill.

Cossu, G., Shankweiler, D., Liberman, I. Y., Katz, L., & Tola, G. (1988). Awareness of phonological segments and reading ability in Italian children. *Applied Psycholinguistics, 9*, 1-16.

Critchley, M. (1970). *The dyslexic child.* London: William Heinemann Medical Books.

CTB/McGraw-Hill. (1981). *Listening test.* Monterey, CA: Publisher.

Cunningham, A. E. (1990). Explicit versus implicit instruction in phonemic awareness. *Journal of Experimental Child Psychology, 50*, 429-444.

Cunningham, A. E., & Stanovich, K. E. (1990). Assessing print exposure and orthographic processing skill in children: A quick measure of reading experience. *Journal of Educational Psychology, 82*, 733-740.

Cunningham, A. E., & Stanovich, K. E. (1991). Tracking the unique effects of print exposure in children: Associations with vocabulary, general knowledge, and spelling. *Journal of Educational Psychology, 83*, 264-274.

Cunningham, A. E., Stanovich, K. E., Wilson, M. R. (1990). Cognitive variation in adult students differing in reading ability. In T. Carr & B. A. Levy (Eds.), *Reading and its development: Component skills approaches.* New York: Academic Press.

Curtis, M. (1980). Development of components of reading skill. *Journal of Educational Psychology, 72*, 656-669.

Daneman, M., & Tardif, T. (1987). Working memory and reading skill re-examined. In M. Coltheart (Ed.), *Attention and performance* (Vol. 12, pp. 491-508). London: Lawrence Erlbaum Associates.

Doehring, D. G. (1978). The tangled web of behavioral research on developmental dyslexia. In A. L. Benton & D. Pearl (Eds.), *Dyslexia* (pp. 123-135). New York: Oxford University Press.

Durrell, D. D. (1969). Listening comprehension versus reading comprehension. *Journal of Reading, 12*, 455-460.

Durrell, D. D., & Hayes, M. (1969). *Durrell listening-reading series.* New York: Psychological Corporation.

Eisenberg, L. (1978). Definitions of dyslexia: Their consequences for research and policy. In A. L.. Benton & D. Pearl (Eds.), *Dyslexia (pp.* 29-42). New York: Oxford University Press.

Ellis, A. W. (1985). The cognitive neuropsychology of developmental (and acquired) dyslexia: A critical survey. *Cognitive Neuropsychology, 2* 169-205.

Ellis, N., & Large, B. (1987). The development of reading: As you seek so shall you find. *British Journal of Psychology, 78*, 1-28.

Evans, M. A., & Carr, T. H. (1985). Cognitive abilities, conditions of learning, and the early development of reading skill. *Reading Research Quarterly, 20.* 327-350.

Fletcher, J. M., Espy, K., Francis, D., Davidson, K., Rourke, B., & Shaywitz, S. (1989). Comparisons of cutoff and regression-based definitions of reading disabilities. *Journal of Learning Disabilities, 22.* 334-338.

Fodor, J. (1983). *Modularity of mind.* Cambridge: MIT Press.

Fox, B., & Routh, D. K. (1975). Analyzing spoken language into words, syllables, and phonemes: A developmental study. *Journal of Psycholinguistic Research, 4,* 331-342.

Frankenberger, W., & Fronzaglio, K. (1991). A review of states' criteria and procedures for identifying children with learning disabilities. *Journal of Learning Disabilities, 24.* 495-500.

Frankenberger, W., & Harper, J. (1987). States' criteria and procedures for identifying learning disabled children: A comparison of 1981/82 and 1985/86 guidelines. *Journal of Learning Disabilities, 20,* 118-121.

Frederiksen, J. R. (1980). Component skills in reading: Measurement of individual differences through chronometric analysis. In R. Snow, P Federico, & W. Montague (Eds.), *Aptitude, learning, and instruction* (Vol. 1, pp. 105-138). Hillsdale, NJ: Erlbaum.

Fredman, G., & Stevenson, J. (1988). Reading processes in specific reading retarded and reading backward 13-year-olds. *British Journal of Developmental Psychology, 6,* 97-108.

Freebody, P, & Byrne, B. (1988). Word-reading strategies in elementary school children: Relations to comprehension, reading time, and phonemic awareness. *Reading Research Quarterly, 23,* 441-453.

Gillet, J. W., & Temple, C. (1986). *Understanding reading problems: Assessment and instruction,* (2nd Ed.). Boston: Little, Brown.

Gough, P B., & Hillinger, M. L. (1980). Learning to read: An unnatural act. *Bulletin of the Orton Society, 30.* 171-176.

Gough, P B., & Tunmer, W. E. (1986). Decoding, reading, and reading disability. *Remedial and Special Education, 7,* 6-10.

Gray, D. B., & Kavanagh, J. K. (1985). *Biobehavioral measures of dyslexia.* Parkton, MD: York Press.

Harris, A. J., & Sipay, E. R. (1985). *How to increase reading ability* (8th Ed.). White Plains, NY: Longman.

Hayes, D. P (1988). Speaking and writing: Distinct patterns of word choice. *Journal of Memory and Language, 27,* 572-585.

Hayes, D. P, & Ahrens, M. (1988). Vocabulary simplification for children: A special case of 'motherese'? *Journal of Child Language. 15,* 395-410.

Hessler, G. L. (1987). Educational issues surrounding severe discrepancy. *Learning Disabilities Research, 3,* 43-49.

Hinshelwood, J.(1895). Word-blindness and visual memory. *Lancet, 2,*1564-1570.

Hinshelwood, J. (1917). *Congenital word-blindness.* London: Lewis, 1917.

Holligan, C., & Johnston, R. S.. (1988). The use of phonological information by good and poor readers in memory and reading tasks. *Memory & Cognition, 16,* 522-532.

Hood, J., & Dubert, L. A.. (1983). Decoding as a component of reading comprehension among secondary students. *Journal of Reading Behavior, 15,* 51-61.

Hoover, W. A., & Gough, P B. (1990). The simple view of reading. *Reading and Writing: An Interdisciplinary Journal. 2* 127-160.

Horowitz, R, & Samuels, S. J. (1985). Reading and listening to expository text. *Journal of Reading Behavior, 17,* 185-198.

Hulme, C. (1988). The implausibility of low-level visual deficits as a cause of children's reading difficulties. *Cognitive Neuropsychology, 5.* 369-374.

Hurford, D. P, & Sanders, R. E. (1990). Assessment and remediation of a phonemic discrimination deficit in reading disabled second and fourth graders. *Journal of Experimental Child Psychology, 50,* 396-415.

Jackson, M. D.. & McClelland, J. L.. (1979). Processing determinants of reading speed. *Journal of Experimental Psychology: General, 108,* 151-181.

Johnson, D. J.. (1988). Review of research on specific reading, writing, and mathematics disorders. In J. F. Kavanagh, & T. J. Truss (Eds.), *Learning disabilities: Proceedings of the national conference* (pp. 79-163). Parkton, MD: York Press.

Jorm, A. (1983). Specific reading retardation and working memory: A review. *British journal of Psychology, 74,* 311-342.

Jorm, A., Share, D., Maclean, R., & Matthews, R. (1986). Cognitive factors at school entry predictive of specific reading retardation and general reading backwardness: A research. *Journal of Child Psychology and Psychiatry, 27,* 45-54.

Judson, H. F (1979). *The eighth day of creation.* New York: Simon and Schuster.

Juel, C. (1988). Learning to read and write: A longitudinal study of 54 children from first through fourth grades. *Journal of Educational Psychology, 80,* 437-447.

Juel, C., Griffith, P. L., & Gough, P B. (1986). Acquisition of literacy: A longitudinal study of children in first and second grade. *Journal of Educational Psychology, 78,* 243-255.

Just, M., & Carpenter, P. A. (1987). *The psychology of reading and language comprehension.* Boston: Allyn and Bacon.

Kamhi, A., & Catts, H. (Eds.) (1989). *Reading disabilities: A developmental language perspective.* Boston: College-Hill Press.

Kavale, K. A. (1987). Theoretical issues surrounding severe discrepancy. *Learning Disabilities Research, 3,* 12-20.

Kavale, K. A., & Nye, C. (1981). Identification criteria for learning disabilities: A survey of the survey of the research literature. *Learning Disability Quarterly. 4,* 363-388.

Kavanagh, J. F., & Truss, T. J. (Eds.), (1988). *Learning disabilities: Proceedings of the national conference.* Parkton, MD: York Press.

Kochnower, J., Richardson, E., & DiBenedetto, B. (1983). A comparison of the phonic decoding ability of normal and learning disabled children. *Journal of Learning Disabilities, 16,* 348-351.

Labuda, M., & DeFries, J. C. (1989). Differential prognosis of reading disabled children as a function of gender, socioeconomic status, IQ, and severity: A longitudinal study. *Reading and Writing: An Interdisciplinary Journal, 1,* 25-36.

Liberman, I. Y. (1982). A language-oriented view of reading and its disabilities. In H. Mykelbust (Ed.), *Progress in learning disabilities* (Vol. 5, pp. 81-101). New York: Grune & Stratton.

Liberman, I. Y., & Shankweiler, D. (1985). Phonology and the problems of learning to read and write. *Remedial and Special Education, 6,* 8-17.

Liberman, I. Y., Shankweiler, D., Fischer, F. W., & Carter, B. (1974). Explicit syllable and phoneme segmentation in the young child. *Journal of Experimental Child Psychology 18,* 201-212.

Lie, A. (1991). Effects of a training program for stimulating skills in word analysis in first-grade children. *Reading Research Quarterly, 26,* 234-250.

Lieberman, P, Meskill, R. H., Chatillon, M., & Schupack, H. (1985). Phonetic speech perception deficits in dyslexia. *Journal of Speech and Hearing Research, 28,* 480-486.

Lindgren, S. D.., De Renzi, E., & Richman, L.C. (1985). Cross-national comparisons of developmental dyslexia in Italy and the United States. *Child Development 56,* 1404-1417.

Lovegrove, W., Martin, F., & Slaghuis, W. (1986). A theoretical and experimental case for a visual deficit in specific reading, disability. *Cognitive Neuropsychology, 3,* 225-267.

Lovegrove, W., & Slaghuis, W. (1989). How reliable are visual differences found in dyslexics? *Irish Journal of Psychology, 10,* 542-550.

Lundberg, I., Frost, J., & Petersen, O. (1988). Effects of an extensive program for stimulating phonological awareness in preschool children. *Reading Research Quarterly, 23,* 263-284.

Lundberg, I., & Høien, T. (1989). Phonemic deficits: A core symptom of developmental dyslexia? *Irish Journal of Psychology. 10,* 579-592.

Lyon, G. R.. (1985). Educational validation studies of learning disability subtypes. In B. P. Rourke (Ed.), *Neuropsychology of learning disabilities* (pp. 228-253). New York: The Guilford Press.

Lyon, G. R.. (1987). Learning disabilities research: False starts and broken promises. In S. Vaughn & C. S. Bos (Eds.), *Research in Teaming disabilities* (pp. 69-85). Boston, MA: College-Hill Press.

Maclean, M., Bryant, P, & Bradley, L. (1987). Rhymes, nursery rhymes, and reading in early childhood. *Merrill-Palmer Quarterly, 33,* 255-281.

Mann, V. (1986). Why some children encounter reading problems. In J. Torgesen & B. Wong (Eds.), *Psychological and educational perspectives on learning disabilities* (pp. 133-159). New York: Academic Press.

McKinney, J. D. (1987). Research on the identification of learning-disabled children: Perspectives on changes in educational policy. In S. Vaughn & C. Bos (Eds.), *Research in_learning disabilities* (pp. 215-233). Boston: College-Hill.

Morrison, F. (1984). Word decoding and rule-learning in normal and disabled readers. *Remedial and Special Education, 5,* 20-27.

Morrison, F. J. (1987). The nature of reading disability: Toward an integrative framework. In S. Ceci (Ed.), *Handbook of cognitive, social, and neuropsychological aspects of learning disabilities* (pp. 33-62). Hillsdale, NJ: Erlbaum.

Morrison, E, & Giordani, B., & Nagy, J. (1977). Reading disability: An information processing analysis. *Science, 196,* 77-79.

Nichols, E. G., Inglis, J., Lawson, J. S., & MacKay, I. (1988). A cross-validation study of patterns of cognitive ability in children with learning difficulties, as described by factorially defined WISC-R verbal and performance IQs. *Journal of Learning Disabilities, 21,* 504-508.

Olson, R., Kliegl, R., Davidson, B., & Foltz, G. (1985). Individual and developmental differences in reading disability. In T. Waller (Ed.), *Reading research: Advances in theory and practice* (Vol. 4, pp. 1-64). London: Academic Press.

Olson, R., Wise, B., Conners, F., & Rack, J. (1990). Organization, heritability, and remediation of component word recognition and language skills in disabled readers. In T. Carr & B. A. Levy (Eds.), *Reading and its development: Component skills approaches* (pp. 261-322). New York: Academic Press.

Olson, R., Wise, B., Conners, F., Rack, J., & Fulker, D. (1989). Specific deficits in component reading and language skills: Genetic and environmental influences. *Journal of Learning Disabilities, 22,* 339-348.

Palmer, J., MacLeod, C. M.., Hunt, E., & Davidson, J. E.. (1985). Information processing correlates of reading. *Journal of Memory and Language 24,* 59-88.

Patterson, K., Marshall, J., & Coltheart, M. (Eds.) (1985). *Surface dyslexia.* London: Erlbaum.

Pennington, B. F. (1986). Issues in the diagnosis and phenotype analysis of dyslexia: Implications for family studies. In S. D. Smith (Ed.), *Genetics and learning disabilities* (pp. 69-96). San Diego: College-Hill Press.

Pennington, B. F., McCabe, L. L., Smith, S., Lefly, D., Bookman, M., Kimberling, W., & Lubs, H. (1986). Spelling errors in adults with a form of familial dyslexia. *Child Development. 57,* 1001-1013.

Pennington, B. F., Van Orden, G. C., Smith, S. D., Green, P A., & Haith, M. M. (1990). Phonological processing skills and deficits in adult dyslexics. *Child Development. 61,* 1753-1778.

Perfetti, C. A. (1985). *Reading ability.* New York: Oxford University Press.

Perfetti, C. A. (1986). Continuities in reading acquisition, reading skill, and reading disability. *Remedial and Special Education, 7,* 11-21.

Perfetti, C. A., Beck, I., Bell, L., & Hughes, C. (1987). Phonemic knowledge and learning to read are reciprocal: A longitudinal study of first grade children. *Merrill-Palmer Quarterly, 33.* 283-319.

Perfetti, C. A., & Lesgold, A. M. (1977). Discourse comprehension and sources of individual differences. In M. Just & P Carpenter (Eds.), *Cognitive processes in comprehension* (pp- 141-183). Hillsdale, NJ: Erlbaum

Pratt, A. C.., & Brady, S. (1988). Relation of phonological awareness to reading disability in children and adults. *Journal of Educational Psychology, 80.* 319-323.

Pressley, M., & Levin, J. R.. (1987). Elaborative learning strategies for the inefficient learner. In S. J. Ceci (Ed.), *Handbook of cognitive, social, and neuropsychological aspects of learning disabilities* (Vol. 2, pp. 175-212). Hillsdale, NJ: Lawrence Erlbaum Associates.

Rack, J. P, Snowling, M. J., & Olson, R. K. (1992). The nonword reading deficit in developmental dyslexia: A review. *Reading Research Quarterly, 27,* 29-53.

Rapala, M. M., & Brady, S. (1990). Reading ability and short-term memory: The role of phonological processing. *Reading and Writing: An Interdisciplinary Journal, 2,* 1-25.

Rayner, K., & Pollatsek, A. (1989). *The psychology of reading.* Englewood Cliffs, NJ: Prentice Hall.

Reed, J. C. (1970). The deficits of retarded readers--Fact or artifact? *The Reading Teacher, 23,* 347-357.

Reed, M. A. (1989). Speech perception and the discrimination of brief auditory cues in reading disabled children. *Journal of Experimental Child Psychology, 48,* 270-292.

Reynolds, C. R. (1985). Measuring the aptitude-achievement discrepancy in learning disability diagnosis. *Remedial and Special Education, 6,* 37-55.

Rispens, J., van Yeren, T., & van Duijn, G. (1991). The irrelevance of IQ to the definition of learning disabilities: Some empirical evidence. *Journal of Learning Disabilities, 24,* 434-438.

Royer, J. M., Kulhavy, R., Lee, S., & Peterson, S. (1986). The relationship between reading and listening comprehension. *Educational and Psychological Research, 6,* 299-314.

Royer, J. M., Sinatra, G. M., & Schumer, H. (1990). Patterns of individual differences in the development of listening and reading comprehension. *Contemporary Educational Psychology, 15,* 183-196.

Rutter, M. (1978). Prevalence and types of dyslexia. In A. Benton & D. Pearl (Eds.), *Dyslexia: An appraisal of current knowledge,* (pp. 5-28). New York: Oxford University Press.

Rutter, M., & Yule, W. (1975). The concept of specific reading retardation. *Journal of Child Psychology and Psychiatry, 16,* 181-197.

Scarborough, H. S. (1984). Continuity between childhood dyslexia and adult reading. *British Journal of Psychology, 75,* 329-348.

Scheffler, I. (1985). *Of human potential.* New York: Routledge & Kegan Paul.

Seidenberg, M. S., Bruck, M., Fornarolo, G., & Backman, J. (1985). Word recognition processes of poor and disabled readers? Do they necessarily differ? *Applied Psycholinguistics, 6,* 161-180.

Seidenberg, M. S., Bruck, M., & Fornarolo, G., & Backman, J. (1986). Who is dyslexic? Reply to Wolf. *Applied Psycholinguistics, 7,* 77-84.

Seidenberg, M. S., & McClelland, J. L. (1989). A distributed, developmental model of word recognition and naming. *Psychological Review, 96,* 523-568.

Senf, G. M. (1986). LD research in sociological and scientific perspective. In J. K. Torgesen & Y. L. Wong (Eds.), *Psychological and educational perspectives on learning disabilities* (pp. 27-53). New York: Academic Press.

Shankweiler, D., Crain, S., Brady, S., & Macaruso, P (1992). Identifying the causes of reading disability. In P Gough, L. Ehri, & R. Treiman (Eds.), *Reading acquisition* (pp. 275-305). Hillsdale, NJ: Erlbaum.

Share, D. L., Jorm, A., McGee, R., Silva, P A., Maclean, R., Matthews, R., & Williams, S. (1987a). Dyslexia and other myths. Unpublished manuscript. University of Otago Medical School. Dunedin, New Zealand.

Share, D. L., McGee, R., McKenzie, D., Williams, S., & Silva, P A. (1987b). Further evidence relating to the distinction between specific reading retardation and general reading backwardness. *British Journal of Developmental Psychology, 5,* 35-44.

Share, D. L., McGee, R., & Silva, P (1989). IQ and reading progress: A test of the capacity notion of IQ. *Journal of the American Academy of Child and Adolescent Psychiatry , 28,* 97-100.

Share, D. L., & Silva, P A. (1987). Language deficits and specific reading retardation: Cause or effect? *British Journal of Disorders of Communication, 22,* 219-226.

Shepard, L. (1980). An evaluation of the regression discrepancy method for identifying children with learning disabilities. *Journal of Special Education, 14,* 79-91.

Siegel, L. S. (1985). Psycholinguistic aspects of reading disabilities. In L. Siegel & F. Morrison (Eds.), *Cognitive development in atypical children* (pp. 45-65). New York: Springer-Verlag.

Siegel, L. S. (1988). Evidence that IQ scores are irrelevant to the definition and analysis of reading disability. *Canadian Journal of Psychology, 42,* 201-215.

Siegel, L. S. (1989). IQ is irrelevant to the definition of learning disabilities. *Journal of Learning Disabilities 22.* 469-478.

Siegel, L. S. (in press). Phonological processing deficits as the basis of developmental dyslexia: Implications for remediation. In J. Riddoch & G. Humphreys (Eds.), *Cognitive neuropsychology and cognitive rehabilitation.* Hillsdale, NJ: Erlbaum.

Siegel, L. S., & Faux, D. (1989). Acquisition of certain grapheme-phoneme correspondences in normally achieving and disabled readers. *Reading and Writing: An Interdisciplinary Journal, 1,* 37-52.

Siegel, L. S.., & Heaven, R. K.. (1986). Categorization of learning disabilities. In S. J.. Ceci (Ed.), *Handbook of cognitive, social, and neuropsychological aspects of learning disabilities* (Vol. 1, pp. 95-121). Hillsdale, NJ: Lawrence Erlbaum Associates.

Siegel, L. S., & Ryan, E. B. (1988). Development of grammatical-sensitivity, phonological, and short-term memory skills in normally achieving and learning disabled children. *Developmental Psychology, 24,* 28-37.

Siegel, L. S., & Ryan, E. B. (1989). Subtypes of developmental dyslexia: The influence of definitional variables. *Reading and Writing: An Interdisciplinary Journal, 1,* 257-287.

Silva, P A., McGee, R., & Williams, S. (1985). Some characteristics of 9-year-old boys with general reading backwardness or specific reading retardation. *Journal of Child Psychology and Psychiatry, 26,* 407-421.

Slaghuis, W. L., & Lovegrove, W. S. (1985). Spatial-frequency dependent visible persistence and specific reading disability. *Brain & Language, 4,* 219-240.

Slaghuis, W. L., & Lovegrove, W. S. (1987). The effect of field size and luminance on spatial-frequency dependent visible persistence and specific reading disability. *Bulletin of the Psychonomic Society, 25,* 38-40.

Snowling, M. (1980). The development of grapheme-phoneme correspondence in normal and dyslexic readers. *Journal of Experimental Child Psychology 29,* 294- 305.

Snowling, M. (1981). Phonemic deficits in developmental dyslexia. *Psychological Research, 43,* 219-234.

Snowling, M. (1987). *Dyslexia.* Oxford: Basil Blackwell.

Snowling, M., Stackhouse, J., & Rack, J. (1986). Phonological dyslexia and dysgraphia--a developmental analysis. *Cognitive Neuropsychology, 3,* 309-339.

Solman, R. T., & May, J. G. (1990). Spatial localization discrepancies: A visual deficiency in poor readers. *American Journal of Psychology, 103,* 243-263.

Spache, G. D. (1981). *Diagnostic reading scales.* Monterey, CA: CTB/McGraw-Hill.

Spring, C., & French, L. (1990). Identifying children with specific reading disabilities from listening and reading discrepancy scores. *Journal of Learning Disabilities, 23,* 53-58.

Stanley, G., Smith, G., & Powys, A. (1982). Selecting intelligence tests for studies of dyslexic children. *Psychological Reports, 50,* 787-792.

Stanovich, K. E. (1986a). Cognitive processes and the reading problems of learning disabled children: Evaluating the assumption of specificity. In J. Torgesen & B. Wong (Eds.). *Psychological and educational perspectives on learning disabilities* (pp. 87-131). New York: Academic Press.

Stanovich, K. E. (1986b). Matthew effects in reading: Some consequences of individual differences in the acquisition of literacy. *Reading Research Quarterly, 21,* 360-407.

Stanovich, K. E. (1988a). Explaining the differences between the dyslexic and the garden-variety poor reader: The phonological-core variable-difference model. *Journal of Learning Disabilities, 21,* 590-612.

Stanovich, K. E. (1988b). The right and wrong places to look for the cognitive locus of reading disability. *Annals of Dyslexia, 38,* 154-177.

Stanovich, K. E.. (1989). Learning disabilities in broader context. *Journal of Learning Disabilities, 22,* 287-297.

Stanovich, K. E. (1991a). Discrepancy definitions of reading disability: Has intelligence led us astray? *Reading Research Quarterly, 26,* 7-29.

Stanovich, K. E. (1991b). Speculations on the causes and consequences of individual differences in early reading acquisition. In P Gough, L. Ehri, & R. Treiman (Eds.), *Reading Acquisition* (pp. 307-342). Hillsdale, NJ: Erlbaum Associates.

Stanovich, K. E., & Cunningham, A. E. (1992). Studying the consequences of literacy within a literate society: The cognitive correlates of print exposure. *Memory & Cognition, 20,* 51-68.

Stanovich, K. E., Cunningham, A. E., & Feeman, D. J. (1984). Intelligence, cognitive skills, and early reading progress. *Reading Research Quarterly, 19,* 278-303.

Stanovich, K. E., Nathan, R., & Vala-Rossi, M. (1986). Developmental changes in the cognitive correlates of reading ability and the developmental lag hypothesis. *Reading Research Quarterly, 21,* 267-283.

Stanovich, K. E., Nathan, R. G., & Zolman, J. E. (1988). The developmental lag hypothesis in reading: Longitudinal and matched reading-level comparisons. *Child Development, 59,* 71-86.

Stanovich, K. E., & West, R. F. (1989). Exposure to print and orthographic processing. *Reading Research Quarterly, 24,* 402-433.

Sticht, T. G.., & James, J. H.. (1984). Listening and reading. In P. D. Pearson (Ed.), *Handbook of reading research* (pp. 293-317). NY: Longman.

Taylor, H. G., Lean, D., & Schwartz, S. (1989). Pseudoword repetition ability in learning-disabled children. *Applied Psycholinguistics, 10,* 203-219.

Thomson, M. (1982). Assessing the intelligence of dyslexic children. *Bulletin of the British Psychological Society, 35,* 94-96.

Tindal, G., & Marston, D. (1986). Approaches to assessment. In J. K.. Torgesen & B. Y. L. Wong (Eds.), *Psychological and educational perspectives on learning disabilities* (pp. 55-84). Orlando, FL: Academic Press, Inc.

Torgesen, J. (1985). Memory processes in reading disabled children. *Journal of Learning Disabilities, 18,* 350-357.

Torgesen, J. K. (1986). Controlling for IQ. *Journal of Learning Disabilities, 19,* 452.

Torgesen, J. K., Dahlem, W. E., & Greenstein, J. (1987). Using text recordings to enhance reading comprehension in learning disabled adolescents. *Learning Disabilities Focus, 3,* 30-38.

Torgesen, J. K., & Wong, B. (1986). *Psychological and educational perspectives on learning disabilities.* New York: Academic Press.

Torneus, M. (1984). Phonological awareness and reading: A chicken and egg problem. *Journal of Educational Psychology, 76,* 1346-1358.

Trieman, R., & Baron, J. (1983). Phonemic-analysis training helps children benefit from spelling-sound rules. *Memory & Cognition, 11,* 382-389.

Treiman, R., & Hirsh-Pasek, K. (1985). Are there qualitative differences in reading behavior between dyslexics and normal readers? *Memory and Cognition, 13,* 357-364.

Tunmer, W. E., & Nesdale, A. R. (1985). Phonemic segmentation skill and beginning reading. *Journal of Educational Psychology, 77,* 417-427.

van den Bos, K. P (1989). Relationship between cognitive development, decoding skill, and reading comprehension in learning disabled Dutch children. In P. G. Aaron & R. M. Joshi (Eds.), *Reading and writing disorders in different orthographic systems.* (pp. 75-86). Dordrecht, The Netherlands: Kluwer Academic.

van der Wissel, A. (1987). IQ profiles of learning disabled and mildly mentally retarded children: A psychometric selection effect. *British Journal of Developmental Psychology, 5,* 45-51.

van der Wissel, A., & Zegers, F. E. (1985). Reading retardation revisited. *British Journal of Developmental Psychology, 3,* 3-9.

Vellutino, F. R. (1978). Toward an understanding of dyslexia: Psychological factors in specific reading disability. In A. L. Benton & D. Pearl (Eds.), *Dyslexia,* (PP. 59-111). New York: Oxford University Press.

Vellutino, F. R. (1979). *Dyslexia: Theory and research.* Cambridge, MA: MIT Press.

Vellutino, F. R., & Scanlon, D. M. (1987). Phonological coding, phonological awareness, and reading ability: Evidence from a longitudinal and experimental study. *Merrill-Palmer Quarterly, 33,* 321-363.

Vogler, G., Baker, L. A., Decker, S. N., DeFries, J. C., & Huizinga, D. (1989). Cluster analytic classification of reading disability subtypes. *Reading and Writing: An Interdisciplinary Journal, 1,* 163-177.

Wagner, R. K.., & Torgesen, J. K. (1987). The nature of phonological processing and its causal role in the acquisition of reading skills. *Psychological Bulletin, 101,* 192-212.

Walberg, H. J., & Tsai, S. (1983). Matthew effects in education. *American Educational Research Journal, 20,* 359-373.

Werker, J. F., & Tees, R. C. (1987). Speech perception in severely disabled and average reading children. *Canadian Journal of Psychology, 41,* 48-61.

Williams, J. P. (1984). Phonemic analysis and how it relates to reading. *Journal of Learning Disabilities, 17,* 240-245.

Williams, J. P. (1986). The role of phonemic analysis in reading. In J. Torgesen & B. Wong (Eds.), *Psychological and educational perspectives on learning disabilities* (pp. 399-416). New York: Academic Press.

Willows, D. M. (1991). Visual processes in learning disabilities. In B. Wong (Ed.) *Learning about learning disabilities* (pp. 163-193). New York: Academic Press.

Wolf, M. (1991). Naming speed and reading: The contribution of the cognitive neurosciences. *Reading Research Quarterly, 26,* 123-141.

FROM RESEARCH TO CLINICAL ASSESSMENT OF READING AND WRITING DISORDERS: THE UNIT OF ANALYSIS PROBLEM

VIRGINIA W. BERNINGER   TERESA M. HART
College of Education DQ-12
University of Washington
Seattle, WA 98195
U.S.A.

ABSTRACT: A battery of developmental measures and achievement measures, which was administered to 100 first grade, 100 second grade, and 100 third grade children, and the theoretical models of reading and writing acquisition underlying the battery are described. An overview is provided of the previous major results based on group analytical techniques (multiple regression, canonical correlational analysis, and structural equation modeling) to be compared with the results of the individual subject analyses, which are the focus of the research reported here. Three criteria (absolute, relative, and combined absolute +relative) were used to identify individuals who had a disorder (low functioning, underachieving, or learning disabled, respectively) on each of the developmental and academic measures and to analyze their profiles in reference to the set of variables validated by the group analyses. Comparison of the group and individual subject analyses indicates that it is difficult to generalize from the group as the unit of analysis to the individual as the unit of analysis in a simple one-to-one fashion. Most identified individuals had a disorder in at least one of the relevant variables identified in the group analysis, but few had disorders in all the relevant variables. The variability across individual profiles for the same reading or writing disorder shows that multiple etiologies or developmental processes can contribute to the same academic achievement disorder.

Results based on data aggregated over individuals and results based on data aggregated over items or trials for a single individual do not necessarily correspond (Berninger & Abbott, 1992b; Burstein, 1980; Cronbach, 1976; Dogan & Rokkan, 1969; Engel, 1960; Peckham, Glass, & Hopkins, 1969; Raudenbush, 1988; Robinson, 1950; Sternbach, 1966). The common practice of drawing inferences at one unit of analysis from data analyses performed on another, higher-unit of analysis has thus been referred to as the ecological fallacy (e.g., Robinson, 1950). In some cases, the fallacy is to draw inferences about classrooms when the unit of analysis is the school as an organizational unit (e.g., Burstein, 1980; Glass & Stanley, 1970; Sirotnik, 1980). In other cases, the fallacy is to draw inferences about the individual when the unit of analysis is a group of research participants (e.g., Berninger & Abbott, 1992b).

The ecological fallacy can be avoided by recognition that the unit of analysis places limitations on the generalizeability of findings. For example, Berninger and Abbott (1992b) have shown that in the case of research on reading acquisition, results of *group analyses,* in which data are aggregated over individuals, are most appropriately *generalized to groups,* whereas the results of *individual analyses,* in which data are aggregated over stimulus trials in an experimental design, are most appropriately *generalized to individuals.* This unit of analysis problem poses special challenges for scientist/practitioners who want to apply their basic research, based on group analysis, to clinical practice in which the individual is the important unit.

R.M. Joshi and C.K. Leong (eds.), Reading Disabilities: Diagnosis and Component Processes, 33–61.
© 1993 *Kluwer Academic Publishers. Printed in the Netherlands.*

The purpose of the research reported here is to investigate the unit of analysis problem further in another sample, to which, instead of an experiment, we administered a large number of tasks measuring developmental skills or reading and writing achievement. First, we summarize briefly those developmental and academic achievement measures for which the scores were aggregated over task or test items and the theoretical models guiding our inquiry. Next, we provide a brief overview of the results of the major group analyses, which were aggregated over individuals and were performed to address basic research issues about reading and writing acquisition. Then, in order to apply the results of our basic research to clinical practice, we consider three alternative approaches for identifying those individuals who have disorders in specific developmental or academic achievement skills. Finally, we discuss how we may have to modify our understanding of reading and writing disorders when we take into account results based on the individual rather than the group unit of analysis.

Description of the Sample and Measures Administered

SAMPLE

Although the ultimate aim of this line of research is to improve assessment of reading and writing disorders, we studied an unreferred, non-clinical sample for two reasons. First, we wanted a sample as free as possible of referral bias, which may affect the sex ratio of a disorder (see Shaywitz, Shaywitz, Fletcher, & Escobar, 1990) or the relative distribution of specific kinds of reading or writing disorders or the co-occurrence of other developmental disorders such as attention deficit or conduct disorder with reading and writing disorders. Second, we believe that reading is a complex mental activity drawing upon multiple brain systems, any one(s) of which may fail to develop efficiently in a given child. Vellutino, Scanlon, and Tanzman (1991) have pointed out the importance of investigating multiple variables rather than single variables in research on reading disorders. Thus, we validated measures of developmental skills based on theoretical models of multiple variables contributing to normal reading and writing achievement; these measures could then be used to construct profiles of relative strengths and weaknesses in developing readers and writers in which each developmental or achievement skill falls along a continuum, ranging from very low to very high.

Three hundred children (grades 1, 2, 3) participated who attended one of eight elementary schools in three school systems located in suburban, suburban/rural, or urban communities in the Northwestern United States. Half the sample (25 girls, 25 boys at each grade level) was representative of the United States population on ethnic and adult level of education variables. The other half was primarily Caucasian and Asian-American and highly educated (high school + or college or college +). Because both samples showed the same pattern of correlations between predictor (developmental) and criterion (achievement measures), the two samples were pooled for further group analyses. For the total sample, 6% were Asian-American, 6% were African-American, 84% were Caucasian, 3% were Hispanic, and <1% were Native American; mother's educational level ranged from <high school (3%) to high school (17%), to high school+ (29%), to college or college+ (51%). Age ranged from a mean of 6 years-11 months for grade 1 (SD = 4.4 months), to 8 years-0 month for grade 2 (SD = 4.8 months), to 8 years-10 months for grade 3 (SD = 4.9 months). Nine percent of the children were left handed.

MEASURES

Sixteen developmental measures (the alphabet task, six finger function tasks, tests of visual-motor integration, expressive vocabulary, syllable segmentation, phonemic segmentation, word finding or verbal fluency, sentence memory, and orthographic coding of whole words, single letters, and letter clusters) and *seven achievement measures* (3 component reading skills--reading real words, reading nonwords, passage comprehension, and 4 component writing skills--handwriting, spelling, narrative composition, and expository composition) were administered in two individual sessions of about 45-60 minutes each. The developmental measures were chosen because they were thought to operationalize skills children bring to the task of learning to read or write, which may constrain or interfere with skill acquisition, but which do not cause learning independent of the constructive processes of the learner, the motivation of the learner, the skill of the teacher, and the nature and appropriateness of learning opportunities (see Berninger, Hart, Abbott & Karovsky, 1992). To control for Type 1 errors alpha was set at $p < .001$ to evaluate the validity of the developmental measures for assessing component reading and writing skills (achievement measures). Each of these measures is described briefly below and more fully in Berninger, Yates, Cartwright, Rutberg, Remy, and Abbott (1992) and Berninger, Hart, Abbott, and Karovsky (1992).

DEVELOPMENTAL MEASURES

Alphabet Task (AT) (Berninger & Alsdorf, 1989). Children were asked to print the alphabet in order in lower case letters on lined paper. The number of correctly produced letters in the first 15 seconds (reversals, transpositions, omissions, and capital letters were counted as errors) correlated with all component reading and writing measures.

Finger Succession (FS) (Wolff, Gunnoe, & Cohen, 1983). Of the six finger function tasks, finger succession had the best interrater and test-retest reliability and validity for writing assessment (Berninger & Rutberg, 1992) and is the only finger task considered in regard to the unit of analysis problem. Children were asked to touch their thumb with each finger, in sequential order, beginning with the little finger and moving to the index finger (first with the right hand out of view, then with the left hand out of view). The time required for five cycles of touching each finger in succession of the dominant hand (no significant differences between it and the non-dominant hand) correlated with handwriting and composition.

Visual-Motor Integration (VMI) (Beery Test), (Beery, 1982). Children copied geometric forms of increasing difficulty. This test correlated with spelling and all component reading measures.

Phonetic/Semantic Code (P/S) (Vocabulary subtest of WISC-R), (Wechsler, 1974). Children defined orally the meaning of words of increasing difficulty. This task correlated with all component reading measures but with no component writing measures.

Syllabic Coding (Syl) (Part I, Modified Rosner Test of Auditory Analysis) (Berninger, Thalberg, DeBruyn, & Smith, 1987, Appendix). Children were asked to repeat a designated polysyllabic word (e.g., cowboy) and then to say it again without a designated syllable (e.g., cow). This task correlated with all component reading and writing measures.

Phonemic Coding (Pho) (Parts II, III, Modified Rosner Test of Auditory Analysis) (Berninger et al.,1987, Appendix). Children were asked to repeat a word (e.g., coat) and then to say it again without a designated phoneme (e.g., /k/). This task correlated with all component reading and writing measures.

Word Finding (WF) (Verbal Fluency Subtest of the McCarthy Scales of Children's Abilities) McCarthy, 1972). Children were asked to tell all the examples they could think of for four designated categories: food, animals, clothing, and things to ride. This task correlated with all component reading and writing measures.

Sentence Memory (SM) (Subject of Stanford-Binet, IV Ed.) (Thorndike, Hagen, & Sattler, 1986). Children were asked to repeat orally presented sentences of increasing length and complexity. This test, which requires syntactic analysis as well as verbatim memory, correlated with spelling and one composition measure (narrative-words), but with all component reading measures.

Whole Word Orthographic Coding (WW) (Berninger, Yates, & Lester, 1991). Children were asked to decide whether a second printed word matched a first printed word, which had been presented for just one second, exactly. This task correlated with all component reading and writing measures.

Letter Orthographic Coding (L) (Berninger, Yates et al., 1991). Children were asked to decide whether a printed letter had appeared in a previously printed word, which had been exposed for just one second. This task correlated with all component reading and writing measures.

Letter Cluster Orthographic Coding (LC) (Berninger, Yates et al., 1991). Children were asked to decide whether a printed letter cluster (2 adjacent letters) had appeared in exactly that order in a previous printed word, which had been exposed for just one second. This task correlated with all component reading and writing measures.

ACHIEVEMENT MEASURES

Reading Real Words or Word Identification (WI) (Woodcock Reading Mastery Test-Revised, Woodcock, 1987). Children were asked to pronounce real words of increasing difficulty.

Reading Nonwords or Word Attack (WA) (Woodcock Reading Mastery Test-Revised, Woodcock, 1987). Children were asked to pronounce nonwords of increasing difficulty, which could be translated into phonology but not meaning via letter-phoneme or letter cluster-syllable/subsyllable connections (Berninger, Yates et al., 1991) abstracted from case by case experience with analogous words (Berninger & Abbott, 1992).

Passage Comprehension (PC) (Woodcock Reading Mastery Test-Revised, Woodcock, 1987). Children were asked to supply a missing word that made sense given the context (immediate sentence and preceding text).

Handwriting (H) (Copying Subtest, Group Diagnostic Test, Monroe & Sherman, 1966). Children were asked to copy a short paragraph. (Time limit was 90 seconds.) The written protocols were scored for accuracy (number of words correctly reproduced).

Spelling (SP) (Wide-Range Achievement Test, Jastak & Wilkinson, 1984). Children spelled words in writing from dictation. (Time limit was 15 seconds per word from the time the examiner finished pronouncing the word for a second time.) The written spellings were scored for accuracy.

Narrative Composition (Berninger, Yates, et al., 1992). Children were asked to write a story beginning with the frame, "One day_____ (choose person) had the best or worst day (choose) at school." (Time limit was 5 minutes.) These were scored for number of words (NW), an index of fluency, and number of clauses, an index of micro-organization (NC) (see Berninger, & Fuller, (1992), for rationale), which correlated on the average, about .60 with mean ratings of quality.

Expository Composition (Berninger, Yates,et al., 1992). Children were asked to write an explanation beginning with the frame, "I like _____ (choose someone, some place, or some thing) because_____ (explain why). (Time limit was 5 minutes.) Again, these were scored for number of words (EW) and number of clauses (EC).

Theoretical Model Guiding Reading Acquisition Research

The Multiple Connections Model (Berninger, Chen, & Abbott, 1988; Berninger & Abbott, 1992), which is grounded in four principles of developmental psychobiology--normal variation, redundancy, alternative pathways, and critical development periods (Berninger & Traweek, 1991), offers a theoretical framework for diagnosing and remediating a specific reading disability in word recognition. According to this model, there are *multiple orthographic codes*--for whole words, single letters, and letter clusters (Berninger, 1987; Berninger, Yates, & Lester, 1991), *multiple phonological codes*--for phonetic, phonemic, and syllabic/subsyllabic units (Berninger, Abbott, & Shurtleff, 1990; Berninger, Proctor, DeBruyn, & Smith, 1988; Studdert-Kennedy, 1974), and *multiple connections between orthographic-phonological codes of corresponding grain size* (Berninger, 1990; Berninger, Chen, & Abbott 1988; Berninger & Abbott, 1992). Each of the multiple connections--whole word-phonetic/semantic, letter-phoneme, and letter cluster-syllable/subsyllable--corresponds to a different instructional technique for word recognition--look-say, phonics, and word families or structural analysis, respectively (Berninger, 1990). (N.B. The phonetic code is referred to as a phonetic/semantic code in our study because for a real word the phonetic code cannot be assessed without also activating the semantic code. The *phonetic code* involves the whole spoken word, whereas the *phonemic* code involves sub-syllable segments. The letter cluster code can map onto syllables or subsyllable units such as the rime [e.g., part of syllable remaining when the onset phoneme(s) is(are) deleted, Trieman, 1985] or onto a single phoneme [e.g., in vowel digraphs or diphthongs].)

The model is subsymbolic (see Van Orden, Pennington, & Stone, 1990) in that codes are conceptualized as procedures for transforming stimulus information into unitary mental representations and not as the information they represent--the content of the code becomes available only after the decoding process is complete (see Johnson, 1978). Thus codes can operate without explicit knowledge of rules. Connections between codes of corresponding grain size can form through abstraction of orthographic-phonological covariance (Van Orden et al., 1990) either inductively from case experience or deductively with explicit instruction.

The Multiple Connections Model differs from Dual Route Theory, which posits a lexical route (for irregular words) and a nonlexical route (for regular words), in that the three orthographic-phonological code connections can operate on either regular or irregular words. Indeed few words are completely irregular; usually the onset phoneme(s) of each syllable is(are) regular and only the remaining rime is irregular (in terms of letter-phonemes but not necessarily in terms of letter cluster-subsyllable). So both letter-phoneme and letter cluster-subsyllable connections can be used to read irregular words (Berninger, 1990). The Multiple Connections Model differs form Connectionist Models that are focused on computational processes in the "hidden units" between input and output in that it is focused on the "visible" units of orthographic and phonological segmentation that educators can manipulate during reading instruction. Indeed, initial instruction focused on development of orthographic and phonological codes resulted in relative gains over subsequent conventional instruction aimed at sight words, phonics, and structural analysis (Berninger & Traweek, 1991).

Developmental dissociations (uneven development) between corresponding orthographic and phonological codes can interfere with acquisition of specific orthographic-phonological code connections and thus with a child's ability to benefit from a particular instructional methodology (sight words, phonics, structural analysis) (Berninger & Hart, in press). Although children can acquire some degree of word recognition skill with one or two orthographic-phonological code connections, optimum proficiency seems to require all three code connections (Berninger & Abbott, 1992a).

Theoretical Model Guiding Writing Acquisition Research

According to the Developmental Constraints Model of Writing Acquisition (Berninger, Mizokawa, & Bragg, 1991), different kinds of constraints operate on the writing acquisition process at different developmental stages. Early in writing acquisition (especially the primary grades), three neurodevelopmental processes may interfere with rapid, automatic production of written language: (a) retrieval of letter symbols; (b) neurological soft signs elicited by finger function tasks (which indicate an immature fine-motor output system, Wolff et al., 1983); and (c) visual-motor integration. Inefficiencies in these low-level processes may contribute to future writing disabilities directly (because of the enormous sustained effort needed to produce written words) or indirectly (because of an aversion to writing that generalizes from the early frustration related to producing written language).

Later in writing acquisition (especially during the intermediate grades), when production of alphabet letters and of a set of functional spelling words has become automatized, the writing process is more likely to be constrained by ability to generate different units of written language-- the word, the sentence, or text-level structures such as the paragraph. Once proficiency in generating different units of language is achieved (especially during the junior high school years), the writing process is more likely to be constrained by cognitive processes such as planning, translating, and revising (Hayes & Flower, 1980) in the construction of larger stretches of text.

Thus, from a developmental perspective, *neurodevelopmental constraints* are more likely to be operating early in writing acquisition, *linguistic constraints* are more likely to be operating next, and *cognitive constraints* are most likely to be operating later in the writing acquisition process. In some cases, particularly beyond the beginning stages constraints may be operating at more than one level and constraints at all levels may need to be addressed. The general principle of intervention, however, is to remediate lower-level neurodevelopmental constraints, if present, to free up attentional resources for the higher-level nonautomatic aspects of writing at the linguistic and cognitive levels.

Major Results Based on Group Analyses for Reading Acquisition

Berninger and Abbott (1992a) used multiple orthographic codes (whole word, letter, and letter cluster) and multiple phonological codes (phonetic, phonemic, syllabic) as predictor measures in multiple regressions in which the criterion measure was reading real words or nonwords in isolation. For primary grade children each of the orthographic and phonological codes above explained unique increments of variance in reading real words, and all of the above except letter coding explained unique increments of variance in reading nonwords.

Structural equation modeling (EQS, Bentler, 1991) was also applied to analyze a structural model of the relationships among a latent *orthographic coding factor* (underlying the whole word, letter, and letter cluster coding measures), a latent *phonological coding factor* (underlying the syllable and phonemic segmentation measures) and a *reading achievement factor* (underlying reading real words and reading nonwords). In grade 1 only the orthographic path to reading was significant; however, in grades 2 and 3 only the phonological path to reading was significant-- orthography contributed to reading indirectly through phonology; at all grade levels both the orthographic and phonological factors contributed to the overall fit of the model (Abbott & Berninger, 1992a).

Major Results Based on Group Analyses for Writing Acquisition

Multiple regression was used to identify the combination of developmental measures accounting for the most variance in each component writing skill. For handwriting, the combination of the alphabet task, whole word and letter cluster orthographic coding, and finger succession accounted for the most variance (R^2 = .66). For spelling, the combination of nonword reading, visual-motor integration, the alphabet task, Verbal IQ, phonemic segmentation, and whole word coding accounted for the most variance (R^2 = .60). For fluency of composition, the alphabet task, letter cluster coding, and finger succession accounted for the most variance (R^2 ranged from .46 to .27 depending on nature of composition--narrative or expository--and dependent measure--words or clauses). In general, for component writing skills, low-level developmental skills were more likely than high-level verbal reasoning (Verbal IQ) to be included in the combination accounting for the most variance and to account for a greater increment of variance than Verbal IQ.

Canonical correlation analysis identified an *orthographic-linguistic dimension* and an *automaticity dimension* in the battery. The measures accounting for the correlation between the first canonical dimension in the ten developmental measures (sentence memory not included because it seemed to be a better predictor of reading than writing) and the six writing measures were primarily lower-level orthographic and phonological measures (whole word and letter cluster orthographic coding, phonemic coding, nonword reading, the alphabet task, and Verbal IQ). The measures accounting for the greatest correlation between the second canonical dimension in the same set of developmental and writing achievement measures were also lower-level skills related to automaticity of retrieval processes in the orthographic and semantic domains (the alphabet task or orthographic fluency and word finding or verbal fluency). The second canonical dimension correlated negatively with measures requiring non-automatic, effortful analytic skills (nonword reading, visual-motor integration, spelling). The results of the multiple regression and canonical correlations, both of which support the importance of low-level constraints on writing acquisition in the primary grades, are reported in Berninger, Yates et al., (1992).

Structural equation modeling (EQS, Bentler, 1991) was also applied to analyze structural models of the relationships among certain developmental skills and component writing skills (Abbott & Berninger, 1991). When the same latent factors--*orthographic* (underlying whole word, letter, letter cluster-coding) and *phonological* (syllable and phonemic) coding were considered, as had been used for reading, in a model of *spelling* achievement (WRAT-R spelling and spelling accuracy on a narrative and expository compositions), only the path from the orthographic factor to the spelling factor was consistently significant (grades 1, 2, and 3). Phonology contributed to the overall fit of the model and thus to spelling only indirectly through orthography.

Likewise, when the relationships among an *orthographic coding factor* (whole word, letter, letter cluster), a *fine motor factor* (finger succession and total score for four finger tasks yielding an accuracy score), and *handwriting factor* (accuracy on the copying task) was modeled, consistently, across grades 1, 2, and 3, only the path from orthographic coding to handwriting was significant. The fine motor factor contributed to overall fit of the model and thus to handwriting only indirectly through orthography.

When the relationships among an *oral language factor* (underlying the information, similarities, vocabulary, and comprehension subtests of the WISC-R, syllable and phoneme segmentation, word finding, and sentence memory), a *reading factor* (underlying reading real and nonwords and passage comprehension) and a *composition factor* (underlying narrative and expository compositions--words and clauses) were modeled, relationships depended on grade level. In grade 1, only the path from reading to composition was significant. In grade 2, the paths from both oral language and reading to composition were significant, but the path from oral language was considerably more sizeable. By grade 3, however, both the paths from oral language and from reading to composition were significant and of comparable magnitude.

Translation of Group Results to the Individual Case

Berninger, Hart, Abbott, & Karovsky (1992) compared three empirical approaches to defining disorders in the predictor developmental measures and criterion reading and writing achievement measures described here (with the exception of sentence memory). In the first approach, absolute criteria were used to identify children who fell in the lowest 5% of the normal distribution (based on the mean and standard deviation for the sample); these children were referred to as the *low functioning group*. In the second approach, relative criteria were used to identify those children who were achieving below ability, based on the Mahalanobis statistic (Stevens, 1986), which like the regression discrepancy model takes into account the correlation between IQ and the other measure, but unlike regression assumes a bi-directional relationship between IQ and the other measure and is based on a random effects rather than fixed effects model; these children were referred to as the *underachieving group*. To make the first approach (based on an absolute criterion) comparable to the second approach (based on a relative criterion), the Chi-square criterion for evaluating the extremeness of individual children's Verbal IQ and developmental or achievement scores was set at the .05 level, one-tail test based on the Mahalanobis statistic. In the third approach, the absolute and relative criteria were combined so that an individual had to meet the criteria for both low functioning and underachieving to qualify for the *learning disabled group*.

Of those individual children who qualified as low functioning (absolute criterion), only 44%, on the average, were also significantly discrepant from their Verbal IQ (relative criterion) and thus learning disabled. Of those individuals who were underachieving (relative criterion), only 36% were also low functioning (absolute criterion) and thus learning disabled. Thus, criteria adopted--absolute, relative, or both--greatly affected which individual children were identified as having a disorder in a developmental skill related to reading or writing or a disorder in a component reading or writing skill.

Berninger and Hart (in press) used the absolute criterion to examine the 300 individuals in the sample on a case by case basis on each of the developmental and achievement measures in the battery. Overall, 38% of the first graders, 37% of the second graders, and 53% of the third graders were in the lowest tail (bottom 5%) of the distribution on at least one measure. Likewise, 36% of the first graders, 33% of the second graders, and 35% of the third graders were in the highest tail (top 5%) of the distribution on at least one measure. Moreover, about 10% of the total sample showed a *developmental dissociation* or uneven development between two developmental and/or achievement skills (lowest tail on at least one measure *and* highest tail on at least one measure): 8% of first graders, 8% of second graders, and 18% of third graders.

The specific aim of the research reported in this paper was to extend individual subject analysis beyond the incidence of disorders in isolated skills using only absolute criteria to the *nature of disorders identified within an individual's profile across the various developmental and achievement measures,* depending on whether absolute, relative, or combined absolute and relative criteria were used. The results of this profile analysis are reported in Appendix 1 for the absolute criteria, in Appendix 2 for the relative criteria, and in Appendix 3 for the combined absolute and relative criteria. In each table results are reported only for individuals who *met the criterion on at least one measure*. Although a child's complete profile is reported in Appendices 1, 2, and 3, we interpret only those developmental (or achievement) measures relevant to the theoretical model for a particular component skill in reading or writing; these latter results are summarized in Tables 1, 2, and 3 for the ease of the reader.

ABSOLUTE CRITERIA FOR PROFILE ANALYSIS OF INDIVIDUALS

To begin, we used absolute criteria to identify those individuals in the lowest tail of the distribution (L) in a component reading and writing skill. We also determined the associated developmental or achievement skills that were also in the lowest tail of the distribution (L). These are reported in Table 1 (reading), Table 2 (writing), and Table 3 (within and between reading and writing domains) for (a) combinations of *two measures at a time* (1 achievement disorder and 1 developmental or achievement disorder) and combinations of *all relevant measures* (shown in research to be theoretically important). For reading real words or non words, individual results were analyzed in reference to the multiple orthographic codes and the multiple phonological codes of the Multiple Connections Model. For passage comprehension, individual results were analyzed in reference to word recognition skills (reading real words and nonwords), which have been shown to constrain reading comprehension (Perfetti & Hogaboam, 1975). For the component writing skills, individual results were analyzed in reference to the measures identified by multiple regression as the combination accounting for the most variance in each component writing skill. Finally, developmental dissociations *within the reading domain* (across component skills) or within the writing domain (across component skills) or across the reading and writing domains (between reading and spelling real words, which should depend on the same letter-sound correspondences, see Joshi & Aaron, 1991) were examined.

Reading Real Words. When skills were considered two at a time, disorders in each of the six relevant orthographic or phonological skills co-occurred with a disorder in reading real words. However, none of the children had disorders in all the orthographic and all the phonological skills, although one had disorders in all phonological skills, and one had disorders in all orthographic skills. (see Table 1 and Apendix 1.)

Reading Nonwords. When skills were considered two at a time, disorders in each of the six relevant orthographic *or* phonological skills co-occurred with a disorder in reading nonwords. However, none of the children had a disorder in all orthographic skills or all phonological skills or in all orthographic *and* phonological skills. (See Table 1 and Appendix 1.)

Reading Comprehension. Disorders in reading real words and in reading nonwords co-occurred with disorders in passage comprehension. However, only half of the individuals had disorders in both word recognition skills. (See Table 1 and Appendix 1.)

Handwriting. When skills were considered two at a time, only disorders on the alphabet task and finger succession co-occurred with a handwriting disorder. None of the children had disorders in all the relevant developmental skills. (See Table 2 and Appendix 1.)

Spelling. When skills were considered two at a time, disorders in each of the six relevant skills co-occurred with a disorder in spelling. In addition to the five skills in the column headings, Verbal IQ was a relevant variable, but only 1 had very low Verbal IQ. None of the children had a disorder on all relevant developmental skills. (See Table 2 and Appendix 1.)

Composition. To qualify as having a reliable disorder in composition, a child had to be in the lowest tail of the distribution on at least two of the four composition measures (narrative-words, expository-words, narrative-clauses, or expository-clauses). Of those who qualified, none had a disorder in any of the relevant developmental measures. (See Table 2 and Appendix 1.)

Table 1. Frequency of disorder in developmental or word recognition skills associated with disorder in component reading skill.

Associated Developmental Skills[a]

		P/S	SYL	PHO	WW	L	LC	All 6
Achievement Disorder								
Reading Real Words	N							
Absolute	16	3	4	4	7	6	6	0
Relative	17	5	8	8	9	7	6	4
Combined	9	0	1	1	2	2	1	0
Reading Nonwords	N							
Absolute	14	3	5	3	5	1	5	0
Relative	16	5	8	2	8	8	7	4
Combined	5	1	1	2	1	0	1	0

Associated Word Recognition Skills[b]

		WI	WA	Both
Passage Comprehension N				
Absolute	14	9	8	7
Relative	16	8	9	8
Combined	7	2	1	1

a See footnote e, Appendices 1, 2, or 3
b See footnote f, Appendices 1, 2, or 3

Developmental Dissociations Within the Reading Domain. Disorders *only* in reading nonwords and in reading real words did not co-occur, but disorders in passage comprehension co-occurred with disorders in both reading real words and reading nonwords. Of those with disorders in *reading real words*, 44% did not have a disorder in any other component reading skill. Of those with disorders in *reading nonwords*, 36% did not have a disorder in any other component reading skill. Of those with disorders in *passage comprehension*, 29% did not have a disorder in any other component reading skill. Thus, when absolute criteria are used, either the whole reading system may be underdeveloped or specific components of it may be underdeveloped. (see STET Table 3 and Appendix 1.)

Developmental Dissociations within the Writing Domain. Only disorders in composition co-occurred with disorders in handwriting. None of the children had disorders on all three component writing skills. Thus, when absolute criteria are used, a specific writing component can be underdeveloped independent of the rest of the components of the system. (see Table 3 and Appendix 1.)

Table 2. Frequency of disorder in developmental skill associated with disorder in component writing skill.

Associated Developmental Skills[a]

Achievement Disorder		AT	FS	WW	LC	All 4	
Handwriting	N						
Absolute	4	2	1	0	0	0	
Relative	8	7	1	5	5	1	
Combined	2	2	0	0	0	0	

Associated   Developmental   Skills[a]

Spelling		AT	VMI	PHO	WW	WA	All 5
	N						
Absolute	11	1	1	5	3	4	0
Relative	12	6	6	7	7	7	0
Combined	4	1	0	1	1	0	0

Associated   Developmental   Skills[a]

Composition		AT	FS	LC	All 3	
	N					
Absolute	3	0	0	0	0	
Relative	9	7	2	6	2	
Combined	9	0	0	1	0	

a See footnote e, Appendices 1, 2, or 3

Developmental Dissociations between Word Identification and Spelling. Of those with disorders in *reading real words,* 44% had disorders in *spelling real words.* Of those with disorders in *spelling real words* 64% had disorders in *reading real words.* (see Table 3 and Appendix 1.)

RELATIVE CRITERIA FOR PROFILE ANALYSIS OF INDIVIDUALS

The same analyses reported in the previous section were repeated using the relative criteria. However, both overachievement (O) (significantly above that predicted by VIQ, based on the Mahalanobis statistic) and underachievement (U) (significantly below that predicted by VIQ based on the Mahalanobis statistic) are reported in Appendix 2.

Reading Real Words. When skills were considered two at a time, disorders in each of the six relevant orthographic or phonological skills co-occurred with disorders in reading real words.

Table 3 Developmental dissociations within the reading domain, within the writing domain, and across domains.

		Associated Achievement Skills		
		WA	PC	All 3 reading components
Achievement Disorder				
Reading Real Words (WI)	N			
Absolute	16	0	2	7
Relative	17	0	1	7
Combined	9	0	2	1
		WI	PC	All 3 reading components
Reading Nonwords (WA)	N			
Absolute	14	0	2	7
Relative	15	2	2	6
Combined	5	0	1	1
		WI	WA	All 3 reading components
Passage Comprehension (PC)	N			
Absolute	14	2	1	7
Relative	16	0	1	8
Combined	7	1	0	1

		Associated Achievement Skills		
		Spelling	Composition	All 3 writing components
Achievement Disorder				
Handwriting	N			
Absolute	4	0	1	0
Relative	8	0	2	4
Combined	2	0	0	0
		Handwriting	Composition	All 3 writing components
Spelling	N			
Absolute	11	0	0	0
Relative	12	4	2	4
Combined	4	0	0	0

Table 3. (continued)

		Handwriting	Spelling	All 3 writing components
Composition	N			
Absolute	3	1	0	0
Relative	9	2	3	2
Combined	1	0	0	0

Associated Achievement Skill
Spelling Real Words

			Spelling Real Words
Reading Real Words	N		
Absolute	16		7
Relative	17		3
Combined	9		1

Reading Real Words

			Reading Real Words
Spelling Real Words	N		
Absolute	1		7
Relative	1		7
Combined	4		2

Only 18% of the children who had disorders in reading real words had disorders in all six of the relevant orthographic and phonological skills; in addition, 6% had disorders in all the orthographic codes and 6% had disorders in all the phonological codes. However, 24% were *overachieving* in phonetic/semantic coding, 6% were *overachieving* in phonemic coding, and 6% were *overachieving* in letter cluster coding! (see Table 1 and Appendix 2.)

Reading Nonwords. When skills were considered two at a time, disorders in each of the relevant orthographic and phonological skills co-occurred with a disorder in reading nonwords. Only 25% had disorders in all orthographic and phonological skills and only 12.5% had disorders in all orthographic skills. However, one (with a low VIQ) was *overachieving* in phonetic/semantic coding, syllabic coding, phonemic coding, whole word coding, and letter coding, while underachieving in letter cluster coding! Two others (both with a very superior VIQ) were *overachieving* in phonetic/semantic coding, while underachieving in all other phonological and orthographic codes. (see Table 1 and Appendix 2.)

Reading Comprehension. When skills were considered two at a time, disorders in each of the word recognition skills co-occurred with disorders in reading comprehension, although only 50% were underachieving in both word recognition skills. However, one (with a very superior VIQ) was *overachieving* in reading real words and not underachieving in reading nonwords despite a disorder in reading comprehension! (see Table 1 and Appendix 2.)

Handwriting. When skills were considered two at a time, disorders in each of the relevant developmental skills co-occurred with disorders in handwriting. Only 12.5% had disorders on all the relevant development skills. However, 4 were *overachieving* on finger succession, consistent with the hypothesis that executing this maneuver too quickly may be associated with impulsivity which may interfere with handwriting. (see Table 2 and Appendix 2.)

Spelling. When skills were considered two at a time, disorders in each of the relevant developmental skills co-occurred with disorders in spelling. None with disorders in spelling had disorders in all relevant skills. However, 1 was also *overachieving* on the alphabet task, 1 was also *overachieving* in visual-motor integration, 1 was also *overachieving* in phonemic coding, and 1 was also *overachieving* in nonword reading! (see Table 2 and Appendix 2.)

Composition. When skills were considered two at a time, disorders in each of the relevant developmental skills co-occurred with disorders in composition. However, only 22% had disorders in all relevant skills. (see Table 2 and Appendix 2.)

Developmental Dissociations within the Reading Domain. Disorders in each of the component reading skills co-occurred. Of those with disorders in *reading real words,* only 41% had disorders in all three component reading skills. Of those with disorders in *reading nonwords,* only 40% had disorders in all three component reading skills. Of those with disorders in *passage comprehension,* only 50% had disorders in all three component reading skills. However, 1 who had a disorder in reading nonwords was *overachieving* in passage comprehension; 1 who had a disorder in reading real words was *overachieving* in the other two component reading skills; another 1 who had a disorder in reading real words was *overachieving* in passage comprehension; and 1 who had a disorder in passage comprehension was *overachieving* in reading real words! Of those with disorders only in passage comprehension, 14% were *overachieving* in reading real words! Thus, when relative criteria are used, either the whole reading system may be underdeveloped or specific components can be underdeveloped or overdeveloped. (see Table 3 and Appendix 2.)

Developmental Dissociations within the Writing Domain. Disorders in each of the component writing skills co-occurred. Of those with disorders in handwriting, 50% had disorders in all three component writing skills but 25% did not have disorders in other component writing skills. Of those with disorders in *spelling,* 33% had disorders in all three component writing skills but 17% did not have disorders in other component writing skills. Of those with disorders in *composition,* 22% had disorders in all three component writing skills, but 22% did not have disorders in other component writing skills. Thus, when relative criteria are used, a specific writing component can be underdeveloped or overdeveloped independent of the other writing components. (see Table 3 and Appendix 2.)

Developmental Dissociation between Word Identification and Spelling. Of those who had a disorder in *reading real words*, 18% had a disorder in *spelling real words*. Of those who had a disorder in *spelling real words*, 64% had a disorder in *reading real words*. However, one of these with a disorder in reading real words was *overachieving* in spelling real words! Given that poor oral reading and good spelling have not been reported to co-occur among English-speaking individuals (Joshi & Aaron, 1991), dissociations in this direction may be found in developing children only when relative, not absolute criteria, are used. (see Table 3 and Appendix 2.)

COMBINED ABSOLUTE AND RELATIVE CRITERIA FOR PROFILE ANALYSES OF INDIVIDUALS

The same analyses were repeated again using the combined absolute and relative criteria. Incidence of both disability (D) (based on the combined criteria) and overachievement (O) (based on relative criteria above) are reported in Appendix 3.

Reading Real Words. When skills were considered two at a time, disorders in each of the orthographic and phonological codes (except phonetic/semantic coding) co-occurred with disorders in reading real words. However, none of the children had a disorder in all the orthographic and phonological codes. (See Table 1 and Appendix 3.)

Reading Nonwords. When skills were considered two at a time, disorders in each of the orthographic and phonological skills (except letter coding) co-occurred with disorders in reading nonwords. None of the children had a disorder in all the orthographic and phonological skills. (See Table 1 and Appendix 3.)

Reading Comprehension. Disorders in reading real words and in reading nonwords co-occurred with disorders in reading comprehension. However only 14% of those with a disorder in reading comprehension had a disorder in both word recognition skills. (See Table 1 and Appendix 3.)

Handwriting. When skills were considered two at a time, only a disorder on the alphabet task co-occurred with a disorder in handwriting. None of the children with a disorder in handwriting had a disorder in all the relevant skills. (See Table 2 and Appendix 3.)

Spelling. When skills were considered two at a time, disorders in the alphabet task, phonemic coding, and whole word coding co-occurred with disorders in spelling. However, none of the children with a disorder in spelling had a disorder in all the relevant developmental skills. One (with a below average VIQ) was *overachieving* on the alphabet task, phonemic coding, and nonword reading! (See Table 2 and Appendix 3.)

Composition. When skills were considered two at a time, only a disorder in letter cluster coding co-occurred with a disorder in composition. None of the children with a disorder in composition had a disorder in all the relevant developmental skills. (See Table 2 and Appendix 3.)

Developmental Dissociations within the Reading Domain. Disorders only in reading real words and passage comprehension or only in reading nonwords and passage comprehension co-occurred, but disorders only in reading real words and in reading nonwords did not co-occur. Of those with disorders in *reading real words,* 11% had disorders in all three component reading skills, but 67% did not have disorders in other component reading skills (including 1 who was *overachieving* in the other two component reading skills!). Of those with disorders in *reading nonwords,* 20% had disorders in all three component reading skills, but 60% did not have disorders in the other component reading skills (including 1[not the same as above] who was *overachieving* in the other component reading skills!). Of those with disorders in *reading comprehension,* 14% had disorders in all component reading skills, but 71% did not have disorders in the other component reading skills. Thus, when combined criteria are used, either the whole reading system may be underdeveloped or specific components can be underdeveloped or overdeveloped. (See Table 3 and Appendix 3.)

Developmental Dissociations within the Writing Domain. None of the disorders in component writing skills co-occurred. When combined criteria are used, the writing components appear to be even more orthogonal than when relative criteria are used and a component writing skill can be underdeveloped independent of another component writing skill. (See Table 3 and Appendix 3.)

Developmental Dissociations between Word Identification and Spelling. Of those with a disorder in *reading real words,* only 11% had a disorder in *spelling real words.* Of those with a disorder in *spelling real words,* 50% had a disorder in *reading real words.* One with a disorder in spelling was overachieving in reading real words--a dissociation in the commonly perceived direction (see Joshi & Aaron, 1991). (See Table 3 and Appendix 3.)

IMPLICATIONS FOR THE NONCONTINGENT, NORMAL VARIATION MODEL

Regardless of whether measures were considered two at a time or simultaneously or whether absolute, relative, or combined criteria were used, results supported the *noncontingent, normal variation model* (Berninger & Hart, in press). Not only was there normal variation on each measure (continuous distribution with considerable range) but also normal variation in combinations of developmental (or achievement) disorders associated with the same disorder in a specific reading or writing skill. Specific combinations did not co-occur across children predictably for the same disorder in reading or writing as is characteristic of a syndrome. Disorders in associated developmental or achievement skills appeared to be fairly independent of one another and not contingent on a particular other disorder also co-occurring.

EFFECTS OF VIQ AND CRITERIA ON IDENTIFYING DISORDERS

The number of cases identified as having a disorder in each component reading and writing measure is reported in Table 4 according to the child's Verbal IQ and the criteria employed (absolute or relative). Clearly relatively more children are identified when the child's *Verbal IQ*

Table 4. Relationship between VIQ, criterion for disorder, and probability of being identified as having a reading or writing disorder.

	Absolute Criteria	Relative Criteria
Reading Real Words		
Average IQ & below[a]	13	8
Superior IQ & above[b]	1	7
Reading Nonwords		
Average IQ & below	13	4
Superior IQ & above	0	10
Passage Comprehension		
Average IQ & below	12	6
Superior IQ & above	1	9
Handwriting		
Average IQ & below	2	1
Superior IQ & above	1	6
Spelling		
Average IQ & below	9	2
Superior IQ & above	1	10
Composition		
Average IQ & below	2	0
Superior IQ & above	1	9

[a] 110 and below on prorated WISC-R VIQ;   [b] 120 and above on prorated WISC-R VIQ

is average or below and the criterion is absolute, or when the child's *Verbal IQ is superior or better and the criterion is relative*. Thus, exclusive use of either absolute or relative criteria in identification of learning disorders may unfairly exclude and discriminate against either average and below average or gifted children in the primary grades.

Implications of Individual Analyses for Modifying Interpretation of Group Analyses

On the one hand, in previous research (Berninger & Abbott, 1992b), group analyses, in which variation among children within achievement-level groups was treated as error, yielded results consistent with the notion of one process of learning to read but variation in individual rates of mastering that process. On the other hand, in that same research other approaches to analyses emphasizing the individual as the unit of analysis (treating variation among children in an instructional group as systematic variance or performing separate analyses for each individual in an instructional group and using the individual's responses over stimulus trials to estimate error), yielded results consistent with the notion of multiple processes or pathways in learning to read.

Similarly, in this research when we used group analyses to compare distributions of scores on developmental measures (or composites of these scores) to distributions of scores on achievement measures, we validated models of reading and writing acquisition for *groups of children in general*. This group approach suggested that there is a set of orthographic and phonological coding skills underlying acquisition of word recognition skills. In applying these findings to clinical practice and the identification of children with disorders we might assume that all of these skills would be underdeveloped in all children who struggle to learn to recognize words. Such an assumption is clearly not supported, however, by the individual subject analyses reported here.

What we found was that individual children may, in some cases, have disorders in all these skills, but more often they had disorders in just one specific skill or disorders in a sub-set of those skills. There appeared to be considerable normal variation in which skill or combination of skills was underdeveloped among the children exhibiting a disorder in the same academic skill. This finding, which held whether absolute, relative, or combined absolute and relative criteria were used to define a learning disorder, indicates that multiple profiles of processing disabilities underlie the same disorder in a component reading or writing skill. Moreover, specific areas of strength, as evidenced by overachievement, were also noted in the profiles of children with specific reading or writing disorders. Of great importance, some children did not exhibit disorders on any of the theoretically-relevant developmental skills (e.g., S1 and S2, handwriting; S1, S8, S9, spelling; all 3 subjects, composition; S1, S2, S5, reading real words; S5, S6, S10, reading nonwords; S1, S2, S7, S10, Appendix 1)!

Taken together, these results illustrate that research findings based on analyses aggregated over individuals will not generalize neatly and simply to clinical assessment focused on a single individual. For one thing, theory-based assessment models for reading and writing need to be broadly-based to encompass all the relevant processes that might go awry during the complex reading and writing acquisition process and not just the variables in our assessment battery or other investigators' favorite variables. For example, although phonological awareness is currently considered the single most important variable in reading acquisition (see Leong,, 1991, for recent review), when we used absolute criteria, never more than 35% of the *individuals* who were in the lowest tail for reading real words or nonwords were also in the lowest tail for the phonological skills of syllabic or phonemic coding. When we used relative criteria, never more than 50% of the *individuals* who were underachieving in reading real words or nonwords, were also underachieving in syllabic or phonemic segmentation. In fact, some were even overachieving on these phonological skills! When we used combined criteria, never more than 40% of the *individuals* who were learning disabled in reading real words or nonwords, were also learning disabled in syllabic or phonemic segmentation. Clearly, phonological awareness is not the only important variable placing constraints on the reading acquisition process.

For another thing, there will be considerable normal variation in just which processes may fail to develop normally; and disorders seem to occur independent of one another rather than to co-occur as in symptom clusters. The developmental skills underlying reading and writing acquisition exhibit *non-contingent, normal variation* (Berninger & Hart, 1991, in press), which has important implications for the search for the genetic bases of reading and writing disorders, namely the high probability of finding polygenic influences.

The individual subject analyses reported here show that developmental dissociations are fairly typical within the reading domain, within the writing domain, and across the reading/spelling domains. These results reinforce the importance of replacing our generic label of learning disability with more specific diagnostic categories linked to component reading and writing skills (see Berninger, Hart, Abbott, & Karovsky, 1992).

In conclusion, our group analyses, which investigated the relationship among individual difference on different theoretically-relevant measures for a large group of beginning readers and writers, provided a theoretical framework for assessing reading and writing disorders. At the same time, the group analyses made nature look simpler than it really is--by reducing literacy acquisition to a small set of quantitative measures (regression analyses) and a straightforward story (structural equation modeling) of one process for all children. In contrast, our individual analyses reminded us of how complex nature really is--multiple processes contributing to the same disorder. Whereas the group analyses took into account the entire distribution of scores on the developmental and academic measures, the individual analyses focused on the extremes of the distribution. Of course, some of the differences between group and individual analyses will be due to this difference. However, clinicians use performance at the extremes of the distribution to diagnose specific reading and writing disorders and we need to *link basic research knowledge with the cognitive activity of clinicians*. Practitioners need to realize that research findings based on group analyses may sometimes apply only in part or not at all to individual cases. We do not believe that the solution to the ecological fallacy problem is to eliminate either group or individual analyses, but rather to be cognizant of the creative tension in traversing the levels of analysis and to examine data sets from both perspectives.

ACKNOWLEDGEMENT

This research was supported by Grant No. 25858-01 awarded by the National Institute of Child Health and Human Development to the first author. We thank the children, teachers, principals, and administrative staff of the Bellevue, Northshore, and Seattle Public Schools who participated in this research and acknowledge the assistance of Judith Rutberg, Ana Cartwright, Cheryl Yates, and Elizabeth Remy in data collection and of Robert D. Abbott in statistical consultation. We appreciate the secretarial assistance of Sylvia Mirsepassi throughout this project and are grateful for the suggestion of C.K. Leong to apply the Mahalanobis statistic to profile analysis and for Robert Abbott's helpful comments on an earlier version of this paper.

REFERENCES

Abbott, R., & Berninger, V. (1991, April). *Structural equation modeling of relationships among verbal intelligence, oral language, reading, and beginning writing.* Society for Research in Child Development, Seattle.

Abbott, R.,& Berninger, V. (1992). Structural equation modeling of beginning and developing writing skills. In revision, *Journal of Educational Psychology.*

Beery, K. (1982). *Revised administration, scoring, and teaching manual for the Development Test of Visual-Motor Integration.* Cleveland, OH: Modern Curriculum Press.

Bentler, P.M. (1991). *Theory and implementation of EQS: A structural equations program,* University of California, Los Angeles.

Berninger, V. (1987). Global, component, and serial processing of printed words in beginning readers. *Journal of Experimental Child Psychology, 43,* 387-418.

Berninger, V. (1990). Multiple orthographic codes: Key to alternative instructional methodologies for developing the orthographic-phonological connections underlying word identification. *School Psychology Review, 19,* 518-533.

Berninger, V. (1991) Overview of "Bridging the Gap between Developmental, Neuropsychological, and Cognitive Approaches to Reading." *Learning and Individual Differences, 3,* 163-179.

Berninger, V., & Abbott, R. (1992a). *Multiple connections model of reading: Cross-validation and extension to spelling.* American Educational Research Association, San Fransisco. Also submitted.

Berninger, V., & Abbott, R. (1992b). The unit of analysis and the constructive processes of the learner: Key concepts for educational neuropsychology. *Educational Psychologist, 27,* 223-242.

Berninger, V., Abbott, R., & Shurtleff, H. (1990). Developmental changes in interrelationships among visible language, oral language, and reading and spelling. *Learning and Individual Differences, 2,* 45-66.

Berninger, V., & Alsdorf, B. (1989). Are there errors in error analysis? *Journal of Psychoeducational Assessment, 7,* 209-222.

Berninger, V., Chen, A., & Abbott, R. (1988). A test of the multiple connections model of reading acquisition. *International Journal of Neuroscience, 42,* 283-295.

Berninger, V., & Fuller, F. (1992). Gender differences in orthographic, verbal, and compositional fluency: Implications for diagnosis of writing disabilities in primary grade children. *Journal of School Psychology, 30,* 363-382.

Berninger, V., & Hart, T. (1991, April). *A developmental neuropsychological perspective for reading and writing acquisition.* American Educational Research Association, Boston. In press, *Educational Psychologist.*

Berninger, V., Hart, T., Abbott, R., & Karovsky, P. (1992). Defining reading and writing disabilities with and without IQ: A flexible, developmental perspective. *Learning Disabilities Quarterly. 15,* 103-118.

Berninger, V., Mizokawa, D., & Bragg, R. (1991). Theory-based diagnosis and remediation of writing disabilities. *Journal of School Psychology, 29,* 57-79.

Berninger, V., Proctor, A., DeBruyn, I., & Smith, R. (1988). Relationship of levels of oral language and written language in beginning readers. *Journal of School Psychology, 26,* 341-357.

Berninger, V., & Rutberg, J. (1992). Relationship of finger function to beginning writing: Application to diagnosis of writing disabilities. *Developmental Medicine & Child Neurology, 34,* 155-172.

Berninger, V., & Thalberg, S., DeBruyn, I., & Smith, R. (1987). Preventing reading disabilities by assessing and remediating phonemic skills. *School Psychology Review, 16,* 554-565.

Berninger, V., & Traweek, D. (1991). Effects of a two-phase intervention on three orthographic-phonological code connections. *Learning and Individual Differences, 3,* 323-338.

Berninger, V., Yates, C., Cartwright, A., Rutberg, J., Remy, E., & Abbott, R. (1992). Lower-level developmental skills in beginning writing. *Reading and Writing: An Interdisciplinary Journal, 4,* 257-280.

Berninger, V., Yates, C., & Lester, C. (1991). Multiple orthographic codes in acquisition of reading and writing skills. *Reading and Writing: An Interdisciplinary Journal, 3,* 115-149.

Burstein, L. (1980). The analysis of multilevel data in educational research and evaluation. In D.C. Berliner (Ed.), *Review of research in education* (pp. 158-233). Washington, DC: American Educational Research Association.

Cronbach, L. (with the assistance of Denken, J., & Webb, N.) (1976). *Research on classrooms and schools: Formulation of questions, design, and analysis.* Occasional paper, Stanford Evaluation Consortium, School of Education, Stanford University.

Dogan, M., & Rokkan, S. (Eds.) (1969). *Quantitative ecological analysis in the social sciences.* Cambridge: MIT Press.

Engel, B. (1960). Stimulus-response and individual-response specificity. *Archives of General Psychiatry, 2,* 305-313.

Glass, G.V., & Stanley, J.C. (1970). *Statistical methods in education and psychology.* Englewood Cliffs, NJ: Prentice-Hall.

Hayes, J., & Flower, L. (1980). Identifying the organization of the writing process. In L.W. Gregg & E.R. Steinberg (Eds.), *Cognitive processes in writing.* (pp. 3-30). Hillsdale, NJ: Erlbaum.

Jastak, S., & Wilkinson, G. (1984). *Wide Range Achievement Test-Revised.* Wilmington, DE: Jastak Associates.

Johnson (1978). Coding processes in memory. In W.K. Estes (Ed.), *Handbook of learning and cognitive processes* (Vol. 6, pp. 87-129). Hillsdale, NJ: Erlbaum.

Joshi, R.M., & Aaron, P. (1991). Developmental reading and spelling disabilities: Are these dissociable? In R.M. Joshi (Ed.), *Written Language Disorders* (pp. 1-24). Dordrecht: Kluwer Academic Publishers.

Leong, C.K. (1991). From phonemic awareness to phonological processing to language access in children developing reading proficiency. In D.J. Sawyer, & B.J. Fox (Eds.), *Phonological awareness in reading: The evolution of current perspectives* (pp. 217-254). New York: Springer-Verlag.

McCarthy, D. (1972). *Manual for the McCarthy Scales of Children's Abilities.* San Antonio: The Psychological Corporation.

Monroe, M., & Sherman, E. (1966). *Group Diagnostic Reading Aptitude and Achievement Tests.* Bradenton, FL: C.H. Nevins Printing Co.

Peckham, P., Glass, G. & Hopkins, K. (1969). The experimental unit in statistical analysis. *Journal of Special Education, 3,* 337-349.

Perfetti, C., & Hogaboam, T. (1975). Relationship between single word decoding and reading comprehension skill. *Journal of Educational Psychology, 67,* 461-469.

Raudenbush, S.W. (1988). Educational applications of hierarchical linear models: A review. *Journal of Educational Statistics, 13,* 85-116.

Robinson, W.S. (1950). Ecological correlations and the behavior of individuals. *American Sociological Review, 15,* 351-356.

Shaywitz, S., Shaywitz, B., Fletcher, J., & Escobar, M. (1990). Prevalence of reading disability in boys and girls. Results of the Connecticut longitudinal study. *Journal of the American Medical Association, 264,* 998-1002.

Sirotnik, K. (1980). Psychometric implications of the unit-of-analysis problem with examples from the measurement of organizational climate. *Journal of Educational Measurement, 17,* 245-282.

Sternbach, R. (1966). *Principles of psychophysiology.* New York: Academic Press.

Stevens, J. (1986). *Applied multivariate statistics for the sciences.* Hillsdale, NJ: Lawrence Erlbaum Associates.

Studdert-Kennedy, M. (1974). The perception of speech. In T.A. Sebeok (Ed.), *Current trends in linguistics,* Vol. 12 (pp. 2349-2385). The Hague: Mouton.

Thorndike, R., Hagen, E., & Sattler, J. (1986). *Guide for administering and scoring the Stanford-Binet Intelligence Scale: Fourth Edition.* Chicago: Riverside Publishing.

Treiman, R. (1985). Onsets and rimes as units of spoken syllables: Evidence from children. *Journal of Experimental Child Psychology, 39,* 161-181.

Van Orden, G., Pennington, B., & Stone, G. (1990). Word identification in reading and the promise of subsymbolic psycholinguistics. *Psychological Review, 97,* 1-35.

Vellutino, F., Scanlon, D., & Tanzman, M. (1991). Bridging the gap between cognitive and neuropsychological conceptualizations of reading disability. *Learning and Individual Differences, 3,* 181-203.

Wechsler, D. (1974). *Manual for the Wechsler Intelligence Scale for Children-Revised.* San Antonio: The Psychological Corporation.

Wolff, P., Gunnoe, C., & Cohen, C. (1983). Associated movements as a measure of developmental age. *Developmental Medicine & Child Neurology, 25,* 417-429.

Woodcock, R. (1987). *Woodcock Reading Mastery Tests-Revised.* Circle Pines, MN: American Guidance Service.

APPENDIX 1. DISORDERS IN DEVELOPMENTAL SKILLS ASSOCIATED WITH DISORDERS IN A SPECIFIC READING OR WRITING SKILL[a] (BASED ON ABSOLUTE CRITERA -- L = LOW FUNCTIONING OR LOWEST TAIL OF DISTRIBUTION.)

Disorder	S	G[b]	S[c]	VIQ[d]	Developmental Skills[e]											Academic Skills[f]								
					AT	FS	VMI	P/S	SYL	PHO	SM	WF	WW	L	LC	WI	WA	PC	HA	SP	NW	EW	NC	EC
Reading Real Words																								
1	1	G		122												L				L				
2	1	G		98												L								
3	1	B		80				L	L	L	L		L			L	L	L		L			L	
4	1	B		88					L	L			L			L	L	L	L	L				
5	1	B		119												L	L	L						
6	2	B		92							L		L			L				L				
7	2	B		98								L				L								
8	2	B		70				L	L	L			L	L	L	L	L	L	L	L				
9	2	B		94														L						
10	2	B		106									L	L	L	L				L				
11	2	B		109									L	L	L	L	L	L		L				
12	3	G		88				L	L		L		L	L	L	L	L	L	L	L				
13	3	G		82								L		L	L	L				L				
14	3	G		87										L	L	L				L				
15	3	B		115												L	L							
16	3	B		94			L	L		L			L	L	L	L	L	L		L				
Reading Nonwords																								
1	1	B		80					L	L	L		L			L	L	L		L		L		L
2	1	B		79						L			L	L	L	L	L	L					L	L
3	1	B		101					L	L	L			L	L	L	L	L		L			L	
4	1	B		88													L	L						
5	1	B		119												L	L							
6	1	B		92																				
7	2	G		106			L																	
8	2	G		70					L	L			L			L	L	L	L					
9	2	B		92				L								L								
10	2	B		92																				
11	2	B		87												L								
12	3	B		88				L	L	L	L		L	L	L	L	L	L	L	L				
13	3	G		82				L	L					L	L	L	L	L		L				
14	3	B		94				L	L	L	L					L	L	L		L				

Appendix 1 (continued)

| | | | | | Developmental Skills[e] | | | | | | | | | | | Academic Skills[f] | | | | | | | | |
Disorder	S	G[b]	S[c]	VIQ[d]	AT	FS	VMI	P/S	SYL	PHO	SM	WF	WW	L	LC	WI	WA	PC	HA	SP	NW	EW	NC	EC
Reading Comprehension																								
	1	1	G	97		L							L					L						
	2	1	G	82									L					L						
	3	1	B	80				L	L	L	L		L			L	L	L						
	4	1	B	79					L	L		L				L	L	L						
	5	1	B	88						L				L	L	L	L	L						
	6	1	B	119														L					L	
	7	2	G	97					L		L		L			L	L	L						
	8	2	B	92										L	L	L		L				L		
	9	2	B	94						L	L		L	L	L	L	L	L						
	10	2	B	130				L					L	L	L	L	L	L						
	11	3	B	88				L						L	L	L		L		L				
	12	3	G	82							L				L			L		L				
	13	3	G	87					L									L		L				
	14	3	B	94			L		L	L					L			L						
Handwriting																								
	1	1	G	91			L																	
	2	3	G	119		L				L									L	L	L	L	L	
	3	3	B	107	L	L						L							L	L		L		
	4	3	B	133	L														L	L				
Spelling																								
	1	1	G	117				L	L	L	L		L	L		L	L			L				
	2	1	B	80														L		L				
	3	1	B	109					L	L	L		L	L	L	L	L	L		L				
	4	1	B	88	L				L	L		L	L		L			L		L				
	5	2	B	70				L						L	L	L	L			L				
	6	2	B	87														L		L				
	7	3	G	88						L	L			L		L	L	L		L			L	
	8	3	G	87							L									L				
	9	3	B	101										L						L				
	10	3	B	133														L		L				L
	11	3	B	94			L		L	L	L			L		L	L	L		L				L

Appendix 1 (continued)

Disorder	S	G[b]	S[c]	VIQ[d]	AT	FS	VMI	P/S	SYL	PHO	SM	WF	WW	L	LC	WI	WA	PC	HA	SP	NW	EW	NC	EC
Composition																								
	1	1	G	91						L							L	L	L	L				
	2	1	B	79						L											L	L	L	
	3	3	B	125																	L	L	L	L

[a] Disorders in first column (component achievement skills) are not mutually exclusive across children; the same child may have more than one disorder

[b] G = grade

[c] S = sex

[d] VIQ = prorated Verbal IQ

[e] AT=alphabet task (Berninger & Alsdorf, 1989); FS=finger succession (Wolff et al., 1983); VMI=Beery Visual-Motor Integration (Beery, 1982); P/S=phonetic/semantic code (Wechsler, 1974); SYL=syllable segmentation (Berninger et al., 1987); PHO=phoneme segmentation (Berninger et al., 1987); SM=sentence memory (Thorndike et al., 1986); WF=word finding (McCarthy, 1972); WW=whole word (Berninger, Yates et al., in press); L=letter coding (Berninger, Yates et al., 1991); LC=letter cluster coding (Berninger, Yates et al., 1991)

[f] WI=word identification (real words) (Woodcock, 1987); WA=word attack (nonwords) (Woodcock, 1987); PC=passage comprehension (Woodcock, 1987); HA=handwriting (Monroe & Sherman, 1966); SP=spelling (Jastak & Wilkinson, 1984); NW=narrative-words (Berninger, Yates et al., 1991); EW=expository-words (Berninger, Yates et al., 1991); NC=narrative-clauses (Berninger, Yates et al., 1991); EC=expository-clauses (Berninger, Yates et al., 1991)

APPENDIX 2. DISORDERS IN DEVELOPMENTAL SKILLS ASSOCIATED WITH DISORDERS IN A SPECIFIC READING OR WRITING SKILL[a]
(BASED ON RELATIVE CRITERIA--U = UNDERACHIEVEMENT AND O = OVERACHIEVEMENT)

Disorder	S	G[b]	S[c]	VIQ[d]	AT	FS	VMI	P/S	SYL	PHO	SM	WF	WW	L	LC	WI	WA	PC	HA	SP	NW	EW	NC	EC
Reading Real Words																								
	1	G		122												U	U	U						
	2	B		80	U	O	U	U	U	U	U	U	U			U	U							
	3	G		109	U	O	U	O	U	U	U	U	U	U	U	U	U	O		O	U	U	U	U
	4	G		146												U	U	U			U	U	U	U	U
	5	B		119	O		U	U	U	U	O	U	U	O	O	U	O	U			O	O	O	O
	6	B		70	U		U	O	O	U	U	U	U	U	U	U	U	O			O	O	O	U
	7	B		152												U									
	8	B		106												U									
	9	B		118												U									
	10	B		149		O	U	U	U	U	U		U	U	U	U	U	U	U	O	O	U	U	U
	11	B		94	U											U	U							
	12	B		109	U	O	U	U	U	U	U	U	U	U	U	U	U	U		U	U	U	U	U
	13	G		82												U									
	14	G		145												U									
	15	B		146												U									
	16	B		94												U									
	17	B														U									
Reading Nonwords																								
	1	G		122	O	U	O	O	O	O	O	O	U	U		U	O	O	U	O		O	O	O
	2	B		118		U		O	U	U	U	U	O	O	O	O	O				U	U	U	U
	3	B		122	U	O	U	U	U	U	U	U	U	U	U	U	U	U	U	U	U	U	U	U
	4	G		70	U	U	U	U	U	U	U	U	U	U	U	U	U	U		U	U	U		U
	5	G		106	U	U	U	U	U	U	U	U	U	U	U	U	U	U		U	U	U		U
	6	B		146											U	O	U				U	O		O	U
	7	B		152	U		U	U	U	U	U	U	U	U	U	U	U	U		U	U	O	O	U
	8	G		88												O									
	9	G		145		O	U	U	U	U	U	U	U	U	U	U	U	U	U	U	U	U	U	U
	10	G		131												U	U							
	11	B		143	U	U	O	U	U	U	U	U	U	U	U	U	U	U	U	U	U	O	O	U
	12	B		133												U	U							
	13	B		149	U	O	U	U	U	U	U	U	U	U	U	U	U		U	O	U	U	U	U
	14	B		146	O	O	U	U	U	U	U	U	U	U	U	U	U		O		U		O	U
	15	B		94		U										U	U			O				
	16	G		146	U	O	O	U	U	U	U	U	U	U	U	U	U	O		O	U	U	U	U

Appendix 2 (continued)

					Developmental Skills[e]												Academic Skills[f]									
Disorder	S	G[b]	S[c]	VIQ[d]	AT	FS	VMI	P/S	SYL	PHO	SM	WF	WW	L	LC	WI	WA	PC	HA	SP	NW	EW	NC	EC

Reading Comprehension
S	G	SC	VIQ
1	G	122
2	G	82
3	G	136
4	B	88
5	B	119
6	G	79
7	G	146
8	B	92
9	B	152
10	B	87
11	G	145
12	B	143
13	B	133
14	B	149
15	B	146
16	B	94

Handwriting
S	G	SC	VIQ
1	G	146
2	G	146
3	G	119
4	B	133
5	B	146
6	G	145
7	B	107
8	B	143

Spelling
S	G	SC	VIQ
1	G	122
2	G	136
3	G	146
4	B	70
5	B	152
6	B	87
7	B	122
8	B	143
9	B	133
10	B	149
11	B	145
12	B	146

Appendix 2 (continued)

Disorder Composition	S	G[b]	S[c]	VIQ[d]	Developmental Skills[e]											Academic Skills[f]								
					AT	FS	VMI	P/S	SYL	PHO	SM	WF	WW	L	LC	WI	WA	PC	HA	SP	NW	EW	NC	EC
1	1	G		136	U		U	O		U			U	U	U	U	U	U		U	O	U	O	U
2	2	G		146		O	U	O	U	U		U	U	U	U	U	U	U	U	U	U	U	U	U
3	2	G		137	U	O	U	U	U	U	U	U	U	U	U	U	U			U	O	O	U	O
4	2	G		146	U	U	U	U	U	U	U	U	U	U	U	U	U	O	U	U	U	U	U	U
5	2	B		152	U	U	U	U	U	U	U	O	U	U	U	U	U			U	O	O	U	U
6	3	G		145	U	O		U			U	U	U	U	U			U	U		U	U	U	U
7	3	B		133	U		U		U	U	U	U	U	U	U	U	U	U	U		U	U	U	U
8	3	B		146	U	O	U	U			U	U	U	U	U		U	U		U	U	U	U	U
9	3	B		143									U	U	U		U	U	U	U	U	U	U	U	U

[a] Disorders in first column (component achievement skills) are not mutually exclusive across children; the same child may have more than one disorder

[b] G = grade

[c] S = sex

[d] VIQ = prorated Verbal IQ

[e] AT=alphabet task (Berninger & Alsdorf, 1989); FS=finger succession (Wolff et al., 1983); VMI=Beery Visual-Motor Integration (Beery, 1982); P/S=phonetic/semantic code (Wechsler, 1974); SYL=syllable segmentation (Berninger et al., 1987); PHO=phoneme segmentation (Berninger et al., 1987); SM=sentence memory (Thorndike et al., 1986); WF=word finding (McCarthy, 1972); WW=whole word (Berninger, Yates et al., 1991); L=letter coding (Berninger, Yates et al., 1991); LC=letter cluster coding (Berninger, Yates et al., 1991)

[f] WI=word identification (real words) (Woodcock, 1987); WA=word attack (nonwords) (Woodcock, 1987); PC=passage comprehension (Woodcock, 1987); HA=handwriting (Monroe & Sherman, 1966); SP=spelling (Jastak & Wilkinson, 1984); NW=narrative-words (Berninger, Yates et al., 1991); NC=narrative-clauses (Berninger, Yates et al., 1991); EW=expository-words (Berninger, Yates et al., 1991); EC=expository-clauses (Berninger, Yates et al., 1991)

APPENDIX 3. DISORDERS IN DEVELOPMENTAL SKILLS ASSOCIATED WITH DISORDERS IN A SPECIFIC READING OR WRITING SKILL [a] (BASED ON COMBINED ABSOLUTE AND RELATIVE CRITERIA FOR D, DISABILITY, AND RELATIVE CRITERIA FOR O, OVERACHIEVEMENT)

Disorder	S	G[b]	Sc[c]	VIQ[d]	Developmental Skills[e]														Academic Skills[f]					
					AT	FS	VMI	P/S	SYL	PHO	SM	WF	WW	L	LC	WI	WA	PC	HA	SP	NW	EW	NC	EC
Reading Real Words																								
	1	G		122															D					
	2	B		80				D	D	D						D	D	D						
	3	B		119							D					D	D							
	4	B		70	O				D	D	O			D	D	D	O	O	O	O	O	O	O	O
	5	B		94			O									D								
	6	B		106												D	D	D						
	7	G		82								D		D	D	D	D	D	O					
	8	G		82										D	D		D	D	O					
	9	B		94						D						D								
Reading Nonwords																								
	1	B		79						D						D	D	D						
	2	G		106	O		O		O	O	O	O			O	O	D	O		O	O	O	O	O
	3	G		70					D	O	O		O	O	D	O	D	D		O	O	O	O	O
	4	G		88												D								
	5	B		94						D			D		D	D	D	D						
Reading Comprehension																								
	1	G		82		D							D		D			D	D					
	2	B		79						D			D					D	D					
	3	B		88					D	D				D				D	D					
	4	B		119												D		D	D					
	5	B		92	D					D			D					D	D					
	6	B		87						D								D	D					
	7	B		94												D	D	D	D					

Appendix 3 (continued)

				Developmental Skills[e]													Academic Skills[f]						
Disorder / S	G[b]	S[c]	VIQ[d]	AT	FS	VMI	P/S	SYL	PHO	SM	WF	WW	L	LC	WI	WA	PC	HA	SP	NW	EW	NC	EC
Handwriting																							
1	3	B	107	D														D					
2	3	B	133	D														D			D		
Spelling																							
1	1	G	122	O											D								
2	2	B	70	D					D	O					D	O	O		D	O		O	
3	2	B	87						D				D	D		O			D				
4	3	B	133																D				D
Composition																							
1	3	B	125																		D	D	

CONSTRUCTING MEANING FROM DIAGNOSTIC ASSESSMENT TEXTS: VALIDITY AS USEFULNESS

PETER AFFLERBACH
National Reading Research Center
University of Maryland at College Park
College Park, MD 20742-1175
U. S. A.

ABSTRACT: This paper focuses on critical, but relatively unexamined aspects of diagnostic assessment: how diagnostic assessment information is read, and the usefulness of the diagnostic information. After a description of the texts of diagnostic literacy assessment, the need for literal readings of these texts is outlined. Next, theories of text interpretation are used to describe how readers may or may not construct meanings similar to those intended by the authors of assessment texts. The influence of readers' values on understanding assessment texts is examined. Implications for diagnostic reading and writing assessment, instruction, and learning are discussed. Lastly, a research agenda for studying the contexts of diagnostic reading and writing assessment, how readers make meaning from these assessments and how this information informs instruction, is proposed.

Much has been written about the appropriateness of different methods of diagnostic reading and writing assessment, and much has been enacted educationally, politically, and socially based on the results of these assessments. In contrast, little is known about the **reading** of these assessments, a critical point which lies between the collection of diagnostic literacy assessment information, and the actions which are informed by this information. Without an understanding of how readers make meaning from diagnostic assessment texts, it is not possible to determine the usefulness and value of particular diagnostic procedures, and the information they yield.

How diagnostic assessment is read and understood influences the usefulness, and validity of the assessment information. In the history of educational measurement, the term **validity** has undergone regular modification and revision (Cronbach, 1988; Messick, 1989). Theorists recently have suggested that the usefulness of information gathered in assessment must be considered when making a determination of the validity of any assessment instrument or procedure (Tittle, 1989). The comprehensibility and usefulness of diagnostic assessment information are closely related. A clinician, teacher, or parent reading diagnostic assessment results and finding them uninterpretable cannot act on the information. Thus, regardless of the psychometric elegance of the assessment instrument and procedure, or the theoretical soundness of the construct(s) to which the assessment is tied, the information is not useful.

How do readers make meaning from diagnostic assessment information? This paper first examines the reading of diagnostic assessment information from a constructivist perspective. Using theories of text comprehension and interpretation, the manner in which diagnostic assessment is understood is examined. Next, the impact of readers' values on interpretation of

63

R.M. Joshi and C.K. Leong (eds.), Reading Disabilities: Diagnosis and Component Processes, 63–69.
© 1993 *Kluwer Academic Publishers. Printed in the Netherlands.*

diagnostic assessment texts is discussed. Finally, a research agenda for studying how people read, understand, and use diagnostic assessment texts is proposed.

The Texts Of Diagnostic Assessment

The diagnostic assessment of reading and writing disorders yields texts. The texts are created by authors to inform the reader about a particular student's reading and writing abilities, and strengths and needs. Diagnostic assessment texts can vary on several continua: the texts may be written or spoken, brief or lengthy, broad or narrow in focus, they may contain formative or summative information, and they may be related to a single assessment event, or many. Typical authors of diagnostic assessment texts include test developers, psychometricians, researchers, clinicians, and teachers. The purpose of diagnostic assessment texts is to provide information about students' reading or writing strengths and needs, and the reader's (i.e., teacher, parent, administrator, clinician, or student) task is to make meaning from the assessment text.

Because diagnostic assessment texts are written to inform the reader about students' literacy development, a literal reading of the text is appropriate. Rosenblatt (1978) calls this "efferent" reading, in which the reader literally "carries away" information. An optimal situation in the communication of diagnostic assessment information would be when the reader carries away the meaning of the diagnostic assessment text exactly as it was intended by the author.

Is it appropriate to assume that readers of diagnostic assessment texts construct the meaning intended by the authors? This question is considered from the perspective of several theories related to constructing meaning from text, including schema theory (Anderson & Pearson, 1984), intertextuality (DeBeaugrande & Dressler, 1981), and the model reader and shared codes (Eco, 1976). Each of the theories describes situations in which the reader may be encouraged to construct meaning from an assessment text, as it was intended by the author. The theories also help anticipate situations in which it may be difficult for the reader to construct a literal meaning of the diagnostic assessment text. Thus, the theories help describe the potential usefulness of diagnostic reading and writing assessment.

Prior Knowledge And Diagnostic Assessment Texts

It is well established that prior knowledge influences comprehension (Anderson & Pearson, 1984), and a reader's prior knowledge related to assessment will influence the reading of diagnostic literacy assessment texts. This prior knowledge is from the reader's experiences with assessment: assessing and being assessed, and partaking in discourse related to diagnostic assessment. When diagnostic assessment texts are read, the reader calls upon prior knowledge, or schemata, to help construct a meaning from text. Readers may have prior knowledge for the content and format of the assessment text, as well as the theory and research on which the assessment is based. Schema theory suggests that if the content and format of the diagnostic assessment text are familiar, they will be more easily integrated into the reader's schemata, and more readily understood by the reader. Once understood, the information may be useful for the design, revision, or maintenance of a remedial instruction program.

In contrast, a lack of prior knowledge may make it difficult for teachers, parents, and students to understand the diagnostic assessment text. If the reader is not familiar with a particular diagnostic assessment finding (or the manner in which it is presented), understanding the text, and acting on the information, will be difficult. Consider, for example, the following excerpt from a hypothetical clinical report, written for the parents of a child with a reading disorder:

> Test results demonstrate that John has difficulties in letter naming and letter recognition. The cause of these difficulties rests in John's visual perception, and cross-modal transfer ability.

The student's difficulties with reading and the causes of the problem are succinctly stated in this excerpt. However, the parents (or teacher) may not understand the stated nature of the cause (e.g., cross-modal transfer ability). Diagnostic assessment information, however important (and however familiar) to a diagnostician or test developer, may not be useful to those readers who often have great potential and responsibility for remediating a student's particular difficulty with reading or writing.

The Intertextuality Of Diagnostic Assessment

Theories of intertextuality (DeBeaugrande & Dressler, 1981) suggest that a reader's understanding of text is influenced by the reading of other texts. Parents and teachers of students with reading and writing disorders may encounter diagnostic assessment texts such as clinicians' reports, test scores, written and spoken comments, narrative reports, formal and informal conversations, and different diagnostic screening results. In this context, the reader makes links between the different sources and types of information which are part of the overall assessment. The reader may seek information from different, but complementary texts to build a rich, composite picture of the student as language user. The combined information can provide greater explanatory power related to the student's areas of relative strengths and needs, and may suggest particular remedial instruction.

Constructing an understanding of a students' strengths and needs using the intertextuality of diagnostic assessment places demands on the reader. The reader must be able to synthesize information about students' reading and writing from different sources. An able synthesis of information (such as the results of clinical screenings, observations, standardized diagnostic scores, and classroom tasks collected by a teacher) may result in a meaningful conglomerate which is useful in guiding instruction. Achieving a balance using this information is a challenge to someone with knowledge of these measures, and it may prove exceedingly difficult for someone who is not familiar with all of them.

Some types of diagnostic information may resist synthesis. Particular diagnostic reading assessments are based on specific etiological perspectives which are used to interpret a student's performance, and to recommend remedial instruction. For example, a clinical assessment based on a medical model of reading disability may suggest the probability of neurological etiology. For the same student, a series of careful teacher observations may suggest a psychoeducational locus to the reading difficulty. With competing explanations, the reader's task becomes more difficult, as does the planning of remediation to address the student's needs. The reader needs to be knowledgeable about the distinct approaches to diagnosing and remediating the student with needs assessed from such approaches. This may require the reader to interpret and combine diagnostic information from disparate sources, based on theoretical models which are not compatible. Here, the reader's disposition to seeking complementary information from disparate sources may be more fruitful than eliminating competing explanations, based on a "zero sum" mentality (Stanovich, 1990).

The Model Reader, Shared Codes, And Diagnostic Assessment

Eco (1976) describes the model reader as one who understands the intentions and purposes of the author. Such a reader also shares with the author a set of codes which point the reader to the meaning intended by the author. When the codes used by the author are not shared by the reader, a "correct" reading of the text may be difficult, or impossible. If the reader is not familiar with the vocabulary used to describe a diagnostic assessment routine, or with the vocabulary used to describe a reader's needs and plan for remediation, a lack of shared codes will lessen the chances of diagnostic information being useful. Similarly, if the author and reader do not share similar theoretical perspectives on the etiology, diagnostic assessment, and remediation of reading and writing difficulties, making meaning from a diagnostic text will be challenging.

To the extent that test developers, test administrators, and test users explain the reasoning and processes which went into the development of a particular diagnostic assessment instrument or procedure, the codes of the assessment text may be "shared". Similarly, if the specialized vocabulary (e.g., dysphasia) is defined, another set of codes is shared. The result of sharing of codes is a reader who is more and more like the model reader: one who understands the author's intention, and the purpose for reading. If codes are not shared, the reader's task is increasingly ill-defined, the reading of diagnostic assessment texts may prove frustrating. The information contained in the text may not be useful, and actions taken based on the reading of diagnostic assessment may be misinformed.

The Role Of The Reader's Values

Theories of prior knowledge, intertextuality, and model readers and shared codes allow us to examine potentially powerful influences on readers' attempts to understand and make usable diagnostic assessment texts. Readers' values can also influence the construction of meaning from diagnostic information. Both readers and authors of diagnostic assessment texts have values related to diagnostic assessment and remedial instruction. Indeed, underlying the field of diagnostic reading and writing assessment and remediation are many different values, and conflicts related to these values (Coles, 1987). The values are related to the etiology of reading and writing disorders, and how best to teach and assess those children who have difficulties (Johnson, 1988; Taylor, 1991).

When an author and a reader of a diagnostic text have diametrically opposed values related to a particular reading or writing disorder, it is possible that a reader will construct an understanding of a diagnostic assessment text which is exactly what the author intended, and then dismiss it outright. A related concern is the reader who has prior knowledge which conflicts with information in the diagnostic text. The information derived from a diagnostic assessment reflects in some way the values of the assessment developer. If the reader of diagnostic assessment texts has conflicting values and beliefs, and firm conviction in her or his knowledge of a student, it will be difficult for that reader to value the information in the text, and to consider the information useful. For example, teachers vary in their beliefs as to the function and value of diagnostic test results, and the validity of different theories used to explain reading disability. A teacher who has strong beliefs about the overuse of the term "dyslexia" may not value diagnostic results which point to dyslexia. Similarly, teachers and parents may differ in the values they hold related to particular assessment information (Afflerbach, 1990).

Implications

This brief and somewhat arbitrary consideration of theories of making meaning from diagnostic reading and writing assessment texts suggests two important considerations which may contribute to the usefulness (and thus, validity) of diagnostic reading and writing assessment: communication and involvement. If the reader is informed about the purpose of the diagnostic assessment text, an accurate reading of the text may be encouraged. An informed reader understands the purpose of a particular diagnostic assessment. Similarly, an informed reader understands why particular diagnostic assessment texts are valued, how they work, and how they fit in with the program of diagnostic assessment and remedial instruction.

A second factor which influences the reading of literacy assessment texts is reader involvement. Diagnostic assessment is often developed by psychometricians, without dialogue (i.e., input from, or explanation to) those who have large stakes in the assessment, particularly students, parents, and teachers. Communication with the community which uses and interprets assessment texts may provide for the increased understanding of rationale and means of diagnostic assessment. This understanding should foster increased usefulness of the diagnostic information.

How Are Diagnostic Assessment Texts Useful?: A Research Agenda

Currently, there is *terra incognita* in the diagnostic assessment and remediation of reading and writing disorders. We have examined the theories which drive diagnostic assessment, and which contribute to the development of diagnostic instruments and materials. We have examined the effectiveness of teaching and remediation, based on diagnostic assessments. However, we lack an understanding of the critical link between effective diagnosis and effective remediation and instruction: the communication and interpretation of diagnostic assessment information. While the aforementioned theories of text interpretation suggest areas of concern, describing this unknown area is needed for realizing effective (i.e., useful) diagnosis and remedial instruction. To gain an understanding of the usefulness of diagnostic assessment it is important to study the contexts of communication of diagnostic information, the interpretation of the information, and how the diagnostic information is acted upon by the reader.

THE CONTEXTS CF DIAGNOSTIC ASSESSMENT

Jakobson (1960) suggests that the nature of communication is influenced by the context in which it occurs. The diagnostic assessment of reading and writing disorders takes place in social, educational, and political contexts. Understanding these value-laden contexts will help reveal the conditions which influence both the reading and writing of diagnostic assessment texts. There are several promising methodologies which might help us to better understand the contexts of communication and interpretation of diagnostic assessment. First, ethnographic methods using clinical and classroom observations should allow for descriptions of the context in which reading and writing assessment are conducted, the context in which results are communicated, and the contexts in which results are interpreted. As a result, we may determine which contexts are supportive of useful dialogue between test developers and test users, and between teachers and parents and students. We may also better understand the conflicts which occur when the results of different assessments (suggesting different etiologies for reading and writing disorders) are encountered by people who must use assessment results.

THE INTERPRETATION OF DIAGNOSTIC ASSESSMENT

Because the information contained in diagnostic assessment texts has the potential to inform remediation and instruction, it is imperative that we more fully understand how the text is interpreted, and made useful. Think-aloud protocols have the potential of providing rich descriptions of both authors' and readers' construction of meaning (Afflerbach & Johnston, 1984; Hayes & Flower, 1980). Verbal report data might be collected from authors to determine the meaning they intend as diagnostic texts are written. Next, the verbal reports of readers reading diagnostic assessment texts could be used to gain an understanding of how readers construct meaning from the texts.

Comparing the verbal reports of authors and readers diagnostic assessment texts may allow for determining the degree of congruence between author's intended message and the reader's interpretation. Verbal reports will also help describe the on-line influences of prior knowledge, intertextuality, shared codes, and readers' values on the interpretation of diagnostic assessment texts. Verbal reports are themselves diagnostic of authors' and readers' abilities to communicate and interpret diagnostic information. Through examination of verbal report data, we may determine the processes and knowledge which help people communicate and interpret diagnostic information. It may be possible to train readers and writers of assessment texts to use particular processes and knowledge (e.g., synthesis of information from multiple sources) to render diagnostic assessment more useful.

Interviews might be used to tap readers' values and serve as a triangulation measure for how readers construct meaning from diagnostic assessment texts. Rank-ordering tasks in which readers rank-order the contents of diagnostic assessment texts in terms of usefulness and importance of the information might also prove useful. The combination of investigative methods will allow for the examination of how the reader's interpretation is mediated, and how information of varied familiarity is interpreted or translated. In addition, it may be possible to determine the most effective means of communicating with specificity and comprehensibility to a variety of audiences.

IMPLEMENTATION OF INSTRUCTION BASED ON DIAGNOSTIC ASSESSMENT

A final area of investigation should examine the actions taken based upon interpretations of diagnostic assessment texts. Currently, there is a wide range of remedial efforts taken on behalf of students with reading and writing disorders. Yet, we lack models which help describe the relationship of these actions to particular diagnostic assessment procedures, and to the interpretation of diagnostic results. Previous research demonstrates the value of examining the planning and decision making processes of teachers (Clark & Peterson, 1986). As teachers and clinicians develop remedial instruction for students with reading and writing disorders, methodologies which tap planning and decision-making processes should prove fruitful. Additionally, videotaped instructional settings in classrooms or tutoring settings will provide further data on how diagnostic assessment information is implemented in instruction. Taken as a whole, research methodologies including verbal reporting, interviews, observations, and teacher decision-making may help us determine what assessment information is most useful, to whom it is useful, and under what conditions it is useful.

Conclusions

The reading of diagnostic assessment texts is critical to helping meet the needs of students with reading and writing disorders. Diagnostic assessment texts signal the stasis or change in progress towards our goals, and it is these texts on which we base our remedial efforts. Effective diagnostic assessment involves valid instruments and procedures which yield texts with **usable** information. While literal readings of diagnostic assessment texts inform our teaching and remediation plans, theories of making meaning from text suggest that literal meanings are not always the ones constructed by readers.

For readers, communication about the nature and purpose of diagnostic assessment texts is extremely important. As demonstrated by theories sampled here, readers of diagnostic assessment texts can be encouraged to construct meaning similar to that intended by the author. From this meaning-making process, improved diagnostic literacy assessment, instruction, and learning may result. Thus, the usefulness and validity of the diagnostic assessment instrument, procedure, and information may be realized. Examining the contexts and processes of making meaning from diagnostic assessment texts should provide information about diagnoses which are valid from a psychometric viewpoint, and which are useful to teachers, parents, and students.

REFERENCES

Afflerbach, P. (1990). *Issues in statewide reading assessment.* Washington, DC: American Institutes for Research.
Afflerbach, P., & Johnston, P. (1984). On the use of verbal reports in reading research. *Journal of Reading Behavior, 16,* 307-322.
Anderson, R., & Pearson, P. (1984). A schema-theoretic view of reading. In P. Pearson (Ed.), *Handbook of reading research.* (pp. 255-291). New York: Longman.
Clark, C., & Peterson, P. (1986). Teachers' thought processes. In M. Wittrock (Ed.), *Handbook of research on teaching.* (pp. 255-296). New York: Macmillan.
Coles, G. (1987). *The learning mystique: A critical look at learning disabilities.* New York: Fawcett Columbine.
Cronbach, L. (1988). Five perspectives on the validity argument. In H. Wainer & H. Braun (Eds.), *Test validity.* (pp. 3-17). Hillsdale, NJ: Erlbaum.
DeBeaugrande, R., & Dressler, R. (1981). *Introduction to text linguistics.* New York: Longman.
Eco, U. (1976). *The role of the reader.* Bloomington, IN: Indiana University Press.
Hayes, J., & Flower, L. (1980). Identifying the organization of writing processes. In L. Gregg & E. Steinberg (Eds.), *Cognitive process in writing.* (pp. 3-30). Hillsdale, NJ: Erlbaum.
Jakobson, R. (1960). Closing statements: Linguistics and poetics. In T. Sebeok (Ed.), *Style in language.* (pp. 350-377) Cambridge, MA: MIT Press.
Johnson, D. (1988). Specific developmental disabilities of reading, writing, and mathematics. in J. Kavanagh & T. Truss (Eds.), *Learning disabilities: Proceedings of the National Conference,* (pp. 79-163). Parkton, MD.: York Press.
Messick, S. (1989). Validity. In R. Linn (Ed.), *Educational measurement,* (3rd ed.) (pp. 13-103). New York: Macmillan.
Rosenblatt, L. (1978). *The reader, the text, and the poem.* Carbondale, IL: Southern Illinois University Press.
Stanovich, K. (1990). A call for the end of the paradigm wars in reading research. *Journal of Reading Behavior, 22,* 221-231.
Taylor, D. (1991). *Learning denied.* Portsmouth, NH: Heinemann.
Tittle, C. (1989). Validity: Whose construction is it in the teaching and learning context? *Educational measurement: Issues and practice, 8,* 5-13.

ALICE IN IQ LAND OR WHY IQ IS STILL IRRELEVANT TO LEARNING DISABILITIES

LINDA S. SIEGEL
Ontario Institute for Studies in Education
252 Bloor Street West
Toronto, Ontario
Canada M5S 1V6

ABSTRACT: In this chapter, I review the assumptions underlying the use of IQ test scores in the definition of a reading disability. I examine the concept of IQ scores as the gold standard to which to compare reading and find no logical reason for considering an IQ score as this gold standard. I illustrate the problems with the use of IQ scores by showing the illogical assumptions and inferences that are made by the use of IQ. I provide empirical data to show that both dyslexics (IQ-reading discrepant) and poor readers (reading discrepant from chronological age not IQ) have difficulties on a variety of tasks central to the reading process and both groups are significantly different from normal readers *but not from each other*. I conclude by questioning the usefulness of the use of IQ tests in the definition of a reading disability.

Alice had been looking over his shoulder with some curiosity. "What a funny watch!" she remarked, "It tells the day of the month, and doesn't tell what o'clock it is!"

"Why should it?" muttered the Hatter. "Does your watch tell you what year it is?"

"Of course not," Alice replied very readily; "but that's because it stays the same year for such a long time together."

"Which is just the case with *mine*," said the Hatter.

Alice felt dreadfully puzzled. The Hatter's remark seemed to her to have no sort of meaning, and yet it was certainly English. "I don't quite understand you," she said as politely as she could. (Lewis Carroll, 1946 Edition pp. 74-75)

Alice was confused because the arguments of the Hatter did not make any sense. In the past several years since I have published articles about the irrelevance of intelligence (IQ) test scores to the diagnosis and analysis of learning disabilities, I have often felt like Alice. The dialogue that has occurred around this issue often seems to resemble Alice's conversation with the Hatter in that there is no real discussion or any attempts to respond to the points that I and others, such as Bryan (1989), Stanovich (1989) and Swanson (1989), have raised. Some experts in the field disagree with my position and it is clearly their right to do so. I welcome a serious discussion of these very important issues. But I would like to see the discussions based on logic and empirical data and not on cherished but unvalidated assumptions.

R.M. Joshi and C.K. Leong (eds.), Reading Disabilities: Diagnosis and Component Processes, 71–84.
© 1993 *Kluwer Academic Publishers. Printed in the Netherlands.*

In an attempt to steer the discussion of the IQ issue on a meaningful course, this chapter will address the conceptual and logical issues and the empirical data that form the basis of this debate. I will show that some of the arguments advanced in connection with this issue are often illogical and fallacious and that the empirical data that are available support the position that IQ tests are not necessary in the diagnosis and analyses of learning disabilities. I will review my discussion of assumptions underlying the use of IQ tests and show that my objections to the use of IQ have not been successfully countered. The debate has been filled with contradictions, logical fallacies, and paradoxes.

The "Gold Standard"

I have argued that IQ tests do not really measure intelligence or potential. I claim that IQ tests are not particularly adequate measures of skills such as problem solving, logical reasoning, and/or adaptation to the environment. Instead, the IQ tests that are in current use measure factual knowledge, language skills, fine-motor coordination, long and short-term memory, etc. There seems to be a great deal of confusion and disagreement, even among those who advocate the use of the IQ test scores, as to what the IQ tests supposedly measure. The confusion seems to revolve around the question of whether the IQ tests measure "potential" that is determined in some unknown amounts by biological factors or environmental factors or, on the other hand, achievement. I have made a case for the biased nature of the content of IQ tests and how performance on the test might be subject to specific knowledge of specific facts, vocabulary, etc. I seem to have convinced some individuals, so now the claim is that IQ tests do not measure potential but "that IQ test results are environmentally influenced and, at best, reflect a momentary level of intellectual functioning." (Baldwin & Vaughn, 1989, p. 513). I could not agree more. If this is the case, I am even more confused as to why we need IQ test scores at all. Baldwin and Vaughn argue that IQ tests are not perfect but that is not sufficient reason for doing away with them. My argument is that they are very far from perfect and measure specific knowledge and not real problem solving or conceptual thinking.

In spite of the obvious problems with IQ tests, many seem unwilling to abandon them. The debate concerning the IQ issue has centered around the justification of the use of IQ scores in the definition of learning disabilities for a number of reasons. One of the major reasons for the use of IQ scores, according to the proponents of their use, seems to be that we must control IQ, presumably to obtain a "true" measure of whether or not there is a reading disability. Let us consider the logic of this position. The claim is made that we need to have a measure of general cognitive ability as a "gold standard" to assess what the reading score really represents. For example, Baldwin and Vaughn (1989), Graham and Harris (1989), Leong (1989), Lyon (1989), Meyen (1989), and Torgesen (1989) appear to argue that if we abandon the IQ test, that we need to replace it with some type of assessment of ability. The assumption of this position is that we need this gold standard to be used in the educational system in order to ascertain whether or not a learning disability exists.

Torgesen argues that we need IQ tests to ensure that differences between learning disabled and normally achieving groups are not primarily the result of differences in "general learning aptitude" which appears to mean learning potential. However, Siegel (1988) has reported that there were significant differences between the reading disabled and normally achieving children at each IQ level, *but no significant differences among reading disabled children at each IQ level.* Furthermore, these differences in whatever IQ tests measure do not seem to be sufficient to explain the differences in cognitive functioning between reading disabled and normally achieving children. Torgesen claims that we need IQ because we want to be certain that the differences in cognitive processing are "not the result of mild but pervasive intellectual differences between groups." The data that I have reported clearly show that the differences between the normally achieving and reading disabled group are not due to differences in IQ. The normally achieving readers had higher scores on the phonological, language and memory tasks than the reading disabled group *at every level of IQ*. In addition, there were no differences on the phonological, reading, spelling, language, and memory tasks among the groups of reading disabled children at each IQ level. I remain perplexed as to why these data are ignored by those who argue for the use of IQ tests.

Will the real IQ please stand up?

Another assumption of the proponents of the use of IQ test scores is that intelligence can be measured in the same way as height or weight. I assume that even the more avid proponents of the validity of IQ test scores as measures of intelligence would agree that the measurement of height is significantly more accurate than the measurement of intelligence. To put it simply, height is a physical dimension that has a physical reality. Intelligence is not a physical dimension but is a *construct*. There is no yardstick for the real IQ. Independent observers with different rulers would arrive at the same number, within a few millimeters, for the height of a person. Independent IQ tests often arrive at quite different numbers for the IQ of a particular individual. There is universal agreement among scientists on what constitutes a millimeter, centimeter, inch, yard, etc.; however, there is endless controversy about the nature of intelligence, how to measure it, and how it is subject to cultural biases, etc. As Stanovich has said, "The popularity of this use of the concept of intelligence as a benchmark in the diagnosis of reading disability is puzzling. Surely one would be hard pressed to find a concept more controversial than intelligence in all of psychology! For decades it has been the subject of dispute, which shows no sign of abating. Current research on individual differences in intelligent functioning continues to produce exciting findings and interesting theories...but still no consensual view of intelligence as a concept." (Stanovich, 1991, p. 9). These divergent views are reviewed in Sternberg and Detterman (1986). I am not aware of endless debates on how to measure height.

As Stanovich has noted there is a great deal of controversy about what constitutes appropriate measures of intelligence. The point is that the nature and content of the questions on the IQ test are arbitrary. As Stanovich has said, "Oblivious to the ongoing debates, specialists in learning disabilities seem to have avoided the issue by adopting a variant of E.G. Boring's dictum and acting as if 'intelligence is what The Psychological Corporation says it is!'" (Stanovich, 1991, p. 10)

The argument that we should use IQ as a general measure in the same way that we use height is fallacious. IQ is not the same type of construct as height, weight, blood pressure, eye color, hair color, etc. Even if one decides to use IQ, which one should we use - Verbal, Performance, Full Scale, PPVT, some other IQ test? As Torgesen (1989, p.484) has written, "Thus, there are no easily defensible conventions about which aspects of 'intelligence' to control when selecting samples of children with LD." There is no way to decide and no evidence that one particular IQ score is better than any other.

IQ and Learning Disabilities

For the purposes of argument, let us consider the proposition that IQ is a measure of general cognitive ability that provides a gold standard against which we can use to measure reading and explore the logic of that position. The IQ tests measure functions such as vocabulary, specific knowledge, memory, fine motor coordination, and short and long term memory. All of these are deficient in children with reading problems. Therefore, the IQ will reflect the difficulties that children have in these areas. Proponents of the use of IQ tests argue children who have low scores on a reading test should not be considered *reading disabled* if they have low scores on an IQ test. This reasoning is the ultimate in circularity because the low scores on the IQ test are a consequence, not a cause, of their reading disability.

Rather than dealing with the issues of the difficulties that learning disabled children have on IQ tests *because of their learning disabilities that create problems in the areas of language, memory, fine-motor coordination,* Baldwin and Vaughn say that I am merely providing "a list of excuses for why children with learning disabilities do poorly on IQ tests." These so called "excuses" are not excuses, but reasons even if Baldwin and Vaughn choose not to recognize the problem. Simply stated, the reason that the IQ score may be an underestimate of the potential of many learning disabled children is that these children have difficulty, with the questions on the IQ test, *because of their learning disability.* It seems circular and even cruel to suggest that someone is not capable, or less capable of learning because the very learning disability that they have affects their memory, language, fine-motor skills, etc. and is responsible for their lower score on an IQ test.

It might be argued that some children who are reading disabled have higher scores on the IQ test than other reading disabled children. Therefore, if my point is that having a reading disability means that the IQ score is an underestimate of "general cognitive ability", it is reasonable to ask why some reading disabled children have higher scores than others. There are several points that are relevant here. The IQ test is a mixture of a variety of skills; the same score can be arrived at with different profiles and there is a premium on the knowledge of specific facts, vocabulary, etc. It is quite reasonable to assume that different children, particularly children of different social class environments, have had different exposure to this material so that the IQ test has a social class bias. In a recent paper, Tunmer (1989) summarizes the political and social class biases that are represented by IQ tests. These biases result in questions about usefulness of IQ as a measure of individual differences to be used as a gold standard.

One of the implications of using the IQ test is that the IQ score "predicts" reading achievement. Olson (1986) analyzes this relationship as follows:

> But, do tests of intelligence measure some underlying quality of mind and thereby explain intelligent performance? Or do they simply, as I prefer to say, sample a domain of competence, thereby providing a *description* of a range of cognitive competence but not an *explanation* of how or why such competence would arise? To focus this question more sharply, do tests of intelligence give access to some underlying quality of mind that would explain a person's performance on cognitive tasks, or do they merely sample that competence in such a way as to give an indication of level of performance in a domain, but in no way explain that level of competence?

> In the simplest case, IQ predicts reading comprehension. But why? What are these tests measuring? A basic quality of the mind that makes learning to read easy? Or a sample of specialized use of language common to both tests of intelligence and tests of reading. If it is the first, the IQ test would explain the good or poor reading competence itself. In that case, it would provide a description of the poor reading but not an explanation for that level of reading competence. (p. 339)

One of the arguments of the proponents of the use of IQ tests scores has been that IQ correlates with achievement. Therefore, as it is a predictor of achievement, it is "useful" according to Graham and Harris (1989). Even if the IQ score was the ultimate measure of general achievement, it only correlates very moderately with school achievement. The best estimates are that the correlation is approximately .50, accounting for, at best, 25% of the variance. Parental educational level or income is also correlated with achievement. Therefore, it would be as logical to use parental income as the gold standard (Tunmer, 1989). The use of parental income makes as much sense as the use of IQ. Of course, I am not seriously making this suggestion but if IQ is used as a gold standard because it correlates with achievement, why not use parental income (or education) by the same logic? Obviously, this type of suggestion is counter to our egalitarian philosophy, but the logic is clear. Remember Alice's confusion in her discussion with the Hatter. In a similar manner, I remain perplexed as why IQ should serve as a gold standard.

Matthew Effects

Another issue is the problem of the Matthew effects as described by Stanovich (1986). Simply stated, children who are good readers read more, gain vocabulary, knowledge, and language skills and, consequently obtain higher IQ scores. Poor readers, on the other hand, show decline in vocabulary, language, and knowledge because of fewer opportunities for exposure to print. Stanovich has provided some compelling arguments for these Matthew effects and there is no point in reiterating them here. Stanovich reviews studies to show that the IQ scores decrease over time for the reading disabled children. There has not been a challenge to Stanovich's concept of Matthew effects. The existence of these Matthew effects is particularly relevant to the discussion of the role of IQ in the measurement of reading disability because the Matthew effects cast doubts on the validity of the IQ measure, particularly for children with reading and other learning problems.

IQ as a Limit on Reading?

The use of IQ scores carries with it the assumption that reading can be predicted from IQ scores, or, more properly, that the IQ score sets a limit on reading. That is, children should not be expected to read above the level of their IQ. Let us examine the premises contained in the assumption that "a child was reading as well as could be expected given his or her overall level of ability" which is used as the rationale for the use of the IQ score. The assumption is that "overall level of ability" should set some kind of limit on how well a child can read. The discussion of this assumption completely ignores the fact that there are hyperlexic children, that is children with low IQ scores who can read words and pseudowords very well. If IQ does set some sort of limit on reading, then these children should not exist and yet they do. Hyperlexic children have been reported who can read words and pseudowords in spite of very low IQ scores (e.g., Cobrinik, 1974; Denckla, 1979; Healy, Aram, Horowitz & Kessler, 1982; Siegel, 1984). The existence of even one of these cases presents a very significant challenge for the position that IQ is relevant because it is an obvious logical paradox that if IQ sets a limit on reading, then children with very low IQ should not be able to read.

I have even reported (Siegel, 1988) that there are children with IQ scores of less than 80 who can read very well. If IQ sets a limit on reading, then logically these children should not exist. How, logically, can someone read significantly better than predicted by their IQ?

Baldwin and Vaughn (1989) have argued, "According to Siegel, the fact that some children with low IQ scores have good reading skills proves that IQ is not a cause of poor reading. This is inferior reasoning because there are also some students with low IQ scores who have poor reading skills. The same bad logic should drive us to the conclusion that low IQ is a cause of poor reading" (Baldwin & Vaughn, 1989, p. 513). This type of reasoning illustrates the logical fallacy of affirming the consequent. If one finds a circumstance in which low IQ is not related to poor reading, finding a circumstance where it does, does *not* prove that low IQ is always related to poor reading.

One of the assumptions of those who use the IQ test is that IQ sets some sort of limit on how well we can expect a child to read so that children with low IQ scores would not be expected to read well. When proponents of the use of IQ scores encounter the paradoxical cases of children with low IQ scores and good reading skills, they choose to ignore them. It is important to note that these cases are devastating to their argument. As I have argued, "According to the discrepancy formulation, it should not be possible for a child with a low IQ to be a good reader; however, as we will see, a significant number of such cases exist. The existence of this type of child, that is, a child with a low IQ score and good reading skills, would seem to be a paradox. Existence of such children means that children with low IQ scores can learn to read, often as well as children with higher IQ scores and no reading disabilities. *Therefore, children with low IQ scores who fail to read are genuinely reading disabled and do not fail to read because of low IQ scores*" (Siegel, 1989, p. 472).

Torgesen (1989) has a different explanation for these children with low IQ test scores but good reading abilities. He notes that they "may have benefited from a variety of other factors that contribute to learning to read, such as a particularly excellent teacher, unusually strong motivation and home support, or even specially developed talents in the phonological processing area" (p. 485). This is exactly my point. If some children with low IQ scores can benefit from good instruction or encouragement, why not give it to all children who need it regardless of their IQ.

The Evidence Against IQ

The assumption of the proponents of IQ is that children who are poor readers and have high IQ scores are somehow different in their reading behavior or patterns of cognitive processing than poor readers with lower IQ scores. Data concerning the validity of this assumption are reported in Siegel (1988). There were *no differences between reading disabled children of different IQ levels* on a variety of reading, spelling, language, and memory tasks. This evidence seems to be the most damaging to the use of IQ test scores. If there are no differences among reading disabled children of different IQ levels, why do we need scores for the definition of reading disability? I am still waiting for a satisfactory answer to this question.

Baldwin and Vaughn do not answer this question but instead propose a different study. "Someone hypothesizes that general athletic ability is unrelated to ability to run fast. His subjects are 50 individuals who are paralyzed from the waist down. He uses a variety of physical assessments, for example, lung capacity, strength, and coordination, to split the group into athletes and nonathletes. The dependent variable is speed in a 100-yard foot race. Voila! Athletic ability is irrelevant" (Baldwin & Vaughn, 1989, p. 513). Baldwin and Vaughn claim to know the results and that athletic ability will be irrelevant to winning the race. First of all, do we know the outcome? Lung capacity, arm strength and coordination might indeed be related to the speed with which an individual can move his or her wheelchair, so we would not conclude, as Baldwin and Vaughn have done, that athletic ability is unrelated to ability to win a foot race. But more importantly, suppose that we hypothesize as I and others have done, that phonological, syntactic awareness, and memory skills are important in reading and that we find that reading disabled children with different IQ scores do not perform differently on these *critical* measures, I am at a loss to explain why we need IQ. If this is the case, and my data show that it is, what additional information do we get from an IQ test score? I am still waiting for an answer. As Graham and Harris have said (1989), "findings that the performance of students with mild retardation or LD is similar across all or most tasks would draw into question the assumption of specificity and the practice of differentially diagnosing underachievers" (p. 501). I certainly agree.

Size of Effect: IQ vs. Phonological Processing

Some of the proponents of the use of IQ scores have argued that because IQ is correlated with reading we should continue to use IQ scores. However, I think that the important question is the relative size of effect of the contribution of IQ test scores and other cognitive processes to reading scores. In other words, we need to know how much is actually gained by using IQ test scores in an attempt to understand what are the important components of the reading process. In one study (Siegel, in press), I compared the relative contribution of IQ test scores and phonological processing to the prediction of reading scores on word recognition and reading comprehension tasks using multiple regression techniques. I found that IQ contributed virtually no independent

Table 1. Results of the multiple regression analyses for WRAT Reading (Word Recognition) and Reading Comprehension Scores.

	WRAT Reading n = 1106 Multiple R	R^2
Order of Entry		
1. Pseudoword Reading	.81	.65
2. IQ	.82	.67
Order of Entry		
1. IQ	.43	.19
2. Pseudoword Reading	.82	.67
	Gilmore Comprehension n -= 412 Multiple R	R^2
Order of Entry		
1. Pseudoword Reading	.51	.26
2. IQ	.54	.30
1. IQ	.40	.16
2. Pseudoword Reading	.54	.30
	Stanford Comprehension n = 170	
1. Pseudoword Reading	.59	.35
2. IQ	.64	.41
1. IQ	.42	.18
2. Pseudoword Reading	.64	.41

variance (actually, it was 2%) to word reading once pseudoword reading had been entered; but if IQ was forced in first, pseudoword reading contributed a great deal of significant independent variance to the prediction of reading score. Similar effects are shown in the case of reading comprehension. These data are shown in Table 1. Phonological processing contributes a great deal of variance to word recognition and pseudoword reading while the contribution of IQ is very small.

The Discrepancy Definition

Often, discrepancy scores are used based on regression scores that are calculated using the correlation between IQ and reading. This method assumes that there is a clear relationship between IQ and reading in the form of a correlation that is a constant and independent of sample characteristics, the particular IQ tests used, the nature of the reading measure, and the age of the subjects. Considering the wide range of correlations that have been reported for the relationship between IQ and reading and considering the critical place that this correlation plays in the calculation of the regression scores, it is clearly premature to assume that there is one appropriate correlation. The calculation of the regression score is problematic. How do we know which is the real correlation to use in the calculation? In addition, arguments have been raised against the regression score on statistical grounds. Ellis and Large (1987) provide an extended discussion of these issues.

One of the arguments advanced for the use of the discrepancy definition is that there is evidence that there are two types of poor readers, that there is a "hump" in the distribution, that is, that the distribution is a bimodal one. There have been several failures to replicate the bimodal distribution found by Rutter and Yule. Neither Rodgers (1983) has, nor Share, McGee, McKenzie, Williams, and Silva (1987) or van der Wissel and Zegers (1985) have replicated the alleged bimodal distribution. In addition, as I have written previously, "Arguments for these two subytpes have been based on difference between them in sex ratio, social disadvantage, and patterns of neurological and motor disorders. However, Share, et al., (1987) did not find significant differences in sex ratios between these two groups. In addition, differences in socioeconomic status would be predicted because IQ (which differentiates the groups) is correlated with socioeconomic status. There does not appear to be any evidence that neurological and motor difficulties are causally related to the reading problems (Share, et al., 1987). Therefore, even if these differences between reading backward and specifically reading retarded exist, the significance is not clear." (Siegel, 1989, p. 471). It seems to me that we need to ask the questions about the differences or lack of them between high and low IQ disabled readers in relationship to the *processes related to reading*. We also need to be sensitive to social class and environmental influences.

As I have noted earlier the critical question is the nature and extent of the difference between the dyslexics (specifically reading retarded) and the reading backward (garden variety) poor readers. I have conducted a study comparing dyslexics and poor readers, ages 7-16 years, on a variety of reading, spelling, phonological processing, language and memory tests (Siegel, in press). Although the dyslexics had significantly higher IQ scores than the poor readers, these two groups did not differ in their performance on reading, spelling, phonological processing and most of the language and memory tasks. In all cases, the performance of *both* reading groups was significantly below that of the normally achieving readers.

Figure 1 shows these data for one measure - pseudoword reading. There was no difference between the dyslexics and the poor readers but both groups had significantly lower scores than

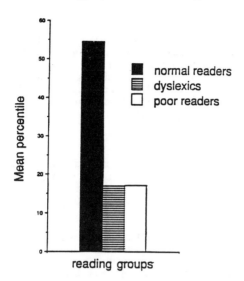

Figure 1. Performance of dyslexics, poor readers, and normal readers on pseudoword reading.

the normally achieving readers. Children with learning problems, whether or not their reading is significantly below the level predicted by their IQ scores, have significant problems in phonological processing, short-term and working memory. There does not appear to be any empirical evidence to justify the distinction between dyslexics and poor readers. There are a number of studies that do not find differences between high and low poor readers (or IQ-reading discrepant and IQ reading non-discrepant). These studies include: Bell and Perfetti (1989), Bloom, Wagner, Resken, and Bergman (1980), Das, Mensink, and Mishra (1990), Ellis and Large (1987), Fischer, Liberman, and Shankweiler (1978), Fredman & Stevenson (1988), Hall Wilson, Humpreys, Tinzmann, and Bower (1983), Johnston, Rugg, and Scott (1987a, 1987b), Jorm, Share, Maclean, and Matthews (1986), Jorm, Share, Matthews, and Maclean (1986), Liberman Shankweiler, Orlando, Harris, and Berti (1971), Rack (1989), Saloner and Gettinger (1985), Scarborough (1989a, 1989b), Seidenberg, Bruck, Fornarolo, and Backman (1985), Share, Jorm, McGee, Silva, Maclean, Matthews, and Williams (1987), Silva, McGee, and Williams (1985), Taylor, Satz, and Friel (1979). Some of these studies found differences between the IQ groups in processes that were not closely related to reading (e.g., mathematics, spatial concepts) but *all* of these studies found that in phonological processing, reading, spelling, and the type of reading errors, there were *no differences* among groups of poor readers who differed in IQ. It seems to me that the weight of the evidence is in favor of the *no difference* position.

Crowder (1984) has argued against the use of IQ scores on methodological grounds and has noted that matching on IQ is particularly dangerous because of the possibility of regression effects. Crowder recommends statistical control. This statistical control is the technique that I have used in a study where I examined whether IQ test scores or phonological processing tasks are better predictors of reading scores.

Listening Comprehension?

Some have proposed that listening comprehension should be used as an alternative to IQ measures. The complexities of measuring reading comprehension and the complex set of variables that are related to reading comprehension make it difficult to measure "comprehension" (Siegel & Heaven, 1986 also provide an extended discussion of these issues.) However, the same issues are relevant to the measurement of listening comprehension. That is, memory, vocabulary size, background knowledge influence listening comprehension scores so it is not clear that listening comprehension is a meaningful general ability control.

Remediation

Meyen (1989) argues that we need to maintain special educational services for individuals who have the most serious problems and that these services should be reserved for individuals of normal intellectual ability. However, there is no evidence that children with higher IQ scores and learning disabilities benefit more from remediation than children with the same learning disabilities but lower IQ scores.

It might be argued that we need to use IQ test scores in the assessment of learning disabilities because these IQ scores could help us determine who would benefit from remediation. Presumably, children with higher IQ scores would be able to benefit more from educational experiences. In fact, the studies that have actually *measured* the relation between IQ and the effects of remediation have found that learning disabled children with lower IQ scores showed *similar* gains from remediation as did those with higher IQ scores (Arnold, Smeltzer, & Barneby, 1981; Kershner, 1990; Lytton, 1967; van der Wissel & Zegers, 1985). Torgesen, Dahlem, and Greenstein (1987) found that, in some cases, gains in reading performance among reading disabled children were not related to IQ scores but in some cases there was a small but statistically significant relationship. One study (Yule, 1973) even found that "reading backward" children with lower IQ scores made *more* gains than "specifically reading disabled" children with higher IQ scores.

The Achievement Test Solution

The solution that I propose is to use achievement test scores and not an IQ achievement discrepancy to define learning disabilities. Various aspects of the rationale for this decision are outlined in Siegel (1991) and Siegel and Heaven (1986). I propose that if an individual has a low score on an achievement test involving reading, spelling, and/or arithmetic, then that individual should be called learning disabled. Of course, certain other criteria called exclusionary criteria need to be applied, such as severe emotional problems, neurological deficits, inadequate educational opportunity, or insufficient knowledge of the language. Why not just use achievement tests? I am still waiting for an answer. Furthermore, Stanovich (1986) and others, including my colleagues and I (Siegel, 1986; 1990; Siegel & Ryan, 1988, 1989), have argued that phonological processing deficits, not low intellectual ability, are the core problems in cases of a reading disability. There is extensive evidence to support this point. (See Siegel, 1992; & Stanovich, 1988a, 1988b for reviews.) We need to develop more extensive and detailed measures of these phonological processing skills. With these types of measures, we will be able to achieve an understanding of the nature of reading disabilities.

The following quote from Gardner (1986) illustrates my view.

If asked to predict, I would guess there will continue to be a search for better and more rapidly administered standardized (group) tests, which can predict more of g with fewer items, or, better yet, with a single neurological measure. In our technologically oriented society, such a search is likely to continue for a long time. My own guess is that such a search will prove as forlorn as the alchemical search for a fountain of youth, but I certainly would not block the road of inquiry.

In my personal vision, I imagine the apparatus of intelligence testing as eventually becoming unnecessary, its waning unmourned. An hour-long standardized test may at certain points in history have served as a reasonable way of indicating who should be performing better at school or who is capable of military service; but as we come to understand the variety of roles and the variety of ways in which scholastic or military accomplishment can come about, we need far more differentiated and far more sensitive ways of assessing what individuals are capable of accomplishing. (pp. 75-76)

Conclusion

On reflecting on the debate that has followed after the publication of my article on this issue (Siegel, 1989), I sometimes feel as if I have entered the world at the bottom of the rabbit hole with Alice.

ACKNOWLEDGMENT

The research discussed in this chapter was supported by a grant from the Natural Sciences and Engineering Research Council of Canada. This chapter was written while the author held a Senior Research Fellowship from the Ontario Mental Health Foundation. The author wishes to thank Keith Stanovich for his helpful contribution to the ideas discussed in this chapter and Letty Guirnela for secretarial assistance.

REFERENCES

Arnold, L. E., Smeltzer, D. J., & Barneby, N. S. (1981). Specific perceptual remediation: Effects related to sex, IQ, and parents' occupational status; behavioral change pattern by scale factors; and mechanism of benefit hypothesis tested. *Psychological Reports, 49,* 198.

Bell, L., & Perfetti, C.A. (1989). Reading ability, "reading disability" and garden variety low reading skill: Some adult comparisons. Unpublished manuscript.

Baldwin, R.S., & Vaughn, S. (1989). Why Siegel's arguments are irrelevant to the definition of learning disabilities. *Journal of Learning Disabilities, 22,* 513, 520.

Bloom, A., Wagner, M., Reskin, L., & Bergman, A. (1980). A comparison of intellectually delayed and primary reading disabled children on measures of intelligence and achievement. *Journal of Clinical Psychology, 36,* 788-790.

Bryan, T. (1989). IQ and learning disabilities: A perspective from research on social factors. *Journal of Learning Disabilities, 22,* 480-481.

Carroll, L. (1946 Edition). *Alice in wonderland and through the looking glass.* Kingsport, TN: Grosset & Dunlap.

Cobrinik, L. (1974). Unusual reading ability in severely disturbed children. *Journal of Autism and Childhood Schizophrenia, 4,* 163-175.

Crowder, R.G. (1984). Is it just reading? *Developmental Review, 4*, 48-61.

Das, J.P., Mensink, D., & Mishra, R.K. (1990). Cognitive processes separating good and poor readers when IQ is covaried. *Learning and Individual Differences, 2*, 423-436.

Denckla, M. B. (1979). Childhood learning disabilities. In K. M. Heilman & E. Valenstein (Eds.), *Clinical Neuropsychology*, (pp. 535-573). New York: Oxford University Press.

Ellis, N., & Large, B. (1987). The development of reading. As you seek so shall you find. *British Journal of Psychology, 78*, 1-28.

Fischer, F.W., Liberman, I.Y., & Shankweiler, D. (1978). Reading reversals and developmental dyslexia: A further study. *Cortex, 14*, 496-510.

Fredman, G., & Stevenson, J. (1988). Reading processes in specific reading retarded and reading backward 13-year-olds. *British Journal of Developmental Psychology, 6*, 97-108.

Gardner, H. (1986). The waning of intelligence tests. In R.J. Sternberg & D.K. Detterman (Eds.), *What is intelligence?* (pp. 73-76). Norwood, N.J.: Ablex.

Graham S., & Harris, K.R. (1989). The relevance of IQ on the determination of learning disabilities: Abandoning scores as decision makers. *Journal of Learning Disabilities, 22*, 500-503.

Hall, J.W., Wilson, K.P., Humphreys, M.S., Tinzmann, M.B., & Bowyer, P.M. (1983). Phonetic similarity effects in good vs. poor readers. *Memory and Cognition, 11*, 520-527.

Healy, J.M., Aram, D.M., Horowitz, S.J., & Kessler, J.W. (1982). A study of hyperlexia. *Brain and Language, 17*, 1-23.

Johnston, R.S., Rugg, M.D., & Scott, T. (1987a) . The influence of phonology on good and poor readers when reading for meaning. *Journal of Memory and Language, 26*, 57-68.

Johnston, R.S., Rugg, M.D., & Scott, T. (1987b). Phonological similarity effects, memory span and developmental reading disorders: The nature of the relationship. *British Journal of Psychology, 78*, 205-211.

Johnston, R.S., Rugg, M.D., & Scott, T. (1988). Pseudohomophone effects in 8 and 11 year old good and poor readers. *Journal of Research in Reading, 11*, 110-132.

Jorm, A.F., Share, D.L., Maclean, R., & Matthews, R. (1986) Cognitive factors at school entry predictive of specific reading retardation and general reading backwardness: A research note. *Journal of Child Psychology and Psychiatry, 27*, 45-54.

Jorm, A.F., Share, D.L., Matthews, R.J., & Maclean, R. (1986). Behavior problems in specific reading retarded and general reading backward children: A longitudinal study. *Journal of Child Psychology and Psychiatry, 27*, 33-43.

Kershner, J.R. (1990). Self-concept and IQ as predictors of remedial success in children with learning disabilities. *Journal of Learning Disabilities. 23*, 368-374.

Leong, C.K. (1989). The locus of so-called IQ test results in reading disabilities. *Journal of Learning Disabilities, 22*, 507-512.

Liberman, I.Y., Shankweiler, D., Orlando, C., Harris, K.S., & Berti, F.B. (1971). letter confusions and reversals of sequence in the beginning reader: Implications for Orton's theory of developmental dyslexia. *Cortex, 7*, 127-142.

Lyon, G.R. (1989). IQ is irrelevant to the definition of learning disabilities: A position in search of logic and data. *Journal of Learning Disabilities, 22*, 504-506, 512.

Lytton, H. (1967). Follow-up of an experiment in selection for remedial education. *British Journal of Educational Psychology, 37*, 1-9.

Meyen, E. (1989). Let's not confuse test scores with the substance of the discrepancy model. *Journal of Learning Disabilities, 22*, 482-483.

Olson, D.R. (1986). Intelligence and literacy: The relationships between intelligence and the technologies of representation and communication. In R.J. Sternberg & R.K. Wagner (Eds.), *Practical intelligence* (pp. 338-360). Cambridge: Cambridge University Press.

Rack, J.P. (1989). Reading-IQ discrepancies and the phonological deficit in reading disability. Paper presented at the biennial meeting of Society for Research in Child Development, Kansas City, MO.

Rodgers, B. (1983). The identification and prevalence of specific reading retardation. *British Journal of Educational Psychology, 53,* 369-373.

Saloner, M.R., & Gettinger, M. (1985). Social interference skills in learning disabled and nondisabled children. *Psychology in the Schools, 2,* 201-207.

Scarborough, H.S. (1989a). A comparison of methods for identifying reading disabilities in adults. Unpublished manuscript.

Scarborough, H.S. (1989b). Prediction of reading disability from familial and individual differences. *Journal of Educational Psychology, 81,* 101-108.

Seidenberg, M.S., Bruck, M., Fornarolo, G., & Backman, J. (1985). Word recognition processes of poor and disabled reader: Do they necessarily differ? *Applied Psycholinguistics, 6,* 161-180.

Share, D.L., Jorm, A.F., McGee, R., Silva, P.A., Maclean, R., Matthews, R., & Williams, S. (1987). Dyslexia and other myths. Unpublished manuscript.

Share, D.L., McGee, R., McKenzie, D., Williams, S., & Silva, P.A. (1987). Further evidence relating to the distinction between specific reading retardation and general reading backwardness. *British Journal of Developmental Psychology, 5,* 35-44.

Siegel, L.S. (1984). A longitudinal study of a hyperlexic child: Hyperlexia as a language disorder. *Neuropsychologia, 22,* 577-585.

Siegel, L.S. (1986). Phonological deficits in children with a reading disability. *Canadian Journal of Special Education, 2,* 45-54.

Siegel, L.S. (1988). Evidence that IQ scores are irrelevant to the definition and analysis of reading disability. *Canadian Journal of Psychology, 42,* 201-215.

Siegel, L.S. (1989). IQ is irrelevant to the definition of learning disabilities. *Journal of Learning Disabilities, 22,* 469-478, 486.

Siegel, L.S. (1990). IQ and learning disabilities: R.I.P. In H.L. Swanson & B. Keogh (Eds.), *Learning disabilities: Theoretical and research issues.* (pp. 111-128) Hillsdale, NJ: Erlbaum.

Siegel, L.S. (1991). The identification of learning disabilities: Issues in psychoeducational assessment. *Education and Law Journal, 3,* 301-313.

Siegel, L.S. (1992). An evaluation of the discrepancy definition of dyslexia. *Journal of Learning Disabilities, 25,* 618-629.

Siegel, L.S., & Heaven, R. (1986). Defining and categorizing learning disabilities. In S. Ceci (Ed.), *Handbook of cognitive, social, and neuropsychological aspects of learning disabilities,* Vol. 1 (pp. 95-121). Hillsdale, N.J.: Erlbaum.

Siegel, L.S., & Ryan, E.B. (1988). Development of grammatical sensitivity, phonological, and short-term memory skills in normally achieving and learning disabled children. *Developmental Psychology, 24,* 28-37.

Siegel, L.S., & Ryan, E.B. (1989). Subtypes of developmental dyslexia: The influence of definitional variables. *Reading and Writing: An Interdisciplinary Journal, 1,* 257-287.

Silva, P.A., McGee, R., & Williams, S. (1985). Some characteristics of 9-year old boys with general reading backwardness or specific reading retardation. *Journal of Child Psychology and Psychiatry, 26,* 407-421.

Stanovich, K.E. (1986). Matthew effects in reading: Some consequences of individual differences in the acquisition of literacy. *Reading Research Quarterly, 21,* 360-407.

Stanovich, K.E. (1988a). Explaining the differences between the dyslexic and garden variety poor reader: The phonological-core variance-difference model. *Journal of Learning Disabilities, 21,* 590-604, 612.

Stanovich, K.E. (1988b). The right and wrong places to look for the cognitive locus of reading disability. *Annals of Dyslexia, 38,* 154-177.

Stanovich, K.E. (1989). Has the learning disabilities field lost its intelligence? *Journal of Learning Disabilities, 22,* 487-492.

Stanovich, K.E. (1991). Discrepancy definition of reading disability: Has intelligence led us astray? *Reading Research Quarterly, 26,* 7-29.

Sternberg, R.J., & Detterman, D.K. (Eds.) (1986). *What is intelligence?* Norwood, N.J.: Ablex.

Swanson, H.L. (1989). Phonological processes and other routes. *Journal of Learning Disabilities, 22,* 493-497.

Taylor, H.G., Satz, P., & Friel, J. (1979). Developmental dyslexia in relation to other childhood reading disorders: Significance and clinical utility. *Reading Research Quarterly, 15,* 84-101.

Torgesen, J.K. (1989). Why IQ is relevant to the definition of learning disabilities. *Journal of Learning Disabilities, 22,* 484-486.

Torgesen, J.K., Dahlem, W.E., & Greenstein, J. (1987). Using verbatim text recordings to enhance reading comprehension in learning disabled adolescents. *Learning Disabilities Focus, 3,* 30-38.

Tunmer, W. (1989). mental test differences as Matthew effects in literacy: The rich get richer and the poor get poorer. *New Zealand Sociology, 4,* 64-84.

van der Wissel, A., & Zegers, F. E. (1985). Reading retardation revisited. *British Journal of Developmental Psychology, 3,* 3-9.

Yule, W. (1973). Differential prognosis of reading backwardness and specific reading retardation. *British Journal of Educational Psychology, 43,* 244-248.

TOWARDS DEVELOPING A FRAMEWORK FOR DIAGNOSING READING DISORDERS

CHE KAN LEONG
Department for the Education of Exceptional Children,
College of Education
University of Saskatchewan,
Saskatoon, Saskatchewan
CANADA. S7N 0W0

ABSTRACT: The main aim of diagnosis of reading disorders is to determine with some degree of accuracy [also fuzziness] and sensitivity the individuals to be served; and from the diagnostic results the components or sub-components of reading that these individuals need to work on. Diagnosis is a more refined process following from that of identification, classification and assessment. This chapter first outlines the refinement of an earlier proposal for a two-stage or two-level approach to diagnosis of individuals with reading disorders (Leong, 1985, 1987, 1989a). Relevant issues in diagnosing developmental dyslexics within the aptitude-achievement discrepancy framework and the role of "intelligence" are revisited (see also Siegel, this volume; Stanovich, this volume). There is convergent evidence of the diagnostic efficacy of pseudoword reading; and this can be enhanced with a broader sampling of pseudowords. Reading of irregular words, morphological and morphemic processing of lexical items all add to the diagnostic process and help to elucidate knowledge of lexical representation. For "garden-variety" poor readers (Gough & Tunmer, 1986) the renewed call to incorporate listening comprehension tasks to gauge language processing needs to consider both theoretical and methodological aspects underpinning auding or listening to text to gain knowledge. Data from the application of text-to-speech computer systems (DECtalk) suggest the greater potency in using simultaneous on-line text reading and synthetic speech auding for both diagnosing and helping language/reading comprehension. General principles of compensation, practice and computer-mediated learning are seen as effective in remediation.

Diagnosis following Assessment -- A Two-Stage Approach

The first stage from assessment to diagnosis serves to screen a group of children with reading disabilities as potential candidates for further study and remediation. The approach is mainly psychometric or quantitative. The aim is to ascertain initially those children needing help based on their discrepant **predicted** and **measured** achievements. How discrepant this difference should be to constitute a significant difference depends on a number of factors, not the least being the prevailing educational philosophy and the material and human resources available to any one community or school system.

The rationale for this aptitude-achievement discrepancy approach to under-achievement is articulated in an elegant monograph by Thorndike (1963). He also explicates the algorithms with the use of multiple regression analysis incorporating psychometric characteristics of reliabilities, inter-correlations and standard errors of measurement of the

R.M. Joshi and C.K. Leong (eds.), Reading Disabilities: Diagnosis and Component Processes, 85–131.
© 1993 *Kluwer Academic Publishers. Printed in the Netherlands.*

different standardized instruments of general ability and achievement. The successful use of the Thorndike concept in predicting reading disabilities can be found in the monumental Isle of Wight study of reading backwardness and reading retardation by Rutter, Tizard and Whitmore (1970). Using the same logic, Yule and his associates reported on the operationalization of under-achievement in children aged six to twelve years (Yule, Lansdown, & Urbanowicz, 1982) as predicted from the WISC-R or Revised WISC full scale IQ (Wechsler, 1974) and chronological ages; and complementary data on academic achievement for a similar battery of tasks with older children (Yule, Gold, & Busch, 1981). More recently, a number of researchers (Reynolds, 1990; Rispens & van Yperen, 1990; Shepard, 1980) have shown the regression prediction model to be preferred over other models in the identification of children with specific reading disorders.

This first-level psychometric or quantitative approach aims at providing a reasonably accurate estimate of "who shall be served". The data could include group tests of general ability, reading and related areas of achievement; and also scaled teachers' estimates and their cumulative observations on individual children. All these measures could be administered by teachers in the course of their teaching and the results analyzed statistically within the multiple regression framework. The advantage of this multi-faceted and multivariate screening approach is the relative ease in administration and data analyses, especially with computerization, to derive a reasonably close estimate of the children to be served. The disadvantage is the likelihood of identifying a larger number of children as reading disabled, who are not actually disabled (false positives or false alarms). To minimize the number of "misfits" the use of flexible thresholds or limen scores is recommended (Leong, 1987). The flexible cutoffs help to maximize the hits and correct rejections, or the congruence of statistical prediction and actuarial prediction. This congruence is enhanced with the second-level process --that of detailed, individual diagnosis by clinicians or school psychologists. This detailed diagnostic process follows from the assessment using group tests and scaled teachers' estimates as outlined in the preceding paragraphs.

Computerized Assessment

To facilitate the gaining of detailed knowledge of the pattern of performance of individuals, automated psychological testing can be used as an adjunct to gather a large body of interview data or self-reporting materials (Angle, 1981), and to administer psychometric tests (Beaumont, 1981). Computerized-adaptive testing makes possible more extensive assessment and provides the opportunity to evaluate learning aptitude while subjects are being coached by computer programs during problem-solving. Such adaptive assessment should lead to improved estimation of abilities and measurement of change over time (Embretson, 1992), especially in the study of individual differences in visual-spatial reasoning, memory and attention tasks (Hunt & Pellegrino, 1985). The earlier reservations expressed about possible misinterpretation of computerized test scores (Matarazzo, 1985, 1986) have given place to much more sanguine predictions of combining salient information of psycho-educational and behavioral profiles of individuals for diagnosis and habilitation (Matarazzo, 1992).

In the area of reading, computerized testing has been shown to be ecologically valid (Aaronson, 1984). Computer-aided reading instruction helps to enhance reading comprehension (Reinking & Rickman, 1990) and to help promote literacy in ways not possible without the computer (Reinking & Bridwell-Bowles, 1991). Further more, sophisticated text-to-speech computer systems such as DECtalk and its variants have been shown by different research groups in Colorado, Guelph, Umea, and Saskatoon (see Leong, 1992a, for details) to be effective in reading intervention and useful in research. The provision of immediate and interactive on-line and high-quality synthetic speech feedback to readers for combinations of vowels, consonants or larger speech segments helps to enhance word identification, phonological awarensss and reading or language comprehension. The efficacy of computer-mediated reading will be discussed in subsequent sections. The keynote in this reference to computerized testing is to emphasize its flexibility and as a complement to, or even substitute for, paper-and-pencil tasks.

Some Evidence for the Two-Stage Approach

The proposal first set out some years ago (Leong, 1985, 1987) for a two-stage or two-level framework of diagnosis offers a viable approach for school systems first to screen subgroups of children with reading and related disorders, and later to diagnose in detail and with greater degrees of accuracy those individuals needing help. The approach takes into account scaled teachers' estimates of children's performance in reading and standardized achievement and diagnostic tests; is administratively convenient; is theory based; and is empirically verifiable.

Empirical support for the two-stage approach is provided by Berninger, Hart, Abbot, and Karovsky (1992). Berninger et al. emphasize the importance of multiple development skills during early stages of emerging literacy as grounded in the Multiple Connections Model of Reading Acquisition of Berninger (1988); and proceed to test three inter-related approaches to defining "disabilities" in an unselected sample of 300 first, second, and third graders. Berninger et al. argue for a two-stage approach analogous to the framework of Leong (1985, 1987), as outlined above. In stage 1 classroom teachers are asked to identify "low functioning" children in orthographic and phonological coding, and some perceptual motor integration skills; and stage 2 concentrates on a comprehensive psychoeducational diagnosis.

This two-stage approach is supported by the Berninger et al. (1992) data analyses using mainly the Mahalanobis generalized distance D Square technique, in which a large distance of a case from the mean of all cases computed from the inverse of the correlation or covariance matrix and standard scores indicates the case as an outlier in the space defined by the individual variable. The Berninger et al. results emphasize that more specific diagnostic categories be linked to multiple components of reading and writing (see also Berninger & Hart, this volume). This emphasis on multiple orthographic-phonological connections and explicit teaching of these connections have been shown to prevent more serious reading disabilities (Berninger & Traweek, 1991).

Refining Assessment and Diagnosis

The **sensitivity** and **specificity** of the two-stage or two-level approach to assessment and diagnosis would also need to be emphasized (Leong, 1985, 1987). This twin emphasis aims at maximizing hits and minimizing negatives, especially false alarms, within the framework of **signal detection** theory (see, Green & Swets, 1966/1974; McNicol, 1972, for details). In addition, false-positive fraction (the ratio of false positives to actual negatives) and false-negative fraction (ratio of false negatives to actual positives) allow for the comparison of actuarial and statistical predictions and help to discriminate disabling conditions from different levels of diagnostic decisions.

By plotting the different combinations of true-positive fraction against the false-positive fraction the resultant **receiver-operating-characteristic** (ROC) curve provides an unbiased estimate of observer sensitivity. This receiver-operating-characteristic curve enables diagnosticians to adjust decision thresholds to enable diagnostic decisions to be made on the weight of evidence, and, as in learning and reading disorders, with some uncertainty or fuzziness. The ROC provides the flexibility for diagnosticians to select a stringent threshold (i.e., fewer cases detected but also fewer false positives or false alarms), or a lax threshold (i.e., more cases detected but also more false alarms). The stringency or laxity of the threshold depends on the purpose of diagnosis, administrative, social and other factors.

Signal detection theory has been used in biostatistics in arriving at reasonably precise diagnosis in confirmed positive cases (sensitivity) and in confirmed negative cases (specificity) (Feinstein, 1975). The key concepts of sensitivity and specificity are applicable to a variety of tasks used in identifying clinical conditions and in discrimination performance in general. A good example of the use of the technique is the discrimination of sensitivity to grammatical structure by agrammatical aphasics (Linebarger, Schwartz, & Saffran, 1983). Given its statistical power, it is surprising that signal detection theory is used only sparingly, if at all, in psycho-educational diagnosis. This is despite some detailed discussions of the rationale and procedures of decision theory in the assessment and diagnosis of children with reading and related disorders (Harber, 1981a, 1981b; Leong, 1985, 1987).

Fuzzy Subset Logic

The actuarial approach incorporating regression and signal detection techniques to assessment and diagnosis of children with reading disorders generally provides an academically sound and administratively defensible basis for dichotomous decisions (e.g., eligible or not-eligible for remediation or special help). However, it should also be recognized that there are measurement and human errors. Issues of assessment cannot be resolved entirely through the use of more refined tasks or better techniques. To be effective, assessment must be cumulative and will need to take into account both quantitative and qualitative aspects of children's reading behavior (Leong, 1987, 1989a). The concept of **sequential decisions** permitting fallible data and resultant decisions to be evaluated is emphasized by Macmann, Barnett, Lombard, Belton-Kocher, and Sharpe (1989).

The parallel fuzzy set or fuzzy subset logic from mathamatics is also appropriate in decision making (Zadeh, 1971, 1984). Zadeh, a mathematician, asserts that human behavior is too complex and too dynamic to be explained fully by conventional mathematical reasoning and computer simulation. He advocates the use of fuzzy logic, where propositions are neither entirely true nor entirely false, but assumes **continuous** values to model human knowledge. Thus the propositions "Most students are literate" and "Most literates have completed high school" mean that these elements are represented by the fuzzy quantifier "most." There is a gradual transition from membership to non-membership such as with the fuzzy sets "literate" to "illiterate", the relationships among which are defined by rigorous mathematical rules. Quantifiers such as "most," "almost most," "usually" and related linguistic variables incorporate "common sense" human knowledge to provide for qualitative approaches. The fuzzy logic of graded statements is illustrated in the schematic in Figure 1.

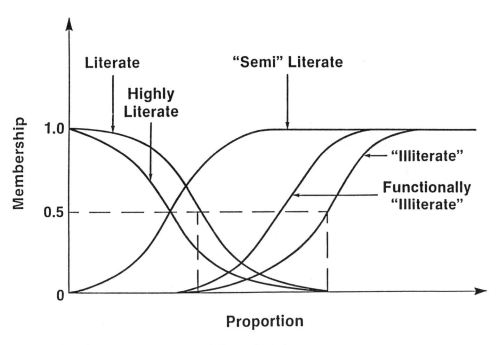

Figure 1. Schematic of fuzzy subset logic applied to diagnosis.

APPLICATION OF FUZZY SUBSET LOGIC TO DIAGNOSIS

The fuzzy subset logic (see also Hersh & Caramazza, 1976) has been used by Horvath, Kass, and Ferrel (1980) to investiage the complex phenomenon of imprecise verbal modelling of learning disabilities by clinicians. The general idea is the comparison of the goodness-of-fit of clinicians' judgment and the verbal modelling. The procedure is as follows: (1) The clinician is asked to specify the characteristics of children with learning [reading] disabilities. (2) The verbal judgment is expressed mathematically as a fuzzy logic composition. (3) The clinician assesses the degree of membership with the fuzzy subset of learning [reading] disabilities from observed data of the children. (4) The clinician assesses the goodness-of-fit of his or her clinical judgment and the children's performance.

Some of the key notions in the goodness-of-fit assessment are: **interaction** (A and B), **union** (A or B), and **complementation** (not A). As an example, learning [reading] disorders may relate to perceptual organization, decoding, working memory, analysis and synthesis of verbal information. Membership in each of these subsets is on a continuum varying from zero to one. From the judgment of the expert clinicians of the composition and strength of these components or subsets, it is possible to work out mathematically the degree of membership of learning [reading] disabilities and to compare the goodness-of-fit of the clinician's judgment and the verbal modelling.

The sketch above suggests that the fuzzy set concept is applicable to the diagnosis of children with reading disorders. The approach provides a formal modelling process using verbal reports and expert judgments as data and does not require large amounts of data as in regression models. The disadvantage is the reliance on the expert judgment of clinicians as input and the difficulty of maintaining within-rater and inter-rater reliabilities. In the last analysis, assessment and diagnosis cannot be exact and should be regarded as problem-solving endeavours. Psychologists, clinicians and teachers should focus their attention more on prevention, intervention, and appropriate service delivery for children with reading disorders (Macmann, et al., 1989).

Mechanisms in Diagnosing Reading Disabilities

Issues Pertaining To Aptitude-Achievement Discrepancy

The **quantitative** and **qualitative** two-stage approach to diagnosis, using regression and signal detection techniques for refinement, is predicated on the assumption that there is a reasonably intact level of aptitude for learning, but the actual learning performance is depressed or impaired in the verbal areas of reading, spelling, and writing. This assumption provides the broad basis from the cognitive-linguistic perspective for usually accepted definitions of learning disabilities (Kavanagh & Truss, 1988), and specific reading disabilities (Leong, 1987, 1989a). The first stage of the two-stage approach summarized above suggests the use of well standardized group general ability tests (The Raven's Progressive Matrices for different levels and ages being possibilities). These well standardized group general ability tests together with other measures including scaled teachers' estimates should serve as indicators of the learning aptitude of individual children in relation to their actual achievement including reading.

At the second stage of the two-stage process, traditional general ability tests still have a place in more refined diagnosis, but may be less relevant above a certain threshold or level (Leong, 1985, 1987, 1989a). Traditional general ability tests need not and should not be confined just to the Wechsler-Revised family of intelligence tests (Wechsler, 1974). Even with current development in the theory and assessment of intelligence, the patterns of cognitive functioning from the WISC-R family of tests provide clinicians with diagnostic and habilitative considerations. Further more, the traditional interpretation of the verbal (comprehension) and performance (perceptual organization) domains of the WISC-R would need to be modified to accommodate the "freedom-from-distractibility" construct (Lezak, 1983). Significant discrepancy between this freedom-from-distractibility factor and the other two factors is indicative of attention deficit disorders in the DSM-III terminology (American Psychiatric Association, 1987). It should also be noted that the new version of WISC-R, the third edition or WISC-III (Wechsler, 1991), is in the direction of current thinking on cognitive abilities.

Changing Concepts Of General Ability Tests

Other traditional intelligence tests of note include the Stanford-Binet Intelligence Scale, Fourth Edition (SB4) (Thorndike, Hagen, & Sattler, 1986) and the British Ability Scales (BAS) (Elliott, 1983). The SB4 with its three levels of tasks culminating in a composite score represents a serious attempt at a broader, multivariate coverage of cognitive ability. The Level II constructs of Crystallized Abilities, subserved by the Level III facets of Verbal and Quantitative Reasoning; and of Fluid-Analytic Abilities, subserved by the facet of

Abstract/Visual Reasoning, are in the tradition of the Cattell-Horn theory of Crystallized (Gc), Fluid (Gf) and Visualization (Gv) intelligences (Horn, 1988; Horn & Cattell, 1966). These three facets of Verbal Reasoning, Quantitative Reasoning and Abstract/Visual Reasoning together with the third Level II construct of Short-Term Memory, subserved by four subtests, represent an integration of some of the current theories of intelligence. These facets provide in greater depth than group tests an indication of learning aptitude.

Another enhanced traditional intelligence test worthy of note is the British Ability Scales (BAS) (Elliott, 1983) because of its theoretical formulation within the Piagetian cognitive-developmental framework; and its item calibration based on the latent trait probabilistic model of Rasch (1960/1980). The BAS provides profiles of: (a) efficiency or speed, (b) reasoning (matrices, formal operation and similarities), (c) spatial imagery, (d) perceptual matching, (e) short-term memory (both recognition and recall), and (f) retrieval and application of knowledge. These profiles also incorporate the processes and cognitive functions involved.

Earlier, reference was made to the use of the standard Raven's Progressive Matrices (Raven, 1960) and its variant forms as an efficient group general ability test at Stage One of diagnosis. The problems posed by the deceptively "simple" culture-fair Raven's can be solved only by "analytic intelligence" involving the induction of relations and correlates, the decomposing of these problems into manageable units or segments and holding these chunks in working memory while operating on them (Carpenter, Just, & Shell, 1990; Hunt, 1974). Performance on the Raven's provides an estimate of differential ability to reason by analogy and higher level abstraction. These are requisites not only for skilled reading, but also for less skilled reading.

This short discussion of both SB4 and BAS and related tests underscores the evolution of traditional intelligence tests from the earlier product-oriented framework to a process-oriented approach. The movement is in the direction of "multiple intelligences" (Gardner, 1983), and the componential analysis of general abilities (Sternberg, 1986). In fact, the underlying notions of intelligence testing from its inception have been on mental functions and psychological processes. Writing in 1903, Alfred Binet (1969 translation by Pollack & Brenner, p. 93) stated that intelligence consisted of: "perceiving the exterior world, and second, reconsidering these perceptions as memories, altering them." Binet considered intelligent behavior as a process of adaptation to a given end and as critical evaluation and that intelligence is educable (see Wolf, 1973). Thus the current notions of components of intelligences, of their modifiability, and of testing for procedural knowledge can be traced to these early formulations.

Relevance Or Irrelevance Of Intelligence Tests In Diagnosis

The summary of the original notions and evolving views of intelligence testing is not meant to be a reentry into an extended discussion of the role of intelligence tests in defining learning [reading] disabilities for diagnostic and remedial purposes. The pros and cons of this important topic have been debated vigorously by a number of researchers, among other places, in a Special Issue of the **Journal of Learning Disabilities** (see Wong, 1989) with a lead article by Siegel (1989) followed by open peer commentaries. Siegel (1990, this volume) has renewed her forceful argument that intelligence test scores are not important or not necessary in diagnosing learning [reading] disabilities and reiterates her evidence that poor readers at varying intelligence score levels show similar patterns of reading, language and memory deficits as indicative of such irrelevance.

It seems that cogent answers to the queries raised by Siegel are provided by Torgesen (1989) and Swanson (1989), among others. Torgesen (1989) reasoned that in learning [reading] disabilities diagnosis, intelligence test controls help to rule out their primary role in achievement differences between contrast groups and between subgroups with and without phonological and orthographic difficulties. Swanson (1989, p. 493) drew attention to "some degree of subjectivity" in Siegel's designation of ability and reading subgroups, and the loss of statistical power in her tripartite division of the continuous variable of intelligence into high, medium and low subgroups. Further more, to the extent that "IQ" scores denote rate of learning, their incorporation in diagnosis provides some indication of the progress that poor readers at different IQ levels will likely make.

It should also be noted that in the **JLD** debate Siegel (1989, p. 477) suggested a compromise solution of using a cutoff score of 80, "if the field is not yet ready to abandon the IQ" (also Siegel, 1990, p. 126). This grudging alternative seems to be an implicit acceptance of the position taken by Torgesen, Swanson, Leong (1989a) and several others. If so, clinical and experimental data suggest that some threshold scores at about one standard deviation below the mean, based on **current**, well standardized general ability tests (not confined to the WISC-R as consistently referred to in much of the 1989 **JLD** debate) should provide some yardstick (with all its inherent measurement errors) to estimate significant discrepancies in actual achievement including reading (Leong, 1985, 1987, 1989a).

Relevance Of Intelligence In Hyperlexia?

A corollary put forward by Siegel (1989, 1990, this volume) to further support her argument that intelligence may not set a limit on reading relates to "hyperlexic" children. These are readers, who purportedly have low intelligence test scores, decode words and pseudowords adequately, but are poor comprehenders. At the outset, it is debatable whether those children with low general ability but good decoding subskills and poor reading comprehension are **true** hyperlexics and can be diagnosed as such.

The early conceptualization of **hyperlexia** as a discrepancy between adequate to proficient decoding (not just "word-calling") and poor reading comprehension needs redefinition and refinement in light of ongoing research (Aaron, 1989; Healy & Aram, 1986; Healy, Aram, Horowitz, & Kessler, 1982; Huttenlocher & Huttenlocher, 1973; Pennington, Johnson, & Welsh, 1987; Rispens & van Berckelaer, 1991; Snowling & Frith, 1986). The consensus finding of these authors is that hyperlexia is not so much a syndrome-specific phenomenon resulting from pathological impairment. Rather, hyperlexia should be defined as a pervasive developmental reading/language disorder characterized by intense and precocious interest in oral word reading together with a significant deficit in language comprehension and development, this language impairment being also reported by Siegel (1984) in her case study of a hyperlexic girl.

The different studies generally show that the purportedly higher decoding subskills of hyperlexic children relate more to rote association and not so much to word-specific processes. Hyperlexics' reading comprehension deficits derive from poor syntactic ability, impaired rule abstraction and generalization abilities, and especially their failure to comprehend larger units of meaning. Among other sets of findings, those by Snowling and Frith (1986) are instructive. In four experiments all focussing on "hyperlexic" children's comprehension of text of varying unit sizes of meaning and using the WISC-R or the British Ability Scales as references, Snowling and Frith (1986, p. 410) suggested that "**true**

hyperlexia is manifested in terms of both (surprising) decoding success **and** (surprising) comprehension failure (the surprise being in relation to verbal ability)" (authors' emphases). This tentative suggestion of "double discrepancy" has been verified by Rispens and van Berckelaer (1991) using the WISC-R as a yardstick in regression prediction models. Thus psychometrically, a general ability test may provide some reference zone to estimate the discrepancy between aptitude and performance; and may afford some theoretically and empirically sound basis for diagnosis.

However, Snowling and Frith (1986, p. 410) also pointed out that the psychometric approach of "double discrepancy does not... constitute a satisfactory definition." They emphasized that an adequate and functional decoding system may operate "in the absence of the usual links with the semantic and or general knowledge systems" and that "true" hyperlexics can be differentiated from the higher verbal ability superior decoders (p. 410). There are also neuropsychological data to consider. Hyperlexics have been shown to rely more on associative mechanisms rather than on word kowledge to recognize and decode words and even pseudowords; and these individuals may be considered to exhibit a weak or extreme form of developmental surface dyslexia showing lexicality effects such as frequency and imageability in reading strategies (Goldberg & Rothermel, 1984; Pennington, Johnson, & Welsh, 1987).

SUMMARY OF HYPERLEXIA IN DIAGNOSIS

As a summary of this part of the argument, it should be recognized that there is the danger of over-extending the concept of hyperlexia (Aaron, 1989; Pennington et al., 1987); and that general ability tests provide a sensitive means to differentiate higher and lower ability superior decoders but poor comprehenders to come closer to define operationally **true** hyperlexics. Over and above this differentiation, if general ability tests seem to be lesspredictive, it is because they are not designed for, and are less sensitive to, teasing out impairments in processing information in general and symbolic and semantic language in particular. These impairments in relation to some general or verbal ability thresholds are characteristics of true hyperlexics and hyperlexia considered as a pervasive developmental disorder (Aaron, 1989; Healy & Aram, 1986; Healy et al., 1982; Rispens & van Berckelaer, 1991; Snowling & Frith, 1986). Where hyperlexia is of particular theoretical interest in the present context is in the analogy with developmental surface dyslexia and the insight it affords in the mechanism of lexical access (Pennington et al., 1987).

Pseudoword Reading as Diagnostic

If Siegel's assertion (1989, 1990, this volume) of the irrelevance of "IQ" scores in diagnosing children with reading disabilities does not meet with consensus (see Wong, 1989; but also Stanovich, 1991, & this volume, for contrary views), her emphasis on the role of decoding, especially using pseudoword tasks, in diagnosing reading disabilities is well grounded and generally accepted. The deceptively "Simple View" of reading (Gough & Tunmer, 1986; Hoover & Gough, 1990) asserts that inability to decode decontextualized words accurately and rapidly (reading aloud or reading silently) is the proximal cause of developmental dyslexia.

Decoding in this context connotes the use of knowledge of "orthographic cipher"; and that decoding ability is a direct function of knowledge of orthographic-phonologic correspondence values of English (Gough & Tunmer, 1986; Hoover & Gough, 1990).

Individual differences in reading comprehension are attributable to differences in word identification or automatic phonological translation of words and memory and this concept is the mainstay of the powerful verbal efficiency theory of Perfetti (1985). This efficient processing of words should be interpreted within the context of "local factors" facilitating the assembly and integration of proposition encoding (Perfetti, 1988). Thus the Siegel proposal and similar ones of using pseudowords conceptualize these tasks as providing an efficient means of selecting those children with "phonological-core" deficits characterizing developmental dyslexics (Stanovich, 1986, 1988a, 1991, this volume).

Variant Findings of Pseudoword Reading

There are studies generally showing significant deficits in phonological coding, derived from pseudoword tests, in small groups of disabled readers compared with reading age controls (Felton & Wood, 1992; Olson, 1985; Olson, Kliegl, Davidson, & Foltz, 1985; Siegel & Ryan, 1988). There are also studies varying in refinement that show only weak trends towards such deficits (Beech & Harding, 1984; Bruck, 1988; Treiman & Hirsh-Pasek, 1985). In their insightful chapter on componential skills analysis of reading disability as part of the detailed longitudinal Colorado Reading Project started in 1982, Olson, Wise, Conners, and Rack (1990) attempted to reconcile some of the variant results of pseudoword reading. They posited explanations in terms of the nature of stimulus materials; power of statistical analyses; and age and developmental status of the target and control subjects, with attendant regression effects in reading age matches.

Olson et al. (1990) agreed that disabled readers in comparison with their reading age controls also use phonological knowledge, although these poor readers are weak in such knowledge and are inefficient in accessing it. Further more, their results suggest that the phonological deficits may be apparent only in older disabled readers from around age twelve onward. Parenthetically, the use of simple difference scores between real word and pseudoword reading as an index of phonological deficit in many of the studies reviewed by Olson et al. (1990) is susceptible to the inequalities of the units of measurements of the two sets of scores. Residualized difference or gain scores between real word and pseudoword reading pose fewer disadvantages and are preferred (Cronbach & Furby, 1970). It should also be noted that elsewhere the Coloradoa group (DeFries, Olson, Pennington, & Smith, 1991) reported small negative correlations of the order of -.28 to -.29 in their samples of 59 and 218 subjects, suggesting that for some of their disabled readers low verbal intelligence may explain in part their low word recognition.

Studying Dyslexia Within A Developmental Context

Olson and his colleagues (Rack, Snowling, & Olson, 1992) have recently carried out a fairly exhaustive review of nonword reading deficits within the framework of phonological deficits in developmental dyslexics. They have reinforced in greater detail the earlier Olson et al. (1990) interpretation of the variant results as attributable to methodological issues relating to stimulus materials, subject selection, and reading age match designs. Rack et al. also report from their calculation of nonword reading relative to word recognition skill in a large sample of over 400 poor readers some prima facie evidence that these subjects could range on a dimension from phonological dyslexics to surface dyslexics within a developmental context.

This observation of ranging dyslexia from phonological to surface dyslexics seems to be analogous to the tentative conclusions of Bryant and Impey (1986) and Baddeley, Logie and

Ellis (1988), derived from their analysis of reading errors of developmental dyslexics. Some of the children in these studies showed considerable difficulties in reading "irrelegular" words but were not specially impaired in pseudoword reading, and their error patterns resembled those of acquired surface dyslexics (Patterson, Marshall, & Coltheart, 1985). Baddeley et al. raised the possibility of fitting normal reading, developmental dyslexia and acquired surface dyslexia within the same theoretical framework. Different studies have shown that young children and developmental dyslexics may have poorly developed lexical knowledge as reflected in their impaired irregular word reading and would need to rely on their also imperfectly developed indirect non-lexical knowledge to assemble phonology from print. Developmental dyslexia should therefore be studied within the context of developmental and normal reading (Baddeley et al., 1988; Frith, 1985; Rack et al., 1992; Snowling, 1983).

"Friendly" and "Unfriendly" Pseudowords

In accepting the central role of pseudoword decoding as diagnostic across different age ranges and different levels of reading disabilities, researchers should pause to reflect on the nature and characteristics of the pseudowords that should be used. This is because not all pseudowords are alike. Some pseudowords have more "friendly neighbors" [with real words] such as <bave> and some have few friendly neighbors and more "unfriendly neighbors" [with real words] such as <baft> (Laxon, Coltheart, & Keating, 1988; Treiman, Goswami, & Bruck, 1990) according to Glushko's (1979, 1981) account of consistency effect.

Consistency or inconsistency is not dichotomous; the concept ranges along a continuum with varying patterns (Patterson & Morton, 1985). Consistency is a **probabilistic** process and refers to the degree of orthographic-phonologic correspondence. In practice, consistency is generally explained in terms of the number of words in which the intrasyllabic unit of rime is pronounced in the same way (e.g., the rime of _AVE in <cave, pave, save, wave> compared with <have> in real words). Consistency effects affect reading not only of young readers (Coltheart & Leahy, 1992; Laxon et al., 1988) but also readers of varying proficiency, especially in the reading of pseudowords (Glushko, 1979; Laxon et al., 1988) and low frequency words (Seidenberg, 1985). Children and poor readers are more accurate in reading pseudowords with rimes shared by many neighbors rather than shared by few neighbors (Goswami & Bryant, 1990).

Some Relevant Data

A just completed study on the **tactics** that elementary school children use in written spelling and reading may add to our understanding of the role of different kinds of pseudowords in reading (Leong, in preparation). The term tactics is used in the sense of both the arrangement of sounds (**phonotactics**) and of letters or spellings (**graphotactics**). In essence, a carefully designed pseudoword reading task with many friendly neighbors is shown to explain considerable individual variations.

In three experiments, 150 grades 3 to 6 children were asked to read and spell sets of real words varying in transparency (e.g., <zebra>) and opacity (e.g., <gnaw>) in grapheme-phoneme correspondence; to read and spell "irregular" or exception words (see next Section) of different printed frequency and orthographic irregularity; and to read and spell sets of pseudowords varying in orthographic-phonologic correspondence. The set of 40 pseudowords with many "friends" (e.g., <wull, blane; stabe, stine>) and the corresponding set of 40 "unfriendly" pseudowords with few friends (e.g., <tras, woln; stult, sturd>) were adapted from the stimulus materials used by Laxon et al. (1988).

In stepwise multiple regression analyses, performance on the Wide Range Achievement Reading Test-Revised (WRAT-R) (Jastak & Wilkinson, 1984) was treated as the dependent variable; and the following tasks or variables formed the predictors: 3 experimental reading tasks (reading of low frequency "irregular" words, of pseudowords with many, and with few friendly neighbors); 5 experimental spelling tasks; a vocabulary test, a short-term memory task, chronological age and grade level. Results show the 40-item "friendly" pseudoword task to be the most predictive of reading (WRAT-R) with a multiple R of 0.74, accounting for some 55% of the variance. However, with the WRAT-R spelling test as the dependent variable, it is the aggregate of the different levels of orthographic-phonological spelling task (e.g., <zebra, gnaw, sobbing>) with 36 items, which is the most predictive of spelling with a multiple R of 0.76, accounting for 58% of the variation.

Further examination of the relationship among certain reading variables in the Leong (in preparation) study reveals some interesting patterns. The product-moment correlations for the 150 children between the WRAT-R reading and that of the exception words is 0.68; between WRAT-R reading and the set of pseudowords with many friends and with few friends are respectively 0.74 and 0.71. Further more, the correlations between the exception words and the friendly and unfriendly sets of pseudowords are respectively 0.72 and 0.65 with an average r (after z-score transformation) of 0.68, while the correlation of the two sets of pseudowords is 0.84.

Related Subskills In Reading Different Kinds Of Pseudowords

It is recognized that correlations do not provide strong explanatory force, as even these high coefficients may implicate some underlying constructs such as phonemic awareness (Ellis, 1991; Goswami & Bryant, 1990). Nevertheless, the absence of covariation, or low correlation, will rule out any presaging effects that pseudowords may have on reading and spelling. The correlation coefficients summarized above seem to bear out the correlations reported by Gough and Walsh (1991) from the reading by 93 first to third grade children of 36-item regular, exception, and "nonsense" words taken from Baron (1979). There is one slight difference between the two sets of data in that Gough and Walsh found a lower correlation between their (or Baron's) "nonsense" and exception words (0.66), as compared with the considerably higher coefficients between regular and exception words (0.80) and regular and their nonsense words (0.76). They interpret this differential to mean different kinds of information or subskills needed to recognize English words, but cast doubt on the use of two independent mechanisms as suggested by Baron and Treiman (1980). Their observation that "... if children can read many pseudowords, they may or may not read many exception words. But if they can read few pseudowords, then they can read few exception words." (Gough & Walsh, 1991, p. 206) is amenable to further testing.

The preliminary results with the 150 children from both the regression analyses and the intercorrelations are from the initial analyses of one study (Leong, in preparation) and will need verification. However, the stimulus items are carefully selected according to psycholinguistic criteria including printed frequency, range of orthographic-phonologic opacity and transparency, and degree of consistency. The data do suggest the potency of pseudoword reading in predicting reading, as discussed by Siegel (this volume) and other authors. The data also emphasize the need to take into account different kinds of pseudowords, and to incorporate the notion of the continuum of consistency and inconsistency (Patterson & Morton, 1985). In agreement with Gough and Walsh (1991), reading pseudowords and exception words may require different kinds of information or subskills, but these subskills may draw on the same underlying representation. Further more, the reading of irregular words correlates with that of pseudowords, but in a different way; and that these different subskills are built on a solid basis of "knowledge of the cipher" as emphasized by Gough and Walsh.

Another theoretical interpretation from orthography to phonology could be the three-route model of Patterson and Morton (1985). The Patterson and Morton orthography-to-phonology system adds to the standard dual-route model (Coltheart, 1978, 1980) of lexical and non-lexical routes in assembling phonology a "**body**" subsystem. This body subsystem incorporates segments of a word left after the initial consonant or consonant cluster or rimes after the onsets. The central notion seems to be one of developing lexical representation in using intralexical information such as letters, phonemes, onsets and rimes and relevant but restricted non-lexical knowledge to activate word identification (Perfetti, 1992).

Reading of "Irregular" Words as Diagnostic

For refined diagnosis different facets of lexical knowledge would need to be assessed: pseudowords sounding like real words (e.g., <kake>), pseudohomophones and pseudowords not sounding like real words (e.g., <dorty>), and those with many or few friendly neighbors. In addition, children's automatic recognition and vocalization of real words carefully selected for frequency and other relevant psycholinguistic factors should also be assessed. In particular, the reading of "irregular" spelling-to-sounds words (e.g., <deny, pint, sword>) in a sentence-frame assessment format as suggested by Adams and Huggins (1985) is a viable diagnostic task.

It is recognized that accuracy and latency of identification and pronunciation of words are affected by the way in which regularity is defined (Parkin, 1982). The consensus finding is that irregular spelling-to-sound sight words of the kind such as <deny> are processed more correctly and more rapidly than those irregular words further confounded by orthographic irregularity or strangeness (e.g., <yacht>)(Patterson & Morton, 1985; Waters & Seidenberg, 1985). To read irregular or unpredictable real words accurately and rapidly, children need to generate some form of phonological recoding of a nonlexical set of rules of the lexical items and process these written words to a "deep" level for articulation (Parkin, 1982). Moreover, unpredictable or exception words that "break the rule" of spelling-to-sound correspondence may be pronounced, in part, by analogy with known words according to the activation-synthesis model of Glushko (1979, 1980).

Some Relevant Data

A sub-part of my developmental study of componential analysis of reading in two cohorts of some 300 grades 4, 5 and 6 children (Leong, 1988, 1992d) has yielded data to support the general finding. In this sub-project, the children were asked to read aloud individually 50 irregular or unpredictable words (divided into 5 blocks by levels of printed frequency and orthographic strangeness) embedded in sentence frames. Predictability is operationally defined as spelling-to-sound patterns predictable on the basis of regular graphemic, morphemic and phonemic features of the words after Venezky (1970). Some sample items were: "The girls rowed the boat to the *island*." (Frequency of 619); "The hot food burned her *tongue*. (Frequency of 281); "Lifting heavy boxes will make your back *ache*." (Frequency of 13).

The irregular word reading task was adapted from that of Adams and Huggins (1985), but unlike these authors who scored only for accuracy, both accuracy and latency in vocalizing the individual target lexical items were emphasized (see Leong, 1992d). The results from both the accuracy and latency scores indicate clearly the efficiency and discriminatory power of this task in separating subgroups of skilled, average, and less skilled readers. Further more, from item-response theory and the use of the Rasch model (Rasch, 1960/1980) in the item analysis of the different tasks in the project, the irregular word reading task is shown to achieve both classical test reliability and a reasonably homogeneous latent trait (Lock & Leong, 1991). A "purer" task (Calfee, 1982) with around 40 items is just as efficient, and provides further validation of the predictive and diagnostic value of a different kind of word reading task.

Irregular Word Reading adding to Dimensions of Diagnosis

The suggestion here of using carefully selected irregular words in addition to pseudowords in the diagnostic process brings us back to the findings by Baddeley et al. (1988), Olson et al. (1990), Rack et al. (1992), among others, of considering dimensions of dyslexia as ranging from phonological dyslexia to surface dyslexia. In terms of the explanation of the tripartite route to lexical access of Patterson and Morton (1985), surface dyslexia is characterized by over-reliance on the "phonological route" to reading because of impairment to the "direct" route and the semantic route, and yet the phonological route is partially impaired. From the work of Coltheart and colleagues (Coltheart, Masterson, Byng, Prior, & Riddoch, 1983; Patterson, Marshall, & Coltheart, 1985) surface dyslexia can be both developmental and acquired. Both types show regularity effects and difficulties with homophonous words and these difficulties could arise from the parsing of words (e.g., <hoped> parsed as <hope + ed>), from the phonological translation and blending.

In the search for dimensions of individual differences in terms of phonological dyslexia and surface dyslexia, the efficiency of reading irregular words as shown by both accuracy and latency scores should add to the diagnostic process. From a similar logic, Høien and Lundberg (1989) demonstrated the usefulness of word recognition strategies from a computer-based test battery in two case studies of fifteen-year-old dyslexic boys. In this and a subsequent study by Lundberg and Høien (1990) with both reading age and chronological age controls it is shown that dyslexics are deficient in phonological processing skills and need to use different strategies to reach a functional level of word recognition.

Incorporating Phonological Awareness Tasks

The proposal by Siegel and others of using pseudowords in diagnosis aims at identifying deficiencies in phonological processing, which are at the core of the problems of children with specific or severe reading disabilities (see Stanovich, 1986, 1988a, 1991, this volume). Strictly, phonological processes encompass both lexical access and phonetic short-term memory (Crowder, 1982). In their insightful review, Wagner and Torgesen (1987) distinguish amongst: (a) Phonological awareness or reflection on the phonological structure of the [English] language; (b) Phonological recoding in lexical access or recoding written symbols into a sound-based representational system; and (c) Phonetic recoding to maintain verbal information in working memory. Much of the discussion in this volume of the use of pseudowords and the differentiation of dyslexics compared with their controls in accuracy and naming speed pertains mainly to domains (b) and (c) as in Wagner and Torgesen.

The important role of phonological awareness and its presaging or reciprocal effect on early reading and reading disabilities is now well documented (see, Stanovich, 1988c; Sawyer & Fox, 1991, for representative views). Space limitation precludes fuller discussion. Indeed, phonological analysis is a central component of early reading and spelling and subserves various phonological awareness tasks such as sensitivity to rhymes, alliterations, onsets and rimes (Cataldo & Ellis, 1988; Goswami & Bryant, 1990). The wider aspect of the development of metalinguistic ability including phonological, syntactic and pragmatic awareness in learning to read is emphasized by Tunmer and Hoover (1992). Tunmer and Hoover (this volume) argue forcefully in their Cognitive-Developmental model for the centrality of this ability and the subtle effect that deficiency in metalinguistic ability has on reading disabilities.

The suggestion here is to incorporate carefully designed tasks measuring different facets of phonological awareness in addition to using pseudoword and irregular word tasks. This broader approach should help us to understand better the "phonological-core variable-difference" model of Stanovich (1988a, 1991, this volume) and of the **garden-variety** poor readers discussed by Gough and Tunmer (1986) in the differential diagnosis of discrepancy-defined poor readers (dyslexics) and of those poor readers less so characterized. The underlying notion of this differentiation is the degree of linguistic coding ability and the quality of word representation (Perfetti, 1986). The crux is **what** is learnt of the alphabetic principle (declarative knowledge) and **how** this is learnt (procedural knowledge) or one of **computational** and **reflective** knowledge (Perfetti, 1986, 1992).

Lexical Representation

The emphasis on both the computational (the how) and the reflective (the what and the why) aspects of lexical representation does not imply that phonology plays a less important role in reading acquisition and reading disabilities. On the contrary, the notion as articulated by the Haskins group (e.g., Liberman & Shankweiler, 1985) is one of "awareness of linguistic structure", of "metalinguistic awareness of the internal structure of words" (p. 10), and of "becoming aware of sublexical structure for the purpose of developing word-recognition strategies" (p. 15). The term **structure** refers to the hierarchical and relational aspects of discourse units. Moreover, linguistically aware persons are those who apply their knowledge of "phonological rules to the morphophonemic forms in the lexicon" to generate phonetic forms (Mattingly, 1984, p. 15). Mattingly (1984, p. 17) further states that during the reading process "lexical items are recognized by virtue of their morphological and (in the case of alphabets and syllabaries) their morphophonemic structure".

Morphophonemic And Morphological Nature Of Alphabetic Languages

In the current Zeitgeist in emphasizing phonological processing as a central component in early reading and reading disabilities, it is instructive to be reminded of the Haskins group's position on the morphophonemic structure and morphological nature of alphabetic languages. There are similar notions from the linguistic perspective. Albrow (1972, p. 10) writes of the English orthography as a system "reflecting the phonological structure of the language" with different conventions representing different lexical elements. The functionalistic postulate of the Prague school holds that grapheme-to-phoneme or phoneme-to-grapheme correspondences should be established at various linguistic levels such as the word and the sublexical unit morpheme (Vachek, 1973).

From a computational linguistic perspective, Venezky (1970) has explicated the morphophonemic nature and the underlying patterns of the English orthography in his seminal computer analysis of spelling-to-sound of 20,000 most commonly used English words. Venezky proposes as significant for the pronunciation of English two kinds of functional units at the graphemic level: (a) **relational units** which correspond to certain morphophonemic clusters and (b) **markers** with the primary function of preserving graphotactical or morphological patterns. Examples of relational units corresponding to certain morphophonemic clusters are the /gn/ in <cognac, poignant>. Examples of markers are the final /e/ in <notice>, which indicates that <c> corresponds morphophonemically to what is usually thought of as "the /s/ sound". The relational units and the markers help to preserve in the English orthography the morphophonemic alternations. Further more, consideration of spelling-to-sound correspondence without regard to morphology and stress would not be adequate linguistically (Venezky, 1970).

From the perspective of the psychology of speaking, Levelt (1989) emphasizes the need to specify the meaning, syntax, morphology, and phonology in the internal structure of a lexical item in the mental lexicon. Meaning and syntax form the non-morphophonological part of a lexical item and constitute its **lemma** or lemma information; while both morphology and phonology are considered important features in the form of the internal lexicon. In her book on the relationship between meaning and form, Bybee (1985) discusses the multiple and diverse patterns of organization of the mental lexicon and the graded relations within and among words. The degree of relatedness varies according to the number and strength of phonological and semantic connections. For example, the lexical coform items <receive, reception> are connected both semantically and phonologically; so do the coforms <perceive, perception>. In each pair of coforms the nominalization is predictable from the base form <receive> and <perceive> respectivelty. The nominalized lexical items <reception, perception> are related much more strongly phonologically, but only weakly in semantic connections. Bybee emphasizes the inter-dependence of meaning (lemma information) and form (morphology and phonology) and the conceptualization of the internal structure of words not only as variant phonological representation of morphemes but also as sets of relations with other words.

Inclusion of Morphology Tasks in Diagnosis

It would appear then a more comprehensive view in relating phonology to reading, and reading to phonology should emphasize also the morphological and morphemic domains of the English orthography. In general, morphology studies word formation and the internal structure of words while morphophonemics usually refers to studies of the relations among allomorphs as discussed earlier. Morphological knowledge is represented in different dimensions (Cutler, 1983) and the two main dimensions are **derivational** and **inflectional** morphology. However, it is not always easy to differentiate derivation and inflection (Matthews, 1974); and the two dimensions should be seen as a gradual, rather than a discrete, distinction (Bybee, 1985).

For the purpose of the present discussion, it is the **productive** aspects of lexical items that we want to develop in children and those with reading disabilities. Productivity is taken to mean the generation of new lexical items derivable from lexically related words according to word formation rules and other complex transformational factors (Stemberger, 1985). For example, the derivation of words such as <beginner> from <begin> requires consonant doubling and stress assignment, while <equality> from <equal> involves vowel alternation pattern and vowel reduction. The production of derived items as illustrated requries an analysis-by-synthesis process in making comparisons "between members of a set of utterances that have identical segments at some ordinal positions but different segments at others" as suggested by Mattingly (1987, p. 489) in his compositional analysis of phonological and morphological structure of segmental awareness.

SOME DATA ON MORPHOLOGICAL AND MORPHEMIC PROCESSING

In a study involving two complementary experiments to examine the productive knowledge of derivational morphology in 75 grade 4, 5, and 6 "poor" readers, further subdivided into those performing better in both reading and spelling (R+S+), those performing worse in reading and spelling (R-S-) and "mixed" subgroups, there is some evidence of the important role of morphological and morphemic structure in reading proficiency (Leong, 1989b).

In the Leong (1989b) study, Experiment 1 required individual subjects to vocalize rapidly and accurately the derived forms of 40 target base words embedded in sentence frames and in four derivational conditions or levels. Some sample target items and derivations were: HAPPY: "The rich man was very sick and sad; and nothing could buy him _____. (HAPPINESS); EQUAL: "In a free country all people are equal and we value our _____. (EQUALITY). The first sample of derivation involves an Orthographic Change condition such as consonant doubling as a function of stress assignment in complex words; and the second set of derivations entails Phonological Change with vowel alternation pattern and vowel reduction. Experiment 2 required the reverse process of vocalizing rapidly and accurately the base forms of 40 different target derived words embedded in sentence frames and again in four different derivational conditions. Samples of some target items and base forms were: USUALLY: "Winter rain in Vancouver is quite _____. (USUAL); ATHLETIC: "She does well in school and in sports. She is a good student and good _____. (ATHLETE). The first set of transformation from derived to base forms involves No Change in the place where stress occurs in the process of transformation; and the second set of samples involves the more complex condition of both Orthographic and Phonological Change.

The lexical items and the different derivational conditions are discriminating amongst subgroups of poor readers and poor spellers and there is also a developmental trend. Figure 2 provides graphic illustrations for the Derived Morphology task (Experiment 1). Similar phenomena have also been observed with a large sample of 298 grades 4, 5 and 6 readers (Leong, 1989c).

Similar suggestions to take into account morphemic principles in the diagnosis and remediation of dyslexics have also been made by Elbro (1989, 1991). In his study of 26 severely impaired developmental dyslexics compared with 26 reading-level controls Elbro found some evidence that the dyslexics seemed to be "arrested" at Frith's (1985) alphabetic phase of reading. While these subjects were specifically impaired in phonological processing, Elbro pointed out that this may not be the only principle underlying alphabetic language systems. The morphemic principles preserving the spelling of the smallest meaning units the morpheme could also be an important one. Support for the role of the morpheme in organizing and accessing the internal lexicon is also offered by Tyler and Nagy (1990) in their study of derivational morphology with tenth and eleventh grade students.

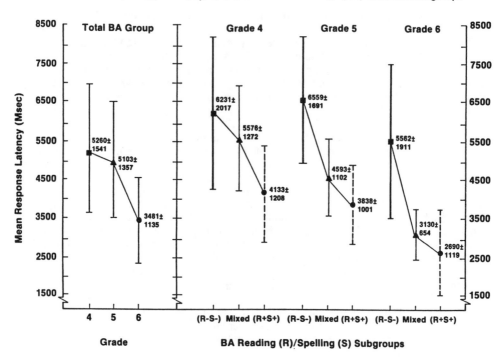

Figure 2. Derived Morphology task (Leong, 1989b, Experiment 1) by grade for below average (BA) total group (n = 75) of readers and BA reading (R) and spelling (S) subgroups.

Summary of Main Issues in Diagnosing Developmental Dyslexics

The argument presented thus far in this chapter pertains to several significant issues on the diagnosis of those poor readers based on their discrepant performance between learning aptitude and achievement in reading (developmental dyslexics). It is suggested that "intelligence" or general ability tests provide some kind of "yardstick" to gauge relative reading performance. Such tests may still be relevant despite their moderate to low correlation with reading and memory tasks and notwithstanding the performance of some "hyperlexics" with purportedly low intelligence. Current formulation and research literature suggest that general ability tests are evolving in the direction of delineating wider areas of cognition including levels tapping Crystallized and Fluid Intelligence, and that **true** hyperlexia is not easy to define.

A two-stage approach involving group tasks including scaled teachers' estimates at the first stage or level followed by more refined diagnosis using individual tasks is seen as effective in the diagnostic process and has some empirical support. Evens if there is no consensus on the role of general ability tests in diagnosis, there is broad agreement that pseudoword reading is diagnostic of developmental dyslexics. However, a wide range of pseudowords will need to be used to incorporate those items with many friendly neighbors and those with few neighbors to accommodate the consistency effect. Further more, unpredictable or exception words will add another dimension to the orthography-to-phonology correspondence; so will tasks tapping phonological awareness. To further understand poor readers' computational and reflective aspects of knowledge of lexical representation, tasks tapping morphological and morphemic knowledge should also be contemplated. The more encompassing battery of tasks including different kinds of pseudowords, exception words and morphological tasks is an attempt to take into account the admonition sounded by Cutler (1981) in including significant variables in diagnosis, without at the same time making them too cumbersome from the point of view of implementation.

The Role of Listening Comprehension Tests

The discussion thus far has focussed on developmental dyslexics or those children with "phonological-core" difficulties according to the **phonological-core variable-difference** model of Stanovich (1988a, 1988b, 1991, this volume). At the outset, we should heed the admonition of Stanovich that estimates for developmental dyslexics with phonological processing difficulties do not seem to run into the 12% to 15% as usually stated; but would be closer to about 3%. From prevalence rate of the early Leadership Training Institute Report commissioned by the U.S. Office of Education (Bryant & Kass, 1972) and other sources to the mid-1980s, it would appear this condition affects up to about 4% of the school population (Leong, 1985, p. 13).

However, there are still large numbers of children (possibly around 10%) who have difficulties in reading. These poor readers form the **"garden- variety"** type as proposed by Gough and Tunmer (1986) in their Simple View of reading. The phonological-core concept of Stanovich posits as the basis of dyslexics' performance deficits in various aspects of phonological processing such as segmental language abilities at the phoneme and onset and rime levels, automaticity in naming, and short-term memory in processing verbal materials. Stanovich (1988a, 1988b,, 1991, this volume) is cautious in pointing out the existence of a group of dyslexics with orthographic processing difficulties. His variable-difference concept compares and contrasts the differences between developmental dyslexics and the garden-variety type of poor readers. These latter disabled readers also share some phonological processing deficits with the phonological-core group, though in a less severe form.

For these "backward" or garden-variety poor readers, they may be impaired in a variety of cognitive domains as compared with their age-matched controls (Stanovich, 1991), and may be described by the developmental lag model (Stanovich, Nathan, & Vala-Rossi, 1986; Stanovich, Nathan, & Zolman, 1988). Further more, listening comprehension tests have been advocated as being "superior" to verbal intelligence tests in isolating separable, modular defitics (Stanovich, 1991, this volume). According to the Simple View, reading disorders could result from difficulties in decoding, in comprehending, or both. Decoding and comprehending could interact not just linearly but multiplicatively, and comprehending could be both of textual materials and in the listening mode (Gough & Tunmer, 1986). Gough and Tunmer and others have alerted us to the possibilities of those individuals who could both decode and listen but could not read; those who could do one but not the other and still read; or those who could neither decode nor listen but still could read with some understanding. One of the claims of the Simple View "may well be...that skilled decoding combined with skilled listening must produce literacy" (Gough & Tunmer, 1986, p. 9).

This claim of decoding and linguistic comprehension as necessary and sufficient for skilled reading is borne out in a longitudinal study of grades 1 to 4 English-Spanish bilingual children (Hoover & Gough, 1990). The results of a series of tight-fitting regression analyses show that the linear combination of decoding and listening comprehension accounted for a substantial proportion of the variation of reading comprehension with enhancement from the product of decoding and listening comprehension, and that both components are needed (Hoover & Gough, 1990). These results also suggest the dissociation of decoding and linguistic comprehension within the "illiterate population" (presumably the garden-variety group) and the emphatic that [these components] "**must** be dissociated if substantial skill is evidenced in either of the two components" (Hoover & Gough, 1990, P. 154, authors' emphasis).

These conclusions provoke further discussion of the concepts and methods pertaining to listening comprehension and the relationship of listening comprehension with reading comprehension [of textual materials] within the language comprehension domain. Subsequent sections attempt to summarize the salient issues and outline some research evidence on listening comprehension with reference to diagnosis of reading disorders. If, as proposed, listening comprehension tests are superior to general ability tests in diagnosis and as listening and reading comprehension tests all assess language comprehension, could it not be that a combination of reading and listening comprehension contributes more to diagnosing reading and learning?

"Learning by Being Told"

Some twenty-five years ago Carroll (1968) discussed the potentials and limitations of print and the importance of "learning by being told". Both print and spoken forms of language should emphasize **epistemic knowledge** or competence an individual has acquired as a result of receiving and comprehending messages in print or aurally. He further elaborated on the "multidimensional" nature of language comprehension: "... with spoken or printed language, the evidence suggests that the individual may have different levels of ability with respect to vocabulary, grammatical features, and other characteristics of texts. In listening comprehension, attention, motivation, auditory, and memory factors may be involved" (Carroll, 1972, p. 3).

The quotation from Carroll indicates some of the challenges in theory formulation and empirical studies of aural and written language comprehension. The literature on reading-listening relationship to the early 1980s was reviewed by Danks (1980), Downing and Leong (1982, pp. 191-194; 225-237). Influential and recent anthologies on language understanding and knowledge acquition include: Freedle and Carroll (1972), Flores d'Arcais and Jarvella (1983); and on comprehending oral and written language: Horowitz and Samuels (1987a), and Olson, Torrance, and Hildyard (1985). Space limitation precludes extensive discussion of these current works except to highlight some of the similarities and differences in the aural/reading continuum with reference to diagnosis of reading disorders and remediation.

Very briefly, spoken language used for listening comprehension is evanescent; while written language is more static, more stable and more lasting. Spoken language involves extra-linguistic or prosodic elements such as gestures, intonation, stress and pause; while written materials are "recontextualized" (rather than decontextualized) with the use of linguistic or lexicalized devices for specific readership. From the linguistic or sociolinguistic perspective, the "oral/literate continuum" should evolve to "oral and literate strategies" to the notion of "features reflecting relative focus on [interpersonal] involvement" (Tannen, 1985, p. 126). There are different ways of learning and knowing with different linguistic strategies; and "Spoken and written language serve as complementary resources for acquiring and organizing knowledge" (Halliday, 1987, p. 80). From the psychological perspective, both forms of language comprehension contain elements of problem solving and both involve processes of encoding, storage, retrieval and integration of linguistic elements within a wider context.

Reading And Listening As Analogous Processes

Careful reading of the above anthologies and related volumes reveal that reading comprehension and listening comprehension are not unrelated. There is general acceptance of "language by ear and by eye" (see Kavanagh & Mattingly, 1972); and of the notion of reading and writing as secondary linguistic activities being parasitic on listening and speaking as primary linguistic activities. This position is espoused by Sticht (1972) in his representing listening and reading comprehension as a single internal conceptualization: "There is only one, holistic ability to comprehend by language, and one should be able to comprehend equally well by listening or by reading, *if one has been taught to decode well and other task variables are equalized.*" (pp. 293-294, original emphasis). This notion leads to the formulation of listening comprehension preceding reading comprehension in language competence; and the prediction of reading comprehension and listening comprehension becoming comparable when decoding subskills are thoroughly mastered at about the seventh grade (see also, Sticht, Beck, Hauke, Kleiman, & James, 1974). A similar view was expressed by Gleitman and Rozin (1977) in relating orthographies to the structure of language. They suggested that a fluently literate person is one who performs about equally in comprehending both spoken materials and the same materials in print form; and that one of the goals in education should be to narrow the initial gap between aural and literate comprehension. All these issues will be further discussed.

All the above views should not be taken to mean that reading and listening are unitary. Massaro (1978, 1979) posited a stage model to study language processing as a sequence of mental operations and suggested that reading and listening be regarded as "independent but analogous processes" (Massaro, 1979, p. 332). Levy (1978) emphasized language processing as involving different levels -- perceptual, syntactic and semantic. Mosenthal (1976-1977) suggested that a common language competence underlies both silent reading and aural processing but not reading aloud. Using the Given-New strategy of Clark and Haviland (1977), Mosenthal tested grades 2, 4, and 6 children in their written and aural language comprehension and presuppositive negatives. He found that different strategies were used in comprehending aurally and visually, with the children tending to treat more information as "given" in the listening mode and more information as "new" in the reading mode. The Mosenthal study underscores the importance of processes and subprocesses in investigating reading and listening comprehension.

To summarize this section thus far, if it is difficult to formulate **generalized** concepts of reading and listening comprehension, it is because of different cognitive and linguistic demands and processing strategies made of these analogous processes (Danks, Bohn, & Fears, 1983; Danks & End, 1987). There are shared and distinctive elements between processing aural and print language and the degrees of commonality vary with reading abilities and levels or stages of reading. For novices [also likely for poor readers] print language is more similar to aural language, and for experts print is more or less equal to speech or heard language in the asymmetrically different and yet shared relationship (Perfetti, 1987).

Some Relevant Factors In Studying Reading And Listening Comprehension

Within the framework of the above variant views a number of factors in relating reading comprehension and listening comprehension will need to be taken into account. One way to achieve some comparability is by manipulating these and other variables: subject characteristics, language materials, presentation conditions, and comprehension measures.

(1) *Subject Characteristics.* Durrell, Hayes, and Brassard (1969) studied reading and listening comprehension across a wide age range (grades 1 to 8) mainly for the purpose of validating their Listening-Reading tests. They found listening vocabulary to be better than reading vocabulary at grade 1 but these scores were comparable at grade 8; while listening comprehension was better than reading comprehension in sentence paragraph comprehension but these scores were comparable at grade 6 and were in the reverse direction by grade 8 (i.e.,reading comprehension superior to listening comprehension). Smiley, Oakley, Worthen, Campione, and Brown (1977) studied grade 7 good and poor readers and found high correlation between reading and listening recall performance.

Kintsch and Kozminsky (1977) found in their college students similar performance in reading and listening of short texts and in answering short factual questions, but they cautioned that the results were restricted to the adult subjects, short texts and factual questions used. Townsend, Carrithers, and Bever (1987) used skilled and average college-age students and skilled and average school-age students and found differential sentence-level and proposition processing. Sticht (1972; Sticht, Beck, Hauke, Kleiman, & James, 1974; Sticht & James, 1984) studied the relationship between reading and listening mainly with U.S. army recruits; and these researchers related pragmatic aspects of language comprehension to on-the-job behaviors and other real-life activities. The general finding of Sticht and colleagues is that reading difficulties stem from reduced ability to comprehend language and that poorer-reading men preferred to learn by listening than by reading.

Even from the above sketch of some of the salient studies it is clear that subject selection and variation in ages may explain individual differences in the differential processing of reading and listening comprehension.

(2) *Language Materials.* Most researchers have used textual materials but these vary in their structure and cohesive devices. In general, listeners or readers may rely more on "lower" level information in processing difficult language materials, while they draw on abstract processing level with complex materials. Different genres of materials will also elicit different responses. This is especially so with poetry as read visually or aurally. Thomas Gray's **Elegy Written in a Country Churchyard** with the opening line of: //The cur/few tolls/ the knell/ of part/ ing day// read aurally (and orally) with the classic metric of iambic pentameter provides the rhythm and cadence which will need to be filled in by visual reading. In this regard, the

study by Walker (1975-1976, 1977) with eleventh grade and college students is notable in using spontaneous speech rather than planned writing. He found a difference in the sampling of linguistic cues and meaningful reconstruction in favor of the readers rather than the listeners, and suggested reading as a more precise form of language processing.

(3) *Presentation Conditions.* The comprehension of spoken or written materials all require the registration, encoding, storage, retrieval and integration of oral or lexicalized linguistic elements and these processes take real time. Since oral/aural materials are processed more slowly than the same materials in print form, there are suggestions to use time-compressed speech to about 275/300 words per minute (wpm) to minimize differential conditions of presentation rates (Danks, 1980).

This relationship between speech rate and reading rate is complex. Carver (1977-1978, 1982) found evidence for a linear relationship under certain conditions. In his detailed formulation, Carver (1990) specifies that the relationship between accuracy of comprehension (A) as expressed in mathematical equations, and the ratio of time allowed for reading passages compared with rate of comprehension (I/R) is linear, provided that the time allowed would not exceed that needed to finish the passage once such that the subject can comprehend almost all of the thoughts during reading. Thereafter the A to I/R relationship becomes linear. Foulke and Sticht (1969) argued for an inverted curvilinear relationship when subjects would habituate at the rate of around 125 to 200 wpm and might still maintain good comprehension to about 275 wpm, while trying harder to comprehend at this much faster compressed rate. To achieve some comparability in presentation rates of aural and written messages, short pauses at structural junctures may be inserted into time-compressed spoken materials to help language comprehension (Sticht, 1972).

However, language comprehension is affected in an interactive manner by the nature and level of difficulty of spoken or written materials and the skill of the individuals (Wilkinson, 1980). The equalizing of presentation rate may help to equalize understanding for both the listening and reading modes for good readers but may lower understanding in reading as compared with listening for poor readers. This differential comprehension was found by Horowitz and Samuels (1985), Smiley et al. (1977), and Sticht (1972). In the Horowitz and Samuels study, their 18 poor and 20 good 6th grade readers listened to tape-recorded expository passages (2 easy ones of 300 words each and 2 hard ones of 367 words each) at the rate of between 96 to 106 wpm, and also read aloud these passages at 121 to 134 wpm. The relatively slow output rate of just over 100 wpm does not allow for efficient listening or reading, and may explain in part their finding of no difference in listening between the poor and good readers. The slower rate also accentuates memory processes and could account in part for the difference in oral reading comprehension in favor of their good readers. Other things being equal, when subjects are given time to complete reading or listening (the completion design) as contrasted with subjects given deadlines (the deadline design) (Wilkinson, 1980), listening tends to produce better comprehension in children. The results of Guthrie and Tyler (1976) were in this direction.

(4) *Comprehension Measures.* Measures of reading and/or listening comprehension vary from the use of multiple choice questions, probe questions, word recognition tasks, specific questions on "who", "when" and "where", to free recall. These different measures likely produce different results. Probably a combination is needed to provide a profile of reading or listening comprehension. Danks and End (1987) suggest sampling these areas: speech perception or print decoding, lexicalization, clause or sentence integration, discourse comprehension, and discourse monitoring.

To summarize this part, it is clear that a careful analysis of subject selection, tasks and processing strategies is needed in the study of oral and written language comprehension. The superiority or otherwise of listening comprehension tests over general ability tests in diagnosis of reading disorders is still an open question; and the interaction of listening comprehension with reading comprehension poses further challenges. These are all issues awaiting exploration.

"Auding" and Computerized Reading and Listening Comprehension Tasks

One of the challenges in the exploration of the use of listening comprehension tests in diagnosing backward or garden-variety poor readers relates to the choice of materials in both the written and oral/aural modes: planned written materials or spontaneous speech or some other means (see also Stanovich, 1991, this volume). In agreement with Hoover and Gough (1990), Stanovich (1991, this volume), and the earlier formulations of Sticht (1972; Sticht et al., 1974; Sticht & James, 1984), it is proposed that **auding** be the preferred approach. Auding refers to listening to orally presented discourse to gain information or knowledge (see Sticht et al., 1974; Sticht & James, 1984). Acceptance and implementation of this notion should be guided by psycholinguistic and psychological considerations (see also above Section on Some Relevant Factors).

Units of Processing

From the psycholinguistic perspective, there should be a happy medium in the search for appropriate units of language processing of what Chafe (1985, p. 105) calls "integrated quality of written language" and "fragmented quality of spoken [language]." Should the units of processing and indices of comprehending be lexical items, clauses or sentences and their integration, or comprehension monitoring, as suggested by Danks and End (1987)? Or should all these units be considered?

It would appear that Chafe's (1985) proposal of using **idea units** as expressing the amount of information a person can focus on at any one time is a viable one. According to Chafe, an idea unit should be at least a clause with a verb phrase along with appropriate phrases and should be uttered as a single coherent intonation contour with intonation or hesitation patterns to show unit boundaries. This view is akin to the **clausal hypothesis** of language comprehension (Fodor, Bever, & Garrett, 1974; Marslen-Wilson, Tyler, & Seidenberg, 1978). The notion of **clause complex** is also espoused by Halliday (1985, pp. 192-251) as maintaining the "dynamic potentials" of the functional organization of sentences and the language system. The general idea of taking clauses as primary units of language comprehension is that listeners or readers organize language materials by clauses, hold them in working memory and integrate them in long-term memory for representation in more abstract forms (Jarvella, 1971).

Clauses as idea units likely serve as good segmentation units for aural and written language comprehension. Such discourse segmentation should take into account appropriate linguistic devices to facilitate the parsing of concepts -- their registering, encoding, storage, retrieval and integration. Structurally, this is the issue of **cohesion** of discourse, which expresses syntagmatic relations and text or discourse structure (Halliday & Hasan, 1976). These cohesive relations are signalled by intonation, stress, juncture and other prosodic elements in the spoken form; and by such lexicalized features in the written form as anaphoras, substitutions, subordinations, decompositions, contrastives, and grammatical complexity to index linguistic information. Functionally, idea units are represented conceptually as **propositions** involving arguments and relations (Kintsch, 1974; Kintsch & Keenan, 1973).

If the same or equivalent idea units or propositions are presented in the reading and auding modes and if some optimal presentation rate can be found, greater comparability may be established. Empirical evidence indicates that an optimal rate of reading prose and of auding prose seems to be "constant across reading and auding and is also constant across prose difficulty levels" (Carver, 1982, p. 85). This constancy has to be interpreted within the framework of what is natural and normal for efficient language comprehension incorporating both accuracy and automaticity (Carver, 1990).

Some Research Findings -- Sentence Verification

In our search for efficient and practical procedures to diagnose listening comprehension within acceptable psychological and psycholinguistic frameworks, there is evidence of the viability of the **Sentence Verification Technique** (SVT) of Royer and his colleagues (Royer, Greene, & Sinatra, 1987; Royer, Hastings, & Hook, 1979; Royer, Kulhavy, Lee, & Peterson, 1986; Royer, Sinatra, & Schumer, 1990). Very briefly, the Sentence Verification Technique was originally developed by Royer, Hastings, and Hook (1979) to assess readers' memory representation of prose passages. The general idea is that good language comprehenders should be sensitive to different test sentences according to whether these are originals (verbatim sentences), paraphrases, meaning changes, or distractors of the sentences in prose passages. Conversely, poor language comprehenders are those who have not established successfully meaning-preservation representations in memory and can expect to show difficulties or inefficiencies in classifying the different test sentence types. Further more, results from several experiments have also established the construct validity of the SVT as a measure both of sentence understanding and of passage comprehension (Royer, Lynch, Hambleton, & Bulgareli, 1984).

Royer, Kulhavy, Lee, and Peterson (1986) subsequently extended the SVT as both reading and listening comprehension tests for fourth and sixth grade students. Both this Royer et al. (1986) study and a later one by Royer, Sinatra, and Schumer (1990) suggest that listening and reading comprehension in children in grades 3 to 6 depends on the subjects' reading ability and the difficulty level of the language materials. Further support for the SVT as a means of evaluating language comprehension and as a diagnostic test is provided by Carlisle (1990) in her study of 60 seventh grade readers (19 poor comprehenders as compared with 41 good comprehenders). However, Carlisle and Felbinger (1991) also cautioned against undue reliance on listening comprehension as an index of overall language comprehension, because of the different demands for memory representation of ideas in the aural and written language modes.

Use of Text-to-Speech Computer Systems

Within the psychological and psycholinguistic constraints discussed in the preceding sections, almost all the studies of the reading-listening comprehension connection have relied on either oral output by the examiners or tape-recorded messages. These modes of generating language materials entail considerable variabilities in the speech parameters and present difficulties in adjusting presentation rates, if necessary. There are also difficulties in the **simultaneous** use of both spoken and print language to assess comprehension. Further more, almost without exception, measures of interest have been accuracy and/or error scores.

While percentage correct provides a reasonable estimate of the subject's level of language understanding, that metric is not sufficiently sensitive to gauge the **efficiency** of languaging comprehension as compared with that indexed by fine-grained response latency. To control all of these and related variables and to present unrestricted texts in listening and reading comprehension, the sophisticated text-to-speech computer system (DECtalk) offers a solution.

This chapter is not the place to go into the theory of text-to-speech conversion, the technical aspects, or details of application of the DECtalk or its variant systems. In a Special Issue on reading and spelling with text-to-speech computer systems (see Leong, 1992a) different groups of researchers in Colorado (R. Olson & B. Wise), Guelph (R. Barron & colleagues), Umea (A. Olofsson) and Saskatoon (C.K. Leong) have demonstrated the actual and potential uses of the systems for beginning reading, for diagnosis and intervention of disorders in reading and spelling (see also Leong, 1992b, 1992c).

DECtalk (or similar high-quality text-to-speech systems) is particularly suited to addressing the issues on hand for several reasons. The system with its large vocabulary uses analysis-by-synthesis principles to extract the underlying phonemic, morphemic and syntactic representations of unrestricted text to produce synthesized utterances with high-quality pause, pitch and stress controls. The system has seven pre-defined male, female adult or child voices (very recent DECtalk PC card has nine voices) and is programmable to switch from one voice to another in the course of narration or exposition; it has a speech rate varying from 120 to 350 wpm (very recent PC card ranges from 120 to 550 wpm); and its speech fidelity has been shown to be highly intelligible to both adults and children including disabled readers (Mackay & Leong, in preparation; Olson, Foltz, & Wise, 1986). In addition to specifications in the technical manuals, a program library with a number of Pascal routines has been prepared (Lock & Leong, 1989) for applied component analysis of reading and its remediation.

Some DECtalk Data On Listening And Reading Comprehension

In the course of investigating computer-mediateded reading (Leong, 1992c), Mackay and Leong (in preparation) have examined the efficacy of using DECtalk for listening comprehension by itself and in combination with on-line reading from the microcomputer. The data from their Experiment 3 are particularly relevant and are summarized below.

The main aim in this third experiment was to examine the efficiency with which 66 sixth grade below average (BA) readers (n=18), average (AV) readers (n=24) and above average (AA) readers (n=24) would process the same language materials in either or both the written mode (on-line and output at 200 msec per word) and the spoken mode (output by DECtalk with "Perfect Paul" voice). The experimental task was modelled after the Sentence Verification Technique (SVT) of Royer, Greene, and Sinatra (1987), as discussed in the preceding sections, with the use of two on-line expository and two on-line narrative passages of between 178 and 183 words each and at grade level of ease or difficulty of reading. Efficiency of processing was defined in terms of both the accuracy and automaticity (guarding against speed and accuracy trade-offs) with which the children could respond to "old" information (Royer et al.'s original and paraphrase sentences) or "new" information (Royer et al.'s meaning change and distractor sentences), and the response metric was expressed as millisecond latency scores recorded on-line. The 18 BA, 24 AV and 24 AA sixth grade subjects were approximately the bottom one-third, the middle one-third and the top one-third readers on both standardized vocabulary and reading comprehension tests. The sample of

BA, AV or AA readers was each trichotomized at random into three subgroups with equal number of children for each of the three experimental conditions in auding the same prose passages: reading on-line only, listening (from DECtalk) only, and on-line reading plus DECtalk listening.

The means and standard deviations for the 3 modes of language presentatin (on-line, DECtalk, on-line plus DECtalk); 3 reading groups (below average, average, above average) and 2 verification conditions ("old & "new" information) are summarized in Figure 3.

Summary results of the means and standard deviations shown in Figure 3 reveal several trends. One is the more efficient performance as shown by msec latency scores of the better reading subgroup(s); the other is the considerable variabilities of the below average readers; the third is the greater efficiency in comprehending "old" as compared with "new" information, and apparently more so with the combination of on-line reading and DECtalk auding.

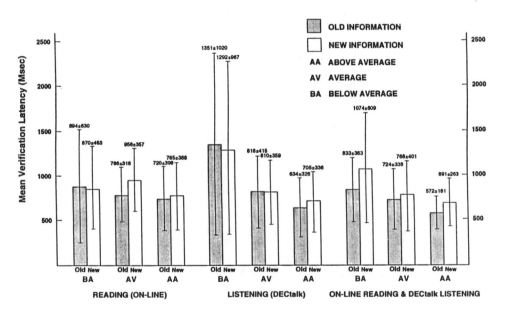

Figure 3. Summary results (means and standard deviations) for 3 modes of language comprehension: reading on-line, listening via DECtalk, on-line reading and DECtalk listening; for 3 reading groups of 66 sixth graders: below average (BA), average (AV) and above average (AA); and for 2 sentence verification conditions: "old" and "new" information.

A 3 (mode of presentation) by 3 (reading level) by 2 (information condition) analysis of variance with the last factor repeated shows a significant main effect for reading level (F (2, 57) = 3.29, p < .05). Multiple comparisons show the effect to be the greatest between the BA subgroup (M = 1053 msec) as compared with the AA (M = 681 msec) subgroup, with no significant difference between the AV subgroup with either the BA or the AA subgroups. There is a significant difference between information condition or sentence type (F (1, 57) = 10.14, p < .01) with greater processing efficiency for old information (M = 795 msec) as compared with new information (M = 863 msec), but there is also an interaction effect between presentation mode and information condition (F (2, 57) = 3.29, p < .05). There is a difference in response latency as a function of passage types in a 3 (mode of presentation) by 3 (reading level) by 2 (passage type) ANOVA with the last factor repeated (F (1, 57) = 26.33, p < .001). Multiple comparisons show that the BA subgroup was much less efficient as compared with the AA subgroup in processing both narratives (mean RTs of 1082 vs. 719 msec) and expository passages (mean RTs of 1023 vs. 643 msec).

ANOVA results show no significant difference between or among the three modes of presentation (F < 1). This lack of statistical significant difference may have come about because of the much poorer performance of the BA subgroups with both passage types and would need to be complemented with some qualitative analyses. Careful study of the data, observations during the experiment, and post-experiment interviews with the children, all suggest that the combination of on-line reading plus the DECtalk speech output helps in comprehending the information, especially for the below average readers. These extrapolations of the data would need to be interpreted cautiously within the contexts of the sentence verification technique, the relatively short prose passages (less than 200 words each), the not-too-large sample size of 66 sixth grade readers, even though the experiment was conducted under rigorous laboratory conditions in school settings and with careful computerized control in equating auding and on-lint reading of the same language materials. Further experiments are being carried out to extend and refine the use of the DECtalk text-to-speech computer system (see Leong, 1992b, 1992c) for both listening and reading comprehension under different conditions.

Summary of Simultaneous On-Line Reading and DECtalk Auding

The Special Issue on the application of DECtalk for research, remediation and intervention (Leong, 1992a) has highlighted some of the psychological and psycholinguistic areas for further study in using text-to-speech computer systems such as the nature of "usable texts" and different presenation formats. The Mackay and Leong (in preparation) data summarized earlier suggest the potency of combining on-line presentation of short texts with simultaneous DECtalk output of the same materials. There are similar findings in auding from less sophisticated speech devices. Reitsma (1988) found that reading with listening (digitized speech and tape-recorded messages) covaries with the reading ability of his six- and seven-year-old Dutch subjects; and van Bon, Boksebeld, Font Freide, and van den Hurk (1991) suggested from their peripheral results with 36 "backward" nine-year-old Dutch readers that simultaneous reading and auding (from tape-recorded messages) might help these children in everyday reading.

These Dutch data and the modest Mackay and Leong Experiment 3 reinforce the early but fairly rigorous study of Wilkinson (1980) using oral presentation that auding in both the written and spoken language modes should improve comprehension, though with varying results for different groups of readers for the different studies. Current technology also allows for the use of the hypertext (high-speed nonlinear text) and hypermedia environment (Hillinger, 1992; Leong, 1992b) to incorporate text, speech and graphics for language learning.

The data outlined here and the summaries of other studies partially validate the statement by Horowitz and Samuels (1987b, p. 15) in their comparison and contrast of oral and written language comprehension for literacy and schooling: "... The incorporation of the oral with the written [language], and the addition of listening with reading, may promote literacy and offers new insights about what literacy is and how it develops." Earlier in the same context, they emphasize that "reading and writing coupled with oral exchange about the ideas are what in the final analysis produce advanced thinking and knowledge." We are thus reminded of the broader and also the deeper issues of language comprehension and the acquisition of knowledge (Freedle & Carroll, 1972). These are clearly complex issues. The formulations and research studies by Gough and his colleagues (Gough & Tunmer, 1986; Hoover & Gough, 1990) on the role of listening in language comprehension in the diagnosis of garden-variety poor readers and the strong support by Stanovich (1991, this volume) have rekindled interests in the topic. What is also needed is a sound theory of the psychology of aural language comprehension, analogous to the elegant psychology of speaking by Levelt (1989), in our quest for better understanding of the nature of listening comprehension or auding.

Issues of Distribution and Specificity in Developmental Dyslexia

Developmental Dyslexia As Bimodal Or Continuous Distribution Of Reading Abilities

Whether the distribution of severe reading disabilities is bimodal with a small mode or "hump" at the lower end of the intelligence continuum (Rutter & Yule, 1975; Yule, Rutter, Berger, & Thompson, 1974) may still need further investigation. This question was revisited by Dobbins (1988) using non-verbal intelligence and reading measures given to 5,000 nine-to ten-year-old children. His results were inconclusive, but may provide some shadowy support for the notion, depending on interpretations. However, his further study using the regression approach with about 600 nine- to eleven-year-old children shows the stability of classification over time and tasks; and adds to the qualified support for the concept of severe under-achieving readers as a "naturally occurring" group different from those merely backward in reading (Dobbins & Tafa, 1991).

In some contrast to Dobbins' psychometric results of severe under-achievement are the findings of the large-scale Connecticut Longitudinal Study of 414 children entering kindergarten in 1983 and followed through as a birth cohort (Shaywitz, Escobar, Shaywitz, Fletcher, & Makuch, 1992; also Shaywitz, Shaywitz, Liberman, Fletcher, Shankweiler, Duncan, Katz, Liberman, Francis, Dreyer, Crain, Brady, Fowler, Kier, Rosenfield, Gore, & Makuch, 1991). The children were followed through with WISC-R intelligence scores from grades 1, 3, and 5 and achievements scores in reading and mathematics from grades 1 through 6. The cohort members were also administered a neurolinguistic and neuropsychological battery including tasks on phonological awareness, short-term memory, vocabulary, word-finding, speech perception and production, morphological awareness, syntactic comprehension, and attention; and a behavior and environment information battery. Using the aptitude-achievement discrepancy approach with discrepancy defined as the difference between observed achievement and achievement predicted by regression on intelligence, Shaywitz et al. (1992) demonstrate a univariate normal distribution pattern for the discrepancy scores.

Their results show dyslexia as occurring at the tail-end of a normal distribution of reading ability with some fluctuation of long-term outcomes in diagnosis. In a commentary on the Shaywitz et al. study, Rosenberger (1992) suggests that reading disabilities as estimated from aptitude-achievement discrepancies may have multiple causes needing different treatments.

The Shaywitz et al. (1992) longitudinal results showing the occurrence of dyslexia along a continuum seem to be at variance with the finding of a bimodal distribution of "reading retardtion" with a "hump" at the lower mode in the Isle of Wight Study (Rutter, Tizard, & Whitmore, 1970; Rutter & Yule, 1975; Yule, Rutter, Berger, & Thompson, 1974). However, Shaywitz et al. (1992) point out that their use of individual tests as compared with the use of group tests by the Rutter group, and the lower statistical power of their tasks in detecting the very low rate of "true" dyslexia may not show up the lower mode or "hump" as with the Isle of Wight study. They further state that: "...it is still possible that a small second mode may have gone unnoticed. Many or even most children who are labeled dyslexic may come from the lower end of the normal distribution; however, we do not wish to rule out the possibility that some may, in fact, have a reading disability of **qualitative different origin** or a unique biologic deficit (Shaywitz et al., 1992, p. 149, emphasis added).

Qualitative Difference in Developmental Dyslexics

The issues of continuity in the distribution of reading ability and of the "specificity" of developmental dyslexics with their phonological core difficulties are very much in the fore of diagnosis (Stanovich, 1989b, 1991, this volume). A Special Series was devoted on "What's specific about specific reading disability" (Foorman, 1989). In that series, Fletcher, Espy, Francis, Davidson, Rourke, and Shaywitz (1989) reported from their aptitude-performance discrepancy analyses, with or without correction for regression, in a large sample of 1,069 Ontario children that specificity in reading disability would depend on its definition or classification. What then might be the specificity or qualitative aspect differentiating developmental dyslexics from other poor readers?

PHONOLOGICAL CODING DEFICITS

In the long-range Colorado Reading Project Olson and his colleagues (DeFries, Olson, Pennington, & Smith, 1991; Olson, Gillis, Rack, DeFries, & Fulker, 1991; Olson, Wise, Conners, & Rack, 1990) use powerful and flexible statistical techniques to differentiate genetic and environmental influences in the behavioral genetic analyses of the reading and language component processes of their normal and disabled cotwin readers. The phonological coding component of word recognition requires subjects to read aloud rapidly and accurately pseudowords (e.g., <stalder>) and is an index of their efficiency in "computing" the phonology for these lexical items. The orthographic coding component requries subjects to designate quickly and accurately the real word in homophonic word-pseudoword pairs (e.g., < rain - rane>). The language tasks are rhyme fluency (generating within unit time all words rhyming with a target word), phoneme segmentation, and oral comprehension. The Colorado longitudinal studies provide compelling and converging evidence to show that the phonological coding deficits of the reading disabled children are significantly heritable and that orthographic coding is linked to environmental variations. Rhyme fluency is also associated with heritable variations and there is a substantial genetic covariation between phonological coding and word recognition. Taken together, Olson and his colleagues in the different studies propose that likely there is some basic segmental language skills which are heritable.

Conceptually, might it not be that the biological substrate shown by the Colorado group constitutes the specificity or the qualitative difference, over and above quantitative difference, in distinguishing developmental dyslexics from the garden-variety poor readers? While emphasizing the domain-specific phonological deficits in developmental dyslexics, the phonological-core variable-difference framework of Stanovich (1991) does not deny the occurrence of these difficulties, though in lesser degrees, in garden-variety readers, except that these latter poor readers also suffer from difficulties in general language comprehension.

Specifically, the primary symptoms of phonological coding deficits, shown to be heritable by the Colorado group (DeFries et al., 1991; Olson et al., 1990), might be complex and manifest themselves in different aspects of phonological processing. This issue of **primary** phonological processing deficits in developmental dyslexics was further addressed by other members of the Colorado team of Pennington, Van Orden, Smith, Green and Haith (1990). In four elegant experiments involving ascertained familial and clinic adult dyslexic groups compared with their chronological age (CA) and reading age (RA) controls, Pennington et al. (1990) studied five spoken language phonological processes of phoneme perception, phoneme awareness, lexical retrieval of phonology, articulatory speed, and phonetic coding in short-term memory; and found that the adult dyslexics show primary deficits relative to their CA and RA controls in phoneme awareness (verifying or producing pig Latin). The finding is robust in that the pattern of results was replicated across tasks and across both accuracy and latency scores. Similar results have been found by Mann (1991), Mann and Ditunno (1990) in their longitudinal study of phonological abilities in kindergarten and grade one children. The primacy of phoneme awareness within the phonological processing framework (see relevant Sections in this volume) also brings us back to pseudoword reading because of the close relationship between the two processes.

Automaticity

If one level of the many-faceted phonological processing is the relatively slow-acting phoneme awareness, there is also the fast-acting automatic level of processing as represented by rapid naming tasks discussed early in the neuropsychological literature (Denckla & Rudel, 1976). Tallal (1980) showed that both developmental dysphasic and developmental dyslexic children were deficient in responding correctly to rapidly presented verbal and nonverbal acoustic stimuli; and suggested the "stretching" technique of extending initial formant transitions of, say, stop consonants (e.g., /ba/) while maintaining the total duration of the consonants as effective in helping these children. Could it not be that naming speed as an index of automaticity be considered another qualitative aspect of developmental dyslexia?

In an insightful review of the cognitive neuropsychological contribution to naming speed and reading, Wolf (1991) argues forcefully for this notion of the slower processing of cognitive and linguistic systems in dyslexics. The complementary nature of automatic processing and phoneme awareness in promoting phonological knowledge critical to reading is well explained by Perfetti's (1992, p. 165) distinction between **computational** and **reflective** knowledge. "Computational knowledge is simply connections between phonemes (or letter names) and letters that allow pronunciations of grapheme strings to be partly or wholly computed. Reflective knowledge is an awareness of the basic nature of these connections, that is, they depend on the fact that words comprise meaningless speech segments. Some computational phonemic knowledge is necessary to gain a functional lexical representation system of any size, and explicit reflective knowledge, or "awareness," is a sign of more powerful learning than implicit knowledge." (Perfetti, 1992, p. 165). In terms of methodology, the reflective and computational aspects of knowledge acquisiton and development in reading and language represent a shift from off-line to on-line data collection procedures with their attendant cognitive and linguistic issues of interpretation (Bierwisch, 1983).

Use of Growth Curves in Studying Individual Poor Readers

Methodologically, detailed answers to the questions of quantitative and qualitative differences will need to come from time series studies of growth curves of individuals receiving different educational treatments for phonological-core deficits and/or variable-difference difficulties. An elegant explication of individual growth curves and trend analysis is provided by Francis, Fletcher, Stuebing, Davidson, & Thompson (1991); and an application of the principle and methodology to the training of phonemic segmentation in relation to reading and spelling in first graders by Foorman, Francis, Novy, and Liberman (1991).

Diagnosis as Guided Learning

The discussion of quantitative and qualitative differences among severely disabled readers and garden-variety poor readers brings us back to the early, prescient work of Alfred Binet the clinician, the developmentalist (Binet & Simon, 1905/1961, 1909; see also Wolf, 1973). In many ways, Binet's ardent advocacy of enhancement of educational experience and the modifiability of intelligence, as shown by his detailed observations of his two daughters and his writings, predated a number of current notions in both diagnosis and remediation (see Leong, 1987, pp. 44-49). These notions include those of critical exploration of learning advocated by Piaget (1963) and of mediated learning experience of Vygotsky (1934/1986, 1978).

In their influential writing predicated on Vygotsky's (1978) concept of zone of proximal development, Campione (1989), Campione and Brown (1990) draw our attention to assisted assessment with a focus on individuals' potential for change. The guided learning and transfer can take different forms, including changing the format of the problems, providing feedback to the children about their performance and generally encouraging reflection and control strategies. The need for iterative, feedback functions in assessing, instructing, and further assessing has also been reiterated by Keating (1990).

Some Principles of Remediation of Reading Disorders

This section outlines some very general principles of remediation of severely disabled readers in elementary school children.

Compensation

If developmental dyslexia has many causes (Duane & Gray, 1991), then these severely disabled readers, especially those in mid- and upper elementary school years, may benefit by a multi-level and multi-component approach to reinforce amelioration of their phonological core deficits (see Carr & Levy, 1990; Frederiksen, 1982; Leong, 1988, 1992d). The componential approach emphasizes the inter-related roles of phonological, morphemic, morphological and syntactic processing with a parallel shift of different processing units -- sublexical units such as syllables, phonemes, morphemes, onsets and rimes; words; phrases; clauses; and sentences. The multi-level and multi-component approach to reading and its difficulties also has the advantage of specifying functionally defined information domains and provides for modules or areas for instruction or remediation.

The concept proposed here is one of **compensation** (Lundberg & Leong, 1986). Within our context of the multi-level and multi-component approach to reading, compensation is conceptualized as emphasizing or enhancing one component of reading more than another to ameliorate decrements or deficiencies in the components. Specifically, compensation can take place via : (a) support provided by the clinician or teacher to enrich the learning situation, (b) improved task properties, and (c) cognitive support systems generally, including the use of technology (Backman, 1985). These forms of compensation are not mutually exclusively and reinforce one another.

The evidence for compensation derives from several inter-related sources. Sensory, physical and communicative disabilities can be compensated for with vicarious modes of learning using materials rich in information content and aided by technology (Hjelmquist & Nilsson, 1986). Neurolinguistic data indicate different processing routes to lexical access in acquired dyslexia and can inform developmental dyslexia (Coltheart, Patterson, & Marshall, 1980; Marshall & Newcome, 1966, 1973). The interactive-compensatory model of reading suggests the use of different cognitive systems and levels of processing to ameliorate reading difficulties (Stanovich, 1980, 1984; Stanovich, West, & Feeman, 1981). Studies of memory and aging with particular reference to prose processing in the elderly show that older adults produce more elaborations in their prose recall, if given prose pasages emphasizing life experience (Backman, 1985; Dixon & Backman, 1988; Hultsch, Hertzog, & Dixon, 1984).

Practice

One way to effect compensation in reading disorders is to emphasize practice. In our earlier writing and drawing on the conceptualization of skill acquisition and development in cognitive psychology (Anderson, 1980, 1982), Downing and Leong (1982, pp. 13-49) considered reading as an integrated skill subsuming a hierarchy of interrelated subskills. We viewed reading as a complex behavior with these phases of development: cognitive, mastering and automaticity. The development of proficient reading, and the amelioration of reading disorders in children can be achieved through: (1) smooth performance, (2) proper timing, pacing and flexibility, (3) anticipation of future events, (4) consciousness of the reading activities and their functions, (5) sensitivity to shifts from external to internal cues, (6) use of increasingly larger units of processing, (7) automaticity beyond mere accuracy for flexible resource allocation for various subskills, and (8) integration of these cascading subskills.

The role of practice beyond accuracy was emphasized by Huey (1908/1968, p. 104): "Repetition progressively frees the mind from attention to details, makes facile the total act, shortens the time, and reduces the extent to which consciousness must concern itself with the process." The "method" of repeated reading of specific passages to attain a certain level of fluency before attempting new ones has been found to work well with low achieving students (C. Chomsky, 1978; Samuels, 1979). The repeated exposure to a word also leads to an increase in the size of the processing unit used in word recognition, although the perceptual learning that occurs is limited to the specific words repeatedly presented (Samuels, Miller, & Eisenberg, 1979).

Computer-Mediated Reading

To help poor readers to compensate for their difficulties, computer-aided reading is useful. One dilemma in such reading instruction is to maintain a balance between the "basic-but-dull" word decoding and the "complex-but-engaging" text comprehension (Perfetti, 1983). Further more, there should be a gradual shift in using context to guide cognitive processes during the real-time reading activity (Wilkinson, 1983). A recent research report with grade 6 subjects showed that by providing them with vocabulary learning on a computer screen their reading comprehension could be increased (Reinking & Rickman, 1990). There is further evidence that computer-aided reading instruction can help promote literacy in ways not possible without the computer (Reinking & Bridwell-Bowles, 1991).

It is instructive to reiterate the potency of the text-to-speech computer environment (DECtalk and its variants) to assist reading as reported by different research groups in a Special Issue on the topic (Leong, 1992a). In Guelph, Barron, Golden, Seldon, Tait, Marmurek, and Haines (1992) train phonological awareness in nonreaders with the aid of the DECtalk system. Their results emphasize the role of knowledge of letter-sound and other print-sound relationships ("proto-literacy"); and support bidirectional causal models of phonological awareness and literacy. In Colorado, Olson and Wise (1992) in their pioneering and long-term research and remediation programs have found significant gains from synthetic speech feedback (DECtalk) in their target children in word recognition, especially phonological coding. Wise and Olson (1992) have devised training programs to use interactive speech feedback from DECtalk to enhance children's phonological subskills in printed word decoding and in spelling. There is evidence for improvement in the children's ability to read nonwords. The Colorado group has progressively varied their training conditions to study individual differences and has made suggestions for future directions in the use of computerized speech for reading instruction and remediation. In Umea, Olofsson (1992) uses the Swedish Infovox text-to-speech system (similar to DECtalk) in two studies with Swedish children. He finds the provisions during text reading of pronunciation of words, on request from Infovox, assists his target group and older children in reading. In Saskatoon, Leong (1992c) provides immediate on-line and DECtalk speech explanations of difficult words and sentence structures to enhance text comprehension in older students. He finds some evidence of enhancement from a pre- and posttest design with open-ended inferencing questions in 67 grades 6, 7, and 8 readers reading 12 computerized expository passages of about 200 words each.

"COMPUTER AS PENCIL"

In all our enthusiasm in using the computer or text-to-speech computer systems to promote reading and writing, we should not overlook the "computer as pencil" concept of Papert (1980). As pencils are used for drawing, scribbling and writing, computers should be used for many different activities. There is something active, motivating learning in the computer environment. In Vygotskyan terms the computer should become a means of mediated experience and social construction of knowledge. The emphasis of diagnosis and coaching with or without the aid of computers should be the promotion of active learning on the part of students. The provision of suitably designed materials in contexts or situations helps to engender what may be known as cognitive bootstrapping or scaffolding to enable these learners to climb higher in the proverbial learning ladder as if they had the full prior knowledge.

A good example of this approach is the sophisticated educational knowledge media system known as Computer-Supported Intentional Learning Environments (CSILE). CSILE is developed by Scardamalia and Bereiter and their team as a "knowledge exploration" system for eventual use at all grade levels and for different school curricula (Scardamalia & Bereiter, in press; Scardamalia, Bereiter, McLean, Swallow, & Woodruff, 1989). CSILE supports learning by building a collection of knowledge base as database in the form of texts and graphics and stores the thoughts, ideas, problems and goals constructed by students to be shared by all. The emphasis is on the active production and use of knowledge and activities by students with the media as the intelligent tutoring system, which is capable of representing knowledge in different ways. Further more, students actively participate in learning, share their contributions and in doing so move to higher levels of learning and control of learning. In this way, technology provides the supportive environment to distribute knowledge and to maximize the expertise of teachers and clinicians.

Without being far-fetched, the notions of mediated experience and social construction of knowledge (Vygotsky, 1934/1986, 1978); computers as objects to think **with** (Papert, 1980); and CSILE as knowledge exploration (Scardamalia & Bereiter, in press; Scardamalia et al., 1989) may be likened to the parallel distributed processing systems of different classrooms discussed by Boden (1989). The general concept is a classroom full of children, who individually discuss with their neighbors some details relevant to the solution of a problem, whether in reading, spelling, or composing. A child's ideas are amenable to reinforcement or inhibition by the suggestions she receives from her immediate neighbors. These same neighbors are also communicating with the children next to them, who in turn are also discussing with their neighbors further away. The first child can then modify her opinions directly as a result of comments by her immediate neighbors and indirectly by neighbors in more distant places. In this way, the ideas and opinions of each child modify, and are modified by, those of her immediate and distant neighbors until all children reach a consensus as to the solution of the problem. This final decision results from: "the **parallel processing** (all the children chatter simultaneously) of **localized computations** (each child speaks to, and is directly influenced by, only her immediate neighbors), and is **distributed** across the whole system (as an internally consistent set of mini-decisions made by all the children)" (Boden, 1989, p. 5, original emphasis).

Experience with the componential analyses of reading using the microcomputer (Leong, 1988, 1992d; Leong & Lock, 1989) and with the text-to-speech computer system to assist readers (Leong, 1992b, 1992c) suggests that computer-mediated reading would need to incorporate the kind of "parallel, distributed" discussion as outlined above. Whether for developmental dyslexics or for garden-variety poor readers, explicit, systematic and sustained guidance is needed to help these readers to internalize their learning. This is done through modelling by the teacher, through the on-line presentation of targeted segments of discourse (onsets, rimes, phonemes and other sublexical units; words, phrases, clauses and sentences) coupled with simultaneous high-quality synthetic speech feedback and reinforced by metacognitive strategies (e.g., prompting of main ideas, key sentences, images, intermediate summaries).

Summary Of Principles Of Remediation

We are reminded by the authors of the IQ test Binet and Simon (1905/1961) that intelligence is a constructive process (see Siegler, 1992) and diagnosis should lead to remediation. The aim of the twin diagnosis-remediation endeavour should be to improve the child's performance in school work with timely, intensive and appropriate intervention. Remediation is cast within the psychological framework of compensation. This concept of the interactive-compensatory approach emphasizes substitutable components, and the activation of inactive or new subskills. Practice to promote automaticity, the covariation of phonology and morphology at the word level, and reflection and discussion at the discourse level all need to be emphasized. Computer-aided learning to ameliorate reading should be seen within the wider context of mediated experience and distributed learning.

Summary and Conclusion of Diagnostic Framework for Reading Disorders

This chapter addresses several interrelated and salient issues in the diagnosis of children with reading disorders, together with an outline of some principles in remediation. The main issues discussed are: (a) the relevance or irrelevance of intelligence tests revisited; (b) the efficacy of pseudoword reading with developmental dyslexics with "phonological-core" deficits; (c) the use of listening comprehension tests in assessing language comprehension in garden-variety poor readers with "variable-difference" performance in language and other domains; and (d) the distribution of reading disabilities with the attendant question of specificity or qualitative difference between developmental dyslexics and other poor readers.

A two-stage or two-level approach incorporating group tests and teachers' estimates at the assessment stage and more refined, individual tasks at the diagnostic stage is proposed. This quantitative and qualitative approach provides an academically sound, empirically verifiable and administratively convenient framework for ascertaining who shall be served. General ability tests, especially those tapping information processing subskills, represent indices of learning aptitude to gauge degrees of discrepancy when compared with actual and predicted reading achievement in regression studies.

If it is difficult to achieve consensus on the aptitude-achievement discrepancy approach incorporating intelligence tests to diagnose severe reading disabilities (developmental dyslexia), there is convergent evidence to support the potency of pseudoword reading in diagnosing dyslexics. Different kinds of pseudowords are needed: those with many "friendly neighbors" and those with few friendly neighbors; and other linguistic dimensions and consistency effects should be taken into account. Phonological awareness; the processing of exception or irregular words; and morphological and morphemic structure of words will also need to be examined to provide a better profile of dyslexics' knowledge of lexical representation.

For the garden-variety poor readers beyond the estimated 3% or 4% of true dyslexics, the proposal to incorporate listening comprehension tests as part of language comprehension rekindles interests in aural/oral language comprehension. The learning by listening approach should be seen as knowledge acquisition at the conceptual level. For language comprehension through the contextualized aural/oral mode and the recontextualized written mode, appropriate units of processing such as idea units and methods of comparable assessment should be aimed at. For more efficient assessment of language comprehension in both modes sophisticated text-to-speech computer systems such as DECtalk provide opportunities to assess reading comprehension on-line simultaneously with auding (listening to gain knowledge) from the same prose materials. Data are presented to buttress the claim that this simultaneous presentation of reading and auding the same language materials facilitates reading and knowledge acquisiton.

Another issue pertains to investigations of the distribution of reading disabilities, including developmental dyslexia, as bimodal with a "hump" as usually accepted or whether as part of a continuum encompassing normal reading. Current data from the Connecticut Longitudinal Study showing a normal distribution does not deny the possible hump and putative specificity of a biological origin with developmental dyslexics. It is suggested that phonological processing, especially in phoneme awareness (e.g., pig Latin), may represent such specific, qualitative differences, over and above quantitative ones, as inferred from the long-term Colorado Reading Project data with cotwins. Neuropsychological literature also suggests automaticity such as rapid naming might be another candidate. Both reflective and fast, automatic language processing contributes to reading and language development.

As enjoined by the pioneer developmentalist Alfred Binet that diagnosis should lead to remediation, it is suggested that substitutable subskills or components in reading disorders can be ameliorated with compensatory mechanisms augmented with available computer technology. The computer environment should be one of the promotion of learning as knowledge exploration.

ACKNOWLEDGMENT

The research reported and the writing of this chapter have been assisted in part by research grants from the Social Sciences and Humanities Research Council of Canada and the University of Saskatchewan. I am grateful for the assistance.

REFERENCES

Aaron, P.G. (1989). *Dyslexia and hyperlexia.* Dordrecht, The Netherlands: Kluwer Academic Publishers.

Aaronson, D. (1984). Computer methods and ecological validity in reading research. *Behavior Research Methods, Instruments, & Computers, 16*, 102-108.

Adams, M.J., & Huggins, A.W.F. (1985). The growth of children's sight vocabulary: A quick test with educational and theoretical implications. *Reading Research Quarterly, 20*, 262-281.

Albrow, K.H. (1972). *The English writing system: Notes towards a description.* London: Longmans.

American Psychiatric Association. (1987). *Diagnostic and statistical manual of mental disorders* (3rd ed., rev). Washington, D.C.: Author.

Anderson, J.R. (1980). *Cognitive psychology and its implications.* San Francisco, CA: Freeman.

Anderson, J.R. (1982). Acquisition of cognitive skill. *Psychological Review, 89*, 369-406.

Angle, H.V. (1981). The interviewing computer: A technology for gathering comprehensive treatment information. *Behavior Research Methods & Instrumentation, 13*, 607-612.

Backman, L. (1985). Compensation and recoding: A framework for aging and memory research. *Scandinavian Journal of Psychology, 26*, 193-207.

Baddeley, A.D., Logie, R.H., & Ellis, N.C. (1988). Characteristics of developmental dyslexia. *Cognition, 29*, 197-228.

Baron, J. (1979). Orthographic and word-specific knowledge in children's reading of words. *Child Development, 50*, 60-72.

Baron, J., & Treiman, R. (1980). Use of orthography in reading and learning to read. In J.F. Kavanagh & R.L. Venezky (Eds.), *Orthography, reading, and dyslexia* (pp.171-189). Baltimore, MD: University Park Press.

Barron, R.W., Golden, J.O., Seldon, D.M., Tait, C.F., Marmurek, H.H.C., & Haines, L.P. (1992). Teaching prereading skills with a talking computer: Letter-sound knowledge and print feedback facilitate nonreaders' phonological awareness training. *Reading and Writing: An Interdisciplinary Journal, 4*, 179-204.

Beaumont, J.G. (1981). Microcomputer-aided assessment using standard psychometric procedures. *Behavior Research Methods & Instrumentation, 13*, 430-433.

Beech, J.R., & Harding, L.M. (1984). Phonemic processing and the poor reader from a developmental lag viewpoint. *Reading Research Quarterly, 19*, 357-366.

Berninger, V. (1988). Acquisition of linguistic procedures for printed words: Neuropsychological implications for learning. *International Journal of Neuroscience, 42*, 276-281.

Berninger, V., & Hart, T.M. (this volume). From research to clinical assessment of reading and writing disorders: The unit of analysis problem.

Berninger, V., Hart, T.M., Abbot, R., & Karovsky, P. (1992). Defining reading and writing disabilities with and without IQ: A flexible, developmental perspective. *Learning Disabilities Quarterly, 15*, 103-118.

Berninger, V., & Traweek, D. (1991). Effects of a two-phase reading intervention on three orthographic-phonological code connections. *Learning and Individual Differences, 3*, 323-338.

Bierwisch, M. (1983). How on-line is language processing? In G.B. Flores D'Arcais & R.J. Jarvella (Eds.), *The process of language understanding* (pp. 113-168). New York: John Wiley.

Binet, A., & Simon, T. (1909). L'intelligence des imbeciles. *L'Annee Psychologique, 15*, 1-147.

Binet, A., & Simon, T. (1961). Upon the necessity of establishing a scientific diagnosis of inferior states of intelligence. In T. Shipley (Ed.), *Classics in psychology*. New York: Philosophical Library. (Originally published in *L'Annee Psychologique*, 1905, 11, 163-190).

Boden, M.A. (1989). *Artificial intelligence in psychology*. Cambridge, MA: MIT Press.

Bruck, M. (1988). The word recognition and spelling of dyslexic children. *Reading Research Quarterly, 23*, 51-69.

Bryant, N.D., & Kass, C.E. (Eds.). (1972). *Leadership training institute in learning disabilities* (Final Report, Project No. 127145). Washington, DC: U.S. Office of Education.

Bryant, P., & Impey, L. (1986). The similarities between normal readers and developmental and acquired dyslexics. *Cognition, 24*, 121-138.

Bybee, J. (1985). *Morphology: A study of the relation between meaning and form*. Amsterdam: Benjamins.

Calfee, R.C. (1982). Cognitive models of reading: Implications for assessment and treatment of reading disability. In R.N. Malatesha & P.G. Aaron (Eds.), *Reading disorders: Varieties and treatments* (pp. 151-176). Hillsdale, NJ: Lawrence Erlbaum.

Campione J.C. (1989). Assisted assessment: A taxonomy of approaches and an outline of strengths and weakness. *Journal of Learning Disabilities, 22*, 151-165.

Campione, J.C., & Brown A.L. (1990). Guided learning and transfer: Implications for approaches to assessment. In N. Frederiksen, R. Glaser, A. Lesgold, & M.G. Shafto (Eds.), *Diagnostic monitoring of skill and knowledge acquisition* (pp. 141-172). Hillsdale, NJ: Lawrence Erlbaum.

Carlisle, J.F. (1990). Diagnostic assessment of listening and reading comprehension. In H.L. Swanson & B. Keogh (Eds.), *Learning disabilities: Theoretical and research issues* (pp. 277-298). Hillsdale, NJ: Lawrence Erlbaum.

Carlisle, J.F., & Felbinger, L. (1991). Profiles of listening and reading comprehension. *Journal of Educational Research, 84*, 345-354.

Carpenter, P.A., Just, M.A., & Shell, P. (1990). What one intelligence test measures: A theoretical account of the processing in the Raven Progressive Matrices Test. *Psychological Review, 97*, 404-431.

Carr, T.H., & Levy, B.A. (Eds.). (1990). *Reading and its development: Component skills approaches*. New York: Academic Press.

Carroll, J.B. (1968). On learning from being told. *Educational Psychologist, 5*, 4-10.

Carroll, J.B. (1972). Defining language comprehension: Some speculations. In R.O. Freedle & J.B. Carroll (Eds.), *Language comprehension and the acquisition of knowledge*, (pp. 1-29). New York: John Wiley.

Carver, R.P. (1977-1978). Toward a theory of reading comprehension. *Reading Research Quarterly, 13*, 8-63.

Carver, R.P. (1982). Optimal rate of reading prose. *Reading Research Quarterly, 18*, 56-88.

Carver, R.P. (1990). *Reading rate: A review of research and theory*. New York: Academic Press.

Cataldo, S., & Ellis, N. (1988). Interactions in the development of spelling, reading and phonological skills. *Journal of Research in Reading, 11*, 86-109.

Chafe, W.L. (1985). Linguistic differences produced by differences between speaking and writing. In D.R. Olson, N. Torrance, & A. Hildyard (Eds.), *Literacy, language, and learning: The nature and consequences of reading and writing* (pp. 105-123). New York: Cambridge University Press.

Chomsky, C. (1978). When you still can't read in third grade: After decoding, what? In S.J. Samuels (Ed.), *What research has to say about reading instruction* (pp. 13-30). Newark, DE: International Reading Association.

Clark, H.H., & Haviland, S.E. (1977). Comprehension and the Given-New contract. In R.O. Freedle (Ed.), *Discourse production and comprehension, Vol. 1. Discourse processes: Advances in research and theory* (pp. 1-40). Norwood, NJ: Ablex.

Coltheart, M. (1978). Lexical access in simple reading tasks. In G. Underwood (Ed.), *Strategies of information processing* (pp. 151-216). San Diego, CA: Academic Press.

Coltheart, M. (1980). Reading, phonological recoding and deep dyslexia. In M. Coltheart, K. Patterson, & J.C. Marshall (Eds.), *Deep dyslexia* (pp. 197-226). London: Routledge & Kegan Paul.

Coltheart, M., Masterson, J., Byng, S., Prior, M., & Riddoch, J. (1983). Surface dyslexia. *Quarterly Journal of Experimental Psychology, 35A,* 469-496.

Coltheart, M., Patterson, K.E., & Marshall, J.C. (Eds.). (1980). *Deep dyslexia.* London: Routledge & Kegan Paul.

Coltheart, V., & Leahy, J. (1992). Children's and adults' reading of nonwords: Effects of regularity and consistency. *Journal of Experimental Psychology: Learning, Memory, and Cognition, 18,* 718-729.

Cronbach, L.J., & Furby, L. (1970). How we should measure change -- or should we? *Psychological Bulletin, 74,* 68-80.

Crowder, R.G. (1982). *The psychology of reading.* New York: Oxford University Press.

Cutler, A. (1981). Making up materials is a confounded nuisance, or: Will we be able to run any psycholinguistic experiments at all in 1990? *Cognition, 10,* 65-70.

Cutler, A. (1983). Lexical complexity and sentence processing. In G.B. Flores D'Arcais & R.J. Jarvella (Eds.), *The process of language understanding* (pp. 43-79). New York: John Wiley.

Danks, J.H. (1980). Comprehension in listening and reading: Same or different? In J. Danks & K. Pezdek (Eds.), *Reading and understanding* (pp. 1-39). Newark, DE: International Reading Association.

Danks, J.H., Bohn, L., & Fears, R. (1983). Comprehension processes in oral reading. In G.B. Flores D'Arcais & R.J. Jarvella (Eds.), *The process of language understanding* (pp. 193-223). New York: John Wiley.

Danks, J.H., & End, L.J. (1987). Processing strategies for reading and listening. In R. Horowitz & S.J. Samuels (Eds.), *Comprehending oral and written language* (pp. 271-294). New York: Academic Press.

DeFries, J.C., Olson, R.K., Pennington, B.F., & Smith, S.D. (1991). Colorado reading project: An update. In D.D. Duane & D.B. Gray (Eds.), *The reading brain: The biological basis of dyslexia* (pp. 53-87). Parkton, MD: York Press.

Denckla, M.B., & Rudel, R.G. (1976). Naming of objects by dyslexic and other learning-disabled children. *Brain and Language, 3,* 1-15.

Dixon, R.A., & Backman, L. (1988). Text recall and aging: Toward research on expertise and comprehension. In M.M. Gruneberg, P.E. Morris, & R.N. Sykes (Eds.), *Practical aspects of memory: Vol. 2. Clinical and educational implications* (pp. 101-106). Chichester, UK: John Wiley.

Dobbins, D.A. (1988). Yule's "hump" revisited. British *Journal of Educational Psychology, 58,* 338-344.

Dobbins, D.A., & Tafa, E. (1991). The 'stability' of identification of underachieving readers over different measures of intelligence and reading. *British Journal of Educational Psychology, 61,* 155-163.

Downing, J., & Leong, C.K. (1982). *Psychology of reading.* New York: Macmillan.

Duane, D.D., & Gray, D.B. (Eds.). (1991). *The reading brain: The biological basis of dyslexia.* Parkton, MD: York Press.

Durrell, D.D., Hayes, M.T., & Brassard. M.B. (1969). *Listening-reading tests.* New York: Harcourt, Brace, and World.

Elliott, C.D. (1983). *The British Ability Scales.* Windsor, UK: NFER-Nelson.

Ellis, N. (1991). Spelling and sound in learning to read. In M. Snowling & M. Thomson (Eds.), *Dyslexia: Integrating theory and practice* (pp. 80-94). London: Whurr Publishers.

Elbro, C. (1989). Morphological awareness in dyslexia. In C. von Euler, I. Lundberg, & G. Lennerstrand (Eds.), *Brain and reading. Structural and functional anomalies in developmental dyslexia with special reference to hemispheric interactions, memory functions, linguistic processes, and visual analysis in reading* (pp. 279-291). London: Macmillan.

Elbro, C. (1991). Dyslexics and normal beginning readers read by different strategies: A comparison of strategy distributions in dyslexic and normal readers. *International Journal of Applied Linguistics, 1,* 19-37.

Embretson, S.E. (1992). Computerized adaptive testing: Its potential substantive contributions to psychological research and assessment. *Current Directions in Psychological Science, 1,* 129-131.

Feinstein, A.R. (1975). On the sensitivity, specificity, and discrimination of diagnostic tests. *Clinical Pharmacology and Therapeutics, 17,* 104-116.

Felton, R.H., & Wood, F.B. (1992). A reading level match study of nonword reading skills in poor readers with varying IQs. *Journal of Learning Disabilities, 25,* 318-326.

Fletcher, J.M., Espy, K.A., Francis, D.J., Davidson, K.C., Rourke, B.P., & Shaywitz, S.E. (1989). Comparisons of cutoff and regression-based definitions of reading disabilities. *Journal of Learning Disabilities, 22,* 334-338, 355.

Flores D'Arcais, G.B., & Jarvella, R.J. (Eds.). (1983). *The process of language understanding.* New York: John Wiley.

Fodor, J.A., Bever, T.G., & Garrett, M. (1974). *The psychology of language.* New York: McGraw-Hill.

Foorman, B.R. (1989). What's specific about specific reading disability: An introduction to the Special Series. *Journal of Learning Disabilities, 22,* 332-333.

Foorman, B.R., Francis, D.J., Novy, D.M., & Liberman, D. (1991). How letter-sound instruction mediates progress in first-grade reading and spelling. *Journal of Educational Psychology, 83,* 456-469.

Foulke, E., & Sticht, T.G. (1969). Review of research on the intelligibility and comprehension of accelerated speech. *Psychological Bulletin, 72,* 50-62.

Francis, D.J., Fletcher, J.M., Stuebing, K.K., Davidson, K.C., & Thompson, N.M. (1991). Analysis of change: Modeling individual growth. *Journal of Consulting and Clinical Psychology, 59,* 27-37.

Frederiksen, J.R. (1982). A componential theory of reading skills and their interactions. In R.J. Sternberg (Ed.), *Advances in the psychology of human intelligence, Vol. 1,* (pp. 125-180). Hillsdale, NJ: Lawrence Erlbaum.

Freedle, R.O., & Carroll, J.B. (Eds.). (1972). *Language comprehension and the acquisition of knowledge.* New York: John Wiley.

Frith, U. (1985). Beneath the surface of developmental dyslexia. In M. Coltheart, K.E. Patterson, & J.C. Marshall (Eds.), *Surface dyslexia: Neurospychological and cognitive studies of phonological reading* (pp. 303-332). London: Lawrence Erlbaum.

Gardner, H. (1983). *Frames of mind: The theory of multiple intelligences.* New York: Basic Books.

Gleitman, L.R., & Rozin, P. (1977). The structure and acquisition of reading I: Relations between orthographies and the structure of language. In A.S. Reber & D.L. Scarborough (Eds.), *Toward a psychology of reading* (pp. 1-53). Hillsdale, NJ: Lawrence Erlbaum.

Glushko, R.J. (1979). The organization and activation of orthographic knowledge in reading aloud. *Journal of Experimental Psychology: Human Perception and Performance, 5,* 674-691.

Glushko, R.J. (1981). Principles of pronouncing print: The psychology of phonography. In A.M. Lesgold & C.A. Perfetti (Eds.), *Interactive processes in reading* (pp. 61-84). Hillsdale, NJ: Lawrence Erlbaum.

Goldberg, T.E., & Rothermel, R.D. (1984). Hyperlexic children reading. *Brain, 107,* 759-785.

Goswami, U., & Bryant, P. (1990). *Phonological skills and learning to read.* East Sussex, UK: Lawrence Erlbaum.

Gough, P.B., & Tunmer, W.E. (1986). Decoding, reading, and reading disability. *Remedial and Special Education, 7,* 6-10.

Gough, P.B., & Walsh, M.A. (1991). Chinese, Phoenicians, and the orthographic cipher of English. In S.A. Brady & D.P. Shankweiler (Eds.), *Phonological processes in literacy* (pp. 199-209). Hillsdale, NJ: Lawrence Erlbaum.

Green, D.M., & Swets, J.A. (1974). *Signal detection theory and psychophysics.* New York: Kriege, Huntington. (Original work published 1966, New York: John Wiley).

Guthrie, J.T., & Tyler, S.J. (1976). Psycholinguistic processing in reading and listening among good and poor readers. *Journal of Reading Behavior, 8,* 415-426.

Halliday, M.A.K. (1985). *An introduction to functional grammar.* Baltimore, MD: Edward Arnold.

Halliday, M.A.K. (1987). Spoken and written modes of meaning. In R. Horowitz & S.J. Samuels (Eds.), *Comprehending oral and written language* (pp. 55-82). New York: Academic Press.

Halliday, M.A.K., & Hasan, R. (1976). *Cohesion in English.* London: Longman.

Harber, J.R. (1981a). Assessing the quality of decision making in special education. *Journal of Special Education, 15,* 77-90.

Harber, J.R. (1981b). Evaluating utility in diagnostic decision making. *Journal of Special Education, 15,* 413-428.

Healy, J.M., & Aram, D.M. (1986). Hyperlexia and dyslexia: A family study. *Annals of Dyslexia, 36,* 237-252.

Healy, J.M., Aram, D.M., Horowitz, S.J., & Kessler, J.W. (1982). A study of hyperlexia. *Brain and Language, 17,* 1-23.

Hersh, H.M., & Caramazza, A. (1976). A fuzzy set approach to modifiers and vagueness in natural language. *Journal of Experimental Psychology, 105,* 254-276.

Hillinger, M.L. (1992). Computer speech and responsive text: Hypermedia support for reading instruction. *Reading and Writing: An Interdisciplinary Journal, 4,* 219-229.

Hjelmquist, E., & Nilsson, L.-G. (Eds.). (1986). *Compensation and handicap: Aspects of psychological compensation and technical aids.* Amsterdam: North-Holland.

Høien, T., & Lundberg, I. (1989). A strategy for assessing problems in word recognition among dyslexics. *Scandinavian Journal of Educational Research, 33,* 185-201.

Hoover, W.A., & Gough, P.B. (1990). The simple view of reading. *Reading and Writing: An Interdisciplinary Journal, 2,* 127-160.

Horn, J. (1988). Thinking about human abilities. In J.R. Nesselroade & R.B. Cattell (Eds.), *Handbook of multivariate experimental psychology* (2nd ed.) (pp. 645-685). New York: Plenum Press.

Horn, J..L., & Cattell, R.B. (1966). Refinement and test of the theory of fluid and crystallized intelligence. *Journal of Educational Psychology, 57,* 253-270.

Horowitz, R., & Samuels, S.J. (1985). Reading and listening to expository text. *Journal of Reading Behavior, 17,* 185-198.

Horowitz, R., & Samuels, S.J. (Eds.) (1987a). *Comprehending oral and written language.* New York: Academic Press.

Horowitz, R.,& Samuels, S.J. (1987b). Comprehending oral and written language: Critical .contrasts for literacy and schooling. In R. Horowitz & S.J. Samuels (Eds.), *Comprehending oral and written language.* (pp 1-52). New York: Academic Press.

Horvath, M.J., Kass, C.E., & Ferrell, W.R. (1980). An example of the use of fuzzy set concepts in modeling learning disability. *American Educational Research Journal, 17,* 309-324.

Huey, E.B. (1968). *The psychology and pedagogy of reading.* Cambridge, MA: MIT Press. (Original work published 1908, New York: Macmillan)

Hultsch, D.F., Hertzog, C., & Dixon, R.A. (1984). Text recall in adulthood: The role of intellectual abilities. *Developmental Psychology, 20,* 1193-1209.

Hunt, E. (1971). What kind of computer is man? *Cognitive Psychology, 2,* 57-98.

Hunt, E. (1974). Quote the Raven? Nevermore! In L. Gregg (Ed.), *Knowledge and cognition* (pp. 129-157). Hillsdale, NJ: Lawrence Erlbaum.

Hunt, E., & Pellegrino, J. (1985). Using interactive computing to expand intelligence testing: A critique and prospectus. *Intelligence, 9,* 207-236.

Huttenlocher, P., & Huttenlocher, J. (1973). A study of children with hyperlexia. *Neurology, 23,* 1107-1116.

Jarvella, R.J. (1971). Syntactic processing of connected speech. *Journal of Verbal Learning and Verbal Behavior, 10,* 409-416.

Jastak, S., & Wilkinson, G.S. (1984). *The Wide Range Achievement Test-Revised: Administration manual.* Wilmington, DE: Jastak Associates.

Kavanagh, J.F., & Mattingly, I.G. (Eds.). (1972). *Language by ear and by eye.* Cambridge, MA: MIT Press.

Kavanagh, J.F., & Truss, T.J. (Eds.). (1988). *Learning disabilities: Proceedings of the national conference.* Parkton, MD: York Press.

Keating, D.P. (1990). Charting pathways to the development of expertise. *Educational Psychologist, 25,* 243-267.

Kintsch, W. (1974). *The representation of meaning in memory.* Hillsdale, NJ: Lawrence Erlbaum.

Kintsch, W., & Keenan, J.M. (1973). Reading rate and retention as a function of the number of propositions in the base structure of sentences. *Cognitive Psychology, 5,* 257-274.

Kintsch, W., & Kozminsky, E. (1977). Summarizing stories after reading and listening. *Journal of Educational Psychology, 69*, 491-499.

Laxon, V.J., Coltheart, V., & Keating, G.C. (1988). Children find friendly words friendly too: Words with many orthographic neighbours are easier to read and spell. *British Journal of Educational Psychology, 58*, 103-119.

Leong, C.K. (1985). Diagnosis for learning in children with special needs. In D.D. Duane & C.K. Leong (Eds.), *Understanding learning disabilities: International and multidisciplinary views* (pp. 49-63). New York: Plenum Press.

Leong, C.K. (1987). *Children with specific reading disabilities.* Lisse, The Netherlands: Swets and Zeitlinger.

Leong, C.K. (1988). A componential approach to understanding reading and its difficulties in preadolescent readers. *Annals of Dyslexia, 38*, 95-119.

Leong, C.K. (1989a). The locus of so-called IQ test results in reading disabilities. *Journal of Learning Disabilities, 22*, 507-512.

Leong, C.K. (1989b). Productive knowledge of derivational rules in poor readers. *Annals of Dyslexia, 39*, 94-115.

Leong, C.K. (1989c). The effects of morphological structure on reading proficiency -- A developmental study. *Reading and Writing: An Interdisciplinary Journal, 1*, 357-379.

Leong, C.K. (Ed.). (1992a). Reading and spelling with text-to-speech computer systems [Special issue]. *Reading and Writing: An Interdisciplinary Journal, 4*, 95-229.

Leong, C.K. (1992b). Introduction: Text-to-speech, text, and hypertext: Reading and spelling with the computer. *Reading and Writing: An Interdisciplinary Journal, 4*, 95-105.

Leong, C.K. (1992c). Enhancing reading comprehension with text-to-speech (DECtalk) computer system. *Reading and Writing: An Interdisciplinary Journal, 4*, 205-217.

Leong, C.K. (1992d). Cognitive componential modelling of reading in ten- to twelve-year-old readers. *Reading and Writing: An Interdisciplinary Journal, 4*, 327-364.

Leong, C.K. (in preparation). Tactics children use in spelling.

Leong, C.K., & Lock, S. (1989). The use of microcomputer technology in a modular approach to reading and its difficulties. *Reading and Writing: An Interdisciplinary Journal, 2*, 51-61.

Levelt, W.J.M. (1989). *Speaking: From intention to articulation.* Cambridge, MA: MIT Press.

Levy, B.A. (1978). Speech analysis during sentence processing: Reading and listening. *Visible Language, 12*, 81-102.

Lezak, M.D. (1983). *Neuropsychological assessment.* New York: Oxford University Press.

Liberman, I.Y., & Shankweiler, D.P. (1985). Phonology and the problems of learning to read and write. *Remedial and Special Education, 6*, 8-17.

Linebarger, M., Schwartz, M., & Saffran, E. (1983). Sensitivity to grammatical structure in so-called agrammatic aphasics. *Cognition, 13*, 361-392.

Lock, S., & Leong, C.K. (1989). Program library for DECtalk text-to-speech system. *Behavior Research Methods, Instruments & Computers, 21*, 394-400.

Lock, S., & Leong, C.K. (1991). An algorithmic implementation of Rasch approach to item analysis with graphical interpretation. *Educational Research Journal, 6*, 40-52.

Lundberg, I., & Høien, T. (1990). Patterns of information processing skills and word recognition strategies in developmental dyslexia. *Scandinavian Journal of Educational Research, 34*, 231-240.

Lundberg, I., & Leong, C.K. (1986). Compensation in reading disabilities. In E. Hjelmquist & L.-G. Nilsson (Eds.), *Communication and handicap: Aspects of psychological compensation and technical aids* (pp. 171-190). Amsterdam: North-Holland.

Mackay, M.E., & Leong, C.K. (in preparation). Readers' comprehension of verbal output from DECtalk.

Macmann, G.M., Barnett, D.W., Lombard, T.J., Belton-Kocher, E., & Sharpe, M.N. (1989). On the actuarial classification of children: Fundamental studies of classification agreement. *The Journal of Special Education, 23*, 127-149.

Mann, V.A. (1991). Phonological abilities: Effective predictors of future reading ability. In L. Rieben & C.A. Perfetti (Eds.), *Learning to read: Basic research and its implications* (pp. 121-133). Hillsdale, NJ: Lawrence Erlbaum.

Mann, V.A., & Ditunno, P. (1990). Phonological deficiencies: Effective predictors of future reading problems. In G. Th. Pavlidis (Ed.), *Perspectives on dyslexia. Vol. 2: Cognition, language and treatment* (pp. 105-131). Chichester, UK: John Wiley.

Marshall, J.C., & Newcombe, F. (1966). Syntactic and semantic errors in paralexia. *Neuropsychologia, 4*, 169-176.

Marshall, J.C., & Newcombe, F. (1973). Patterns of paralexia: A psycholinguistic approach. *Journal of Psycholinguistic Research, 2*, 175-199.

Marslen-Wilson, W.D., Tyler, L.K., & Seidenberg, M. (1978). Sentence processing and the clause boundary. In W.J.M. Levelt & G.B. Flores D'Arcais (Eds.), *Studies in the perception of language.* (pp. 219-246) Chichester, UK: John Wiley.

Massaro, D.W. (1978). A stage model of reading and listening. *Visible Language, 12*, 3-26.

Massaro, D.W. (1979). Reading and listening (Tutorial paper). In P.A. Kolers, M.E. Wrolstad, & H. Bouma (Eds.), *Processing of visible language.* Vol. 1 (pp. 331-354). New York: Plenum Press.

Matarazzo, J.D. (1985). Clinical psychological test interpretations by computer: Hardware outpaces software. *Computers in Human Behavior, 1*, 235-253.

Matarazzo, J.D. (1986). Computerized clinical psychological test interpretations: Unvalidated plus all mean and no sigma. *American Psychologist, 41*, 14-24.

Matarazzo, J.D. (1992). Psychological testing and assesment in the 21st century. *American Psychologist, 47*, 1007-1018.

Matthews, P.H. (1974). *Morphology.* Cambridge, UK: Cambridge University Press.

Mattingly, I.G. (1984). Reading, linguistic awareness, and language acquisition. In J. Downing & R. Valtin (Eds.), *Language awareness and learning to read* (pp. 9-25). New York: Springer-Verlag.

Mattingly, I.G. (1987). Morphological structure and segmental awareness. *Cahiers de Psychologie Cognitive, 7*, 488-493.

McNicol, D. (1972). *A primer of signal detection theory.* London: George Allen & Unwin.

Mosenthal, P. (1976-1977). Psycholinguistic properties of aural and visual comprehension as determined by children's abilities to comprehend syllogisms. *Reading Research Quarterly, 12*, 55-92.

Olofsson, Å. (1992). Synthetic speech and computer aided reading for reading disabled children. *Reading and Writing: An Interdisciplinary Journal, 4*, 165-178.

Olson, D.R., Torrance, N., & Hildyard, A. (Eds.). (1985). *Literacy, language, and learning: The nature and consequences of reading and writing.* New York: Cambridge University Press.

Olson, R.K. (1985). Disabled reading processes and cognitive profiles. In D.B. Gray & J.F. Kavanagh (Eds.), *Biobehavioral measures of dyslexia* (pp. 215-244). Parkton, MD: York Press.

Olson, R.K., Foltz, G., & Wise, B. (1986). Reading instruction and remediation with the aid of computer speech. *Behavior Research Methods, Instruments, & Computers, 18*, 93-99.

Olson, R.K., Gillis, J.J., Rack, J.P., DeFries, J.C., & Fulker, D.W. (1991). Confirmatory factor analysis of word recognition and process measures in the Colorado Reading Project. *Reading and Writing: An Interdisciplinary Journal, 3*, 235-248.

Olson, R.K., Kliegl, R., Davidson, B.J., & Foltz, G. (1985). Individual and developmental differences in reading disability. In G.E. Mackinnon & T.G. Waller (Eds.), *Reading research: Advances in theory and practice. Vol. 4* (pp. 1-64). New York: Academic Press.

Olson, R.K., & Wise, B.W. (1992). Reading on the computer with orthographic and speech feedback: An overview of the Colorado remediation project. *Reading and Writing: An Interdisciplinary Journal, 4*, 107-144.

Olson, R.K., Wise, B., Conners, F., & Rack, J. (1990). Organization, heritability, and remediation of component word recognition and language skills in disabled readers. In T.H. Carr & B.A. Levy (Eds.), *Reading and its development: Component skills approaches* (pp. 261-322). New York: Academic Press.

Papert, S. (1980). *Mindstorms: Children, computers, and powerful ideas.* New York: Basic Books.

Parkin, A.J. (1982). Phonological recoding in lexical decision: Effects of spelling-to-sound regularity depend on how regularity is defined. *Memory & Cognition, 10*, 43-53.

Patterson, K.E., Marshall, J.C., & Coltheart, M. (Eds.). (1985). *Surface dyslexia: Neuropsychological and cognitive studies of phonological reading.* Hillsdale, NJ: Lawrence Erlbaum.

Patterson, K.E., & Morton, J. (1985). From orthography to phonology: An attempt at an old interpretation. In K.E. Patterson, J.C. Marshall, & J. Morton (Eds.), *Surface dyslexia: Neuropsychological and cognitive studies of phonological reading* (pp. 335-359). Hillsdale, NJ: Lawrence Erlbaum.

Pennington, B.F., Johnson, C., & Welsh, M.C. (1987). Unexpected reading precocity in a normal preschooler: Implications for hyperlexia. *Brain and Language, 30,* 165-180.

Pennington, B.F., Van Orden, G.C., Smith, S.D., Green, P.A., & Haith, M.M. (1990). Phonological processing skills and deficits in adult dyslexics. *Child Development, 61,* 1753-1778.

Perfetti, C.A. (1983). Reading, vocabulary, and writing: Implications for computer-based instruction. In A.C. Wilkinson (Ed.), *Classroom computers and cognitive science* (pp. 145-163). New York: Academic Press.

Perfetti, C.A. (1985). *Reading ability.* New York: Oxford University Press.

Perfetti, C.A. (1986). Continuities in reading acquisition, reading skill, and reading disability. *Remedial and Special Education, 7,* 11-21.

Perfetti, C.A. (1987). Language, speech and print: Some asymmetries in the acquisition of literacy. In R. Horowitz & S.J. Samuels (Eds.), *Comprehending oral and written language* (pp. 355-369). New York: Academic Press.

Perfetti, C.A. (1988). Verbal efficiency in reading ability. In M. Daneman, G.E. Mackinnon, & T.G. Waller (Eds.), *Reading research: Advances in theory and practice.* Vol. 6 (pp. 109-143). New York: Academic Press.

Perfetti, C.A. (1992). The representation problem in reading acquisition. In P.B. Gough, L.C. Ehri, & R. Treiman (Eds.), *Reading acquisition* (pp. 145-174). Hillsdale, NJ: Lawrence Erlbaum.

Piaget, J. (1963). *The child's conception of the world.* Paterson, NJ: Littlefield, Adams.

Pollack, R.H., & Brenner, M.W. (Eds.). (1969). *The experimental psychology of Alfred Binet: Selected papers.* New York: Springer-Verlag.

Rack, J.P., Snowling, M.J., & Olson, R.K. (1992). The nonword reading deficit in developmental dyslexia: A review. *Reading Research Quarterly, 27,* 28-53.

Rasch, G. (1980). *Probabilistic models for some intelligence and attainment tests.* Chicago: University of Chicago Press. (Original work published 1960, Copenhagen: The Danish Institute for Educational Research.)

Raven, J.C. (1960). *Guide to using the Standard Progressive Matrices.* London: Lewis.

Reinking, D., & Bridwell-Bowles, L. (1991). Computers in reading and writing. In R. Barr, M.L. Kamil, P. Mosenthal, & P.D. Pearson (Eds.), *Handbook of reading research.* Vol. 2 (pp. 310-340). New York: Longman.

Reinking, D., & Rickman, S.S. (1990). The effects of computer-mediated texts on the vocabulary and comprehension of intermediate-grade readers. *Journal of Reading Behavior, 22,* 395-411.

Reitsma, P. (1988). Reading practice for beginners: Effects of guided reading, reading-while-listening, and independent reading with computer-based speech feedback. *Reading Research Quarterly, 23,* 219-235.

Reynolds, C.R. (1990). Conceptual and technical problems in learning disability diagnosis. In C.R. Reynolds & R.W. Kamphaus (Eds.), *Handbook of psychological and educational assessment of children: Intelligence and achievement* (pp. 571-592). New York: Guilford Press.

Rispens, J., & Van Berckelaer, I.A. (1991). Hyperlexia: Definition and criterion. In R.M. Joshi (Ed.), *Written language disorders* (pp. 143-163). Dordrecht, The Netherlands: Kluwer Academic Publishers.

Rispens, J., & van Yperen, T.A. (1990). The identification of specific reading disorders: Measuring a severe discrepancy. In G. Th. Pavlidis (Ed.), *Perspectives on dyslexia. Vol. 2: Cognition, language and treatment* (pp. 17-42). Chichester, UK: John Wiley.

Rosenberger, P.B. (1992). Dyslexia -- Is it a disease? *The New England Journal of Medicine, 326,* 192-193.

Royer, J.M., Greene, B.A., & Sinatra, G.M. (1987). The sentence verification technique: A practical procedure for testing comprehension. *Journal of Reading, 30,* 414-422.

Royer, J.M., Hastings, C.N., & Hook, C. (1979). A sentence verification technique for measuring reading comprehension. *Journal of Reading Behavior, 11,* 355-363.

Royer, J.M., Kulhavy, R.W., Lee, J.B., & Peterson, S.E. (1986). The sentence verification technique as a measure of listening and reading comprehension. *Educational and Psychological Research, 6,* 299-314.

Royer, J.M., Lynch, D.J., Hambleton, R.K., & Bulgareli, C. (1984). Using the sentence verification technique to assess the comprehension of technical text as a function of subject matter expertise. *American Educational Research Journal, 21*, 839-869.

Royer, J.M., Sinatra, G.M., & Schumer, H. (1990) Patterns of individual differences in the development of listening and reading comprehension. *Contemporary Educational Psychology, 15*, 183-196.

Rutter, M., Tizard, J., & Whitmore, K. (Eds.). (1970). *Education, health, and behaviour.* London: Longman.

Rutter, M., & Yule, W. (1975). The concept of specific reading retardation. *Journal of Child Psychology and Psychiatry, 16*, 181-197.

Samuels, S.J. (1979). The method of repeated readings. *The Reading Teacher, 32*, 403-408.

Samuels, S.J., Miller, N.L., & Eisenberg, P. (1979). Practice effects on the unit of word recognition. *Journal of Educational Psychology, 71*, 514-520.

Sawyer, D.J,, & Fox, B.J. (Eds.). (1991). *Phonological awareness: Recent advances in theory and research.* New York: Springer-Verlag.

Scardamalia, M., & Bereiter, C. (in press). Schools as knowledge-building communities. In S. Strauss (Ed.), *Human development.* Norwood, NJ: Ablex.

Scardamalia, M., Bereiter, C., McLean, R., Swallow, J., & Woodruff, E. (1989). Computer-supported intentional learning environments. *Journal of Educational Computing Research, 5*, 51-68.

Seidenberg, M. (1985). The time course of phonological code activation in two writing systems. *Cognition, 19*, 1-30.

Shaywitz, B.A., Shaywitz, S.E., Liberman, I.Y., Fletcher, J.M., Shankweiler, D.P., Duncan, J.S., Katz, L., Liberman, A.M., Francis, D.J., Dreyer, L.G., Crain, S., Brady, S., Fowler, A., Kier, L.E., Rosenfield, N.S., Gore, J.C., & Makuch, R.W. (1991). Neurolinguistic and biologic mechanisms in dyslexia. In D.D. Duane & D.B. Gray (Eds.), *The reading brain: The biological basis of dyslexia* (pp. 27-52). Parkton, MD: York Press.

Shaywitz, S.E., Escobar, M.D., Shaywitz, B.A., Fletcher, J.M., & Makuch, R. (1992). Evidence that dyslexia may represent the lower tail of a normal distribution of reading ability. *The New England Journal of Medicine, 326*, 145-150.

Shepard, L.A. (1980). An evaluation of the regression discrepancy method for identifying children with learning disabilities. *The Journal of Special Education, 14*, 79-91.

Siegel, L.S. (1984). A longitudinal study of a hyperlexic child: Hyperlexia as a language disorder. *Neuropsychologia, 22*, 577-585.

Siegel, L.S. (1989). IQ is irrelevant to the definition of learning disabilities. *Journal of Learning Disabilities, 22*, 469-478, 486.

Siegel, L.S. (1990). IQ and learning disabilities: R.I.P. In H.L. Swanson & B. Keogh (Eds.), *Learning disabilities: Theoretical and research issues* (pp. 111-128). Hillsdale, NJ: Lawrence Erlbaum.

Siegel, L.S. (this volume). Alice in IQ land or why IQ is still irrelevant to learning disabilities.

Siegel, L.S., & Ryan, E.B. (1988). Development of grammatical sensitivity, phonological, and short-term memory skills in normally achieving and learning disabled children. *Developmental Psychology, 24*, 28-37.

Siegler, R.S. (1992). The other Alfred Binet. *Developmental Psychology, 28*, 179-190.

Smiley, S.S., Oakley, D.D., Worthen, D., Campione, J.C., & Brown, A.L. (1977). Recall of thematically relevant material by adolescent good and poor readers as a function of written versus oral presentation. *Journal of Educational Psychology, 69*, 381-387.

Snowling, M.J. (1983). The comparison of acquired and developmental disorders of reading -- A discussion. *Cognition, 14*, 105-118.

Snowling, M.J., & Frith, U. (1986). Comprehension in "hyperlexic" readers. *Journal of Experimental Child Psychology, 42*, 392-415.

Stanovich, K.E. (1980). Toward an interactive-compensatory model of individual differences in the development of reading fluency. *Reading Research Quarterly, 16*, 32-71.

Stanovich, K.E. (1984). The interactive-compensatory model of reading: A confluence of developmental, experimental and educational psychology. *Remedial and Special Education, 5*, 11-19.

Stanovich, K.E. (1986). Matthew effects in reading: Some consequences of individual differences in the acquisition of literacy. *Reading Research Quarterly, 21*, 360-407.

Stanovich, K.E. (1988a). Explaining the differences between the dyslexic and garden-variety poor readers: The phonological-core variable-difference model. *Journal of Learning Disabilities, 21,* 590-612.

Stanovich, K.E. (1988b). The right and wrong places to look for the cognitive locus of reading disability. *Annals of Dyslexia, 38,* 154-177.

Stanovich, K.E. (Ed.) (1988c). *Children's reading and the development of phonological awareness.* Detroit, MI: Wayne State University Press.

Stanovich, K.E. (1991). Discrepancy definitions of reading disability: Has intelligence led us astray? *Reading Research Quarterly, 26,* 7-29.

Stanovich, K.E. (this volume). Problems in the differential diagnosis of reading disabilities.

Stanovich, K.E., Nathan, R.G., & Vala-Rossi, M. (1986). Developmental changes in the cognitive correlates of reading ability and the developmental lag hypothesis. *Reading Research Quarterly, 21,* 261-283.

Stanovich, K.E., Nathan, R.G., & Zolman, J.E. (1988). The developmental lag hypothesis in reading: Longitudinal and matched reading-level comparisons. *Child Development, 59,* 71-86.

Stanovich, K.E., West, R.F., & Feeman, D.J. (1981). A longitudinal study of sentence context effects in second grade children: Tests of an interactive compensatory model. *Journal of Experimental Child Psychology, 38,* 175-190.

Stemberger, J.P. (1985). *The lexicon in a model of language production.* New York: Garland Publishing, Inc.

Sternberg, R.J. (1986). *Intelligence applied: Understanding and increasing your intellectual skills.* San Diego: Harcourt, Brace, Jovanovich.

Sticht, T.G. (1972). Learning by listening. In R.O. Freedle & J.B. Carroll (Eds.), *Language comprehension and the acquisition of knowledge,* (pp. 285-314). New York: John Wiley.

Sticht, T.G., Beck, L.J., Hauke, R.N., Kleiman, G.M., & James, J.H. (1974). *Auding and reading: A developmental model.* Alexandria, VA: Human Resources Research Organization.

Sticht, T.G., & James, J.H. (1984). Listening and reading. In P.D. Pearson, R. Barr, M.L. Kamil, & P. Mosenthal (Eds.), *Handbook of reading research* (pp. 293-317). New York: Longman.

Swanson, H.L. (1989). Phonological processes and other routes. *Journal of Learning Disabilities, 22,* 493-497.

Tallal, P. (1980). Auditory temporal perception, phonics, and reading disabilities in children. *Brain and Language, 9,* 182-198.

Tannen, D. (1985). Relative focus on involvement in oral and written discourse. In D.R. Olson, N. Torrance, & A. Hildyard (Eds.), *Literacy, language, and learning: The nature and consequences of reading and writing* (pp. 124-147). New York: Cambridge University Press.

Thorndike, R.L. (1963). *The concepts of over- and under-achievement.* New York: Columbia University Teachers College.

Thorndike, R.L., Hagen, E.P., & Sattler, J.M. (1986). *Stanford-Binet Intelligence Scale:* Fourth edition. Chicago: Riverside.

Torgesen, J.K. (1989). Why IQ is relevant to the definition of learning disabilities. *Journal of Learning Disabilities, 22,* 484-486.

Townsend, D.J., Carrithers, C., & Bever, T.G. (1987). Listening and reading processes in college- and middle school-age readers. In R. Horowitz & S.J. Samuels (Eds.), *Comprehending oral and written language* (pp. 217-242). New York: Academic Press.

Treiman, R., Goswami, U., & Bruck, M. (1990). Not all nonwords are alike: Implications for reading development and theory. *Memory & Cognition, 18,* 559-567.

Treiman, R., & Hirsh-Pasek, K. (1985). Are there qualitative differences in reading behavior between dyslexic and normal readers? *Memory & Cognition, 13,* 357-364.

Tunmer, W.E., & Hoover, W.A. (1992). Cognitive and linguistic factors in learning to read. In P.B. Gough, L.C. Ehri, & R. Treiman (Eds.), *Reading acquisition* (pp. 175-214). Hillsdale, NJ: Lawrence Erlbaum.

Tunmer, W.E., & Hoover, W.A. (this volume). Components of variance models of language-related factors in reading disability: A conceptual overview.

Tyler, A., & Nagy, W. (1990). Use of derivational morphology during reading. *Cognition, 36,* 17-34.

Vachek, J. (1973). *Written language.* The Hague: Mouton.

van Bon, W.H.J., Boksebeld, L.M., Font Freide, T.A.M., & van den Hurk, A.J.M. (1991). A comparison of three methods of reading-while-listening. *Journal of Learning Disabilities, 24,* 471-476.

Venezky, R.L. (1970). *The structure of English orthography.* The Hague: Mouton.

Vygotsky, L.S. (1978). *Mind in society: The development of higher psychological processes.* (Eds.: M. Cole, V. John-Steiner, S. Scribner, & E. Souberman). Cambridge, MA: Harvard University Press.

Vygotsky, L.S. (1986). *Thought and language* (A. Kozulin, Ed. & Trans.). Cambridge, MA: MIT Press. (Original work published 1934)

Wagner, R.K., & Torgesen, J.K. (1987). The nature of phonological processing and its causal role in the acquisition of reading skills. *Psychological Bulletin, 101,* 192-212.

Walker, L. (1975-1976). The comprehension of speech and writing. *Reading Research Quarterly, 9,* 144-167.

Walker, L. (1977). Comprehension of writing and spontaneous speech. *Visible Language, 11,* 37-51.

Waters, G.S., & Seidenberg, M.S. (1985). Spelling-sound effects in reading: Time-course and decision criteria. *Memory & Cognition, 13,* 557-572.

Wechsler, D. (1974). *Manual for the Wechsler Intelligence Scale for Children -- Revised.* New York: Psychological Corporation.

Wechsler, D. (1991). *Manual, WISC-III: Wechsler Intelligence Scale for Children -- Third Edition.* San Antonio: TX: Psychological Corporation.

Wilkinson, A.C. (1980). Children's understanding in reading and listening. *Journal of Educational Psychology, 72,* 561-574.

Wilkinson, A.C. (Ed.). (1983). *Classroom computers and cognitive science.* New York: Academic Press.

Wise, B.W., & Olson, R.K. (1992). How poor readers and spellers use interactive speech in a computerized spelling program. *Reading and Writing: An Interdisciplinary Journal, 4,* 145-163.

Wolf, M. (1991). Naming speed and reading: The contribution of the cognitive neurosciences. *Reading Research Quarterly, 26,* 123-141.

Wolf, T.H. (1973). *Alfred Binet.* Chicago, IL: University of Chicago Press.

Wong, B.Y.L. (Ed.). (1989). Is IQ necessary in the definition of learning disabilities? Introduction to the Special Series [Special issue]. *Journal of Learning Disabilities, 22,* 468-520.

Yule, W., Gold, R.D., & Busch, C. (1981). WISC-R correlates of academic attainment in 16 1/2 years. *British Journal of Educational Psychology, 51,* 237-240.

Yule, W., Lansdown, R., & Urbanowicz, M.-A. (1982). Predicting educational attainment from WISC-R in a primary school sample. *British Journal of Clinical Psychology, 21,* 43-46.

Yule, W., Rutter, M., Berger, M., & Thompson, J. (1974). Over- and under-achievement in reading: Distribution in the general population. *British Journal of Educational Psychology, 44,* 1-12.

Zadeh, L.A. (1971). Quantitative fuzzy semantics. *Information Sciences, 3,* 159-176.

Zadeh, L.A. (1984). Making computers think like people. *IEEE Spectrum, 21,* 26-32.

**PART II   ACCESS TO LANGUAGE-RELATED COMPONENT PROCESSES --
EDITORS' INTRODUCTION**

The term model or paradigm denotes at one level "the entire constellation of beliefs, values, techniques, and so on shared by the members of a given [scientific] community" and at a deeper level some "concrete puzzle-solutions" which "can replace explicit rules as a basis for the solution of the remaining puzzles of normal science" (Kuhn, 1970, p. 175). Components of reading acquisition and development generally refer to functionally identifiable language-related subsystems interacting with one another to produce more skilled, more complex reading behavior. Within this componential paradigm, the various chapters of this part generally focus on molar and molecular aspects of phonological processing and their differential effects on literacy acquisition and development.

Tunmer and Hoover explicate theoretical concepts and empirical evidence to support the deceptively Simple View of reading (see also, Gough, Ehri, & Treiman, 1992). Longitudinal data show that individual differences in reading comprehension can be explained maximally as the linear combination and the interaction of "decoding" (efficient access to the lexicon) and listening comprehension; and that there are developmental changes in the relative contribution of this combination. Tunmer and Hoover then detail arguments and data from various studies to consider three variant models to account for differences in decoding and listening comprehension. These mutually facilitating models are: their "environmental model" emphasizing exposure to print and "text-like language" prior to formal schooling and orthographic knowledge during schooling; their more broadly based [than the phonological-core variable-difference model of Stanovich] "phonological 'g' model" incorporating encoding, retrieving, manipulating and retaining phonological information; and their "cognitive-developmental model" incorporating intrinsic and extrinsic language-related factors especially executive control. Their longitudinal studies with path analyses show that the cognitive-developmental model best explains differences in a broad range of metalinguistic abilities necessary for both efficient access to the internal lexicon (decoding) and language comprehension.

Following the Kuhn tradition of hypothesis testing, **Olofsson** summarizes and discusses a series of Scandinavian (Sweden, Denmark and Norway) longitudinal studies of phonological processing and emergent literacy. Using confirmatory linear structural equation modelling analyses with latent variables, Olofsson suggests a "causal" chain from phonemic awareness to phonological recoding contributing to efficient reading and spelling.

On the relatedness of phonemic awareness and phonological awareness, **Morais** raises the pertinent and searching question of the parameters of the latter constraining those of the former. Awareness of articulatory gestures used in producing speech could be one aspect of phonological awareness. We would interpret this notion of abstract motor gestures as primitive linguistic units in the production of significant speech sounds (Liberman & Mattingly, 1985). In concrete terms, children with a past history of phonological disorders tend to be more at risk for later literacy difficulties, as reported in the chapter by **Dodd, Russell and Oerlemans**. Indeed, even for adolescents inefficient formation of phonological codes as shown by pseudoword repetition may also explain their reading and spelling difficulties as suggested by **Schwartz**. Morais brings a further fresh perspective in emphasizing that "conscious representation" of phonology and orthography are mutually supportive and may have the same underlying neural mechanisms.

R.M. Joshi and C.K. Leong (eds.), Reading Disabilities: Diagnosis and Component Processes, 133–134.
© 1993 *Kluwer Academic Publishers. Printed in the Netherlands.*

The mapping between phonology and alphabetic orthography is explored by **Hulme and Snowling** in their long-term cognitive, neuropsychological study of a dyslexic boy JM. In addition to invoking extant stage or phase models, Hulme and Snowling also consider JM's delayed and aberrant mapping between orthography and phonology within the parallel distributed processing (PDP) model. The PDP model can provide a unified and computationality explicit account of the knowledge and procedures needed in the acquisition, development and breakdown of word identification (see, Patterson, Seidenberg, & McClelland, 1989, for details). The distributed representations involve encoding orthographic and phonological knowledge in terms of the weights on connections between units; and the approach may generate patterns of dyslexic reading with further "puzzle-solutions" for component reading processes.

REFERENCES

Gough, P.B., Ehri, L.C., & Treiman, R. (Eds.). (1992). *Reading acquisition*. Hillsdale, NJ: Lawrence Erlbaum.

Kuhn, T.S. (1970). *The structure of scientific revolutions* (2nd ed. enlarged). Chicago: The University of Chicago Press.

Liberman, A.M., & Mattingly, I.G. (1985). The motor theory of speech perception revised. *Cognition, 21,* 1-36.

Patterson, K., Seidenberg, M.S., & McClelland, J.L. (1989). Connections and disconnections: Acquired dyslexia in a computational model of reading processes. In R.G.M. Morris (Ed.) *Parallel distributed processing: Implications for psychology and neurobiology* (pp. 131-181). Oxford, UK: Clarendon Press.

COMPONENTS OF VARIANCE MODELS OF LANGUAGE-RELATED FACTORS IN READING DISABILITY: A CONCEPTUAL OVERVIEW

WILLIAM E. TUNMER   and   WESLEY A. HOOVER
Massey University   Southwest Educational
Palmerston North   Development Laboratory
New Zealand   Austin, Texas, 78701 USA

ABSTRACT: We argue in this chapter that reading skill is best described as the product of decoding and listening comprehension skills. After summarizing both the theoretical arguments and empirical evidence in support of this simple view of the proximal causes of reading, we consider the question of reading failure, reviewing evidence bearing on three models that attempt to account for differences in the two proximal causes of reading. The environmental model proposes that extrinsic factors are primarily responsible for early reading difficulties, focusing on inadequate exposure to print and text-like language prior to schooling and inadequate instruction during schooling. The phonological "g" model focuses on intrinsic factors, hypothesizing that differences in both decoding and listening comprehension stem from constitutional differences in the phonological processing component of working memory. The cognitive-developmental proposes that beginning reading difficulties are the result of both intrinsic and extrinsic factors. This model focuses on intrinsic differences in the capacity of the central executive that operates control processes in working memory, holding that developmental differences in control processing ability produce differences in developing metalinguistic abilities that are necessary for acquiring basic decoding and comprehension skills. Further, the cognitive-developmental model argues that insufficient exposure to the kinds of language activities that focus children's attention on the structural features of spoken language are also linked to reading difficulties. After reviewing the available evidence, we conclude that the most supportable model is the cognitive-developmental model.

Introduction

In this chapter we present three components of variance models of language-related factors in reading disability. Each of the models incorporates the simple view of reading, a model of the proximal causes of reading performance differences. In the first section of the paper we briefly examine the theoretical arguments and empirical evidence in support of the simple view. We then describe how each of the components of variance models attempts to account for deficiencies in the proximal causes of reading difficulties. The first model, the environmental model, focuses on extrinsic factors; the second model, the phonological "g" model, focuses on intrinsic factors; and the third model, the cognitive-developmental model, proposes that beginning reading difficulties are the result of both intrinsic and extrinsic factors. Despite the different theoretical orientations of the models, they should not be seen as mutually exclusive. It is possible that reading disability comes about, or is "triggered," in more than one way.

R.M. Joshi and C.K. Leong (eds.), Reading Disabilities: Diagnosis and Component Processes, 135–173.

The Simple View

The simple view (Gough & Tunmer, 1986; Hoover & Gough, 1990; Juel, Griffith & Gough, 1986; Tunmer & Hoover, 1992) proposes that differences in reading comprehension are a function of the product of two factors, decoding (i.e., word recognition) and listening comprehension (see Figure 1). Each of these factors is assumed to be necessary, but not sufficient, for success in reading. Stated simply, if a child does not understand the language being read, he or she will have trouble understanding the text. Similarly, if a child cannot recognize the words of text, he or she will again have trouble understanding the text.

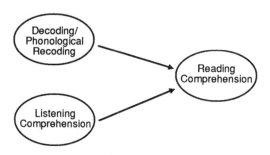

Figure 1. Model of proximal causes of individual differences in reading.

The simple view equates decoding with efficient access of the mental lexicon, regardless of how such access is accomplished. However, there is substantial evidence, consistent with the simple view, that the development of decoding skills in beginning readers of alphabetic writing systems is based on phonological recoding, the ability to translate letters and letter patterns into phonological forms. Beginning readers must eventually discover that there are systematic correspondences between elements of written and spoken language to advance beyond an initial stage of reading in which words are recognized by selective association (the pairing of a partial stimulus cue to a response) (Byrne, 1991, 1992; Byrne & Fielding-Barnsley, 1989; Gough & Hillinger, 1980; Gough & Juel, 1991; Gough, Juel & Roper-Schneider, 1983). There is now considerable convergent evidence indicating that knowledge of grapheme-phoneme correspondences (as measured by pseudoword naming; e.g., *toin, sark*) is intimately related to the acquisition of basic reading skills (Backman, Bruck, Hebert & Seidenberg, 1984; Hoover & Gough, 1990; Jorm, Share, MacLean & Matthews, 1984; Juel, 1988; Juel, Griffith & Gough, 1986; Lundberg & Hoien, 1991; Manis & Morrison, 1985; Olson, Wise, Conners, Rack & Fulker, 1989; Perfetti & Hogaboam, 1975; Snowling, 1980, 1981; Stanovich, Cunningham & Feeman, 1984; Thompson, 1986; Tunmer, 1989; Tunmer, Herriman & Nesdale, 1988; Tunmer & Nesdale, 1985; Vellutino & Scanlon, 1987b).

There is even evidence suggesting that phonological recoding ability is essential for acquiring word-specific knowledge. In a study of beginning readers, Gough and Walsh (1991) found a positive correlation between pseudoword naming and exception word naming ($r = .66$). A scatterplot of the data revealed that there were many children who performed reasonably well on the pseudoword naming test but recognized few exception words.

However, there were no children who performed poorly on the pseudoword naming test but well on the exception word naming test. These results suggest that phonological recoding ability is necessary but not sufficient for the development of word-specific knowledge. Consistent with this interpretation, Gough and Walsh also found that first grade readers with higher levels of phonological recoding skill required fewer trials to learn unfamiliar exception words than did children with lower levels of phonological recoding ability.

In support of the simple view are results from a longitudinal study by Hoover and Gough (1990) which showed that phonological recoding and listening comprehension, and the interaction between these two variables, accounted for 73% of the variance in reading comprehension in first grade, 75% in second grade, 85% in third grade, and 90% in fourth grade (see Table 1). Similar to findings reported in earlier studies (e.g., Juel, Griffith & Gough, 1986; Sticht & James, 1984; Tunmer, 1989), the results also revealed developmental changes in the relative contributions of recoding and listening comprehension to the variance in reading comprehension, with recoding accounting for more of the variance in the lower grades. These results suggest that recoding skills are critical in the beginning stages of learning to read and that listening comprehension becomes more important at somewhat later stages after children have begun to master basic word recognition skills, and when children's reading materials have become more advanced in components of language that are common to both listening and reading comprehension (e.g., semantics, syntax, pragmatics).

Table 1. Summary of regression analyses in support of simple view.

Variable	Multiple R	Increase in R^2
	Grade 1 ($n = 210$)	
Linear	.849	.721**
Product	.856	.011*
	Grade 2 ($n = 206$)	
Linear	.853	.728**
Product	.865	.020**
	Grade 3 ($n = 86$)	
Linear	.884	.782**
Product	.921	.067**
	Grade 4 ($n = 55$)	
Linear	.922	.851**
Product	.948	.048**

Note:
Linear = Linear combination of phonological recoding and listening comprehension.
Product = Product of phonological recoding and listening comprehension.
*$p < .005$
**$p < .001$

This latter finding is related to another prediction of the model, which is that beginning readers should be able to read as well as they can listen provided that inadequate recoding skills are not holding them back. That is, when listening comprehension is represented on the horizontal axis and reading comprehension on the vertical axis, the model predicts that at increasing levels of recoding skill there should be positive slope values between listening and reading comprehension of increasing magnitudes. In addition, the intercept values for the slopes should all be zero because reading comprehension should be zero if listening comprehension is zero irrespective of the level of recoding skill. These predictions were confirmed by Hoover and Gough (1990).

A third prediction of the model is that within the population of poor readers, recoding and listening comprehension should be negatively correlated. If reading comprehension is the product of phonological recoding and listening comprehension, then to achieve a low score on reading comprehension, a child who performs at a high level on recoding must achieve a low score on listening comprehension, and vice versa (poor reading comprehension also occurs when both recoding and listening comprehension skills are weak). Thus, for increasing sample reductions based on successively removing from the sample students of higher levels of reading comprehension skill, correlations between recoding and listening comprehension should go from positive to negative. This prediction was also confirmed by Hoover and Gough (1990).

Another finding reported in the study was that the correlation between phonological recoding and listening comprehension increased with grade level (from 0.42 in first grade to 0.72 in fourth grade). Hoover and Gough suggest that this developmental pattern is probably a consequence of the reciprocal nature of the relationship between reading and other skills (in this case, decoding and listening comprehension; see Figure 2). The process of becoming a fluent reader itself produces "spinoff" skills that provide the basis for further growth in reading and other areas, a phenomenon referred to as *reciprocal causation* (Stanovich, 1986). As children become better readers, both the amount and difficulty of the material they read increases, which leads to further development of vocabulary knowledge, syntactic knowledge, and general knowledge (all of which improves listening comprehension), and to increased knowledge of the orthographic cipher (which improves decoding skills).

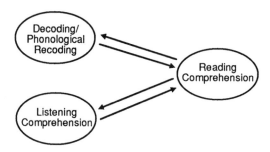

Figure. 2. Reciprocally facilitating relationships between reading and the proximal causes of reading performance differences.

If there are many children in the population under study with relatively severe listening comprehension deficiencies (due to low intelligence, impoverished early language environment, or hearing difficulties), it is likely that listening comprehension will directly influence the development of phonological recoding/decoding, as shown in Figure 3. This may come about in a number of ways. For example, children who are unable to discriminate easily between different speech sounds (perhaps because of a history of recurrent otitis media) will likely encounter difficulty in segmenting speech, which, in turn, will hamper the development of their phonological recoding skill (Morais, 1991).

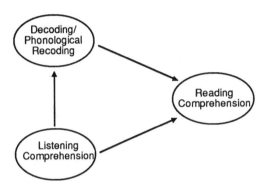

Figure 3. Direct influence of listening comprehension ability on the development of decoding/phonological recoding skills.

Relatedly, children with deficient morphophonemic rule knowledge will be disadvantaged in using this knowledge to break the orthographic code of an alphabetic writing system such as English. For example, the letter *s* represents regular noun plural inflection, even though it is not always realized as the /s/ phoneme, as is true of words like *dogs* and *cars,* in which the final sound is /z/. However, for beginning readers with morphophonemic rule knowledge it is not necessary to learn the exceptions on a case-by-case basis. In acquiring spoken English, these children unconsciously learn a phonological rule that specifies that plural inflection is realized as /s/ when it follows a voiceless stop consonant, as in *cats,* and as /z/ when it follows a voiced phoneme, as in *dogs.* When children with such knowledge confront an unfamiliar word, such as the nonsense word spelled *z-o-g-s,* they automatically know that it is pronounced /zogz/, not /zogs/.

Poorly developed lexical representations will also limit the development of children's decoding skills. When beginning readers apply their incomplete knowledge of grapheme-phoneme correspondences to unfamiliar words (including irregular ones), the result will often be close enough to the correct phonological form that they can correctly identify the word and thus increase both their word-specific knowledge and their knowledge of grapheme-phoneme correspondences. However, this can occur only if the unfamiliar word is in their *listening* vocabulary (for related arguments and supportive evidence, see Vellutino & Denckla, 1991; Vellutino & Scanlon, 1987a, 1987b, 1989).

Deficiencies in syntactic knowledge may also impair the development of decoding skills by limiting beginning readers' ability to use sentence contexts as an aid to word identification (Vellutino & Denckla, 1991; Vellutino & Scanlon, 1987a, 1987b). Syntactic knowledge enables beginning readers to monitor accuracy in word identification by providing them with immediate feedback when their responses to the words of text fail to conform to the surrounding grammatical context (such as when their attempted response results in either a violation of a strict sub-categorization rule, which governs the syntactic structures into which a word can enter, or a violation of a selectional restriction rule, which places constraints on how words of different form classes can be combined). Beginning readers may also combine knowledge of the constraints of sentence context with incomplete graphophonemic information to identify unfamiliar words (which further increases their knowledge of grapheme-phoneme correspondences) and to discover homographic spelling patterns (letter sequences that have different pronunciations in different words; e.g., *own,* as in *clown* and *blown*; and *ear,* as in *bear* and *clear).* When confronted with an unfamiliar word containing a homographic spelling pattern, beginning readers who have acquired knowledge of such patterns can generate alternative pronunciations until one matches a word in their listening vocabulary.

Although severe deficiencies in oral language may result in listening comprehension having a direct influence on the development of decoding skills, we shall limit our discussion in the following sections to children who *unexpectedly* fail to learn to read. These are children who satisfy the standard exclusionary criteria for reading disability. Their difficulties in reading are assumed not to be due to factors that would be expected to cause problems in reading, and in other areas as well. These factors include intellectual impairment, gross neurological disorders, severe physical disabilities, sensory deficits, attentional problems, emotional and social difficulties, poor motivation, inadequate early language environment, socioeconomic disadvantage, poor school attendance, and inadequate or inappropriate school instruction. With respect to language development, it is important to note that the children under consideration are "not ostensibly impaired in language and suffer no gross debilitating disorders in this function" (Vellutino & Scanlon, 1982, p. 191). If some aspect of language processing is causally related to reading disability, it must be of a more subtle nature.

For children who satisfy standard exclusionary criteria, the key question, then, is what causes deficiencies in the two proximal causes of reading performance differences, decoding and listening comprehension? Recent theories of reading disability have tended to reject non-verbal deficit theories in favor of explanations that focus on deficiencies in aspects of language processing. Vellutino and Scanlon (1982, 1987a), for example, review the theoretical arguments and empirical evidence in support of theories of reading disability that assume deficits in visual processing, cross-modal transfer, serial memory, attention, association learning, or rule learning and conclude that all these theories are untenable. They propose instead that reading disability is due primarily to deficits in verbal processing. We agree with this general conclusion and for that reason the models we describe in the following sections focus on language-related factors in reading disability.

The Environmental Model

The environmental model, which is illustrated in Figure 4, proposes that inadequate exposure to print-related activities and text-like language prior to schooling and inadequate instruction during schooling are responsible for differences in early reading. Reading difficulties are thought to be the result of experiential factors, not vaguely specified constitutional shortcomings.

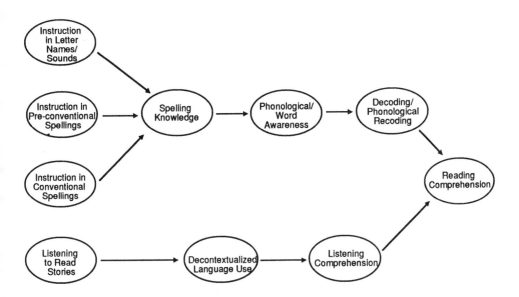

Figure 4. The environmental model.

In general the practice of defining reading disability by exclusion is problematic. With respect to environmental factors, it is extremely difficult to completely rule out the possible adverse effects of all such factors because some may be present to a limited degree and therefore operate in a very subtle manner. Morrison (1991), for example, argues that because of the use of inadequate assessment procedures, "children with significant though non-traumatic emotional problems could easily be included in samples of children selected for studies of reading disability" (p. 167). This leaves open the possibility that the poor reading performance of some "reading disabled" children is due to family or social problems that are not sufficiently severe to produce the kind of readily identifiable emotional disturbance that would exclude these children from consideration.

With regard to educational deficits, Stanovich (1991) notes that "very little effort is expended in ascertaining whether adequate instruction has been provided..." and that "in actual educational practice the key defining feature [of reading disability] is a discrepancy between reading achievement and aptitude as measured by an individually administered intelligence test" (p.9). Similarly, Vellutino and Denckla (1991) state that "virtually all of the research available has failed to evaluate or adequately control for the environmental and/or educational deficits that may cause a reading disorder" (p.603).

A consequence of the discrepancy-based assessment procedure is that reading disabled children are not identified until after they have been exposed to reading instruction for 1 to 3 years, in which case inadequate or inappropriate instruction cannot be ruled out as a possible cause (Ehri, 1989). This is an important consideration because research has shown that learning to read is not a "natural" process that occurs simply through exposure to print (Masonheimer, Drum & Ehri, 1984). Byrne (1991, 1992) has reported the results of a series of experiments demonstrating that pre-readers are largely ignorant of phonological segments, adopting instead a "nonanalytic" strategy in which new words are learned by associating some distinguishing feature of the printed word with its spoken counterpart as a whole. He argues that the failure of pre-readers to develop analytic links between print and speech results from the extension of this natural strategy, a strategy that can, however, be altered by explicit instruction in phonological awareness and letter-phoneme relations (Byrne & Fielding-Barnsley, 1989).

Research by Tunmer and Nesdale (1985) suggests that Byrne's experimental findings can be extended to natural classroom settings. In a study of the relation of phonemic segmentation skill to beginning reading achievement, they examined the reading achievement of first-grade children from classes (six altogether) that differed markedly in the instructional strategy used by the teacher. Classroom observations and teacher interviews revealed that three teachers employed the "psycholinguistic" approach to teaching reading in which very little incidental or formal instruction in phonological recoding skills was provided in either reading or spelling. This approach reflects the view that the amount of graphophonemic knowledge required by beginning readers is extremely small. In contrast, the three remaining teachers used a combination of different methodologies, including a heavy emphasis on the teaching of phonological recoding skills. Despite the fact that the six classes were selected from three schools located relatively close to one another in an average socioeconomic status area, the reading performance (as measured by separate tests of real word decoding, pseudoword decoding, and reading comprehension) of the children from the classes that included the teaching of recoding skills was strikingly superior to that of the children from the classes that emphasized the exclusive use of contextual guessing and sight word learning. The instructional methodology that is used by the teacher can have an enormous impact on the development of basic reading skills (see also Seymour & Elder, 1986).

Returning to the model shown in Figure 4, a leading proponent of the upper portion of this model is Linnea Ehri (1984, 1986, 1987, 1989). She argues that children who are exposed to instruction (including instruction of a less formal nature) in letter names/sounds and spelling are able to use their developing knowledge of letters and printed words as mediators in conceptualizing separate phonemes and words. This, in turn, enables them to acquire basic decoding skills. Ehri (1989) rejects the view that the phonological deficits of poor readers are the result of more basic phonological deficiencies that existed in the children before reading instruction began (see the model of reading disability described in the next section). Rather, she maintains that it is instruction that fails to provide beginning readers with full knowledge of the spelling system that is responsible for limited reading and spelling development and limited phonological awareness, not speech-based neurological deficits. Children who lack the skills necessary to succeed in reading are more likely to develop inappropriate or ineffective learning strategies (such as exclusive reliance on contextual guessing to identify unfamiliar words) and associated feelings of learned helplessness, which, in turn, contribute to further learning problems (a phenomenon referred to as *negative Matthew effects;* Stanovich, 1986). In short, these children "learn to be learning disabled" (Clay, 1987).

According to Ehri (1989), then, orthographic knowledge is essential for children to be able to manipulate aspects of speech. This suggests that phonological awareness, the ability to decompose spoken words into their constituent phonemic elements, is a consequence of exposure to print, a view that would appear to conflict with the widely held view that deficient phonological awareness is a major cause of reading disability (see Tunmer & Rohl, 1991, for a review of research). As evidence in support of this claim Ehri (1989) cites the results of several studies showing that orthographic knowledge influences children's performance on phonemic segmentation tasks. Tunmer and Nesdale (1982, 1985) found that in a phoneme-counting task beginning readers were much more likely to make overshoot errors (i.e., errors in which the response given exceeds the number of phonemes in the item) on orally presented words containing digraphs (letter pairs that represent single phonemes; e.g., *sh, oo*) than on similar words not containing digraphs. Similarly, Ehri and Wilce (1980) found that fourth-grade children were more likely to make overshoot errors on a word like *pitch* than on the matched control word *rich*.

Ehri (1989) discounts findings from studies showing that training in phonological awareness produces significant experimental group advantages in reading achievement because, she maintains, such training was combined with *spelling* training that teaches learners how to symbolize sounds with letters. For example, in the frequently cited study by Bradley and Bryant (1985), the group of children that received training in *both* sound categorization and spelling with plastic letters outperformed the control group on tests of reading and spelling achievement, whereas the group that received training only in sound categorization failed to show significant gains over the control group. As Wagner and Torgesen (1987) point out, it cannot be determined from Bradley and Bryant's (1985) study whether a group that received training only in spelling with plastic letters would have made gains comparable to that of the group that received training in both sound categorization and spelling.

Longitudinal studies have shown that phonological awareness in children prior to school entry is related to later reading achievement even when children showing any preschool reading ability are excluded (Bradley & Bryant, 1985; Tunmer, Herriman & Nesdale, 1988), or when the influence of preschool reading ability is statistically controlled (Vellutino & Scanlon, 1987b). However, Ehri (1989) points out that preliterate children may nevertheless possess substantial knowledge of letter names and sounds, knowledge which may enable them to acquire rudimentary phonological awareness skills. Consistent with this suggestion, Tunmer, Herriman and Nesdale (1988) found a positive correlation between letter-name knowledge and preliterate phonemic segmentation ability ($r=0.38$). Ehri (1989) further argues that prior to school entry children may be exposed to activities in the home that lead to the development of preliterate phonological awareness. These activities include looking at books and playing games that increase knowledge of letter names and their relation to sounds in words (e.g., "Z is for Zebra"), playing rhyming and sound analysis games that increase phonological sensitivity, and manipulating movable letters to form preconventional spellings of words (e.g., *FRE* for *fairy*). Ehri (1989) suggests that these "informal experiences with print ... may account for the variation in phonemic awareness scores observed among pre-readers before they begin kindergarten" (p.363). Finally, Ehri (1989) notes that a post hoc analysis of the data from Bradley and Bryant's (1985) longitudinal study revealed that only a minority of pre-readers who performed poorly on a phonological awareness task at school entry became disabled readers. On the basis of this finding, Ehri (1989) concludes that "among pre-readers who have not yet begun instruction, children who subsequently become dyslexic may differ relatively little from non-dyslexics" (p.363).

Ehri (1986) also discounts findings from studies employing reading-age match designs which show that younger, normal readers perform better than older, poor readers on measures of phonological awareness (e.g., Bradley & Bryant, 1978). She cites research indicating that as reading disabled children grow older, their spelling age falls increasingly behind their reading age. This means that if normal and backward readers are matched on reading age, the backward readers will be behind the normal readers in spelling ability. Thus, argues Ehri (1986), "dyslexics may exhibit phonological deficits because they have not advanced as far in acquiring working knowledge of the orthographic system as a map for speech.... In short, poor spelling skill may be the cause of phonological deficits rather than phonological deficits being an aberrant property of dyslexics and causing their poorer reading and spelling performance" (p. 173).

To investigate this claim, Rohl and Tunmer (1988) used a spelling-age match design to determine whether deficits in phonologically-related skills were related to difficulties in acquiring basic spelling knowledge. Poor fifth-grade spellers, average third-grade spellers, and good second grade spellers matched on a standardized spelling test, and a group of good fifth-grade spellers matched by chronological age with the poor fifth-grade spellers, were administered a phoneme segmentation test containing 20 non-digraph pseudowords (e.g., *ip*, *wob*, *slint*) and an experimental spelling test containing 72 words, 18 of each of the following four types: exception (e.g., *have*), ambiguous (e.g., *town*), regular (e.g., *rush*), and pseudowords (e.g., *teb*). In support of their hypothesis, Rohl and Tunmer (1988) found that when compared with the poor fifth-grade spellers, the average third-grade and good second-grade spellers performed significantly better on the phonological awareness test, made fewer errors in spelling pseudowords, and made spelling errors that were more phonetically accurate. Interestingly, when percentage of orthographically legal misspellings to total errors was the dependent variable, there were no significant differences among the three spelling-matched groups. All three groups performed well, suggesting that even the poor spellers were familiar with legal English letter sequences. Their errors, which were poor phonetic representations of the target words, conformed reasonably well to rules about how letters can be combined, thus emphasizing the specific phonological problems of these children. These findings appear to contradict Ehri's view that it is lack of orthographic knowledge *per se* that causes deficits in phonological awareness and related skills.

In support of this conclusion are the results of a training study by Lundberg, Frost and Petersen (1988) indicating that exposure to print is not a *necessary* condition for the development of phonological awareness, as Ehri (1989) seems to claim. They found that preliterate children with very limited letter-name knowledge could be successfully trained in phonological awareness skills during their kindergarten year without the use of letters. These children and a matched control group were given spelling and reading tests in first and second grade. The training group outperformed the control group only in spelling in first grade, but in both spelling and reading in second grade. Ehri (1989) suggests that a possible explanation of this pattern of results is that phonological awareness training *combined* with spelling development, which then provided the basis for progress in reading.

There is, however, an alternative explanation. Because phonemic segmentation ability has been shown to influence reading achievement through phonological recoding skill (Juel, Griffith & Gough, 1986; Stanovich, Cunningham & Feeman, 1984; Tunmer, 1989; Tunmer & Nesdale, 1985), and because children tend to rely heavily on nonanalytic word recognition strategies in the early stages of learning to read (see earlier discussion), it is possible that differences in reading performance would have been obtained in first grade if a measure of phonological recoding had been used. Evidence in support of this suggestion comes from a longitudinal study of beginning reading by Jorm, Share, MacLean and Matthews (1984). They formed two groups of first-grade readers who were matched on sight word vocabulary, verbal intelligence, gender and school at the end of their first year of instruction but differed in phonological recoding skill. They found that the difference in phonological recoding ability gave rise to steadily increasing differences in future reading achievement that favored the group that initially had higher levels of phonological recoding skill.

Ehri (1989) states that "according to our theory of printed word learning, when readers know the spelling system, they can store the spellings of individual words as visual *phonemic* symbols for the pronunciations" and that "letters enter memory by being interpreted as symbols for *phonemes*" (p.359, emphasis added). A key feature of this view, however, is that children learning to read must be phonologically aware, for how else could they discover connections between letters and *phonemes*? Because there is no one-to-one correspondence between phonemes and segments of the acoustic signal, it is not possible to pronounce in isolation the sound corresponding to most phonemes. Consequently, most letter sounds and letter names are only imprecise physical analogues of the phonemes in spoken words. Whether children learn to associate the sound "duh" or the name "dee" or both with the letter *d*, they must still be able to segment the sound or name to make the connection between the letter *d* and the phoneme /d/. This suggests that Ehri's (1989) argument that spelling knowledge is a prerequisite for the development of phonological awareness may be circular.

On logical grounds alone, it would appear that at least some minimal level of phonemic segmentation ability is necessary for children to be able to acquire knowledge of the correspondences between phonemes and graphemes. Supporting this claim are the results of studies in which scatterplots were generated of the relationship between phonological awareness and phonological recoding, as measured by pseudoword decoding (Juel, Griffith & Gough, 1986; Tunmer, 1989; Tunmer & Nesdale, 1985). The scatterplots revealed that although many children performed well on phoneme segmentation but poorly on pseudoword decoding, no children performed poorly on phoneme segmentation but well on pseudoword decoding. Explicit phonological awareness appears to be necessary, but not sufficient, for acquiring phonological recoding skill.

A closely related finding is that some minimal level of phonological awareness appears to be necessary for children to profit from letter-*name* and/or letter-*sound* knowledge in the acquisition of phonological recoding skill. Tunmer and Lally (1986) conducted a training study in which four groups of pre-readers who varied orthogonally in letter-name knowledge and phonemic segmentation skill received four computer-monitored training sessions in basic word recognition skills. The computer program was designed to draw children's attention to grapheme-phoneme correspondences by presenting them with sequences of words in which only one letter or letter group was varied at a time while all else remained constant. In a word-recognition post-test of the generalization of the correspondences that were taught, the high letter-name/high phonemic segmentation group performed significantly better than any of the other three groups. The latter groups (low letter-name, low phonemic segmentation; high letter-name, low phonemic segmentation; low letter-name, high phonemic segmentation) did not differ significantly from one another. This finding was confirmed in natural classroom settings by Tunmer, Herriman and Nesdale (1988) who found that beginning readers with low phonological awareness scores performed poorly on a test of phonological recoding skill regardless of their level of letter-name knowledge.

Similar results were obtained by Byrne and Fielding-Barnsley (1989) in the series of experiments mentioned earlier. Preschool children with no knowledge of reading or the sounds of individual letters were able to achieve criterion performance on a word learning task *only* when letter-sound training was accompanied by training in phonemic segmentation. On the basis of this finding Byrne (1991) concluded that "learning the sounds that the letters represent is not sufficient.... It needs to be supplemented by appropriate insights into segment separability and segment identity" (p. 83).

This finding was recently confirmed in a training study by Ball and Blackman (1991). Two groups of kindergarten children received training in letter names and letter sounds but only one of these groups received training in phonological awareness as well. Results indicated that only the children in the group that received phonological awareness instruction showed significant gains over a control group in spelling and reading performance, and phonemic segmentation skill. The group that received instruction in letter names and letter sounds alone did not differ from the control group on post-test measures of reading, spelling and phoneme segmentation. In summary, contrary to Ehri's (1989) views, it appears that knowledge of letter names and/or sounds is neither necessary for acquiring phonological awareness (as demonstrated by the training study by Lundberg, Frost & Petersen, 1988) nor is it sufficient (as demonstrated by the training studies by Ball & Blackman, 1991; Byrne & Fielding-Barnsley, 1989; Tunmer & Lally, 1986).

The likelihood that some minimal level of phonemic segmentation ability is necessary for learning to read does not preclude the possibility that some skills that are acquired or improved as a result of learning to read and spell may greatly improve performance on phonological awareness tasks (Tunmer & Rohl, 1991). Some of these spinoff skills, which include the ability to maintain and operate on verbal material in working memory, to generate orthographic images, and to apply phoneme-grapheme correspondence rules, may even be necessary to perform more advanced phonological awareness tasks (see Figure 5).

Figure 5. Reciprocal relationship between development of phonological awareness and learning to read.

The assumption of a reciprocal relationship between phonological awareness and learning to read would explain why children who have acquired basic reading skills tend to make overshoot errors on phonemic segmentation test items containing digraphs or silent letters (see earlier discussion). The children appear to segment on the basis of the number of letters in the word, or on the number of letters and letter groupings in the word that they believe (perhaps mistakenly) represent individual phonemes in the corresponding spoken word. The assumption of reciprocal causation would also explain why beginning readers (Yopp, 1988), illiterate adults (Morais, Cary, Alegria & Bertelson, 1979), and adults literate only in non-alphabetic orthographies (Read, Zhang, Nie & Ding, 1986) are unable to perform well on phonological awareness tasks that draw heavily on the spinoff skills of reading, such as the phoneme reversal task (say *pat* backwards) and the phoneme deletion task (say *skip* without the *kuh* sound). Such tasks may amount to little more than indirect measures of reading achievement (Tunmer, 1991; Tunmer & Rohl, 1991).

Although Ehri (1989) appears to be incorrect in suggesting that orthographic knowledge is necessary for children to acquire phonemic segmentation ability, she may nevertheless be correct in arguing that phonological awareness develops mostly during the course of learning to read, and that phonological awareness is not a prerequisite for deriving benefit from beginning reading instruction. Supporting the latter claim are results from a longitudinal study by Tunmer, Herriman and Nesdale (1988). They found that many preliterate 5-year-old children who performed very poorly on a phoneme-counting task at the beginning of reading instruction nevertheless showed average to above-average performance on phoneme-counting and pseudoword-decoding tasks at the end of the school year. Despite this finding, however, a contingency analysis of the data from the same study indicated that phonological awareness is necessary for acquiring basic phonological recoding skills. The claim that phonological awareness is not a cognitive prerequisite for taking advantage of reading *instruction* is not inconsistent with the claim that phonological awareness is a cognitive prerequisite for reading *acquisition*. As Stanovich (1989) points out in a commentary on Ehri's (1989) paper, the key question is what causes differences in individual *responsiveness* to instructional activities, both formal and informal. The models we describe in the next two sections of the paper attempt to address this issue.

The environmental model further proposes that listening to read stories during the preschool years is an important factor in reading development because it facilitates the development of decontextualized language use (see Figure 4). In general, preschool speech is highly concrete and bound to the specific situation. Young children are relatively effective communicators when language is embedded in familiar perceptual and social contexts and is used for instrumental purposes. The language of text, however, is a more context independent, elaborated form of code. Idea units in written language are longer and more syntactically complex than they are in spoken language (Chafe, 1985). Such linguistic devices as nominalization, subordination, and modification are used to pack many idea units into a single sentence. In addition, cohesion, the process of linking together the sentences of running discourse, is lexicalized in written language; the sentences of text are tied together by cohesive elements. In contrast, spoken discourse cohesion is accomplished primarily through situational context and paralinguistic and prosodic cues.

In a widely cited study, Wells (1985) suggests that listening to and discussing stories during the preschool years facilitates the development of decontextualized language use which, in turn, helps beginning students acquire reading comprehension skills and cope with the more disembedded uses of spoken language in the classroom. In support of this suggestion, he found that of three preschool activities -- drawing, looking at picture books, and listening to stories -- only the latter was significantly related to later reading comprehension performance.

There are major difficulties with this study, however. Wells (1985) failed to control for the educational attainment level of the children's parents, the children's general level of intelligence, and the children's exposure to other preschool activities that might have been more directly related to future growth in reading, such as rhyming and sound analysis games that increase phonological sensitivity. Regarding the latter, Bryant and colleagues (Bryant, Bradley, MacLean & Crossland, 1989; Bryant, MacLean, Bradley & Crossland, 1990; MacLean, Bryant & Bradley, 1987) found in a longitudinal study that knowledge of nursery rhymes in children as young as 3 years of age was strongly related to subsequent development of phonological awareness, which, in turn, predicted early reading ability. Relatedly, Hall (1990) reported that the development of phonological awareness in preschool children was significantly correlated with "language play" but not with story listening. In a longitudinal study of beginning reading, Juel (1988) found that reading achievement itself was the major factor influencing growth in listening comprehension skills among disadvantaged children with below average school language and listening comprehension abilities at school entry. Reading achievement, in turn, was influenced primarily by level of phonological awareness at the beginning of school. It seems likely that any positive effects that preschool story listening may have on the development of children's comprehension processes are probably washed out by reading (see also Ellis & Large, 1988; Share & Silva, 1987).

The Phonological "g" Model

The second model, which we have named the phonological "g" model, proposes that early reading problems are the result of deficits in various aspects of language processing: phonological perception, phonological awareness, lexical retrieval and short-term verbal recall (see Figure 6). The model further proposes that these language processing deficits are the reflection of a more general underlying deficiency in the phonological processing component of working memory (Brady & Fowler, 1988; Liberman & Shankweiler, 1985, 1991; Liberman, Shankweiler & Liberman, 1989; Mann, 1987; Mann, Cowin & Schoenheimer, 1989; Shankweiler & Crain, 1986; Stanovich, 1987, 1988a, 1988b, 1991). The four language processes shown in Figure 6 are concerned with encoding phonological information (phonetic perception); gaining access to and performing mental operations on phonological information (phonological awareness); retrieving phonological information from semantic memory (lexical retrieval); and retaining phonological information in working memory (short-term verbal recall). If there is indeed an underlying deficiency in the generation and/or processing of phonological representations, all of these processes would be adversely affected. This points to an attractive feature of the phonological "g" model, which is that the assumption of a more basic deficiency in the ability to generate, maintain and operate on phonological representations in working memory provides a unified account of the various verbal processing skill deficiencies observed in disabled readers (Shankweiler & Crain, 1986).

There appear to be sound theoretical arguments and considerable empirical evidence in support of the phonological "g" model. With respect to phonetic perception, Brady, Shankweiler and Mann (1983) found that poor eight-year-old readers made more errors than did good readers of the same age in identifying speech stimuli degraded by noise. However, the poor readers did not differ from the good readers in perceiving non-speech environmental sounds masked by noise, suggesting that the subtle deficit displayed by the poor readers may be related to an impairment in the ability to encode phonological information, not to an impairment in auditory perception in general. Difficulties in discriminating between different types of phonemes would be expected to interfere with the development of knowledge of grapheme-phoneme correspondences.

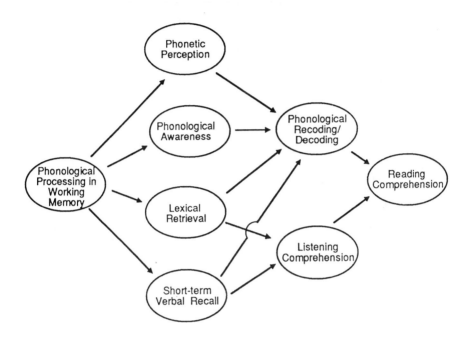

Figure 6. The phonological "g" model.

Several studies in a number of languages indicate that lack of phonological awareness is related to failure in reading and writing (see Tunmer & Rohl, 1991, for a review of research). In the preceding section, we presented arguments and evidence in support of the claim that phonological awareness is causally related to learning to read. To discover correspondences between graphemes and phonemes children must be able to segment spoken words into their constituent phonemic elements. However, if phonological representations in working memory are poorly differentiated, children would be expected to encounter difficulty in becoming aware of the phonological segments of spoken words. As Liberman, Shankweiler and Liberman (1989) argue, "if the underlying biology tends to set up phonological structures weakly, then it should follow that these structures would be much harder for the child to bring to a level of explicit awareness" (p. 17).

Poor readers also perform less well than good readers on tasks requiring retrieval of the phonological codes associated with nameable objects. They make more errors than good readers when naming pictured objects (Katz, 1986) and tend to be slower on tasks that require the rapid naming of colors, letters, numbers or objects (Denckla & Rudel, 1976). Wolf (1984) found that naming speed for objects in kindergarten was related to later reading achievement.

An important aspect of the study by Katz (1986) was that he was able to show that the naming problems of the poor readers were phonological in nature, rather than semantic. When questioned about the characteristics of the objects they had misnamed, the poor readers were generally able to respond accurately, indicating that they were familiar with the objects. Consistent with this finding, the poor readers were able to correctly identify the misnamed items in a recognition post-test in which they were given the names of the items and asked to select them from a group of pictured objects. Finally, the naming errors of the poor readers were often related to the target word phonologically (number of syllables, stress pattern, vowels), but not semantically. These findings suggest that the lexical retrieval deficits of poor readers are due to phonological representations that are incomplete, or to deficient retrieval and processing of phonological representations (Katz, 1986; Liberman, Shankweiler & Liberman, 1989). Such problems would be expected to adversely affect word recognition processes, and possibly listening comprehension as well.

Research further indicates that poor readers are deficient in their ability to maintain a phonological code in working memory (for reviews of research see Liberman & Shankweiler, 1985; Liberman, Shankweiler & Liberman, 1989; Mann, 1986; Mann, Cowin & Schoenheimer, 1989; Shankweiler & Crain, 1986). They perform less well than normal readers in tasks requiring the ordered recall of strings of digits, letters, nameable objects, nonsense syllables, or words. In addition, they are less sensitive to phonologically confusable items in recall tasks. These deficiencies appear to be limited to the language domain, since other kinds of materials, such as nonsense designs and faces, can generally be retained in working memory without deficit by poor readers.

Deficiencies in the ability to retain phonological information in working memory could interfere with the development of phonological recoding/decoding skills in at least three ways. First, because English orthography is primarily a system for relating phonemes to patterns of graphemes co-occurring within words, and because there is no one-to-one correspondence between phonemes and segments of the acoustic signal, it is not possible to directly teach children individual grapheme-phoneme correspondences. Children must therefore discover the correspondences by reflecting upon the elements of written and spoken *words*. As Gough and Hillinger (1980) argue, "the crucial learning event occurs when the child perceives (or thinks of) a printed word at the same time he perceives (or thinks of) its spoken counterpart" (p. 192). This, of course, requires the ability to maintain phonological material in working memory.

Second, beginning readers who rely on "sounding out" strategies in identifying unfamiliar words must perform blending operations that require serial processing of isolated sounds (e.g., *buh, ah, guh* for the printed word *bag*). Each non-continuant sound must be segmented to isolate the initial phoneme, which is then stored in working memory while the next sound is "cleaned up" (Perfetti, Beck, Bell & Hughes, 1987). The phonemes held in memory are then combined to form a candidate word, which is then compared with word candidates from the mental lexicon. The process of performing blending operations clearly places great demands on working memory. In support of this claim, positive correlations have been reported between blending ability and performance on short-term memory tasks (Wagner et al., 1987).

Third, sentence context that is stored in working memory can be used to facilitate word identification. As noted earlier, the constraints of sentence context enable beginning readers to monitor accuracy in word identification by providing them with feedback when their responses fail to conform to the surrounding grammatical context. In addition, beginning readers can combine sentence context information with (possibly incomplete) knowledge of grapheme-phoneme correspondences to identify unfamiliar regular and irregular words, which further increases their knowledge of grapheme-phoneme correspondences. Deficient working memory ability could prevent beginning readers from taking full advantage of sentence context as an aid to word identification.

Limitations in verbal working memory would also be expected to affect the listening comprehension processes of poor readers. As spoken words are processed, their phonological representations are stored in working memory until sufficient information has accumulated to permit assembly of the lexical entries into larger units of relational meaning. A deficit in the ability to retain recently accessed lexical information would directly impair the ability to comprehend spoken sentences, especially those containing complex syntactic structures. Research indicates that poor readers do in fact encounter difficulties in comprehending syntactically complex sentences (Stein, Cairns & Zurif, 1984). However, research further indicates that the poor performance of disabled readers is not due to insufficient syntactic knowledge. When listening comprehension tasks are changed in various ways to reduce the demands on working memory, poor readers perform as well as normal readers, which again points to the specific phonological processing deficiencies of poor readers (Liberman & Shankweiler, 1991; Shankweiler, 1989; Shankweiler & Crain, 1986).

Despite the arguments and evidence in support of the phonological "g" model, there are major difficulties, one of which relates to the notion of Matthew effects, or rich-get-richer and poor-get-poorer effects, in reading achievement (Stanovich, 1986). In the past reading researchers devoted most of their efforts towards discovering how children acquired reading skills and why some children encountered unusual difficulty in learning to read. More recently, however, researchers have begun to focus more attention on the negative consequences of early reading failure. Because of their deficient word recognition skills poor readers not only receive much less practice in reading but soon begin to confront materials that are too difficult for them. To quote Stanovich (1986),

> Reading becomes less and less pleasurable as the poor reader spends an increasing amount of time in materials beyond his or her capability. He or she avoids reading, and the resultant lack of practice relative to his or her peers widens achievement deficits. (p.394)

Poor readers are thus prevented from taking full advantage of the "bootstrapping" relationships between reading and other aspects of development, such as vocabulary growth, ability to comprehend more syntactically complex sentences, and development of richer and more elaborated knowledge bases, all of which facilitate *further* growth in reading by enabling readers to cope with more difficult textual materials. What began as a relatively small difference in basic reading skills soon develops into what Stanovich (1986) describes as a downward spiral of achievement deficits and negative motivational spin-offs. The longer this situation is allowed to continue, the more generalized the deficits become, affecting more and more areas of cognition and behavior.

A major difficulty with the evidence cited in support of the phonological "g" model is that it is based largely on studies comparing good and poor readers of similar age and intelligence (see Shankweiler & Crain, 1986, p.173). A problem with this type of design is that it yields uninterpretable results when a difference in some reading-related variable is found (Bryant, 1986; Bryant & Bradley, 1985). The difference observed between good and poor readers could be either a cause or a consequence of reading failure.

This is an important consideration in relation to positive Matthew effects because good beginning readers are able to take advantage of the reciprocally facilitating relationships between reading and other reading-related skills (e.g., phonological awareness, phonological recoding) and are therefore able to progress at a faster rate. As a consequence, they read much more than poor readers and receive larger amounts of practice in reading and processing verbal material. In support of this claim, research indicates that large differences between good and poor readers in exposure to print begin to emerge as early as the first year of formal instruction (see Stanovich, 1986, for a review of research).

This additional reading experience may improve the efficiency of phonological processing in working memory in a number of ways. For example, as noted earlier, it has been found that idea units in written language are significantly longer and more syntactically complex than those of spoken language (Chafe, 1985). Since better readers are exposed to more written language, and more linguistically advanced written language, than poor readers, they receive more practice in maintaining complex linguistic structures in working memory, a possible consequence of which is an improvement in their ability to make effective use of phonological representations in working memory.

As noted earlier, deficiencies in the ability to retain phonological information in working memory may hinder the development of phonological recoding/decoding skills in several ways. However, given the nature of Matthew effects, the suggested cause and effect relationships may go in the opposite direction. Blending operations, for example, stress verbal working memory. Because better readers read more than poor readers, they receive more practice in performing blending operations, a likely consequence of which is an improvement in their ability to maintain and operate on verbal material in working memory.

Moreover, as we shall argue in the next section, both phonological and syntactic awareness are essential for acquiring phonological recoding skill. The ability to analyze the internal structure of spoken words enables children to discover how phonemes are related to graphemes, and the ability to reflect on sentence structures in order to combine knowledge of the constraints of sentence context with incomplete graphophonemic information helps children to identify unfamiliar words, and thus increase both their word specific knowledge and their knowledge of grapheme-phoneme correspondences. It is possible that repeated occurrences of reflecting on spoken words and sentence structures to discover grapheme-phoneme correspondences improves children's ability to maintain a phonological code in memory. That is, improved efficiency in verbal working memory may be a spin-off effect of the metalinguistic operations that children must perform to become skilled readers.

There is considerable evidence in support of these suggestions. Studies employing reading-age match, rather than mental-age match, designs have failed to show differences between good and poor readers in either short-term verbal recall or phonological confusability (Bisanz, Das & Mancini, 1984; Hulme, 1981; Johnston, 1982; Johnston, Rugg & Scott, 1987). The major advantage of the reading-age match design over the mental-age match design is that, because reading levels are the same, it reduces the possibility that any differences that emerge between good and poor readers are merely the product of reading ability differences. The results of studies employing the reading-age match design indicate that the phonological coding processes in working memory of older, disabled readers are comparable to those of younger, normal readers of similar reading ability.

Several investigations have found a significant relationship between short-term verbal recall in kindergarten and reading achievement in first grade (Mann, 1984; Mann & Liberman, 1984; Share, Jorm, MacLean & Matthews, 1984). However, because these studies failed to control for reading skill in kindergarten, it cannot be concluded that efficiency of phonological coding in working memory is causally related to the acquisition of reading skills. If, as suggested earlier, the process of learning to read itself is largely responsible for the development of verbal working memory ability, then children who possess some reading ability at school entry would be expected to perform better on short-term verbal recall tasks than children with no reading ability. Preschool reading ability might therefore produce a spurious correlation between preschool verbal working memory ability and later reading achievement.

In support of this suggestion are the results of longitudinal studies in which children showing any preschool reading ability were excluded. Bradley and Bryant (1985), for example, gave a short-term verbal recall task to a group of pre-readers who were four or five years old. Eighteen months later the children were given tests of reading and spelling ability. Bradley and Bryant found that preschool performance on the recall task was not related to later reading achievement. However, they did find a significant relationship between reading ability at age seven and verbal working memory ability (as measured by a test of memory for words) when the children were eight or nine years of age. Similar findings have been reported by Gathercole (1990).

In a longitudinal study, Ellis and Large (1987) monitored children's performance on several variables (including auditory short-term memory and reading) as they developed from five to seven years of age. To analyze their data they divided the children into three groups based on their IQ and reading scores at age seven: high IQ/low reading, high IQ/high reading, and low IQ/low reading. At age five the two high IQ groups performed at approximately the same level on an auditory word span task, whereas the low IQ/low reading group performed at a below average level. Over the three year period the relative performance of the high IQ/high reading group gradually increased, whereas the relative performance of the low IQ/low reading group remained constant. Most importantly, the relative performance of the high IQ/low reading group steadily declined over the three year period to a level that was similar to that of the low IQ/low reading group. These results strongly suggest that the development of verbal working memory is tied to learning to read.

In a later study Ellis (1990) used LISREL analyses to examine further the relationship between verbal working memory development and learning to read. Because the children in the study were tested on reading and verbal working memory ability at several points, Ellis was able to make cross-lag comparisons of LISREL path coefficients at two developmental stages: from age five to six years and from age six to seven years. Ellis summarizes his findings as follows:

> At each of the two developmental stages Reading skill contributes more to later proficiency in Auditory STM (0.31, 0.36) than the reverse (0.06, 0.18). Indeed Reading is the *best* predictor of Auditory STM at 6 years old (0.31), better than prior levels of Auditory STM itself (0.21). (p.117)

These results led Ellis (1990) to conclude that "the acquisition of reading skills makes relevant active phonological processing in short-term memory and thus stimulates the development of these skills" (p.107).

Further evidence that the development of verbal working memory ability during the school years is largely a consequence of reading development comes from a series of experiments conducted by Torgesen and colleagues (see Torgesen, 1988). Torgesen was interested in comparing the processing deficiencies of two groups of learning disabled children, those who did not have memory span difficulties (LD-N) and those with severe problems in the short-term retention of information (LD-S). The children were between nine and eleven years of age. Torgesen presented several kinds of evidence in support of the hypothesis that LD-S children are deficient in their ability to process phonological information in working memory. First, the LD-S children did not show a performance deficit when asked to recall sequences of visual figures that were difficult to label verbally. Second, performance differences between the LD-S children and the LD-N children (and a control group of normal children) were greater when less familiar verbal items were used. Third, performance differences between the LD-S children and other groups decreased when phonologically confusable items were used.

Although these findings are *consistent* with Torgesen's (1988) claim that "the performance problems of LD-S children on memory span tasks are *caused* by difficulties utilizing verbal/phonological codes to store information" (p.608, emphasis added), the results could also be related to reading ability differences between the LD-S and LD-N children. Torgesen's data show just that. The two groups performed at a similar level on a standardized test of math achievement. However, the LD-S children were one grade level behind the LD-N children in reading achievement. Torgesen argues that "the children with LD in each group were not selected because of one type of academic disability or another, so the differences between the LD groups in reading skill may reflect a special relationship between deficient phonological skills and difficulties acquiring good reading skills" (p.609). Given the evidence and arguments presented earlier, it seems more likely that Torgesen's findings support the opposite conclusion, namely, that differences in reading ability are "driving" differences in phonological processing in working memory.

In addition to accounting for differences in verbal working memory between good and poor readers of the same age, reading ability differences may also account for differences in lexical retrieval and phonetic perception. With respect to performance differences on object naming tasks, Katz (1986) offers the following account as a possible explanation of the findings he obtained in his study (which we described earlier):

> It is plausible that the better readers had previously been exposed to many of the object names in print. Possibly, having read the object names repeatedly, the good readers' representations of the names could have been more elaborate than those of poor readers, thus allowing the good readers to name more objects correctly. It is possible, therefore, that reading experience resulted in an improvement in the ability of the better readers to name objects. (p.239)

The larger amounts of practice that good readers receive may produce stronger linkages between words and the concepts they represent, which would explain why good readers appear to be able to access more readily the names of concepts that pictured objects represent. Consistent with this suggestion is the finding reported by Katz (1986) that poor readers have particular difficulty in naming objects with low-frequency names. Because good readers not only read more than poor readers but also tend to read more difficult materials, they are more likely to have been exposed to less frequently occurring words.

With regard to differences in object naming speed between good and poor readers, Bryant and Bradley (1985) argue that such differences may be a consequence of learning to read. They point out that "reading must give children extensive practice in thinking up the right words speedily" (p.33). Earlier we mentioned a longitudinal study by Wolf (1984) showing that naming speed for objects in kindergarten was related to later reading achievement. However, as Wagner and Torgesen (1987) point out, Wolf did not control for reading ability in kindergarten. This is an important consideration because "the substantial correlations between the kindergarten reading test scores and the naming measures indicate that a non-trivial proportion of the kindergarten sample possessed some reading skills when the naming tasks were first administered, and thus, the observed differences in naming speed might have been caused by differential prior practice of reading" (p.204).

Finally, it is also highly likely that differences in phonetic perception are a reflection rather than a cause of reading ability differences. For example, recall the study that we described earlier by Brady, Shankweiler and Mann (1983) in which poor readers performed less well than good readers of the same age in identifying speech stimuli degraded by noise. To perform this task it appears that children must retain a degraded phonological representation in working memory as they search their mental lexicon for a possible match. The task may therefore be measuring differences in the ability to maintain a phonological representation in working memory rather than differences in phonetic perception per se. If efficiency of retaining a phonological code in working memory is tied to the development of reading skills as the research discussed earlier seems to suggest, then this would account for the differences in performance observed between good and poor readers on the task used by Brady et al. (1983).

Consistent with this suggestion are results from a study reported by Snowling, Goulandris, Bowlby and Howell (1986). They found, as did Brady et al. (1983), that disabled readers made more errors than did normal readers of the same age in recognizing words presented in noise. However, when the performance of the disabled readers was compared to that of reading age matched controls, there were no differences in performance.

Stanovich (1988a, 1991) has developed a particular version of the phonological "g" model of reading disability that he calls the phonological-core variable-difference model. A major feature of this model is the "assumption of specificity", which Stanovich (1991) argues underlies the concept of dyslexia. He describes it as "the idea that a child with this type of learning disability has a brain/cognitive deficit that is reasonably specific to the reading task" (p. 12). The model further proposes that the key deficit is in the phonological domain and is modular in nature (following Fodor, 1983). Dyslexic children, argues Stanovich, display performance deficits in various aspects of phonological processing: "They have difficulty making explicit reports about sound segments at the phoneme level, they display naming difficulties, their utilization of phonological codes in short-term memory is inefficient, their categorical perception of certain phonemes may be other than normal, and they may have speech production difficulties" (p. 12).

Stanovich's model does not appear to allow for the possibility that dyslexia may result from a developmental *delay* in phonological processing (due to constitutional or environmental factors) rather than from a specific phonological processing *deficit*. As

Snowling (1987) points out, children who do not possess phonemic segmentation ability *at the critical time* will initially fail to learn to read and spell. If they are developmentally delayed in phonological processing skills, these children may gradually develop along normal lines as they mature. However, it is also possible, perhaps even more likely, that most of these children "will not await phonological development but will start to read using compensatory visual strategies guided by contextual cues" (Snowling, 1987, p. 143). This, in turn, would result in negative Matthew effects in the phonological domain.

In considering the question of whether dyslexia is due to a developmental delay or developmental disorder (i.e., a specific brain/cognitive deficit), it is important to recognize that "a delay in the acquisition of prerequisite skills can precipitate *either* a delay *or* a disorder of literacy" whereas "a disorder always leads to an atypical pattern of reading and spelling" (Snowling, 1987, p. 143). If a disordered pattern of reading and spelling development with associated deficiencies in the phonological domain could conceivably result from either a developmental delay or a developmental disorder, and if "parsimony should be the order of the day in reading theory" (Stanovich, 1989, p.366), then it would seem to be more scientifically parsimonious not to *assume* that dyslexia is caused by a specific cognitive/brain deficit in phonological processing.

Another potential difficulty with Stanovich's (1988, 1991) model is the assumption that the various phonological processing deficits displayed by dyslexics reflect a more basic deficiency in a modular processing system. Stanovich (1988b) describes modular cognitive subsystems as those that are "fast, automatic, and informationally encapsulated" (p.212). The latter property means that a module operates autonomously; that is, "it is not under the control of higher level cognitive structures" (p.212). The problem here is that, although the notion of modularity may apply to many aspects of phonological processing, it does not apply to metalinguistic operations. This point is stressed by Shankweiler and Crain (1986): "Reasoning, planning actions, inference and metalinguistic operations are not taken to be parts of the language module, though they operate on its contents" (p.151). Similarly, Mattingly (1988) states that

> To write or to read... I have to be aware of the phonological structure of the cognitive representation.... It would seem that this secondary, cognitive role of phonology has to be distinguished from the primary, modular role of phonology. No phonological awareness at all is required for speaking and listening. (pp. 5-6)

In the next section we shall argue that the development of metalinguistic abilities such as phonological awareness is related to the development of metacognitive functioning.

Stanovich (1991) argues that his model predicts performance contrasts between dyslexic poor readers and "garden-variety" poor readers (whose below average reading levels are not associated with severe discrepancies between reading ability and measured intelligence). Although the reading-related cognitive performance profiles of garden-variety poor readers should be very similar to those of reading-level matched controls (see Stanovich, Nathan & Vala-Rossi, 1986; Stanovich, Nathan & Zolman, 1988, for supportive evidence), the performance profiles of dyslexic children should reveal deficits that are localized in the phonological domain. More specifically, the phonological processing deficits of dyslexic children should be greater than those of both (1) reading-level matched controls and (2) garden-variety controls (children of the same age and reading level but who are not classified as dyslexic because of their low IQs). Although the evidence in support of the first prediction is reasonably consistent, the evidence in support of the second is less so (Stanovich, 1991).

There are, however, problems of interpretation associated with the evidence in support of these two predictions. As pointed out by Goswami and Bryant (1989), "a positive result in a RL [reading-level] match may not signify the existence of a specific deficit at all" (p.420). This is because:

> A significant difference between disabled readers and their reading level controls could be due to a developmental lag rather than to a specific deficit. This lag could in turn serve to increase group differences in the variable being measured through its effects on reading. (p. 420)

For example, as we noted earlier, the use of visually- and contextually- based compensatory strategies could result in negative Matthew effects in the phonological domain. This would explain why the evidence from garden-variety control designs is inconsistent. Regardless of whether a child is a garden-variety poor reader or a dyslexic poor reader, he or she would not be able to benefit from the reciprocally facilitating relationships between reading development and phonological processing skills. In short, a developmental lag in phonemic segmentation ability may initiate a sequence of events that results in performance deficits in *both* reading skills and phonological processing skills.

The Cognitive-Developmental Model

The cognitive-developmental model proposes that deficient metalinguistic ability may be the subtle language deficiency that is most closely related to problems in learning to read. Metalinguistic ability may be defined as the ability to reflect on and manipulate the structural features of spoken language, where the phrase "structural features" refers to the intuitive notion that words are built up from phonemes, sentences are built up from words, and sets of interrelated propositions are built up from the propositions underlying individual sentences. Research suggests that metalinguistic ability is a distinct kind of linguistic functioning that develops separately from and later than basic speaking and listening skills; the ability to perform metalinguistic operations does not come free with the acquisition of language. Rather, metalinguistic ability begins to emerge somewhat later, when children are around 4 to 6 years of age (see Tunmer, Pratt & Herriman, 1984, for reviews of research on the development of metalinguistic abilities in children).

Metalinguistic operations differ from normal language operations in the type of cognitive processing that is required. Normal language processing is modular in nature, involving component operations that are fast, automatic, and largely sealed off from conscious inspection. Listeners, for example, are normally unaware that anything has intervened between their being aware of the speaker's voice and being aware of having understood the message. Similarly, speakers are aware of what they want to say but not of the cognitive processes required to convert their intended meaning into speech.

Unlike normal language operations, metalinguistic operations require control (or executive) processing, which entails an element of choice in whether or not the operations are performed, as well as relative slowness and deliberateness in the application of such operations. Control processing characterizes the kind of linguistic functioning that is associated with metalinguistic operations because the latter involve deliberately reflecting on the *products* of modular sub-processes by means of a conscious analytic ability.

The relationship between normal language processing and metalinguistic operations can be expressed in terms of a model of sentence comprehension that specifies a set of interacting processors in which the output of each becomes the input to the next (Tunmer & Herriman, 1984; Tunmer, Herriman & Nesdale, 1988). According to the model, a speech perception mechanism converts the acoustic signal into a sequence of phonemes. The phonemes then serve as the input to a lexical access mechanism that groups the phonemes and searches a mental lexicon to find the meanings of the words in the utterance. Another processor, called the parser, takes the words retrieved from the lexicon and builds a structural representation of them, from which the utterance's meaning is derived. Individual propositions, however, do not normally stand in isolation but are integrated into larger sets of propositions through the application of pragmatic and inferential rules.

The model provides the basis for a definition of metalinguistic operations in information processing terms as the use of control processing to perform mental operations on the products (i.e., the phonemes, words, sentences, and sets of interrelated propositions) of the modular sub-systems involved in sentence comprehension. The model also provides the basis for classifying the various manifestations of metalinguistic awareness into four broad categories: phonological, word, syntactic and pragmatic (or discourse) awareness. Phonological awareness refers to the ability to perform mental operations on the output of the speech perception mechanism (e.g., segmentation of words into phonemic segments, phoneme blending). Word awareness refers to the ability to perform mental operations on the output of the lexical access mechanism (e.g., segmentation of spoken sentences into words, separation of words from their referents). Syntactic awareness refers to the ability to perform mental operations on the output of the mechanism responsible for assigning intrasentential structural representations to groups of words (e.g., correction of word order violations, completion of sentences with missing words). And pragmatic awareness refers to the ability to perform mental operations on the output of the mechanism responsible for integrating individual propositions into larger sets of propositions through the application of pragmatic and inferential rules (e.g., detection of inconsistencies between sentences, recognition of message inadequacy).

Research indicates that metalinguistic development is related to a more general change in information processing capability that occurs during the early stages of middle childhood, the development of metacognitive control over the information processing system. The results of several studies suggest that during this period children become increasingly aware of how they can control their intellectual processes in a wide range of situations and tasks, including those requiring metalinguistic skills (see Flavell, 1981, 1985 for reviews). This linkage of metalinguistic development to metacognitive development helps to explain why the ability to treat language as an object of thought is not an automatic consequence of language acquisition. Because the gradual increase in children's control of their cognitive processes does not begin until around age 4 or 5 years for most children, and even later for some, metalinguistic abilities would not be expected to develop concomitantly with the acquisition of language.

This general theoretical framework also provides an explanation for what at first seems rather puzzling; namely, that many 5 and 6 year old children who appear to possess normal language comprehension and speaking abilities are nevertheless unable to perform simple metalinguistic operations such as segmenting familiar spoken words into their constituent phonemes, or correcting word order violations in simple sentence structures. The important distinction is that *using* (tacit) knowledge of the grammatical rules of spoken language to construct and comprehend meaningful utterances, which is done intuitively and at a sub-conscious level, is not the same as the metalinguistic act of deliberately performing mental operations *on* the products of the mental mechanisms involved in comprehending and producing utterances.

In contrast to the phonological "g" model, which focuses on differences in the phonological storage and processing component of working memory, the cognitive-developmental model ascribes greater importance to differences in the limited capacity central executive that is used to operate control processes in working memory. Metalinguistic performances such as separating a word from its referent, dissociating the meaning of a sentence from its form, and reflecting on the phonemic constituents of words require the ability to *decenter,* to shift one's attention from message content to the properties of language used to convey content. An essential feature of both metalinguistic operations and decentration is the ability to control the course of one's thoughts; that is, to invoke control processing. According to the cognitive-developmental model, then, developmental differences in control processing ability (due to maturational delay or cognitive deficit) produce differences in the development of the metalinguistic abilities necessary for acquiring basic decoding and comprehension monitoring skills (see Figure 7).

The claim that the development of metalinguistic ability is related to the development of decentration processes is not to suggest that metalinguistic skills emerge spontaneously in development; that is, without specific stimulation. Children must be exposed to language activities in the home and classroom that focus their attention on the structural features of language (see Figure 7). These activities include rhyming and sound analysis games and

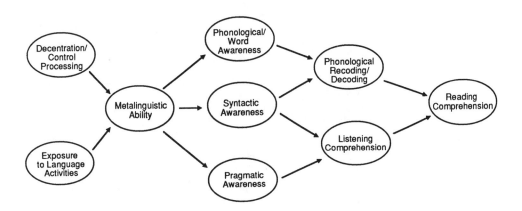

Figure 7. The cognitive-developmental model.

books that increase phonological sensitivity (e.g., pig Latin, I spy, nursery rhymes, Dr. Seuss books), letter games and books that increase letter-name knowledge, games that involve the manipulation of movable letters to form pre-conventional spellings of words, and games and activities that involve listening to and producing "linguistic" jokes and riddles (i.e., those depending on sound similarity or structural ambiguity). The cognitive-developmental model therefore proposes that, although some children possess the level of decentration ability necessary for acquiring metalinguistic skills, their metalinguistic development may be delayed by inadequate environmental stimulation. Reading development may suffer as a result.

Nevertheless, a significant number of children fail to respond to adequate instruction. As noted earlier, a key question is what causes differences in individual responsiveness to instructional activities, both formal and informal (Stanovich, 1989). For example, research indicates that some children derive little or no benefit from explicit training in metalinguistic abilities. In a large-scale training study of phonological awareness abilities in pre-school children, Lundberg, Frost and Petersen (1988) found that 6% of the children in the training group showed virtually no gains in phonemic segmentation ability, despite having received daily lessons in phonological awareness skills over an eight month period. They also found that the children who scored in the lowest quartile on various pre-test measures of phonological awareness benefitted much less from the training than the children in the highest quartile (see Lundberg, 1988). Similarly, Bradley and Bryant (1985) found that phonological awareness training was helpful for some beginning readers who were not phonologically aware, but not others (see Bryant & Goswami; 1987). As noted earlier, Tunmer, Herriman and Nesdale (1988) found in a longitudinal study that preliterate children who performed very poorly on a phonemic segmentation test at the beginning of first grade varied greatly in phonemic segmentation and phonological recoding ability at the end of the year.

As an explanation of such findings, the cognitive-developmental model proposes that during the early stages of middle childhood (from 4 to 6 years of age), children develop the *capacity* for performing metalinguistic operations when confronted with certain kinds of tasks, such as learning to read (Tunmer, Herriman & Nesdale, 1988). However, as a result of a deficit or developmental delay in control processing ability, some children fail to reach the threshold level of decentration ability required to perform the low level metalinguistic operations necessary for developing basic reading skills. Morais, Alegria and Content (1987) argue along similar lines with regard to the development of phonological awareness:

> The concept of capacity is useful to understanding both at what age appropriate experience may produce the expected effects, and why, given appropriate age and experience, the ability develops in some individuals but not in others. These questions concern the conditions of cognitive development and the problem of learning disabled people. (p. 431)

As noted earlier, Snowling (1987) argues that children who do not possess the necessary metalinguistic skills *at the right time* will encounter problems in learning to read. A lag in the development of metalinguistic ability may delay early progress in reading to such an extent that it initiates what Stanovich (1986) describes as a "cascade of interacting achievement failures and motivational problems" (p.393). Children who are developmentally delayed in control processing (or who have not received adequate environmental stimulation) may therefore suffer a "double whammy," as shown in Figure 8. These children's level of decentration ability may be such that they cannot readily perform the low level metalinguistic operations necessary for acquiring basic reading skills. Consequently, they will not be able to

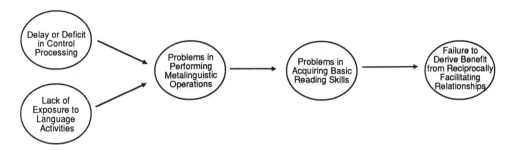

Figure 8. Negative consequences of developmental delays or deficits in control processing ability and/or environmental deficits.

derive maximum benefit from reading instruction and will be prevented from taking advantage of the reciprocally facilitating relationships between reading achievement and other aspects of development (such as growth in vocabulary, syntactic knowledge, and phonological processing skills), which facilitate further growth in reading.

The cognitive-developmental model is consistent with the widely held view in the learning disabilities field that learning disabled children have the necessary knowledge to learn but either cannot access it or do not know how to use it (Swanson, 1988, 1989). Learning disabled children, according to this view, fail to develop effective learning strategies, relying instead on ineffective or inappropriate learning strategies, a problem that is thought to be due to their inability to adequately reflect upon and control their strategic processes. The cognitive-developmental model proposes that, although preliterate children satisfying standard exclusionary criteria possess tacit knowledge of language (as reflected in their ability to produce and comprehend spoken sentences), some of these children are unable to gain *access* to the products of the component processes of the language system because of insufficient development of their metacognitive abilities. This may be due to maturational delay or an underlying neurological deficit, either of which may be related to genetic factors.

Regarding the latter possibility, Olson, Wise, Conners, Rack and Fulker (1989) obtained data from identical and fraternal twins indicating that the phonological coding deficit of reading disabled children is highly heritable. Olson et al. hypothesize that "the underlying causal factor for the heritable phonological coding deficit of the subjects with RD is a heritable weakness in segmental language skills" (p.346). Although these results are consistent with the phonological "g" model of reading disability, they are also consistent with the cognitive-developmental model. A delay in the development of phonemic segmentation skills due to genetically-linked metacognitive deficits could act as a triggering mechanism for negative Matthew effects in the phonological domain.

Stanovich (1988a, 1988b, 1991) argues against conceptualizing reading disability as resulting from a deficit or delay in metacognitive functioning as this would undermine the assumption of specificity, the notion that the reading disabled child has a deficit that is reasonably specific to the reading task: "The concept of dyslexia requires that the deficits displayed by such children not extend too far into other domains of cognitive functioning;

otherwise, the constellation of abilities we call intelligence would also be impaired, reducing the reading/intelligence discrepancy that is central to all current definitions" (Stanovich, 1991, p. 12).

However, it is not clear that a delay or deficit in metacognitive reflection and control would necessarily generalize to other aspects of cognitive functioning. First, as noted earlier, a developmental *delay* in control processing could lead to the use of visually- and contextually-based compensatory strategies in reading that eventually result in negative Matthew effects in phonological processing skills but with development in other areas (such as mathematics) largely unaffected. Second, with respect to the possibility of a neurological deficit, Vellutino and Denckla (1991) cite research indicating that "frontal lobe deficit does not measurably decrease psychometric intelligence, but, rather, impairs general 'control' processes" (p.601). They further note that:

> Currently in usage is the term *executive dysfunction,* the neuropsychological equivalent of what some researchers call *metacognitive control processes....*Persons who suffer from executive dysfunction secondary to frontal deficit fail... when old information must be analyzed or synthesized in new ways. (p. 601)

A neurological deficit resulting in executive dysfunction would clearly impair the performance of metalinguistic operations but not necessarily other areas of cognition, such as general language processing. The extent to which more global aspects of cognitive functioning might be affected by such a deficit would probably depend on the severity of the deficit (if indeed such a deficit even exists).

With respect to the relation of metalinguisitic abilities to the proximal causes of individual differences in reading comprehension, the cognitive-developmental model proposes that phonological and syntactic awareness influence the development of phonological recoding skill, and that along with pragmatic awareness, syntactic awareness also influences the development of listening comprehension by enabling children to monitor their on-going comprehension processes more effectively (see Figure 7). Earlier we presented arguments and evidence in support of the claim that phonological awareness is necessary for acquiring phonological recoding skill. A question that remains is whether deficient phonemic segmentation skill is the result of a developmental delay. Pratt and Brady (1988) claim that it is not on the basis of their finding of phonological awareness deficits in adult poor readers.

The problem with this study, however, is that Pratt and Brady administered relatively difficult phonological awareness tasks (such as the phoneme deletion task) to their adult poor readers. As noted earlier, some skills that are acquired or improved as a result of learning to read and spell (such as the ability to maintain and operate on verbal material in working memory, to generate orthographic images, and to apply phoneme-grapheme correspondence rules) may be necessary to perform more advanced phonological awareness tasks, in which case such tasks would amount to little more than indirect measures of reading achievement. In support of this suggestion are the results of a longitudinal study by Perfetti, Beck, Bell and Hughes (1987) in which the phonological awareness skills and pseudoword decoding skills of first-grade children were assessed at four points throughout the year. The results of partial time-lag correlations suggested that the development of phoneme-deletion ability was largely a consequence of learning to read. It is therefore not surprising that the adult poor readers in the Pratt and Brady study performed poorly on the phoneme deletion task (see Tunmer & Rohl, 1991, for further discussion).

Syntactic awareness, or grammatical sensitivity, is also hypothesized to play a major role in learning to read. Several studies using a variety of different tasks (e.g., judgement of grammaticality, correction of word order violations or morpheme deletions, oral cloze) have demonstrated that syntactic awareness is related to beginning reading achievement (see Ryan & Ledger, 1984, for a review). Willows and Ryan (1986) found that measures of syntactic awareness were related to beginning reading achievement even when general cognitive ability and vocabulary level were controlled. Using a reading-level match design in which good, younger readers were matched with poor, older readers on reading ability and verbal intelligence, Tunmer, Nesdale and Wright (1987) found that the good readers scored significantly better than the poor readers on two measures of syntactic awareness (an oral cloze task and a word order correction task), suggesting the possibility of a causal connection between syntactic awareness and learning to read. Consistent with these results, Bohannon, Warren-Leubecker and Hepler (1984) found that sensitivity to word-order violations at the beginning of kindergarten, first grade and second grade was strongly related to beginning reading achievement at the end of each grade even when verbal intelligence was held constant.

Tests of syntactic awareness impose processing demands on working memory (as would any metalinguistic task). It is therefore possible that inferior working memory ability rather than deficient metalinguistic ability is the reason why poor readers perform less well on syntactic awareness tasks than good readers. However, Fowler (1988) found that performance on a grammatical error correction task was significantly correlated with reading performance (as measured by pseudoword decoding) even after the effects of verbal working memory had been partialled out. The strength of this relationship ($r = 0.39$) was as great as that between phoneme segmentation and pseudoword decoding ($r = 0.37$), again with the effects of verbal working memory held constant.

As indicated in Figure 7, there are two ways in which syntactic awareness may influence reading development. One way is by enabling readers to monitor their on-going comprehension processes more effectively. Many poor readers appear to encounter difficulty in following the content and structure of the passage they are reading (or hearing). When a breakdown in comprehension occurs, these children either fail to detect it, or if they do detect it, they are unable to employ the "fix-up" strategies necessary to improve their understanding of text. One strategy that syntactically aware children are able to use is to check that their responses to the words of the text conform to the surrounding grammatical context. A second strategy these children can employ is to make intelligent guesses about the meanings of unfamiliar words in written or spoken language. Supporting these claims are results from a study by Bowey (1986) showing that performance on a syntactic awareness task was related to measures of on-going reading comprehension and comprehension monitoring even when general intelligence was taken into account.

The second way that syntactic awareness may influence reading is by helping children acquire phonological recoding skill. When confronted with an unfamiliar word, syntactically aware beginning readers would be able to combine knowledge of the constraints of sentential context with incomplete graphophonemic information to identify the word, and thus increase their knowledge of grapheme-phoneme correspondences. In support of this claim are several studies reporting positive correlations between syntactic awareness and decoding and/or phonological recoding (Bowey, 1986; Bowey & Patel, 1988; Bryant, MacLean & Bradley, 1990; Fowler, 1988; Siegel & Ryan, 1988; Stanovich, Cunningham & Freeman, 1984; Tunmer, 1989; Tunmer, Herriman & Nesdale, 1988; Willows & Ryan, 1986). Research further indicates that syntactic awareness typically correlates more strongly with context free decoding than with reading comprehension (Bowey, 1986; Bowey & Patel, 1988; Siegel & Ryan, 1988; Stanovich et al., 1984; Tunmer, 1989; Willows & Ryan, 1986). And when measures of both decoding and phonological recoding are included in a study, syntactic awareness usually correlates more highly with phonological recoding. Siegal and Ryan (1988), for example, found that each of three measures of syntactic awareness correlated more strongly with phonological recoding (as measured by pseudoword decoding) than with real word recognition. Stanovich et al. (1984) found that performance on an oral cloze task correlated more highly with phonological recoding than did their measure of phonological awareness (0.37 vs 0.33). In fact, the oral cloze task correlated more highly with phonological recoding than with any of the other variables included in the study (general intelligence, listening comprehension, word recognition speed, and reading comprehension). Stanovich et al. (1984) also found that in a factor analysis the oral cloze task loaded most highly with the phonological awareness factor, not with listening comprehension as they had anticipated.

It must be emphasized that it is the *combination* of language prediction skills (i.e., syntactic awareness) and emerging phonological recoding skills that provides the basis for acquiring basic reading skills. Language prediction skills will only be useful if they are applied to the problem of breaking the orthographic code. Exclusive reliance on contextual *guessing* to identify unfamiliar words will result in little progress (see Tunmer & Hoover, 1992, for further discussion). Evidence in support of this claim comes from a study by Evans and Carr (1985) that compared the effects of two instructional approaches (decoding-oriented vs language experience-oriented) on beginning reading achievement. They found that the use of context to make predictions was positively correlated with reading achievement, but *only* in the group that had received instruction in decoding skills. Evans and Carr concluded from their findings that "a focus on predictive context utilization 'worked' in the [decoding-oriented] classrooms because it was combined with print-specific skills taught through word analysis activities, but did not work in the [language experience-oriented] classrooms because the children had few resources for dealing with unfamiliar words" (pp. 343-344).

Although syntactic awareness is clearly related to phonological recoding skills, it must be demonstrated that syntactic awareness makes an *independent* contribution to phonological recoding skill when phonological awareness is included in the analysis. It is possible that syntactic awareness is related to phonological recoding simply because syntactic awareness, like phonological awareness, is a metalinguistic ability and therefore shares in common with phonological awareness many of the same component skills (invoking control processing, performing mental operations on the structural features of language, etc.). However, if syntactic awareness facilitates the development of phonological recoding skill by enabling children to use context to identify unfamiliar words, which, in turn, increases their knowledge of grapheme-phoneme correspondences, then syntactic awareness should make a contribution to the development of phonological recoding skill that is distinct from that made by phonological awareness. In support of this claim are the results of three separate studies by Tunmer and colleagues (Tunmer, 1989; Tunmer, Herriman & Nesdale, 1988; Tunmer & Nesdale, 1986) showing that phonological and syntactic awareness in beginning readers each makes an independent and approximately equal contribution to phonological recoding.

In a recently reported longitudinal study, Bryant, MacLean and Bradley (1990) found strong predictive correlations between measures of phonological and syntactic awareness and later reading achievement. However, in a multiple regression analysis that included three "extraneous" variables (age at test of reading, mother's educational level, IQ), four linguistic variables (vocabulary, expressive language, receptive language, sentence imitation) and two measures of phonological sensitivity (rhyme and alliteration oddity tasks), syntactic awareness failed to make an independent contribution to future reading achievement. The two phonological sensitivity measures, however, did make independent contributions to reading.

A possible explanation of this finding is that, unlike phonological awareness, syntactic awareness, as argued earlier, also influences the development of listening comprehension by enabling children to monitor their on-going comprehension processes more effectively and to make intelligent guesses about the meanings of unfamiliar words. Syntactic awareness would therefore be expected to be related to aspects of general language development. In the Bryant et al. (1990) study, syntactic awareness did, in fact, correlate much more highly with the four language measures than did either of the phonological sensitivity measures. This alone would account for the pattern of results obtained by Bryant and colleagues. Consistent with this interpretation, Tunmer (1989) found in a longitudinal study that syntactic awareness was related to later achievement in real word decoding, pseudoword decoding, listening comprehension, and reading comprehension. The same was true for phonological awareness with the exception of *listening* comprehension, where there was no relationship ($r = 0.04$).

The cognitive-developmental model also proposes that pragmatic awareness may influence reading development through its effects on comprehension processes. Whereas syntactic awareness is concerned with *intra*sentential relations, pragmatic, or discourse, awareness is concerned with *inter*sentential relations. Research by Tunmer and colleagues (Tunmer, Nesdale & Pratt, 1983; Nesdale, Pratt & Tunmer, 1985; Nesdale, Tunmer & Clover, 1985) has shown that children's ability to detect inter-sentence inconsistencies in orally presented passages begins to develop around 5 years of age. They also found that difficulty of detecting inconsistencies was greater when the principle upon which a story's consistency depended was implicitly rather than explicitly stated, when the inconsistent sentences were interspersed among other sentences, or when the inconsistent sentences were embedded in larger segments of communication.

Pragmatic awareness may influence reading development by enabling readers to monitor their comprehension of text at the inter-sentence level. Unlike syntactic awareness, however, for pragmatic awareness there seems to be little theoretical justification for supposing that it facilitates the acquisition of phonological recoding skills (Tunmer & Hoover, 1992). This suggests that pragmatic awareness may not be particularly important in the early stages of learning to read, when the focus is primarily on the acquisition of decoding skill. In support of this suggestion are the results of a path analysis by Tunmer, Herriman and Nesdale (1988) showing that although phonological and syntactic awareness each influenced first grade reading comprehension performance indirectly through phonological recoding, pragmatic awareness failed to make an independent contribution to either phonological recoding or reading comprehension.

In support of the overall cognitive-developmental model are the results of two longitudinal studies (Tunmer, 1989; Tunmer, Herriman & Nesdale, 1988). In the first study (Tunmer et al., 1988), 118 pre-readers were administered three tests of metalinguistic ability (phonological, syntactic and pragmatic awareness), three pre-reading tests (print awareness, letter identification, and a word recognition test containing frequently occurring sight words), a test of verbal intelligence, and a test of decentration ability (measured by concrete operations) at the beginning of first grade. At the end of first grade, the children were re-administered the metalinguistic and pre-reading tests, and three tests of reading achievement (real word decoding, pseudoword decoding, and reading comprehension). The latter tests were re-administered at the end of second grade.

A particularly noteworthy finding was that decentration ability in pre-literate children was more strongly correlated with overall metalinguistic ability at the beginning and end of first grade than was any other school-entry variable. The results further revealed that pre-literate children with low levels of phonological awareness at school entry but above-average levels of decentration ability showed significantly greater improvement in phonological awareness during the school year than children with similarly low levels of phonological awareness but below-average levels of decentration ability at school entry. The mean phonological awareness score of the high-decentration ability group was above the mean of all children's phonological awareness scores at the end of the year, whereas the low-decentration ability group mean was one standard deviation below the overall mean. This finding supports the claim that preliterate children with high levels of decentration ability possess greater cognitive capacity for acquiring the metalinguistic skills necessary for learning to read than do children with low levels of decentration ability.

As noted earlier, a path analysis of the data revealed that phonological and syntactic awareness each made an independent contribution to phonological recoding. A scatterplot was generated to examine further the relationship between syntactic awareness and phonological recoding. Similar to what has been observed in studies of the relationship between phonological awareness and phonological recoding (Juel, Griffith & Gough, 1986; Tunmer & Nesdale, 1985), the scatterplot revealed that although many children performed well on syntactic awareness but poorly on pseudoword decoding, only one child performed moderately well on pseudoword decoding, but poorly on syntactic awareness (see Tunmer, 1989, for a replication of this finding, but without the one exception). This finding suggests that syntactic awareness, like phonological awareness, may be essential for acquiring knowledge of grapheme-phoneme correspondences.

In the second longitudinal study (Tunmer, 1989), 100 first grade children were administered tests of phonological and syntactic awareness, a test of verbal intelligence, a test of decentration ability, and four achievement tests (real word decoding, pseudoword decoding, listening comprehension, and reading comprehension). At the end of second grade, these tests were re-administered to 84 children from the original sample.

A path analysis of the data revealed that Grade 1 phonological awareness influenced Grade 2 reading comprehension indirectly through Grade 2 phonological recoding, and that Grade 1 syntactic awareness influenced Grade 2 reading achievement through *both* phonological recoding and listening comprehension (see Figure 9). Neither decentration ability (as measured by concrete operations) nor verbal intelligence in Grade 1 made an independent contribution to the variability of any of the Grade 2 variables. However, decentration ability made a relatively strong independent contribution to both phonological and syntactic awareness, whereas verbal intelligence made a relatively small independent contribution to syntactic awareness only. Overall, these findings are impressive because they show that metalinguistic abilities in the beginning stages of learning to read are significantly related to later listening and reading achievement, even after the effects of verbal intelligence and decentration ability have been removed. The results further showed that decentration ability was more strongly related to metalinguistic development than was verbal intelligence, as expected.

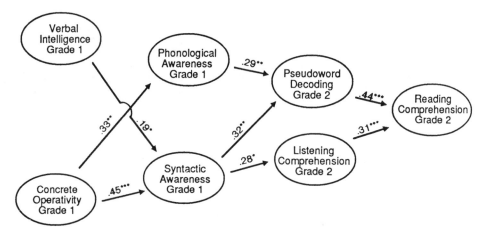

Figure 9. Path diagram displaying structure of relationships between first grade ability measures and second grade achievement measures (standardized beta weights are shown on each path. *p < .05, **p < .01, *** p < .001).

With respect to reading disability, there were three children whose reading comprehension scores in second grade were more than two standard deviations below the mean for all the children. Because these children's verbal intelligence scores in second grade were in the normal range (124, 94, 118), they would be classified as reading disabled under standard criteria. Significantly, for *both* phonological and syntactic awareness, the mean of these children's first grade scores was two standard deviations below the corresponding mean for all children. This suggests that markedly deficient metalinguistic ability in the early stages of learning to read may be the subtle language deficiency that is responsible for the severe reading problems experienced by some beginning readers.

Concluding Remarks

In this paper we presented three components of variance models of language-related factors in reading disability. We began with a description of a model of the proximal causes of reading performances differences. This model, referred to as the simple view, proposes that individual differences in reading comprehension are a function of two factors, decoding and listening comprehension, each of which is assumed to be necessary for reading. We then considered three models that attempt to account for differences in decoding and listening comprehension. The first model, the environmental model, proposes that inadequate exposure to print and text-like language prior to schooling and inadequate instruction during schooling are responsible for early reading difficulties. The second model, the phonological "g" model, proposes that differences in decoding and listening comprehension are primarily the result of constitutional differences in the phonological processing component of working memory. The third model, the cognitive-developmental model, proposes that beginning reading difficulties are the result of both intrinsic and extrinsic factors. In contrast to the phonological "g" model, which focuses on differences in the phonological storage and processing component of working memory, the cognitive-developmental model ascribes greater importance to differences in the limited capacity central executive that is used to operate control processes in working memory. Developmental differences in control processing ability are hypothesized to produce differences in the development of the metalinguistic abilities necessary for acquiring basic decoding and comprehension monitoring skills. In addition, reading difficulties are thought to result from insufficient exposure to the kinds of language activities that focus children's attention on the structural features of spoken language.

On the basis of the research that is currently available, we conclude that the most supportable model is the third model, the cognitive-developmental model.

REFERENCES

Backman, J., Bruck, M., Hebert, M. & Seidenberg, M. (1984). Acquisition and use of spelling-sound correspondence in reading. *Journal of Experimental Child Psychology, 38*, 114-133.
Ball, E. & Blackman, B. (1991). Does phoneme awareness training in kindergarten make a difference in early word recognition and developmental spelling? *Reading Research Quarterly, 26*, 46-66.
Bisanz, G.L., Das, J.P. & Mancini, G. (1984). Children's memory for phonemically confusable and non-confusable letters: Changes with age and reading ability. *Child Development, 51*, 1845-1854.
Bohannon, J., Warren-Leubecker, A. & Hepler, N. (1984). Word awareness and early reading. *Child Development, 55*, 1541-1548.
Bowey, J.A. (1986). Syntactic awareness in relation to reading skill and ongoing reading comprehension monitoring. *Journal of Experimental Child Psychology, 41*, 282-299.
Bowey, J.A. & Patel, R.K. (1988). Metalinguistic ability and early reading achievement. *Applied Psycholinguistics, 9*, 367-383.
Bradley, L. & Bryant, P. (1978). Difficulties in auditory organization as a possible cause of reading backwardness. *Nature, 271*, 746-747.
Bradley, L. & Bryant, P. (1985). *Rhyme and reason in reading and spelling.* Ann Arbor: University of Michigan Press.
Brady, S.A. & Fowler, A.E. (1988). Phonological precursors to reading acquisition. In R. Masland & M. Masland (Eds.), *Preschool prevention of reading failure* (pp.204-215). Parkton, MD: York Press.
Brady, S.A., Shankweiler, D., & Mann, V.A. (1983). Speech perception and memory coding in relation to reading ability. *Journal of Experimental Child Psychology, 35*, 345-367.
Bryant, P. (1986). Phonological skills and learning to read and write. In B. Foorman & A. Siegal (Eds.), *Acquisition of reading skills: Cultural constraints and cognitive universals* (pp.51-69). Hillsdale, NJ: Lawrence Erlbaum Associates.
Bryant, P. & Bradley, L. (1985). *Children's reading problems.* Oxford: Blackwell.
Bryant, P., Bradley, L., MacLean, M. & Crossland, J. (1989). Nursery rhymes, phonological skills and reading. *Journal of Child Language, 16*, 407-428.
Bryant, P. & Goswami, U. (1987). Beyond grapheme-phoneme correspondence. *Cahiers de Psychologie Cognitive, 7*, 439-443.
Bryant, P., MacLean, M., & Bradley, L. (1990). Rhyme, language and children's reading. *Applied Psycholinguistics, 11*, 237-252.
Bryant, P., MacLean, M., Bradley, L. & Crossland, J. (1990). Rhyme and alliteration, phoneme detection and learning to read. *Developmental Psychology, 26*, 429-438.
Byrne, B. (1991). Experimental analysis of the child's discovery of the alphabetic principle. In L. Rieben & C. Perfetti (Eds.), *Learning to read: Basic research and its implications* (pp.75-84). Hillsdale, NJ: Lawrence Erlbaum Associates.

Byrne, B. (1992). Studies in the acquisition procedure for reading: Rationale, hypotheses, and data. In P. B. Gough, L. Ehri & R. Treiman (Eds.), *Reading acquisition* (pp.1-34). Hillsdale, NJ: Lawrence Erlbaum Associates.

Byrne, B. & Fielding-Barnsley, R. (1989). Phonemic awareness and letter knowledge in the child's acquisition of the alphabetic principle. *Journal of Educational Psychology, 81*, 313-321.

Chafe, W. (1985). Linguistic differences produced by differences between speaking and writing. In D. Olson, N. Torrance & W. Hildyard (Eds.), *Literacy, language and learning: The nature and consequences of reading and writing* (pp. 105-123). London: Cambridge University Press.

Clay, M. (1987). Learning to be learning disabled. *New Zealand Journal of Educational Studies, 22*, 155-173.

Denckla, M.B. & Rudel, R. (1976). Naming of pictured objects by dyslexic and other learning disabled children. *Brain and Language, 39*, 1-15.

Ehri, L. (1984). How orthography alters spoken language competencies in children learning to read and spell. In J. Downing & R. Valtin (Eds.), *Language awareness and learning to read* (pp. 119-147). New York: Springer-Verlag.

Ehri, L. (1986). Sources of difficulty in learning to spell and read. In M. Wolraich & D. Routh (Eds.), *Advances in developmental and behavioral pediatrics* (pp. 121-195). Greenwich, CT:JAI Press, Inc.

Ehri, L. (1987). Learning to read and spell words. *Journal of Reading Behavior, 19*, 5-31.

Ehri, L. (1989). The development of spelling knowledge and its role in reading acquisition and reading disability. *Journal of Learning Disabilities, 22*, 356-365.

Ehri, L. & Wilce, L. (1980). The influence of orthography on readers' conceptualization of the phonemic structure of words. *Applied Psycholinguistics, 1*, 371-385.

Ellis, N. (1990). Reading phonological skills and short-term memory: Interactive tributaries of development. *Journal of Research in Reading, 13*, 107-122.

Ellis, N. & Large, B. (1987). The development of reading: As you seek so shall you find. *British Journal of Psychology, 78*, 1-28.

Ellis, N. & Large, B.(1988). The early stages of reading: A longitudinal study. *Applied Cognitive Psychology, 2*, 47-76.

Evans, M. & Carr, T. (1985). Cognitive abilities, conditions of learning and the early development of reading skill. *Reading Research Quarterly, 20*, 327-350.

Flavell, J. (1981). Cognitive monitoring. In W. Dickson (Ed.), *Children's oral communication* (pp.35-60). New York: Academic Press.

Flavell, J. (1985). *Cognitive development.* Englewood Cliffs, NJ: Prentice-Hall.

Fodor, J. (1983). *The modularity of mind.* Cambridge, MA: MIT Press.

Fowler, A. (1988). Grammaticality judgements and reading skill in Grade 2. *Annals of Dyslexia, 38*, 73-94.

Gathercole, S. (1990). Working memory and language development: How close is the link? *The Psychologist, 2*, 57-60.

Goswami, U. & Bryant, P. (1989). The interpretation of studies using the reading level design. *Journal of Reading Behavior, 21*, 413-424.

Gough, P. & Hillinger, M. (1980). Learning to read: An unnatural act. *Bulletin of the Orton Society, 30*, 179-196.

Gough, P. & Juel, C. (1991). The first stages of word recognition. In L. Rieben & C. Perfetti (Eds.), *Learning to read: Basic research and its implications* (pp.47-56). Hillsdale, NJ: Lawrence Erlbaum Associates.

Gough, P., Juel, C. & Roper-Schneider, D. (1983). Code and cipher: A two-stage conception of initial reading acquisition. In J.A. Niles & L.A. Harris (Eds.), *Searches for meaning in reading/language processing and instruction* (pp. 207-211). Rochester, New York: The National Reading Conference.

Gough, P.B. & Tunmer, W. (1986). Decoding, reading and reading disability. *Remedial and Special Education, 7*, 6-10.

Gough, P.B. & Walsh, M. (1991). Chinese Phoenicians and the orthographic cipher of English. In S. Brady & D. Shankweiler (Eds.), *Phonological processes in literacy* (pp.199-209). Hillsdale, NJ: Lawrence Erlbaum.

Hall, A. (1989, November). *Correlates of phonemic awareness.* Paper presented at the National Reading Conference, Austin, Texas.

Hoover, W. & Gough, P. (1990). The simple view of reading. *Reading and Writing: An Interdisciplinary Journal, 2,* 127-160.

Hulme, C. (1981). *Reading retardation and multi-sensory teaching.* London: Routledge and Kegan Paul.

Johnston, R. (1982). Phonological coding in dyslexic readers. *British Journal of Psychology, 73,* 455-460.

Johnston, R., Rugg, M. & Scott, T. (1987). Phonological similarity effects, memory span and developmental reading disorders: The nature of the relationship. *British Journal of Psychology, 78,* 205-21 1.

Jorm, A., Share, D., MacLean, R. & Matthews, R. (1984). Phonological recoding skills and learning to read: A longitudinal study. *Applied Psycholinguistics, 5,* 201-207.

Juel, C. (1988). Learning to read and write: A longitudinal study of 54 children from first through fourth grades. *Journal of Educational Psychology, 80,* 437-447.

Juel, C., Griffith, P. & Gough, P. (1986). Acquisition of literacy: A longitudinal study of children in first and second grade. *Journal of Educational Psychology, 78,* 243-255.

Katz, R. (1986). Phonological deficiencies in children with reading disability: Evidence from an object-naming task. *Cognition, 22,* 225-257.

Liberman, I. & Shankweiler, D. (1985). Phonology and the problem of learning to read and write. *Remedial and Special Education, 6,* 8-17.

Liberman, I. & Shankweiler, D. (1991). Phonology and beginning reading. A tutorial. In L. Rieben & C. Perfetti (Eds.), *Learning to read: Basic research and its implications* (pp. 317). Hillsdale, NJ: Lawrence Erlbaum Associates.

Liberman, I., Shankweiler, D. & Liberman, A. (1989). The alphabetic principle and learning to read. In D. Shankweiler & I. Liberman (Eds.), *Phonology and reading disability: Solving the reading puzzle* (pp. 1-33). Ann Arbor, MI: University of Michigan Press.

Lundberg, I. (1988). Preschool prevention of reading failure: Does training in phonological awareness work? In R. Masland & M. Masland (Eds.), *Preschool prevention of reading failure* (pp. 163-176). Parkton, MD: York Press.

Lundberg, I., Frost, J. & Petersen, 0. -P. (1988). Effects of an extensive program for stimulating phonological awareness in preschool children. *Reading Research Quarterly, 23,* 267-284.

Lundberg, I. & Hoien, T. (1991). Initial enabling knowledge and skills in reading acquisition: Print awareness and phonological segmentation. In D. Sawyer & B. Fox (Eds.), *Phonological awareness in reading: The evolution of current perspectives* (pp.73-95). New York: Springer-Verlag.

MacLean, M., Bryant, P. & Bradley, I. (1987). Rhymes, nursery rhymes and reading in early childhood. *Merrill-Palmer Quarterly, 33,* 255-281.

Manis, F. & Morrison, F. (1985). Reading disability: A deficit in rule Learning? In L. Siegel & F. Morrison (Eds.), *Cognitive development in atypical children* (pp. 1-26). New York: Springer-Verlag.

Mann, V. (1984). Longitudinal prediction and prevention of early reading difficulty. *Annals of Dyslexia, 34,* 117-136.

Mann, V. (1986). Why some children encounter reading problems: The contribution of difficulties with language processing and language sophistication to early reading disability. In J. Torgesen & B. Wong (Eds.), *Psychological and educational perspectives on learning disabilities* (pp. 113-159). New York: Academic Press.

Mann, V. (1987). Phonological awareness and alphabetic literacy. *Cahiers de Psychologie Cognitive, 7,* 476-481.

Mann, V., Cowin, E. & Schoenheimer, J. (1989). Phonological processing, language comprehension and reading ability. *Journal of Learning Disabilities, 22,* 76-89.

Mann, V. & Liberman, I. (1984). Phonological awareness and verbal short-term memory. *Journal of Learning Disabilities, 17*, 592-599.

Masonheimer, P., Drum, P. & Ehri, L. (1984). Does environmental print identification lead children into word reading? *Journal of Reading Behavior, 16*, 257-271.

Mattingly, I. (1988, November). *A binary phonological deficit?* Paper presented at 39th Annual Conference of the Orton Dyslexia Society, Tampa, Florida.

Morais, J. (1991). Phonological awareness: A bridge between language and literacy. In D. Sawyer & B. Fox (Eds.), *Phonological awareness in reading: The evolution of current perspectives* (pp.31-71). New York: Springer-Verlag.

Morais, J., Alegria, J. & Content, A. (1987). The relationship between segmental analysis and alphabetic literacy: An interactive view. *Cahiers de Psychologie Cognitive. 7*, 415-438.

Morais, J., Cary, L., Alegria, J. & Bertelson, P. (1979). Does awareness of speech as a sequence of phones arise spontaneously? *Cognition, 7*, 323-331.

Morrison, F. (1991). Learning (and not learning) to read: A developmental framework. In L. Rieben & C. Perfetti (Eds.), *Learning to read: Basic research and its implications* (pp. 163-174). Hillsdale, NJ: Lawrence Erlbaum Associates.

Nesdale, A., Pratt, C. & Tunmer, W. (1985). Young children's detection of propositional inconsistencies in oral communications. *Australian Journal of Psychology, 37*, 289-296.

Nesdale, A., Tunmer, W. & Clover, J. (1985). Factors influencing young children's ability to detect logical inconsistencies in oral communications. *Journal of Language and Social Psychology, 4*, 39-49.

Olson, R., Wise, B., Conners, F., Rack, J. & Fulker, D. (1989). Specific deficits in component reading and language skills: Genetic and environmental influences. *Journal of Learning Disabilities, 22*, 339-348.

Perfetti, C., Beck, I., Bell, L. & Hughes, C. (1987). Phonemic knowledge and learning to read are reciprocal: A longitudinal study of first grade children. *Merrill-Palmer Quarterly, 33*, 283-319.

Perfetti, C. & Hogaboam, T. (1975). The relationship between single word decoding and reading comprehension skill. *Journal of Educational Psychology, 67*, 461-469.

Pratt, A. & Brady, S. (1988). Relation of phonological awareness to reading disability in children and adults. *Journal of Educational Psychology, 80*, 319-323.

Read, C., Zhang, Y., Nie, H. & Ding, B. (1986). The ability to manipulate speech sounds depends on knowing alphabetic reading. *Cognition, 24*, 31-44.

Rohl, M. & Tunmer, W. (1988). Phonemic segmentation skill and spelling acquisition. *Applied Psycholinguistics, 9*, 335-350.

Ryan, E. & Ledger, G. (1984). Learning to attend to sentence structure: Links between metalinguistic development and reading. In J. Downing & R. Valtin (Eds.). *Language awareness and learning to read* (pp. 149-171). New York: Springer-Verlag.

Seymour, P. & Elder, L. (1986). Beginning reading without phonology. *Cognitive Neuropsychology, 3*, 1-36.

Shankweiler, D. (1989). How problems of comprehension are related to difficulties in decoding. In D. Shankweiler & I. Liberman (Eds.), *Phonology and reading disability: Solving the reading puzzle* (pp.35-68). Ann Arbor, MI: University of Michigan Press.

Shankweiler, D. & Crain, S. (1986). Language mechanisms and reading disorder: A modular approach. *Cognition, 24*, 139-168.

Share, D.L., Jorm, A.R., MacLean, R. & Matthews, R. (1984). Sources of individual differences in reading acquisition. *Journal of Educational Psychology, 76*, 1309-1324.

Share, D.L. & Silva, P.A. (1987). Language deficits and specific reading retardation: Cause and effect? *Journal of Disorders of Communication, 22*, 219-226.

Siegel, L. & Ryan, E. (1988). Development of grammatical-sensitivity, phonological, and short-term memory skills in normally achieving and learning disabled children. *Developmental Psychology, 24*, 28-37.

Snowling, M. (1980). The development of grapheme-phoneme correspondences in normal and dyslexic readers. *Journal of Experimental Child Psychology, 29*, 294-305.

Snowling, M. (1981). Phonemic deficits in developmental dyslexia. *Psychological Research, 43,* 219-234.

Snowling, M. (1987). *Dyslexia: A cognitive developmental perspective.* Oxford: Basil Blackwell.

Snowling, M., Goulandris, N., Bowlby, M. & Howell, P. (1986). Segmentation and speech perception in relation to reading skill: A developmental analysis. *Journal of Experimental Child Psychology, 41,* 489-507.

Stanovich, K.E. (1986). Matthew effects in reading: Some consequences of individual differences in the acquisition of literacy. *Reading Research Quarterly, 21,* 360-406.

Stanovich, K.E. (1987). Perspectives on segmental analysis and alphabetic literacy. *Cahiers de Psychologie Cognitive, 7,* 514-519.

Stanovich, K. (1988a). Explaining the difference between the dyslexic and garden-variety poor readers: The phonological-core variable-difference model. *Journal of Learning Disabilities, 21,* 590-604.

Stanovich, K. (1988b). Science and learning disabilities. *Journal of Learning Disabilities, 21,* 210-214.

Stanovich, K. (1989). Various varying views on variation. *Journal of Learning Disabilities, 22,* 366-369.

Stanovich, K. (1991). Discrepancy definitions of reading disability: Has intelligence led us astray? *Reading Research Quarterly, 26,* 7-29.

Stanovich, K.E., Cunningham, A.E. & Feeman, D.J. (1984). Intelligence, cognitive skills and early reading progress. *Reading Research Quarterly, 19,* 278-303.

Stanovich, K.E., Nathan, R. & Vala-Rossi, M. (1986). Developmental changes in the cognitive correlates of reading ability and the developmental lag hypothesis. *Reading Research Quarterly, 21,* 267-283.

Stanovich, K.E., Nathan, R.G. & Zolman, J.E. (1988). The developmental lag hypothesis in reading: Longitudinal and matched reading-level comparisons. *Child Development, 59,* 71-86.

Stein, C.L., Cairns, H.S. & Zurif, E.B. (1984). Sentence comprehension limitations related to syntactic deficits in reading-disabled children. *Applied Psycholinguistics, 5,* 305-322.

Sticht, T. & James, J. (1984). Listening and reading. In P. Pearson, R. Barr, M. Kamil & R. Mosenthal (Eds.), *Handbook of reading research* (pp.293-317). New York: Longman.

Swanson, H.L. (1988). Toward a metatheory of learning disabilities. *Journal of Learning Disabilities, 21,* 196-209.

Swanson, H.L. (1989). Strategy instruction: Overview of principles and procedures for effective use. *Learning Disability Quarterly, 12,* 3-14.

Thompson, G. (1986). When nonsense is better than sense: Non-lexical errors to word reading tests. *British Journal of Educational Psychology, 56,* 216-219.

Torgesen, J. (1988). Studies of children with learning disabilities who perform poorly on memory span tasks. *Journal of Learning Disabilities, 21,* 605-612.

Tunmer, W. (1989). The role of language-related factors in reading disability. In D. Shankweiler & I. Liberman (Eds.), *Phonology and reading disability: Solving the reading puzzle* (pp.91-131). Ann Arbor, MI: University of Michigan Press.

Tunmer, W. (1991). Phonological awareness and literacy acquisition. In L. Rieben & C. Perfetti (Eds.), *Learning to read: Basic research and its implications* (pp. 105-119). Hillsdale, NJ: Lawrence Erlbaum Associates.

Tunmer, W.E. & Herriman, M.L. (1984). The development of metalinguistic awareness: A conceptual overview. In W.E. Tunmer, C. Pratt & M.L. Herriman (Eds.), *Metalinguistic awareness in children: Theory, research and implications* (pp. 12-35). New York: Springer-Verlag.

Tunmer, W.E., Herriman, M.L. & Nesdale, A.R. (1988). Metalinguistic abilities and beginning reading. *Reading Research Quarterly, 23,* 134-158.

Tunmer, W.E. & Hoover, W. (1992). Cognitive and linguistic factors in learning to read. In P. Gough, L. Ehri & R. Treiman, (Eds.), *Reading acquisition* (175-214). Hillsdale, NJ: Lawrence Erlbaum Associates.

Tunmer, W.E. & Lally, M.R. (1986, July). *The effects of letter-name knowledge and phonological awareness on computer-based instruction in decoding for pre-readers.* Paper presented at annual meeting of the Australian Reading Association, Perth, Western Australia.

Tunmer, W.E. & Nesdale, A.R. (1982). The effects of digraphs and pseudowords on phonemic segmentation in young children. *Applied Psycholinguistics, 3,* 299-311.

Tunmer, W.E. & Nesdale, A.R. (1985). Phonemic segmentation skill and beginning reading. *Journal of Educational Psychology, 77,* 417-427.

Tunmer, W.E. & Nesdale, A.R. (1986). [Path analysis of the relation of phonological and syntactic awareness to reading comprehension in beginning readers.] Unpublished raw data.

Tunmer, W., Nesdale, A. & Pratt, C. (1983). The development of young children's awareness of logical inconsistencies. *Journal of Experimental Child Psychology, 36,* 97-108.

Tunmer, W.E., Nesdale, A.R. & Wright, A.D. (1987). Syntactic awareness and reading acquisition. *British Journal of Developmental Psychology, 5,* 25-34.

Tunmer, W., Pratt, C. & Herriman, M. (Eds.). (1984). *Metalinguistic awareness in children: Theory, research and implications.* New York: Springer-Verlag.

Tunmer, W. & Rohl, M. (1991). Phonological awareness and reading acquisition. In D. Sawyer & B. Fox (Eds.), *Phonological awareness in reading: The evolution of current perspectives* (pp. 1-30). New York: Springer-Verlag.

Vellutino, F. & Denckla, M. (1991). Cognitive and neuropsychological foundations of word identification in poor and normally developing readers. In R. Barr, M.L. Kamil, P.B. Mosenthal & P.D. Pearson (Eds.), *Handbook of reading research* (Vol. 2) (pp.571-608). New York: Longman.

Vellutino, F. & Scanlon, D. (1982). Verbal processing in poor and normal readers. In C.J. Brainerd & M. Pressley (Eds.), *Verbal processing in children* (pp.189-264). New York: Springer-Verlag.

Vellutino, F. & Scanlon, D. (1987a). Linguistic coding and reading ability. In S. Rosenberg (Ed.), *Advances in applied psycholinguistics* (Vol. 2) (pp. 1-69). New York: Cambridge University Press.

Vellutino, F. & Scanlon, D. (1987b). Phonological coding, phonological awareness and reading ability: Evidence from a longitudinal and experimental study. *Merrill Palmer Quarterly, 33,* 321-363.

Vellutino, F. & Scanlon, D. (1989). Auditory information processing in poor and normal readers. In J.J. Dumont & H. Nakken (Eds.), *Learning disabilities, Vol, 2: Cognitive, social and remedial aspects* (pp. 19-46). Lisse, Netherlands: Swets & Zeitlinger.

Wagner, R., & Torgesen, J. (1987). The nature of phonological processing and its causal role in the acquisition of reading skills. *Psychological Bulletin, 101,* 192-212.

Wagner, R., Balthazar, M., Hurley, S., Morgan, S., Rashotte, C., Shaner, R., Simmons, K. & Stage, S. (1987). The nature of pre-readers' phonological processing abilities. *Cognitive Development, 2,* 355-373.

Wells, G. (1985). Preschool literacy-related activities and success in schools. In D. Olson, N. Torrance & A. Hildyard (Eds.), *Literacy, language and learning: The nature and consequences of reading and writing* (pp.229-255). London: Cambridge University Press.

Willows, D. & Ryan, E. (1986). The development of grammatical sensitivity and its relationship to early reading achievement. *Reading Research Quarterly, 21,* 253-266.

Wolf, M. (1984). Naming, reading and the dyslexias: A longitudinal overview. *Annals of Dyslexia, 34,* 87-115.

Yopp, H. (1988). The validity and reliability of phonemic awareness tests. *Reading Research Quarterly, 23,* 159-177.

PHONEMIC AWARENESS, LANGUAGE AND LITERACY

JOSÉ MORAIS
Laboratoire de Psychologie Expérimentale
Université libre de Bruxelles
1050 Brussels, Belgium

ABSTRACT: The capacity to consciously represent phonemes in isolation appears in the course of learning to read and write in the alphabetic system. In this chapter, it is proposed that, besides this learning setting, some perceptual cues obtained during the activities of either speech comprehension, or speech production, or both, must be crucial for the acquisition of phonemic awareness. This view sheds a new light on the relations between phonemic awareness and phonological awareness. The whole set of conscious phonological representations may serve very different functions. Phonemic awareness depends on the capacity to focus attention on the perceptual representations of speech, rather than on a particular form of phonological awareness. At the end of this chapter, it is also suggested, on the basis of neuropsychological data, that phonemic awareness and knowledge of alphabetic correspondences either constitute the same mental capacity, or at least, rely on the same neural structures.

Phonemic awareness is a metalinguistic capacity. It is the set of conscious representations of the individual phonemes of a language. We can, for example, mentally represent /b/ in isolation, although we cannot produce it in isolation. We may think about /b/ as one part of the word /bat/. Moreover, we take /b/ in "bat", "bed", "black" or "cab" as being the same, thus regardless of context and word position. We have similar conscious representations for the other consonants, some of which we can produce in isolation, as well as for vowels. This is phonemic awareness.

Phonemic awareness should be distinguished from the ability to use the conscious representations of phonemes. This ability requires of course phonemic awareness, but it also depends on processing and memory capacities. Given these capacities, phonemic awareness gives us the possibility to equate our phonological representation of, for example, "Bonas" with the sequence of five phonemic representations /b/, /o/, /n/, /a/, /s/. Adults may easily segment a five-phoneme word such as "Bonas"; however, young children, even if they are aware of the individual phonemes, may find this task rather difficult. And if the task presented to the subject is for example to enunciate the five constituent phonemes of "Bonas" in reverse order, i.e., from the end of the word to its beginning, then even most of the adults may need to think for a rather long time in order to respond without any mistake.

The distinction between phonemic awareness and conscious phonemic segmentation ability is practically important, because some individuals may possess phonemic awareness but be deficient in some of the additional cognitive requirements of phonemic operations. On the other hand, it may also happen that phonemic operations are impaired not because of general processing limitations but because of some weakness in the conscious representations

R.M. Joshi and C.K. Leong (eds.), Reading Disabilities: Diagnosis and Component Processes, 175–184.
© 1993 *Kluwer Academic Publishers. Printed in the Netherlands.*

of phonemes. For instance, the initial matching between the speech stimulus and a sequence of phonemes may imply too much effort or time and therefore render processing at later stages of the task inefficient.

The present chapter examines some of the relationships between phonemic awareness, on the one hand, and language and literacy, on the other hand. Some, at least of the roots of phonemic awareness, should be looked for among language capacities. I propose that both some form of phonological awareness, to be defined later, and accurate and stable perceptual representations of speech are conditions for the emergence of phonemic awareness. Learning alphabetic literacy is a third condition.

In the past, many authors have polemized about whether phonemic awareness is cause or consequence of alphabetic literacy. Now, the most widely accepted position seems to be that the acquisition of alphabetic literacy and the acquisition of phonemic awareness are two interacting processes. Each could be both cause and consequence of the other. However, at the end of this chapter, I suggest that phonemic awareness and knowledge of alphabetic correspondences may constitute the same mental capacity. They might be, introspectively or taken from different viewpoints, the two faces of one and the same reality.

Phonemic awareness and language

The function of language is the communication of meaning. In the case of spoken language, meaning must be coded in a way compatible with the possibilities and constraints of the speech apparatus. In other words, a phonological system is needed, between the representation of meaning and its expression in spoken language. The phonological system includes a layer of phonemic representations. However, phonemic representations are not immediately available to consciousness. They are part of the hidden machinery. Thus, the problem, so far as phonemic awareness is concerned, is either how to gain conscious access to the phonemic units in the language machinery, or how to elaborate conscious representations that would be at least analogous to some extent to these hidden units.

The preliterate speaker-listener disposes of only two types of conscious representations. One is the conscious representation of the meaning of the planned or heard message. This representation is helpless for the purpose of acquiring phonemic awareness. The other conscious representation is twofold. For the listener, it is the conscious perceptual representation of the speech sounds he/she listens to. And for the speaker, it is the conscious perceptual representation of both the sounds he/she produces and the gestures used to produce these sounds. This type of conscious representation provides the material for the elaboration of conscious representations of phonemes. Thus, the acquisition of phonemic awareness by people engaged in learning to read and write in the alphabetic system is constrained by two capacities or properties of their language and cognitive apparatus. One is the capacity to focus attention on the perceptual representations of speech. This capacity allows one to become aware of phonological properties of the spoken language, i.e., to develop some form of phonological awareness. The other is the quality of the perceptual representations of speech (the preciseness, robustness, and stability of these representations across different occurrences), which presumably depends on the nature and efficiency of the mechanisms that are responsible for them.

One of these two conditions for phonemic awareness, namely the capacity to focus attention on the perceptual representations of speech, is examined below. The other, namely, the quality of these representations, is examined in a further paper (Morais & Mousty, 1992).

I think that it is important to distinguish between the notions: attention to the perceptual representations of speech, phonological sensitivity, phonological awareness and phonemic awareness.

Attention to the perceptual representations of speech is necessary to develop any form of phonological awareness. What distinguishes phonological sensitivity and phonological awareness is not so much the intervention of attention but the object attended to.

Phonological sensitivity is a component of spoken language comprehension, which allows the listener, for instance, to recognize correctly the French pronouns "mon", "ton", "son", and to distinguish between the Spanish words "'bebe" and "be'be", even when these utterances are represented in isolation. Sensitivity to phonology, be it to segmental or stress differences, allows people to focus on meaning. It is demonstrated by appropriate behavior, but it does not imply phonological awareness. People can be sensitive to phonological properties without being aware of them.

What, then, is phonological awareness? In a first approximation, phonological awareness is the very large and heterogeneous set of conscious representations that are acquired by focusing attention on the perceptual representations of speech. Thus, it is a general concept. It is relatively unuseful unless one specifies the phonological properties of the individual is aware of.

Some form of phonological awareness is certainly necessary to language development. For example, the self-corrections of word pronunciation that are exhibited by the child in the course of language acquisition provide a testimony of his/her awareness of the incorrect pronunciation. The child realizes the difference between the incorrect and the correct pronunciation.

Some form of phonological awareness is also necessary when people asked to say, for instance, which of two evoked names is longer, and whether or not two nonsense utterances are identical or different. These tasks imply intentional judgments on phonology rather than simply the activation of a phonological structure among other phonological structures. In the same vein, people are not aware of semantics but of phonology when they appreciate or use rhyme, alliteration and other phonological resemblances in poetry, slogans and certain word games.

Although all these forms of conscious phonological capacities largely differ between individuals, they do not necessarily require specific forms of instruction. They develop under the usual conditions of experience with spoken language, even if some of them can perhaps improve after special exercise.

Depending on how one chooses to define phonological awareness in a narrow or large sense, phonological awareness is either a condition for phonemic awareness, or the general category to which phonemic awareness belongs. Phonemes are part of the phonological structure of language. Thus, awareness of phonemes may be considered as a case of phonological awareness. However, it is very important not to confound phonemic awareness and phonological awareness. The reason is that the conscious phonological representations that can be attained by simply focusing on the perceptual representations of speech do not include representations of phonemes. Corrections of word pronunciation, even if they concern a phonemic discrepancy between token and target, do not lead to phonemic awareness. Likewise, expertise in rhyming production and evaluation does not render this type of phonological experts, for instance, poets more ready to acquire conscious representations of phonemes, as it is demonstrated by comparison with non-poets.

The distinction between phonological awareness and phonemic awareness is appropriate because phonemic awareness requires a specific form of instruction. This is the instruction to read and write using an alphabetic representation of the spoken language. The idea that only this particular instruction can elicit phonemic awareness has not been refuted so far. Of course, it cannot be demonstrated, either. However, it should be stressed that no other instruction, from among the many types of instruction to which non-alphabetic people are submitted in the modern society, seems to promote phonemic awareness.

Regardless of whether phonemic awareness is best defined as a special case of phonological awareness or as a separate capacity, it is hardly conceivable that phonemic awareness could be elicited in the absence of any kind of phonological awareness. As indicated above, phonological awareness or some of its forms intervene in the acquisition of spoken language. Thus, it would probably be a desperate enterprise to look for human beings without any phonological awareness and then check if they possess phonemic awareness or if they can acquire it by any mean. A more interesting question is whether there are forms of phonological awareness which are absent or deficient in people who simultaneously display either insufficient phonemic awareness or insufficient abilities of conscious phonemic segmentation.

As a first attempt to answer this question, let us take people who, despite having been offered the appropriate instructional conditions (i.e., instruction on alphabetic literacy) for the acquisition of phonemic awareness, remain poor in conscious phonemic segmentation. Would they exhibit significant deficits in some particular forms of phonological awareness? As a matter of fact, the literature presents many observations of these relations between phonemic segmentation ability and phonological awareness. Phonemic segmentation frequently correlates, for instance, with rhyming ability and with syllabic segmentation. Thus, it is tempting to attribute the deficiency in phonemic awareness to impairments in these forms of phonological awareness. The reason for choosing this direction of causality rather than the opposite direction is that syllabic awareness and rhyming ability appear intuitively to be more primitive than phonemic awareness. According to the continuity postulate (each capacity grows from another capacity), which is very much used implicitly in developmental psychology, a deficiency in capacity n should affect negatively the subsequent capacities n', n'', etc..

The problem is that, as it has been recalled so often, correlations do not inform about causality issues. Thus, it is also possible that the apparent impairment in some forms of phonological awareness is due to a deficiency in phonemic awareness rather than the reverse. Indeed, by acquiring phonemic awareness one acquires also a very useful and efficient tool to deal with other phonological units or properties. In the case of rhyme judgment, for instance, the knowledge that rhyme is phonemic identity from the last stressed vowel to the end of the utterances may allow a much more precise evaluation of rhyme than the rather global sensitivity to phonological similarities to which illiterate people must resort to.

How to escape from this dilemma in considering causality relations? Rather than looking for an impairment in some form of phonological awareness which would necessarily occur in any individual who exhibits an impairment in phonemic awareness, one may employ a differential approach. There still is, in the world, a large number of humans who have not acquired phonemic awareness for reasons that have nothing to do with deficiencies in underlying capacities. They simply have never received instruction on the alphabetic code. The inquiry into the different forms of phonological awareness of these people may be very helpful to locate the aspects of phonological awareness that constrain the acquisition of phonemic awareness. The discovery that, in such or such aspect of phonological awareness, illiterates are inferior to alphabetic literates does not permit an unambiguous interpretation. By contrast, the discovery that illiterates are at least very good, if not equal to the alphabetic literates, is of potential importance. When this condition is met, it is especially relevant to consider the case of subjects who, like most dyslexics, have problems in conscious phonemic segmentation in spite of having received appropriate instruction on the alphabetic code. If dyslexic children display a striking deficiency in some form of phonological awareness that is well developed in illiterates, then this deficiency cannot be a by-product of their low phonemic awareness. We would then locate a form of phonological awareness which may not be strictly necessary but should at least be of great help in the acquisition of phonemic awareness. For practical reasons, namely the relative difficulty of finding dyslexics and illiterates for testing, one probably has to reverse the sequence of operations: the discovery of a specific difficulty in dyslexics is followed by the checking of the corresponding competence in illiterates.

One aspect of phonological awareness that may fall in this category is the awareness of the articulatory gestures used to produce speech. There is dramatic evidence of dyslexics being very poor in articulatory awareness (Montgomery, 1981). They are unable to indicate which of several schematic drawings corresponds to the position of the tongue, teeth and lips for a given phoneme. However, with Luz Cary, I have found that illiterate adults are very good in this test. Moreover, Jesus Alegria, and myself also found a similar good performance in five-year-old children. Thus, preliterate children are prepared, in their great majority, to use articulatory cues as a means to acquire phonemic awareness. This articulatory awareness may be of great help, in particular, for deaf children whose articulation capacities are relatively good compared to their hearing. Alegria and I have tested 23 five-year-old deaf children with these characteristics and found that their performance in Montgomery's test was also relatively good, although lower on the average than the performance of the hearing children of the same age. (All the mentioned observations by our group are still unpublished).

Articulatory awareness is certainly not the only form of phonological awareness that constrains the acquisition of phonemic awareness. Given the well-known difficulty of deaf children in acquiring both phonemic awareness and alphabetic literacy, observations such as the one mentioned above with deaf children who are good articulators suggest that articulatory awareness is not the whole story. On the other hand, to exploit the articulatory awareness of these children to promote phonemic awareness in the context of literacy acquisition seems to be a reasonable idea.

Articulatory awareness may not be absolutely necessary to the emergence of phonemic awareness, as suggested by the studies of Bishop (Bishop, 1985; Bishop & Robson, 1989) with congenitally speechless (anarthric) children. Some of these subjects could indicate the orthography of monosyllabic nonwords nearly correctly. If nonword spelling constitutes evidence for phonemic awareness, then it seems that articulatory awareness (although this was not examined in the mentioned studies, one can presumably consider it nonexistent) is not a necessary condition for phonemic awareness. Attention to phonetic cues present in heard speech could be sufficient to allow the emergence of phonemic awareness in the context of alphabetic literacy acquisition. On the other hand, the fact that the lack of articulation abilities, and therefore of articulatory awareness, leads to poorer nonword spelling as compared to control children i.e., children with cerebral palsy but with normal speech (Bishop & Robson, 1989), stresses the utility of articulatory awareness for phonemic awareness.

We still know too little about the forms of phonological awareness that may constrain phonemic awareness. Much work has been devoted to the relationships between rhyming abilities, phonemic awareness and alphabetic literacy. This work is certainly very important. However, the ability to appreciate rhyme, when it does not use phonemic awareness, is probably only one manifestation of the capacity to focus attention on the speech sounds and to evaluate phonological relations. Illiterates, asked to say whether two words rhyme or not, display a gradient of "rhyme" responses for different types of non-rhyming pairs which share some other type of phonological resemblance (Bertelson, de Gelder, Tfouni & Morais, 1989). For instance, rhyming is more frequently falsely detected in pairs that share the stressed syllable but not the final unstressed syllable than in pairs that show the opposite property. We should probably study the rhyming abilities in the context of the general capacity to appreciate phonological properties and relations. There are indications that this capacity, in preliterate individuals, is wholistic rather than analytical. But wholistic capacities may also be studied in an analytical way. It is necessary to discover which phonetic cues contribute, and in which ways, to judgments of phonological similarity and distance between utterances. By doing so, we may perhaps eventually locate the phonetic cues that people use to realize, when provided with an alphabetic representation of their spoken language, that speech is a sequence of phonemes.

Phonemic awareness and literacy

Since the paper our group published in Cognition twelve years ago (Morais, Cary, Alegria & Bertelson, 1979), I have had many occasions to reaffirm that the acquisition of phonemic awareness depends on receiving instruction on the alphabetic code i.e., on a corpus of grapheme-phoneme correspondences. A relatively neglected issue is what happens to phonemic awareness after people have acquired knowledge of the alphabet. Many people become functionally illiterate, in the sense that they cease to read and write for socio-professional reasons and most become unable to do it. Other people may become "alliterate" to some extent as a consequence of a cerebral lesion affecting the regions that underlie the literacy capacities. As far as normal ex-literates are concerned, very few observations of phonemic awareness have been collected. One study by Scliar-Cabral, Morais, Nepomuceno and Kolinsky (in preparation), in Brazil, suggests that adults who learned to read and write in normal classes in their childhood but who now either completely fail in reading or read at a very rudimentary level are unable to perform simple tasks of phonemic awareness. More studies are needed, taking into account different levels of literacy and making an assessment of the mechanisms employed.

The case of loss of literacy capacities as a result of cerebral damage allows one to ask a very interesting question. What is the relation between the use of phonological assembling in the skilled readers and their phonemic awareness? Is the conservation of phonemic awareness dependent on the availability of the phonological access route to the mental lexicon? The introspective feeling of many literate people is that they can think about word phonology and about phonemes without mentally evoking the corresponding written representations. In some cases, for example in cases of irregular orthography, or in cases governed by contextual rules, it may be necessary to avoid the written representation to make judgments about phonemes. Thus, the idea that phonemic awareness has become a capacity independent from the use of alphabetic literacy in literate people may seem quite plausible.

However, from a different perspective, this idea may also appear implausible. As a matter of fact, deep and phonological dyslexics have lost the phonological assembling procedure. But if phonemic awareness is spared in these patients, in other words if they still possessed conscious representations for phonemes, why should they be unable to use at least the non-contextual rules of grapheme-phoneme correspondences? Both visual identification and associative capacities may be preserved in these patients. Thus, if assembling constitutes a problem for them, the difficulty should be attributed to the phonemic component of the process.

In the classic neuropsychological approaches to literacy, the observations made on phonemic awareness are of little help to answer this question, especially because they were not put in relation with selective types of literacy impairment. One recent study (Bisiacchi, Cipolotti & Denes, 1989) has addressed the question explicitly. Their patient, presented as a phonological dyslexic, was still capable of performing phonemic manipulations. The authors claim, in their conclusion, that the operations involved in phonological processing and in pseudo-word reading, although probably interdependent in the initial stages of acquisition, become independent in the final stages.

I disagree with Bisiacchi et al.'s (1989) conclusions. Actually, the impairment of their patient in pseudo-word reading was not very severe (only 37% of errors, even when long pseudo-words are included), and these errors were most of the time substitutions or additions of a single phoneme. This performance could not be obtained if the patient was not using her knowledge of grapheme-phoneme correspondences to a large extent. Moreover, the same type of behavior happened in pseudo-word writing. In addition, the patient knew the phonemic counterparts of all the letters of the alphabet, and she was able to read and write correctly 14 meaningless syllables out of 15. Given these spared abilities, it is not at all surprising that the patient could perform intentional manipulations of phonemes. As the authors indicate, memory anomalies may have been at the origin of the difficulties shown in literacy abilities.

With Philippe Mousty, I have examined several dyslexic patients who display relatively specific deficits in terms of lexical access procedures. A very short description, first of their reading behavior, and then of their performance on different metaphonological tests, is presented below.

JS was a surface-like dyslexic. He showed a large effect of regularity in reading. There was no effect of lexicality (words versus pseudo-words) in either reading or writing. He thus seemed to be strongly impaired in the direct or addressed procedure. However, a relatively large number of single consonant confusions in reading also suggests a slight impairment in his phonological procedure.

PR was a phonological-like dyslexic. She did not read irregular words less well than regular ones. There was a very strong effect of lexicality, both in reading and writing. But she was not a pure phonological dyslexic, since she made some phonological paralexias consisting of pseudo-words. Likewise, some of her spelling errors were phonological. Her phonological procedure was severely impaired, but probably not completely abolished.

VD could read irregular words as well as regular ones. He was completely unable to read or spell pseudo-words. Almost 40% of his errors in word reading were semantic paralexias. Thus, it seems that his phonological procedure was severely impaired, maybe completely, and there was an additional trouble in the association with semantics, allowing a diagnosis of deep dyslexia.

RV had no effect of regularity, but a huge effect of lexicality. He produced many semantic errors in reading. Like VD, he could thus be considered as a deep dyslexic.

These patients were given several metaphonological tests. All with the exception of RV (untested) were perfect in a test that requires the subject to judge the relative phonological length of two words regardless of the physical size of their referents.

The other tests were a test of rhyme judgment, a test of syllable and phoneme detection, and oddity tests based either on the syllable or on the phoneme.

JS, who was only slightly impaired in his phonological procedure, was also only slightly impaired in his conscious phonemic abilities. PR, who had great difficulties in using the phonological procedure, also displayed great difficulties in the phonemic tests. VD, who was probably completely impaired in his phonological procedure, performed around chance level in all the phonemic tests. Finally, RV, like VD, was at chance level in the phonemic tests, and in a clearer way than VD, he performed much better in the rhyming and syllabic tests than in the phonemic ones.

To sum up, there seems to be a clear association between the abilities of phonological transcoding and of conscious phonemic segmentation in this set of patients, who exhibit different types of selective impairment in literacy capacities. When the cerebral lesion spares the mechanism of phonological assembling, phonemic awareness is still present. However, when it is this mechanism that is damaged, then corresponding deficits appear in phonemic awareness. It was dramatic to see, during the testing, how unable these patients were to understand the notion of phoneme. Their behavior closely resembled, in this respect, the behavior of illiterate adults.

One may ask again the question of causality. Did some of these patients lose their knowledge of grapheme-phoneme correspondences because they had become unaware of phonemes, or did they lose phonemic awareness because they had become unable to use phonological transcoding mechanisms? This question has no answer. We can only observe that coincidence. Had the patients recovered phonemic awareness, then they would have been able to use phonological transcoding again, and vice versa.

There might be no cause and no effect, because both competencies might actually be only one competence. Phonemic awareness might be the subjective version of our alphabetic knowledge, but this would not exist without the awareness of phonemes, like a body and its surface. The impression that phonemes are a reality of their own, independent of their graphemic counterpartners, is reinforced by the fact that biunivocal correspondence is transgressed quite often. But the complexity of the relation does not make the two concepts more independent of each other than they need to be. The conscious representations of phonemes and the conscious representations of graphemes may have to support each other in order to be evoked.

However, this is not the only possible interpretation. Indeed, these two types of conscious representations may actually be separate, but served by the same cerebral areas, so that a lesion cannot disturb one and spare the other. The intricate interdependence of these two competencies in the course of acquisition may have required the involvement of the same neural layers. Furthermore, it is hard to figure out that subsequent separate use of one competence ought to lead to reduplication of this particular type of representation in a different area.

Converging and very impressive evidence for the common fate of phonemic awareness and phonological transcoding comes from new observations of PS, a deep dyslexic patient described by de Partz (1986), who kindly made this testing possible. Marie-Pierre de Partz carried out a very long and theoretically motivated re-education of this patient. At the beginning, PS, a previously highly educated man, was completely unable to associate phonemes with letters. Most probably, but no such information is contained in the paper, he was also completely unable to analyze speech into phonemes intentionally. The re-education technique consisted in teaching him to associate the letters with a word code, and then to try to separate the first phoneme of the word-code in order to associate it with the corresponding letter. This was easy to do for vowels, but much more difficult for stop consonants. Three months of such exercises were needed. Finally, the patient was taught to read words by finding the phonemes for each letter and trying to blend them. In other words, PS received training in phonemic segmentation coupled with training in phoneme-grapheme correspondences. As most beginning readers, he was taught again to read according to a phonic method.

Our testing of PS took place in 1988. He was almost completely correct for both words and pseudo-words, in both reading and writing, although he manifested some slowness. Most interestingly, he obtained an almost perfect performance in the phonemic tests presented to the other patients described above. Thus, a deep dyslexic who has re-acquired the use of the phonological assembling mechanism has also become aware of the phonemic constituents of language, and vice versa. Training phonemic awareness alone might have remained ineffective. My guess is that PS would not have understood what the trainer had tried to do, and that he would have discovered nothing but a few tricks to cope with the exercises. On the other hand, training reading and writing with a look-and-say method would have left the patient at the same point.

Phonemic awareness and the knowledge of the alphabetic code only make sense together. They are acquired, lost, and re-acquired together. The mind of PS was not like the mind of an illiterate. Despite his brain lesion, he may have kept a considerable part of the knowledge and analytic abilities which he had acquired for many years by means of his literacy capacities. Yet, all this knowledge and analytic abilities do not seem to have compensated in the slightest degree for the effects of the lesion on his mental representation of the alphabetic principle. This competence seems to be highly specific, and the conditions of its acquisition seem to be highly constrained.

ACKNOWLEDGMENT

This work has been supported by the Belgian "Fonds de la Recherche fondamentale collective". Thanks are due to Régine Kolinsky for fruitful discussions of the present issues.

REFERENCES

Bertelson, P., De Gelder, B., Tfouni, L. V., & Morais, J. (1989). Metaphonological abilities of adult illiterates: New evidence of heterogeneity. *European Journal of Cognitive Psychology, 1,* 239-250.

Bishop, D. V. M. (1985). Spelling ability in congenital dysarthria: Evidence against articulatory coding in translating between phonemes and graphemes. *Cognitive Neuropsychology , 2,* 229-250.

Bishop, D. V. M. & Robson, J. (1989). Accurate non-word spelling despite congenital inability to speak: Phoneme-grapheme conversion does not require subvocal articulation. *British Journal of Psychology, 80,* 1-13.

Bisiacchi, P. S., Cipolotti, L. & Denes, G. (1989). Impairment in processing meaningless verbal material in several modalities: The relationship between short-term memory and phonological skills. *Quarterly Journal of Experimental Psychology, 41A,* 293-319.

de Partz, M. P. (1986). Re-education of a deep dyslexic patient: Rationale of the method and results. *Cognitive Neuropsychology, 3,* 149-177.

Montgomery, D. (1981). Do dyslexics have difficulty accessing articulatory information? *Psychological Research, 33,* 235-243.

Morais, J., Cary, L., Alegria, J. & Bertelson, P. (1979). Does awareness of speech as a sequence of phones arise spontaneously? *Cognition, 7,* 323-331.

Morais, J. & Mousty, P. (1992). The causes of phonemic awareness. In J. Alegria, D. Holender, J. Junça de Morais & M. Radeau (Eds.), *Analytic approaches to human cognition,* Amsterdam: North-Holland.

Scliar-Cabral, L., Morais, J., Nepomuceno, L., & Kolinsky, R. *Phonemic awareness versus phonemic sensitivity: A study of Brazilian adults of different literacy levels.* (in preparation).

THE RELEVANCE OF PHONOLOGICAL AWARENESS IN LEARNING TO READ: SCANDINAVIAN LONGITUDINAL AND QUASI-EXPERIMENTAL STUDIES

ÅKE OLOFSSON
Department of Psychology
University of Umea
S-901 87 Umea, Sweden

ABSTRACT: Skills in analysis of speech sounds and synthesis of phonetic segments into real words (e.g., phonemic or phonological awareness) have often been found to correlate with success in reading acquisition. The nature of this relationship was investigated in a series of Scandinavian longitudinal studies. First, the quantitative relationships between kindergarten measures, including several metaphonological and metacognitive tasks, and reading and writing achievement in grades 1 to 3, were estimated. The most stable and important determinant of basic reading and spelling skills was the preschool child's ability to analyze simple words into phonemic units. In two quasi-experimental studies the effects of kindergarten phonemic awareness training were tested. The training programs consisted of metalinguistic games and exercises, implemented prior to formal reading instruction. The programs did affect positively metalinguistic skills, especially phoneme handling tasks, and also facilitated reading and spelling acquisition in the lower grades. Positive effects were also found in the subgroup of low-achieving children. The validity of the phonological awareness construct and the quality of the measurement variables used were further tested applying structural equation modeling with latent variables. In independent samples, models with a separate phonological awareness factor showed the best fit, thus confirming the existence of a phonological awareness factor.

The nature of the close relationship between phonemic, or phonological, awareness and success in learning to read and spell has received much attention in recent years (For reviews, see e.g., Adams, 1990; Brady & Shankweiler, 1991; Sawyer & Fox, 1991). The object of the present paper is, first, to summarize a series of Scandinavian studies on phonological awareness and reading acquisition, and second, to present additional analyses and data based on this empirical work. The previous work is followed up with new longitudinal data, extended analysis of the effect of phonological awareness training on low-achieving children, and with structural equational modeling using longitudinal data.

A Causal Model for Reading Acquisition

The aim of the first study (Lundberg, Olofsson & Wall, 1980) was to further elucidate the relationship between learning to read, different aspects of linguistic awareness and measures of cognitive ability and finally to extend previous correlational findings by estimating the predictive power of linguistic awareness through a longitudinal study. A rather broad variety of metalinguistic tasks was used. The linguistic unit of analysis was varied by using both syllables and phonemes in all tasks. Further, the cognitive requirement was varied by placing

R.M. Joshi and C.K. Leong (eds.), Reading Disabilities: Diagnosis and Component Processes, 185–198.

different demands on the operations to be carried out with the units and different demands on working memory.

The postulated model assumed that metalinguistic skills are dependent on previous development of general intelligence and decentering and that metalinguistic skills cause differences in development of reading and spelling skills. The direct influence of cognitive abilities was postulated to be minor. Two hundred children were tested in kindergarten whereof 143 were identified one year later in grade 1 and 133 two years later in grade 2, and finally, 114 in grade 3. The dependent variables included teacher ratings of reading and spelling, as well as silent word decoding tests, spelling tests and ratings of language production and understanding. The quantitative implications of the postulated model were worked out by path analysis. For each dependent variable an ordinary least squares (OLS) multiple regression analysis was computed using all prior causal variables as predictors. In Lundberg et al. (1980) the model was estimated with data from kindergarten to grade 2. In the present paper we will estimate the same model using grade 3 measures.

Lundberg et al. (1980) found a clear superiority in predictive power for the phonemic tasks. The cognitive and perceptual tasks influenced reading and spelling almost exclusively in an indirect way mediated by the phonemic awareness tasks. Totally, about 50% of the variance in reading and spelling ability in grade 2 was accounted for. The best single predictor was found to be a task demanding the segmentation of two and three-syllabic words into phonemes, then the reversal of the order of the segments and pronunciation of the new "reversed" word. Nearly as good a predictor was a task allowing the child to analyze picture-presented three-phoneme words into phonemes by concretely representing the phonemes with pegs on a board. This task was designed to minimize the working-memory load and other extraneous cognitive requirements. The same pattern was found in a separate analysis applied to children with no preschool reading ability. Here the phoneme reversal task showed less importance and the analysis and synthesis tasks with concrete representations more importance.

Table 1 presents the results from the follow up in grade 3 (compared to the grade 2 results). The same path model as for the grade 2 variables was estimated using test-results in grade 3 as dependent variables. The predictive power of the kindergarten tests is, as expected, slightly lower, but for the kindergarten test measuring analysis of concretely represented phonemes (in the test situation a plastic peg is used to represent the sounds) the predictive power is not attenuated from grade 1 to 3. This reflects the validity of analyzing concretely represented phonemes as a measurement of stable and genuine individual differences related to reading acquisition. The power of gender as a significant (but weak) predictor of grade 3 spelling skill may reflect the girls' higher sensitivity to linguistic norms, a finding not uncommon in sociolinguistics. Still after three years almost 50% of the variance is explained.

More recent studies using the same path-analytical approach have supported to a great extent the findings in Lundberg et al. (1980), yielding similar causal ordering and effect estimates of cognitive variables upon phonemic awareness and reading and spelling (e.g., Leong, 1984; Stanovich, Cunningham & Feeman, 1984).

It was suggested that the high predictive power of a small set of phonemic awareness tasks -- over 50% of the variance in basic reading and spelling skills -- should not primarily be applied in selecting high-risk cases for intervention. On the contrary, the theoretical clarification gained through the explicitness forced by the use of path analysis implied that a

Table 1. Comparison of path coefficients (standardized regression coefficients) for the path models in Lundberg et al. (1980) and the same models using grade 3 data as dependent variables. N > 114

	Dependent Variables								
	Word decoding[a]		(Rating) Reading[a]		Spelling[b]		(Rating) Writing[a]		Total sum Basics[a]	
Phoneme Reversal	.56	.31	.36	.36	.31	.38	.40	.45	.50	.43
Phoneme analysis (concrete)			.20	.24			.21	.25	.30	.30
Phoneme synthesis (concrete)			.24	.18						
Phoneme synthesis			.23	.08						
Sex[c]	-.17	-.14	-.04	-.04	-.14	-.22	-.05	-.19		
R^2	.39	.16	.50	.40	.43	.39	.33	.49	.54	.45

Note. For simplicity the complete set of predictor variables is not reported. The omitted variables all had lower coefficients than the included variables.
a Measured in grade 1 and grade 3.
b Measured in grade 2 and grade 3.
c This variable was coded as 0 for girls and 1 for boys.

general stimulation of the development of phonemic skills in the kindergarten group should positively affect learning to read and spell in school for all children.

In the literature it is often repeated that findings such as the present ones are correlational and that correlation is not causation. The best way to test the causal power of phonemic awareness is to manipulate it experimentally and evaluate the effects on reading acquisition. Many pioneer researchers commented upon the difficulty in instructing children in phonemic awareness tasks (e.g., Rozin & Gleitman, 1977; Savin, 1972; Zhurova, 1966-67) but later several studies indicated training effects (e.g., Content, Morais, Alegria & Bertelson, 1982; Farmer, Nixon, & White, 1976; Marsh & Mineo, 1977).

Phonemic Awareness Training in Preschool

Olofsson & Lundberg (1983) evaluated a training program designed to develop phonemic awareness skills through playful activities carried out within ordinary kindergarten groups. The program did not emphasize explicit instruction, but on the contrary, in a playful context stimulated the children to construct and develop actively their own representation of the phonemic aspects of speech. This approach to phonemic awareness training, which contrasts sharply with the method of teaching speech sounds in most phonics based reading programs, was stressed already by Elkonin (1973; see also Downing & Leong, 1982, p. 108).

In Olofsson & Lundberg (1983) the three experimental groups had different amounts of phonemic awareness training and one of the control groups participated in a similar program dealing only with non-verbal sounds. Initially, and after about 8 weeks of training, the children were tested with highly equivalent tests measuring the ability to blend concretely represented phonemes into words and to analyze words into their phonemic constituents. (The same as the *concrete* tests in Table 1). The analysis was affected by ceiling effects but clear improvement was found for the children with medium and low abilities in the experimental groups with the most structured training. Based on the observations of spontaneous activities, using phonemic segmentation and blending, it was concluded that the more advanced children also gained from the training program.

No apparent problems were found in the implementation of the exercises or games. The most crucial difficulty for many children was to discover the phoneme and a great deal of the games had to center around tasks of isolating the first phoneme. Despite great individual differences it was possible to carry out exercises and games in a way that all the children enjoyed. It was concluded that phonemic awareness can be developed in prereaders outside the context of formal reading instruction. Attention can be directed to the formal aspects of language by appropriate activities encouraging them to approach their language in a playful and creative way.

Effects on Reading and Spelling in Grades 1 and 2

The long-term effects of the kindergarten training program was evaluated by a follow-up in grade 1 (Olofsson & Lundberg, 1985). In the middle of the spring semester, 83 out of the original 95 children were identified in 9 different school classes. A broad set of measures was used (see also Table 2), capturing phonemic synthesis and analysis ability, reading and spelling of nonsense words, reading and spelling of common words with (for Swedish spelling) more complex or "irregular" spelling-sound relations and a silent word decoding test.

Effects of the training program were found on the phonemic awareness tests. For the subgroup of children with beginning knowledge about reading and spelling in kindergarten, effects were found on reading and spelling of nonsense and 'irregular' words. No effects were found on the silent word reading test. The analysis was affected by ceiling effects and unequal control groups.

The analysis of individual cases indicated that the treated children may, to a greater extent, have avoided failure in reading and spelling. In the experimental groups all the children mastering the phonemic awareness tasks in kindergarten seemed to have acquired satisfactory reading and spelling ability in grade 1. Among the control children with equal kindergarten phonemic awareness there were several with poor development in reading and spelling.

Effects on Reading and Spelling in Grade 2

Further long-term effects of the phonemic awareness training in kindergarten were evaluated in grade 2 (Olofsson, 1989) by repeating the silent word decoding test and the irregular-word spelling test. A nonsense word spelling test was developed in order to tap more effectively the children's use of more complex spelling-sound rules.

The trained children were found to create qualitatively different spellings compared to the untrained children but the groups did not differ on the silent word reading test. The experimental groups made significantly more highly rule-governed spellings, reflecting a correct phonemic analysis of the spoken words as well as knowledge of spelling sound rules. The untrained children created more spellings that could not be explained from spelling-sound rules or conventions in Swedish spelling. These spellings rather reflected poor knowledge of spelling-sound rules or poor phonemic analysis ability.

Kindergarten phonemic awareness training seems to have a long-term effect on the children's ability to learn spelling-sound rules. However, the short training period, the relatively small size of the groups and the ceiling effects called for a new, more extensive investigation.

A Large Scale Training Study

In a Danish study by Lundberg, Frost & Petersen (1988) the general design (quasi-experimental, longitudinal) was similar to the Swedish one, but the training was more extensive and covered 8 months of the preschool year with daily training. The experimental group consisted of 235 children and the control group 155. The assessment now also included general language and intellectual ability as well as letter knowledge. Mathematics was included in the school assessment to permit evaluation of the specificity of the preschool training effect.

Pre- and posttest before and after the kindergarten training program revealed a very strong positive effect on the children's phonemic awareness. Significant but smaller effects were found on syllable manipulation skills and rhyming. No differences between the groups were found on language comprehension and letter knowledge. Sentence reading, word reading and spelling tests in grades 1 to 3 all showed a significant advantage for the experimental group. But, on the mathematics test, given at the end of grade 1, the control group had a significantly higher mean than the experimental. (It should be noted that the regular Danish national assessment had demonstrated a slight advantage for the control group areas.) The difference in this direction justifies the conclusion that the preschool training is specifically related to literacy.

In summary, phonological skill can be developed outside the context of formal reading instruction, and the effect is specific to skills involved in phonemic analysis and synthesis. Preschool training in phonological awareness facilitates reading and spelling development later in school, and the effect persists to at least until grade 3. However, these positive effects need to be further investigated with regard to how low-achieving children are effected, since it can be argued that these children are most in need to be helped. Even if there are constitutional causes behind their disabilities (see Olson, Wise, Conners, Rack, & Fulker, 1989) the idea of prevention should not be forgotten.

The Effect on Low-achieving Children

On the basis of the first assessment prior to the training period (pretest) 25 (extreme) children from each group were selected according to the following criteria: (a) less than 3 points out of 24 possible on the phonological awareness test, (b) recognition of not more than 2 letters, (c) no sign of reading ability. A careful match between experiment and control children ensured almost perfect equivalence in performance on all pretests. Both groups consisted of 16 boys and 9 girls. Below the groups will be termed LPE (Low, Pretest, Experimental) and LPC (Low Pretest, Control).

The development of reading and spelling skills in school for the two groups of low-achieving children (LPE and LPC) was compared and also related to the corresponding development of the total sample of experimental and control children.

WORD-READING SPEED

Figure 1 presents the development of word-reading speed from the end of grade 1 to the middle of grade 3. The slowest development was observed for the LPC-children, whereas the LPE-children matched the performance of the total control group. The total experimental group consistently outperformed the other groups indicating a general positive effect of the preschool program. The differences were statistically significant.

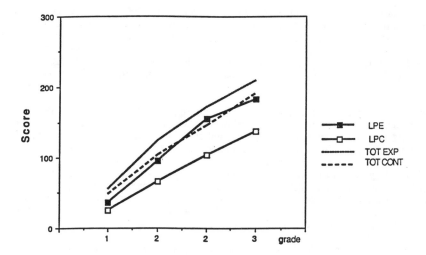

Figure 1. Development of word-reading speed over four occasions of assessment (grade 1-3) for the LPE- and LPC-groups as compared to the total experiment and control groups.

The most interesting finding in the present context, however, is the wide gap between LPC- and LPE-children. The gap between the groups tends to increase over successive measurements, possibly indicating the operation of a Matthew effect (Stanovich, 1986).

SENTENCE READING

The LPE-children, despite their initial handicap, in grade 3 read and understood sentences with the same speed and accuracy as normal children. The untrained children with low preschool score (LPC) on the other hand were significantly behind normal performance.

SPELLING

The spelling results are presented in Figure 2. To facilitate comparisons, the performance scores have been transformed to z-scales with the total control group as reference norm, i.e., all values have been expressed as standardized deviations from the mean of the total control group mean for the given test occasion. The total control group was judged as an appropriate reference, since no specific intervention had taken place there, and the sample seemed to be fairly representative of a normal Danish school population. Again, we can see the LPE-children performing very close to the reference norm ($z = 0$), whereas the LPC-children are consistently far below normal spelling performance.

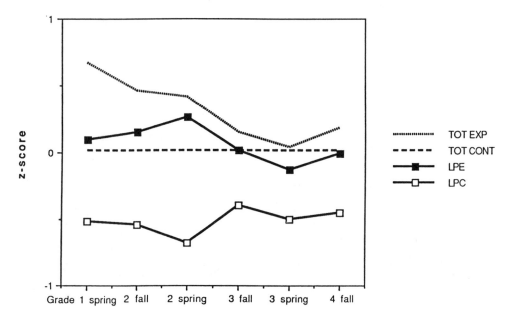

Figure 2. Spelling performance over occasions (grade 1-4) expressed as z-scores with the total control groups as reference.

Conclusions

The findings above are quite clear and straightforward. The low achieving group of children who received extensive training in phonological awareness during the preschool year (LPE) clearly and consistently outperformed a matched group of non-trained children (LPC) in word-reading speed, sentence reading and spelling.

Our interpretation of these findings is that the preschool program in phonological awareness had a strong preventive power (Olofsson & Lundberg, 1985). Children at risk for developing reading disabilities in school could profit from the training in kindergarten and enter formal reading instruction in school better prepared than non-trained children to meet the cognitive requirements of the alphabetic code.

Causal Modeling with Latent Variables

The latent structure hypothesized to account for the relation between kindergarten phonemic awareness and reading and spelling in the first grades can be explicitly formulated and tested using the technique of linear structural relationships (LISREL, see Jöreskog & Sörbom, 1984). Three different models is evaluated using data from Olofsson & Lundberg (1983, 1985) and Olofsson (1989). The 48 subjects having no missing data (from kindergarten to grade 3) were included in the present analysis. At schoolstart the children were about 7 years old, which is the common age for schoolstart in the Scandinavian countries. The tests used are presented in Table 2.

In *Model* 1 we have the traditional formulation of reading tests and spelling tests and the assumption of a greater importance of a phonological strategy in spelling than in reading. Reading is thought to be more dependent on visual or lexical processing. Thus phonemic awareness should have a stronger influence on the latent variable behind spelling tests than on the reading variable.

Model 2 uses nonsense word tests as a measure of spelling-sound rule usage and the ordinary reading and spelling tests as measures of word-specific associations.

Model 3. Within the framework of limited capacity models of reading (Stanovich, 1980), automatic word recognition develops rapidly during the first school years and frees capacity for higher levels processing.

Automaticity is thought to increase as a function of training and the children who grasp the alphabetical principle feel motivated and are more likely to engage in training. Knowledge about how orthography systematically maps speech may also be necessary for the training to have this effect. The use of phonological recoding for lexical access of novel words and for keeping the words in short-term memory may make reading easier to master and training a more pleasant task. Phonological awareness is thought to be important for the understanding of the alphabetical principle. This leads to a model with a causal chain from phonemic awareness to a phonologic (using phonological recoding) reading and spelling factor (latent variable) and further to easy and fast word recognition which then finally enhance comprehension.

STRUCTURAL EQUATION MODELING

In structural equational modeling using LISREL there are basically two types of relationships that have to be defined. First, the relations between observed variables and the latent variables have to be stated. This is called the measurement model and is analogous to the factor-analysis approach in psychometrics. Second, the relations among the latent variables are defined in a structural equation model that, in some sense, can be viewed as a path analysis with latent variables (or factor scores). LISREL then simultaneously computes estimates for all unknown parameters in the model using all information in the data. Several methods for obtaining the estimates are available. The present sample size is critically low, generally samples smaller than 100 cases are not recommended. A careful inspection of raw data revealed departures from normality for several of the variables. Thus, the distribution-free method of Unweighted Least Squares (ULS) was used in the present analysis. However,

Table 2. Tests used in kindergarten, grade 1 and grade 2 (Olofsson & Lundberg, 1985; Olofsson, 1989). (The labels are used in Figure 3.)

PreSyn, PreAn, PostSyn, PostAn	Phonemic synthesis and analysis ability in kindergarten, individually assessed assessed with highly equivalent tests before and after a kindergarten program.
Syn	Synthesis of orally presented speech sounds in grade 1. The test consisted of 17 Swedish words arranged in increasing difficulty from cvcv words to cccvccv words.
An	Analysis of words into phonemes in grade 1.
SpelN	Spelling of nonsense words in grade 1. 12 pseudo words (in the order 4 cvc, 3 ccvc and 5 more complex pseudo words) were dictated to the children. The children were told that the words belonged to a secret language and that they were going to spell them "just like they sounded."
ReadN	Reading of nonsense words in grade 1. The same 12 words as in the nonsense spelling test were used.
ReadI	Reading of irregularly spelled words in grade 1. The material consisted of 12 common words (presumably familiar to most school children of this age), with spelling different from the phonetic structure (7 with 3 letters, 2 with 4 letters and 3 with 5 letters).
Spel1 and Spel2	The same words as in the irregular reading test (ReadI) were used. The words were read to the children who, in turn, were to write them down. Exactly the same test was used both in the grade-I and the grade-2 testing.
OS1 and OS2:	Silent word reading, the same test used in grade 1 and 2, consists of 400 words presented in columns. To the right of each word four pictures are given, one of which illustrates the word. Reading performance is expressed as the number of correct responses during a period of 15 minutes.

this method is statistically and psychometrically less well grounded than the maximum likelihood method. Hence, the distribution of the available goodness of fit indices is not known and the method provides no standard errors for the parameter estimates (and thus their significance cannot be tested). The assumption of multinormally distributed variables may be relaxed only at the expense of a loss of knowledge about the estimates.

Results

Model 1 included latent variables for kindergarten phonemic awareness, grade 1 phonemic awareness, a reading factor and a spelling factor. The solutions obtained were found to have unreasonable values. Several runs were done with fixed parameters, with different variables deleted and without grade 2 variables but the estimates were always found to be outside the admissible parameter space. The best interpretation would be that the model is wrong although this situation is somewhat inconclusive due to the small sample.

Model 2 with the nonsense word tests measuring letter-sound rule use and Spell and ReadI measuring word-specific learning. Root Mean Residual (RMR) = .070, Adjusted Goodness of Fit (AGFI) = .973. The variable ReadN showed a very low reliability. The highest modification index (MI = 4.5) was found for correlated measurement errors between the silent word tests (Residual = 0.29). Thus, the model fails to account sufficiently for the correlation between the silent word reading tests. Correlated measurement errors may be conceptualized as an unspecified (omitted) latent variable. Relaxing the model and allowing these measurement errors to correlate reduced the RMR to .055 and the highest residual between OS2 and Spel2 (0.19, MI = 2.44). This may be taken as a support for the third model.

Model 3 is shown in Figure 3. The nonsense word reading variable is omitted because of the occurrence of improper solutions when it was included. This can be used as an additional argument against its validity. The latent variables for phonological awareness and phonological recoding are collapsed into a single variable for phonological recoding. The first run showed a very low discriminant validity for keeping these variables separate (beta = .99).

Nonsense word spelling to a considerable degree consists of unexplained variance. Analysis of the residuals shows that the input correlation between the synthesis test in grade 1 and OS2 is 0.17 lower than predicted from the model. OS2 probably contains a greater cognitive component than a test of word recognition ideally should. The spelling tests in grade 1 and 2, which were actually a repetition of the same test, correlate 0.13 higher than predicted.

The RMR in the figure clearly indicates that the fit is not perfect but, on the other hand, there are no indications beside the one mentioned where in the model it should be improved. In proceeding model testing the risk is high trying to extract more information than there really is in the data.

The present data are congruent with theories emphasizing the importance of phonemic awareness and phonological processing in learning to read. Phonological recoding is seen as an important factor for the development of automatic and context-free word recognition and decoding speed. The model is also in line with several recent stage models for decoding development (Frith, 1986; Høien & Lundberg, 1988; Seymour, 1986).

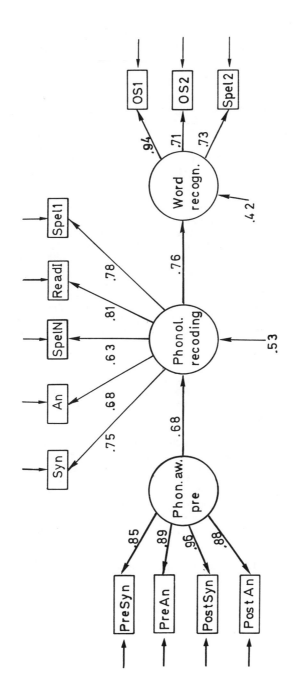

Figure 3. Model for preschool phonemic awareness, grade 1 phonological coding and grades 1 and 2 automatic and effortless word recognition. Standardized ULS solution. RMR = .068, AGFI = .977

The fit of the measurement model for the kindergarten tests is evidence for the construct validity of phonemic awareness. The present findings add further evidence to similar results reported for the Danish sample by Lundberg et al. (1988). (See also Stanovich, Cunningham & Cramer (1984).

The phonemic awareness tests in grade 1 were found to have low discriminant validity compared with the tests thought to measure spelling-sound rule use. This may be an effect of low reliability in combination with highly related latent variables (as indeed postulated). The design of the grade 1 phonemic awareness tests enables the child to benefit by the mental representation of the phonemes with letter (names) and thus the grade 1 Synthesis and Analysis tests to some degree resemble a letter-sound rule task. Such a "reading-contamination" of phonemic awareness tasks is well known from observations of some children's use of letter names in the testing situations. (The effect of letters and spelling are treated by Ehri 1989).

The dissociation between the identical tests, *Spell and Spel2*, supports the notion about a change in word processing between grade 1 and 2. However, the time lag is rather long and its effect is hard to estimate. The means for the 13 items for *Spell* was 5.8 and for *Spel2* 9.4 (SD 1.8 vs. 2). Hence, it seems possible that *Spel2* to a large extent discriminates through the most difficult and irregularly spelled items. On *Spell* most children only succeeded on the most regularly spelled items. Thus, identical tests can measure different traits, and LISREL seems to reveal the same fact as traditional item analysis.

Finally, the importance of theory in causal modeling should be emphasized. The relationships formulated in the model can be quantified by LISREL but the meaning and nature of these relationships must be well grounded on theory (cf. Olofsson, 1985).

Conclusion

Two main conclusions may be drawn from this series of studies. First, phonemic awareness in kindergarten is a good predictor of success in reading acquisition. Second, systematic training in phonemic awareness prior to reading instruction facilitates the acquisition of reading and spelling.

Although we have restricted our focus to the impact of phonological awareness in the present research, we also recognize the importance of other aspects of emergent literacy among preschool children. Pretend writing, invented spelling, letter recognition, story reading, environmental print reading and other natural experiences with print are all possible components in a broad preschool program, of emergent literacy (However, see Ehri & Wilce, 1985). Hagtvet (1989) has convincingly demonstrated how training in phonological awareness can be integrated in a broad program of preschool writing. When practical implications are drawn from our research such a broad perspective of emergent literacy should be considered.

The findings presented here, and by other researchers, provide an optimistic direction for intervening measures in early education.

REFERENCES

Adams, M. J. (1990). *Beginning to read: Thinking and learning about print.* Cambridge, MA.: MIT Press.

Brady, S. & Shankweiler, D. (Eds.), (1991). *Phonological processes in literacy.* Hillsdale, N.J.: Erlbaum.

Content, A., Morais, J., Alegria, J., & Bertelson, P. (1982). Accelerating the development of phonetic segmentation skills in kindergartners. *Cahiers de Psychologie Cognitive, 2,* 259-269.

Downing, J. & Leong, C. K. (1982). *Psychology of reading.* New York: Macmillan.

Ehri, L.C. (1989). The development of spelling knowledge and its role in reading acquisition and reading disability. *Journal of Learning Disabilities, 22,* 356-365.

Ehri, L.C. & Wilce, L. S. (1985). Movement into reading: Is the first stage of printed word learning visual or phonetic? *Reading Research Quarterly, 20,*163-179.

Elkonin, D.B. (1973). U.S.S.R. In J. Downing (Ed.), *Comparative reading* (pp. 551-579). New York: Macmillan.

Farmer, A. R., Nixon, M., & White, R. T. (1976). Sound blending and learning to read: An experimental investigation. *British Journal of Educational Psychology, 46,* 155-163.

Frith, U. (1986). A developmental framework for developmental dyslexia. *Annals of Dyslexia, 36,* 69-81.

Hagtvet, B. E. (1989). Emergent literacy in Norwegian six-year-olds: From pretend writing to phonemic awareness and invented writing. In F. Biglmaier (Ed.), *Reading at the cross- roads.* Proceedings from the 6th European Conference on Reading. Berlin, 1989. Berlin: Freie Universität.

Høien T, Lundberg I. (1988). Stages of word recognition in early reading development. *Scandinavian Journal of Educational Research 32,* 163-182.

Jöreskog, K. G. & Sörbom, D. (1984). *LISREL VI.* Mooresville, IN.: Scientific Software, Inc.

Leong, C. K. (1984). Cognitive processing, language awareness, and reading in grade 2 and grade 4 children. *Contemporary Educational Psychology, 9,* 369-383.

Lundberg, I., Frost, J., & Petersen, O.-P. (1988). Effects of an extensive program for stimulating phonological awareness in preschool children. *Reading Research Quarterly, 23,* 263-284.

Lundberg, I., Olofsson, Å, & Wall, S. (1980). Reading and spelling skills in the first school years predicted from phonemic awareness skills in kindergarten. *Scandinavian Journal of Psychology, 21,* 159-173.

Marsh, G. & Mineo, R. J. (1977). Training preschool children to recognize phonemes in words. *Journal of Educational Psychology, 69,* 748-753.

Olofsson, Å. (1985). On the role of theory in structural equation modeling. *Scandinavian Journal of Psychology, 26,* 377-378.

Olofsson, Å. (1989). Phonemic awareness training before reading instruction: Effects on learning to spell. Paper presented at V Simposio Escuelas de Logopedia y Psicologia del Lenguaje, Salamanca, Spain, 24-28 April 1989.

Olofsson, Å., & Lundberg, I. (1983). Can phonemic awareness be trained in kindergarten? *Scandinavian Journal of Psychology, 24,* 35-44.

Olofsson, Å., & Lundberg, I. (1985). Evaluation of long-term effects of phonemic awareness training in kindergarten: Illustrations of some methodological problems in evaluation research. *Scandinavian Journal of Psychology, 26,* 21-34.

Olson, R., Wise, B., Conners, F., Rack, J., and Fulker, D. (1989). Specific deficits in component reading and language skills: Genetic and environmental influences. *Journal of Learning Disabilities, 22,* 339-348.

Rozin, P. & Gleitman, L. R. (1977). The structure and acquisition of reading II: The reading process and the acquisition of the alphabetic principle. In A. S. Reber & D. L. Scarborough (Eds.), *Toward a psychology of reading* (pp. 55-141). Hillsdale, NJ: Erlbaum.

Savin, H. B. (1972). What the child knows about speech when he starts to learn to read. In J. F. Kavanagh & I. G. Mattingly (Eds.), *Language by ear and language by eye* (pp. 319-326). Cambridge, MA: MIT Press.

Sawyer, D. E. & Fox, B. J. (Eds.), (1991). *Phonological awareness in reading: The evolution of current perspectives.* New York: Springer-Verlag.

Seymour, P. H. K. (1986). *Cognitive analysis of dyslexia.* London: Routledge & Kegan Paul.

Stanovich, K, E. (1980). Towards an interactive-compensatory model of individual differences in the development of reading fluency. *Reading Research Quarterly, 16,* 32-71.

Stanovich, K. E. (1986). Matthew effects in reading: Some consequences of individual differences in the acquisition of literacy. *Reading Research Quarterly, 21,* 360-407.

Stanovich, K. E., Cunningham, A. E., & Cramer, B. B. (1984). Assessing phonological awareness in kindergarten children: Issues of task comparability. *Journal of Experimental Child Psychology, 38,* 175-190.

Stanovich, K, E., Cunningham, A. E., & Feeman, D. J. (1984). Intelligence, cognitive skills and early reading progress. *Reading Research Quarterly, 14,* 278-303.

Zuhrova, L. E. (1966-1967). The development of analysis of words into their sounds by preschool children. *Soviet Psychology and Psychiatry, 2,* 17-27.

DOES A PAST HISTORY OF SPEECH DISORDER PREDICT LITERACY DIFFICULTIES?

BARBARA DODD, TANIA RUSSELL AND MICHAEL OERLEMANS
Department of Speech and Hearing, University of Queensland,
St. Lucia, Queensland 4072
AUSTRALIA

ABSTRACT: Spoken phonological disorder affects 4% of the infant and primary school population. The disorder is associated with behavior disorder, and academic failure primarily due to poor written language, particularly spelling. It has been possible to classify children with spoken disorders into four groups; children with an **articulation** disorder who cannot produce specific speech sound(s), and three groups of children who can pronounce speech sounds but make errors of omission, substitution or addition. These phonologically disordered children may show error patterns reflecting delayed phonological development, **consistent** (non-developmental) errors, or **inconsistent** errors. Children with different patterns of spoken surface errors may have differing underlying deficits which, despite therapy, persist to affect, the acquisition of literacy. Past research suggests that children with a current phonological disorder have problems with spelling (Dodd & Cockerill, 1985). In a pilot study, children with a past history of speech disorder were found to have poor spelling in relation to controls with no previous spoken disorder. The study reported here investigated the spelling and related cognitive abilities of groups of children with past histories of the four types of speech disorder. The results indicated that any type of phonological disorder places children at risk of later reading and spelling difficulties.

Unintelligible speech is the most common communication disorder in childhood. One Australian survey estimated that as many as 4% of 5 year olds mispronounce so many words that their speech is difficult or impossible to understand (Kirkpatrick & Ward, 1984). However, this 4% is not a homogeneous group in terms of the number and type of errors they make, the cause of their disorder or their response to treatment. There is, therefore, an apparent need to classify speech disordered children into subgroups. What is controversial is how they should be categorized. The American literature favors a medical model: classifying in terms of causal factors. One major difficulty with this approach is that by the time a speech pathologist assesses a child's disordered speech at age 3 or more, the causal factors are almost impossible to determine. In fact, most cases of unintelligible speech are dubbed "functional", that is, no known cause.

An alternative classification system relies on the type of errors children make. This approach has been around for a long time, but done very badly. For example, consider a child who says:

tep for step	sing for swing
poon for spoon	seep for sleep
ky for sky	sow for snow

R.M. Joshi and C.K. Leong (eds.), Reading Disabilities: Diagnosis and Component Processes, 199–212.
© 1993 *Kluwer Academic Publishers. Printed in the Netherlands.*

Obviously the child can articulate an /s/, so an articulation problem can be ruled out, but he only does so 50% of the time: 'he' because there are three speech disordered boys for every one girl. Counting correct production of particular speech sounds (the taxonomic approach) is therefore fairly fruitless, and has been justifiably abandoned. However, there is an alternative description of the above data. In /s/ plus consonant clusters, /s/ is deleted when the other consonant is a plosive (t, p, k), but when that consonant is a continuant (w, l, n), that consonant deletes. That is, the child is using a rule. If the speech pathologist analyses the child's speech to discover what rules the child is using, then she should be able to predict how any word will be pronounced. Ultimately, once a child's speech has been described in this way, it is possible to assign that child to one of a number of subgroups according to the type of errors made. Using such an approach, there are at least four groups of spoken disordered children.

i) There are those children who always mispronounce a particular speech sound in the same way wherever it occurs: the classic examples are lisps (shkool for school and shmile for smile) and w for r substitutions. These children have an articulation disorder, that is, they have not learned how to pronounce a particular speech sound or sounds.

ii) There are those children who make consistent rule-governed errors that are inappropriate for their chronological age, but would be normal in a younger child. For example, reducing /s/ plus consonant clusters as shown above would be normal for a 2 year old, but indicate delayed development in a child over 4 years.

iii) A smaller group of children makes consistent errors that are bizarre: for example omitting all word initial consonants. Such a rule does not occur during normal phonological development so the child's speech is disordered, rather than delayed.

iv) Finally, there is another group of children whose errors are inconsistent: that is, every time they pronounce a word it is likely to be pronounced differently: e.g., orsh, orsi, ossi for horse. It is impossible to describe these children's errors in terms of rules.

The usefulness of our method of classification has been assessed in two ways. One method is to compare the groups of children with different speech error patterns on a series of tasks tapping the mental processes thought to underlie speech production to see if different specific deficits can be identified. Further, different treatment approaches may be used with the subgroups to find out if they are differentially effective.

Experiments comparing the three subgroups of phonologically disordered children have revealed that the deviant consistent group performs poorly on tasks involving detection of phonological legality of spoken nonsense words, recognition of their own phonological forms and awareness of alliteration and rhyme (Dodd, Leahy & Hambly, 1989). These findings suggest that the use of consistent but unusual phonological rules might be attributed to an impaired ability to abstract knowledge from the mental lexicon about the nature of the phonological system to be acquired (Duggirala & Dodd, 1991). Leonard (1985) views children as active learners of their phonological system, who seek to mark, in their speech output, the contrasts between words. Consistent but bizarre solutions to the problem of marking differences might result from selecting the wrong parameters of the perceived speech signal as salient in their native phonology. If this were so, these children's specific deficit could be cognitive and lie at the organizational level of the speech chain. That is, children who make deviant consistent errors may have a linguistic deficit.

Phonologically disordered children who make inconsistent errors appear to have intact knowledge of their phonological system, not differing from controls on tasks distinguishing the deviant consistent sub-group. However, their performance on a series of fine motor tasks indicated that they performed particularly poorly on tasks requiring the use of complex motor programs compared to the two other phonologically disordered groups and controls (Bradford, 1990). A deficit in planning sequences of phonemes might, then, account for children who produce inconsistent phonological errors.

Children whose errors are due to the use of normal developmental processes that are inappropriate for their chronological age did not appear to have any specific deficit on the tasks that discriminated the two other subgroups of phonological disorder. This is not surprising, since they are following the normal course of development, albeit slowly. The factors underlying their delay may be more general: impoverished language learning environment or general cognitive delay.

There is now considerable evidence that many children who have a spoken phonological disorder also have literacy difficulties, especially spelling problems. Robinson, Beresford & Dodd (1982), in a study of the spelling errors of eleven phonologically disordered children compared with reading age matched controls, reported no relationship between words misarticulated and the correctness of spelling, thus confirming the earlier work of Ham (1958). However, the phonologically disordered children's *pattern* of spelling errors differed markedly from that of the controls. Whereas the controls made more errors on irregularly spelled words than those words spelled regularly, the phonologically disordered children made approximately the same number of errors for both types of words. The disordered subjects made significantly more errors on the regularly spelled words than the control subjects. It appears that the phonologically disordered subjects have difficulty with assembling the spelling of a word from the spoken form.

Stackhouse (1982) investigated the reading, spelling and phonological skills of developmental verbal dyspraxics (who make inconsistent errors), cleft palate children and normal controls. Both cleft palate children and the dyspraxics had spoken problems, however, the dyspraxics' difficulties were thought to be at a more central level of processing. She found the developmental verbal dyspraxics to be poorer spellers and readers than controls and cleft palate children. There was a significant correlation between phonological coding ability as measured on a nonword matching task, and reading age for control and cleft palate children, but not for the dyspraxics. The deficits in spelling and phonological coding suggest a difficulty in extracting the spelling of a word from its phonological form, that is, sound-letter conversion. A further study of four dyspraxic children (Snowling & Stackhouse, 1983) suggested that the difficulty occurred before actual phoneme-grapheme conversion, represented in a difficulty in segmenting the phonological trace prior to generation of an orthographic form.

Further evidence for the relationship between spelling and spoken disorders is found in a study by Dodd & Cockerill (1985) comparing spelling of words which were either regular, rule-governed or irregular and rare. Comparing phonologically disordered children with hearing impaired subjects and normal controls, the authors found that hearing impaired children made significantly fewer errors on spelling than matched controls, and that phonologically disordered children made the most errors. Normal controls made fewer errors when spelling regular words than rule-governed words and made the most errors on rare words. Hearing impaired subjects spelled all types of words equally well.

Phonologically disordered children spelled regular words better than rule-governed and rare words, for which there was no difference. Critically, phonologically disordered children made more errors on rule governed words than reading-age matched controls. The authors argued that while phonologically disordered children "had mastered simple phoneme-grapheme conversion rules, they had difficulty with the more complex [rule-governed] relationships between sound and orthography" (Dodd & Cockerill, 1985 p. 413).

Even those children whose spoken phonological disorder has resolved through therapy may also be at risk for literacy difficulties. For example, detailed histories of one group of poor spellers indicated four of the five children had a history of a previous spoken disorder. All performed poorly on a task requiring repetition of complex polysyllabic words, suggesting persisting difficulties in speech when the speech production system was placed under stress (Dodd *et al*, 1989). This would suggest that the impact of speech therapy for those groups showing evidence of disordered (rather than delayed) phonology is to provide a cognitive 'super-structure' for converting disordered phonology into normal phonological patterns, rather than replacing incorrect processes. The central hypothesis of this study was, therefore, that children with a history of disordered speech would, even when the spoken deficit was corrected, show evidence of the prior impairment in their written performance, and tasks such as segmentation, word repetition and phonological awareness tasks previously shown to be associated with disordered spelling. The main prediction was that children with a past history of phonological disorder would be impaired on standard measures of reading and spelling compared to children with a past history of articulation disorder and controls.

Method

Subjects: Thirty-seven subjects who had a past history of speech disorder participated in the study. They were drawn from the files of the Department of Speech and Hearing Clinic and community speech therapy clinics in Brisbane. Children were classified into one of four groups on the basis of phonetic transcriptions of whole words available in the records. Two therapists independently assigned subjects to groups. The few disagreements occurring about group categorization were resolved through discussion. Three children were discarded because no agreement could be reached, and were replaced. Articulation disordered children were defined as children whose only speech difficulty was being unable to pronounce one or more sounds. Phonologically disordered children were identified as having been one of types at initial assessment: delayed - using normal developmental phonological processes that were inappropriate for their chronological age; deviant consistent - using two or wore phonological rules that do not occur during normal phonological development (for lists of normal and deviant processes, see Dodd & Iacono, 1989); and deviant inconsistent exhibiting spoken phonological errors which were inconsistent. None of the children had a current speech disorder, and all had been discharged from therapy at least one year before participating in the current experiment. A control group of 10 subjects matched for chronological age, gender and socio-economic status was also tested. None had a history of speech disorder. The description of the subjects is in Table 1. A one factor analysis of variance showed that the chronological age of the groups did not differ (F = 0.28; df = 4,42; NS).

Materials: Each subject completed the following tasks:

- Reading was measured using the Neale Analysis of Reading Ability-Revised (1988) from which a reading age score based on the accuracy of reading aloud was obtained;

Table 1. Description of Subjects: Number, Mean Age and Age Range.

Group	N	Age	Age range
Control	10	8.6	7.3-10.2
Articulation disordered	9	8.5	7.1-10
Phnologically disordered:			
Delayed	10	8.3	6.8-9.7
Deviant consistent	11	8.4	7.3-10
Deviant inconsistent	7	8.2	7.8-9.5

- Spelling was assessed using the South Australian spelling test to give a spelling age and the percentage of misspellings which were phonologically plausible;

- A nonword spelling task consisted of 18 nonwords; six of which had regular sound-letter correspondences, six of which were rule-governed and six of which had rare spelling patterns.;

A word repetition task: subjects were required to repeat aloud 20 complex polysyllabic words. The words had the character of "tongue twisters" and were designed to highlight any existing spoken difficulties.;

- A rhyme identification task: subjects were required to decide if a written pair of words rhymed. The words were varied along two dimensions; orthographic similarity and rhyme, giving four sets of words; orthographically similar/rhyme (pair/hair), orthographically similar/non-rhyme (steak/teak), orthographically dissimilar/rhyme (night/kite) and orthographically dissimilar/non-rhyme (boy/bad);

- A spoonerisms task (adapted from Perin, 1983): subjects had to create spoonerisms from 9 pairs of words (e.g., yellow duck -> dellow yuck). Four pairs began with a single letter/sound (e.g., yellow duck), three pairs with a single letter/sound for one word and a digraph for the other word (e.g., big thing) and two pairs with digraphs for both words (e.g., sharp chain);

- A rule derivation task involved the presentation of a number of words to each of the subjects. Three words ended in a nasal (/m/, /n/, /ŋ/, three words began with a plosive (/b/, /t/, /k/) and three words began with a liquid or semi-vowel (/w/, /l/, /r/). Each of these words were represented on pictures (see Appendix I for word lists) and subjects were told that each word had a "new language" name derived from the real name. The words were modified in three ways. Words beginning with a plosive had /w/ as the second sound (e.g., bottle > bwottle), words beginning with a liquid or semi-vowel had /s/ as the initial sound (whistle > swhistle) and words ending in a nasal were followed by an /i/ sound (e.g., plane > plani). In trials 1-5 subjects identified the pictures when they were named by the experimenter using the altered phonological form. Subjects were then required to provide the 'novel' names. In trial 6 subjects were given a new set of words matched to the learning set and asked to provide the "new language" names to see if the rules had generalized. After this trial the original set of pictures was presented again and subjects were informed of the rules for changing the words, for example, "if the word ends in /n/, /m/ or /ŋ/ put an /i/ sound after the last sound; plane, /pleIni/". Finally, the second set of words was again presented and subjects were required to name them. Therefore, there were three sets of scores; rule learning (trials 1-5), derivation and generalization of rules (trial 6) and use of rules after explicit instruction (trial 7);

- Knowledge of phonological and orthographic forms. Subjects were presented with pairs of words which were either spoken or written (Appendix 2). One word in each pair was phonotactically correct for English, while the other was not (e.g., slatchi/svatchi). Subjects were required to select which word would be the best name for a new product or toy. The order of items was randomized and counter-balanced between conditions.

Procedure: The experimenter who carried out testing was 'blind' to the groups to which the previously speech disordered subjects belonged. Subjects were tested in a quiet room at their home or school. Order of presentation was the same for each subject. Testing took approximately sixty minutes. Consent forms were obtained and subjects were instructed that they could discontinue testing at any time, although no subjects did so.

Results

The prediction that children with a history of phonological disorder would perform poorly on standard tests of reading and spelling was tested first. Two one-way analyses of variance compared the performance of a combined group of previously phonologically disordered children (N=28) and a combined group of previously articulation disordered children and controls (N=18). Difference scores between chronological age and test age were used. The results showed that children who had been phonologically disordered performed poorly in comparison to the other group on both the Neale Analysis of Reading Ability ($F = 6.312$; df = 1,44; $P < 0.02$) and the spelling test ($F = 5.826$; df = 1,44; $P < 0.025$). Table 2 shows the means and standard deviations.

Table 2. Reading and Spelling Age Difference Scores for Combined Phonological Group vs Combined Articulation Plus Control (months)

	Reading		Spelling	
	Mean	S.D.	Mean	S.D
Articulation Plus Control	+11	15	+4	14
Phonological Groups	-3	15	-10	15

The five groups' performance on each of the tasks was then compared using a series of analyses of variance:

Neale Analysis of Reading Ability. The mean reading ages of the groups are contained in Table 3. A one-way analysis of variance with group as a factor showed there was no difference between the groups ($F = 1.413$; df = 4,42; NS) indicating that the groups were matched for reading age.

Table 3. Reading age of groups

Group	Mean	SD.	Range
Control	9.6	1.7	6.1-12
Articulation disordered	9.1	1.9	6.0-12-1
Delayed	8.5	2.0	6.0-12.2
Deviant consistent	8.1	1.7	6.2-11.4
Deviant inconsistent	8.0	1.5	6-0-10-7

South Australian Spelling Test. The mean spelling ages of the groups are contained in Table 4. A one-way analysis of variance with group as a factor was not significant ($F = 1.8$; df = 4,42; NS). Surprisingly, there was no difference in the real word spelling ability of the groups.

Table 4. Spelling age of groups.

Group	Mean	S.D.	Range
Control	8.7	1.7	6.3-11.9
Articulation disordered	9.0	1.8	6.5-11.3
Delayed	8.1	1.8	6-0-10.9
Deviant consistent	7.3	1.3	6-0-9.4
Deviant inconsistent	7.5	1.6	6.0-10.4

Nonword Spelling. The mean percent correct scores of the groups are contained in Table 5. A one-way analysis of variance with group as a factor was significant ($F = 3.12$; df = 4,42; $P = 0.025$). Multiple comparisons using the Bonferroni method with a significance level of 0.01 to account for the number of comparisons showed both groups of children who had a past deviant phonological disorder were poorer at spelling nonwords than children with a past disorder of articulation. While the articulation disordered group did not differ significantly from controls or delayed spellers, the means showed a strong tendency.

Table 5. Nonword spelling - percentage of plausible spellings.

Group	Mean	S.D.	Range
Control	45	24.4	11.1-77.8
Articulation disordered	68.5	17.3	38.9-100
Delayed	43.9	31-3	0.0-83.3
Deviant consistent	28.8	25.6	0.0-77.8
Deviant inconsistent	33.3	32.8	0.0-77.8

Word Repetition. The mean percent correct scores of the groups are contained in Table 6. A one-way analysis of variance with group as a factor showed an effect of group. There was a significant difference between the groups (F = 3.4; df = 4,42; P < 0.01). Post-hoc tests using Bonferroni comparisons showed that the two groups of children who had a treated deviant phonological disorder were poorer than controls at a significance level below 0.01. The other groups showed no difference.

Table 6. Word repetition: Percentage of correct repetitions.

Group	Mean	S.D.	Range
Control	88	9.5	70-100
Articulation disordered	66.9	29.2	2-100
Delayed	72.5	19.3	35-95
Deviant consistent	60.5	22.2	35-90
Deviant inconsistent	55	20.8	30-85

Rhyme Identification. The mean percent correct scores of the groups are contained in Table 7. A three-factor analysis of variance (group, orthographic similarity and rhyme) showed significant effects for similarity (F = 6.0; df = 1,42; P = 0.019), rhyme (F = 11.7; df = 1,42; P < 0.001) and the rhyme by similarity interaction (F = 80.185; df = 1,42; P < 0.001). There was no difference between the groups (F = 0.2; df = 4,42; NS) in their judgments of written rhyming pairs. An examination of the interaction between rhyme and orthographic similarity using the Bonferroni correction showed judgments were poorest for orthographically similar non-rhyming pairs (mean 39.7), better for orthographically different rhymes (mean 54.3), and best when orthographic and phonological information concurred (mean ODNR = 88.3; OSR = 91.8).

Table 7. Rhyme recognition: Percentage of Correct Judgements.

Group	OSR	OSNR	ODR	ODNR	Total
Control	91.7	48.3	56.7	95.0	73.0
Articulation	100	46.3	59.3	92.6	73.1
Delayed	93.3	38.3	51.7	88.3	67.9
Consistent	86.4	30.3	48.5	81.8	61.7
Inconsistent	88.1	35.7	57.1	83.3	66.1

The subscores are:
OSR — orthographically similar, rhyming pairs
OSNR — orthographically similar, non-rhyming pairs
ODR — orthographically different, rhyming pairs
ODNR — orthographically different, non-rhyming pairs

Spoonerisms. The mean percent correct scores of the groups are contained in Table 8. A two-factor analysis of variance (group; type of initial letter: -- single/single; single-digraph; digraph-digraph) showed there was no difference between the groups ($F = 0.968$; df = 4,42; NS). There was an effect of initial letter however. Comparison using univariate F-tests with a Bonferroni critical value of 0.01 showed children performed best at creating spoonerisms when both words began with a single letter (mean 58.6) and were significantly poorer when one (mean 37.8) or both (34.0) of the words began with a digraph.

Table 8. Spoonerism: Percentage of correct spoonerisms.

Group	S - S	S - D	D - D	Total
Control	58.8	41.7	35.0	47.8
Articulation	62.5	29.6	25.0	43.8
Delayed	75.0	53.3	52.5	62.8
Consistent	53.4	31.8	25.0	38.9
Inconsistent	44.6	26.2	32.1	35.7

The subscores are:
SS — both words in the pair begin with a single letter
SD — one word in the pair begins with a digraph
DD — both words in the pair begin with a digraph

Rule derivation. The mean percent correct scores of the groups are contained in Table 9. A two-factor analysis of variance with group as a factor and trial as a repeated measure was used. Trials 5, 6, and 7 were included; trial 5 occurring at the end of the learning period, trial 6 examining if the learned rules would generalize, and trial 7 testing use of the rules after they were explicitly stated. There was no difference between the groups (F = 1.89; df = 4,42; NS) and the interaction was not significant (F = 1.12; df = 8,84; NS). There was an effect of trial, however (F = 109.8; df = 2,84; P < 0.001), and post hoc comparisons showed all differences to be significant. Children knew most of the names for the pictures at the end of the learning trial. Performance during the generalization trial was poor (mean 2.0 - equivalent to learning less than one of the three rules, or more precisely, one rule poorly) and better after rules were explicitly stated (mean = 3.3; learning one rule well).

Table 9. Rule derivation: Mean performance on trial 5 (learning), trial 6 (generalization) and trial 7 (rule-given)

Group	Trial 5	Trial 6	Trial 7
Control	7.6	1.7	3.7
Articulation	7.1	2.3	4.1
Delayed	6.9	2.8	3.9
Consistent	6.1	1.4	2.2
Inconsistent	5.3	2.1	2.7

Knowledge of phonological and orthographic forms. The mean percent correct scores of the groups are contained in Table 10. A two-way analysis of variance with group as one factor and spoken/written as the other factor showed no significant effects (group: F = 1.16; df = 4,84; NS; mode: F = 0.862; df = 1,84; NS; and interaction: F = 0.655; df = 4,84; NS). All children could judge whether a pair of words were phonologically and orthographically legal, at least to the level of control performance.

Discussion

Four groups of children with a past history of speech disorder plus a control group with reported normal speech development were assessed on a battery of tests measuring literacy and phonological coding skills. Comparison of children who had been phonologically disordered with children who had been articulation disordered or had no history of speech disorder revealed that a previous history of phonological disorder is associated with poor performance on standard tests of both reading and spelling. These findings fit with previous research showing that low phonological awareness in the preschool years foreshadows later literacy difficulties (e.g., Bryant & Bradley, 1985). The result also confirms the categorization of articulation disorder as a peripheral problem in motor speech production rather than a cognitive-linguistic deficit.

Table 10. Knowledge of forms: mean correct.

Group	Written presentation		Spoken presentation	
	Mean	S.D.	Mean	S.D.
Control	68.3	24.2	60.0	19.6
Articulation	75.9	29.0	75.9	22.2
Delayed	56.7	31.6	67.6	20.2
Consistent	70.0	25.8	75.0	18.1
Inconsistent	54.8	34.3	71.4	25.0

However, statistical analyses using the five groups revealed few significant differences. Only two tasks discriminated between the groups:

1. *Nonword Spelling.* Those children who had a history of deviant phonological disorder (both consistent and inconsistent groups) performed poorly compared to children who had been articulation disordered when asked to spell nonsense words. This result suggests that children with a past history of phonological disorder continue to have difficulty manipulating phonological information despite therapy that successfully resolved their spoken phonological disorder. The finding is surprising in that it was the previously articulation disordered group who performed significantly better than those children who had been treated for phonological disorder. One possible explanation of the result relies on the type of therapy typically provided for speech disordered subgroups. Therapy for both groups is likely to have focussed on individual phonemes. The articulation disordered children may have consequently enhanced segmentation skills in relation to controls. However, the phonologically disordered children's central deficit may limit their ability to generalize segmentation skills learned in speech therapy to phoneme-grapheme conversion.

2. *Word Repetition.* These same two groups of children with a history of deviant phonological disorder also performed poorly (compared to controls) on a task assessing their ability to imitate spoken unfamiliar multisyllabic words, despite having currently error-free spontaneous speech. The finding suggests that therapy does not 'cure' an underlying deficit, but rather, provides compensatory strategies for speech production that breaks down under stress.

Nevertheless, most tasks failed to discriminate the groups of previously phonologically disordered children. This may be a result of methodological problems such as small group size or inaccurate group categorization leading to large variance in performance. Alternatively, phonological disorder may be associated with later literacy learning difficulties in a general way. Unintelligible speech influences the amount and type of language addressed to children, and being unintelligible may affect children's self esteem. Both these factors could contribute to later difficulties in the acquisition of reading and spelling skills. However, the finding that those children whose phonological development was deviant had particular difficulty generating spellings for nonsense words suggests that they have an impaired ability to use the phonological route for assembling spelling. They may, therefore, rely more on the direct lexical access route when spelling real words. That is, children with a history of phonologically deviant development would still appear to have phonological coding deficit despite therapy that resolved their spoken phonological disorder.

In conclusion, the main finding of the study reported here is that children with a past history of phonological disorder are likely to have difficulties acquiring both reading and spelling competence. The results confirm previous research showing the strong link between the mental processes serving speaking, reading and spelling. The clinical and educational implications of the findings concern the need for monitoring the acquisition of literacy by children who have had a phonological disorder to identify those in need of appropriate intervention.

ACKNOWLEDGMENT

This work was supported by the NHMRC, Australia.

APPENDIX 1: RULE DERIVATION

Word	Word altered by rule
Rule derivation and generalization trials	
fan	fani
sum	sumi
thong	thongi
bottle	bwottle
table	twable
camel	cwamel
rattle	srattle
leaf	sleaf
whistle	swhistle
Rule utilization trials	
swan	swani
thumb	thumbi
swing	swingi
toaster	twoaster
book	bwook
cat	cwat
record	srecord
locket	slocket
whale	swhale

APPENDIX 2: KNOWLEDGE OF FORMS

	Legal form	Illegal form
List 1		
	slatchi	svatchi
	thrip	thrlip
	fring	fning
	stuleg	shtuleg
	shropi	shlopi
	srutow	stutow
List 2		
	flet	vlet
	smebi	zmebi
	grup	gyup
	sletem	zletem
	froodi	vroodi
	strayp	glrayp

REFERENCES

Bradford, A. (1990). The motor planning skills of subgroups of speech disordered children. Unpublished thesis: University of Queensland.

Bryant, P. & Bradley, L. (1985). *Children's reading problems: Psychology and education.* Oxford: Blackwell.

Dodd, B. & Cockerill, H. (1985). Phonological coding deficit: A comparison of spelling errors made by deaf, speech disordered and normal children. *Beitrage zur Phonetik und Linguistik, 48,* 405-415.

Dodd, B. & Iacano, T. (1989). Phonological disorders in children: Changes in phonological process use during treatment. *British Journal of Disorders of Communication, 24,* 333-351.

Dodd, B., Leahy, J. & Hambly, G. (1989). Phonological disorders in children: Underlying cognitive deficits. *British Journal of Developmental Psychology, 7,* 55-71.

Dodd, B., Sprainger, N. & Oerlemans, M. (1989). The phonological skills of spelling disordered children. *Reading and Writing, 1,* 333-355.

Duggirala, V. & Dodd, B. (1991). A psycholinguistic assessment model for disordered phonology. *Proceedings of the XII Congress of Phonetic Sciences, Aix-en-Provence,* (Vol 3), 342-345.

Ham, R.E. (1958). Relationship between misspelling and misarticulation. *Journal of Speech and Hearing Disorders, 23,* 294-297.

Kirkpatrick, E. & Ward, J. (1984). Prevalence of articulation disorders in New South Wales primary school pupils. *Australian Journal of Human Communication Disorders, 12,* 55-62

Leonard, L.B. (1985). Unusual and subtle phonological behavior in the speech of phonologically disordered children. *Journal of Speech and Hearing Disorders, 50,* 4-13.

Neale, M. (1988). *Neale Analysis of Reading Ability-Revised,* Hawthorn: Australian Council for Educational Research Limited.

Perin, D. (1983). Phonemic segmentation and spelling. *British Journal of Psychology, 74,* 9-44.

Robinson, P., Beresford, R. & Dodd, B. (1982). Spelling errors made by phonologically disordered children. *Spelling Progress Bulletin, 12,* 19-20.

Snowling, M. & Stackhouse, J. (1983). Spelling performance of children with developmental verbal dyspraxia. *Developmental Medicine and Child Neurology, 25,* 430-437.

Stackhouse, J. (1982). An investigation of reading and spelling performance in speech disordered children. *British Journal of Disorders of Communication, 17,* 53-60.

PHONOLOGICAL PROCESSING IN LEARNING DISABLED ADOLESCENTS

SYBIL SCHWARTZ
The Learning Centre of Québec
The Montreal Children's Hospital
McGill University
Montreal, Quebec
Canada H3G 2A8

ABSTRACT: Research has concentrated on the investigation and development of phonological skill in young children. Clinical evidence suggests that phonological processing skills thought to be crucial to the acquisition of written language continue to mature into adolescence. This study was undertaken to investigate deficits in phonological processing in learning disabled adolescents. Learning disabled students have difficulty articulating phonological sequences like those found in unfamiliar multisyllabic words. The Pseudoword Repetition Test (PSWRT), developed to study this difficulty, was found to be a reliable measure which was able to distinguish younger learning disabled children from normal learners independent of IQ. In the present study the PSWRT was administered to 26 learning disabled adolescents and 21 normal controls. Results indicate that there is a close relationship between pseudoword repetition ability and reading and spelling skills, independent of IQ in the LD adolescent group. The LD adolescents had significantly less difficulty on the PSWRT than the younger LD group. To the extent that the PSWRT is measuring phonological processing, then one can say that phonological processing continues to improve or mature into adolescence, but is still a factor in the reading and spelling problems encountered by LD adolescents.

Several researchers have studied the phonological deficit in learning disabled subjects by means of a real or nonsense word repetition test. Clinical observations have frequently noted that learning disabled students have difficulty articulating phonological sequences like those found in multisyllabic words. This is particularly so when the words are unfamiliar.

Snowling, (1981) found that dyslexics repeated high frequency words as well as Reading and Age matched normals but made more errors when repeating polysyllabic words of low frequency or nonwords. She argued that the difficulty with nonword repetition reflected difficulties with phoneme segmentation and/or possibly assembly of articulatory instructions.

Catts (1986, 1989) compared dyslexics and normally achieving adolescents and college students in their production of phonologically complex multisyllabic words and phrases. Dyslexics were slower and made significantly more speech sound errors. Catts suggested that dyslexics had difficulty in the process of articulation and/or planning stage of speech production. He hypothesized that dyslexics appear to be less proficient in selecting and ordering phonological segments for speech production.

R.M. Joshi and C.K. Leong (eds.), Reading Disabilities: Diagnosis and Component Processes, 213–223.
© 1993 Kluwer Academic Publishers. Printed in the Netherlands.

Taylor, Lean, and Schwartz, (1989) compared a group of 6-12 year old learning disabled poor readers and a group of normal readers on the Pseudoword Repetition Test. Here again the learning disabled group had significantly more difficulty in Pseudoword repetition. The Pseudoword Repetition Test was found to be a reliable measure which was able to distinguish learning disabled children from normal learners independent of IQ.

Gathercole, Willis, Emslie, and Baddeley (1992) used pseudoword repetition to assess the association between phonological memory and vocabulary knowledge in a longitudinal study of children during the early school years. Vocabulary scores were found to be significantly associated with pseudoword repetition at ages 4, 5, and 6. At age 8 the relationship fell to a nonsignificant level when nonverbal intelligence and reading were controlled. Comparison of crosslegged partial correlations indicated that before age 5 pseudoword repetitions predicted vocabulary knowledge one year later to a significantly greater degree than early vocabulary knowledge predicted age 5 pseudoword repetition. After age 5 vocabulary knowledge became the major pacemaker in the developmental relationship.

Hulme & Snowling (1992) investigated the cause of difficulty in pseudoword repetition in a detailed case study of a 13-year-old-dyslexic. They concluded that the underlying deficit was in output phonology (segmentation or premotor articulatory planning) as opposed to input phonology.

Bruck (1992) found little change in phonological awareness skills of dyslexics as a function of age or reading level. Clinically it has been noted that some learning disabled students are better able to learn decoding skills or profit from remediation in adolescence than they had been when younger, as if a necessary underlying skill had developed or matured.

The present study was undertaken to investigate the usefulness of the PSWRT as a measure of phonological processing in distinguishing between readers of differing ability in an adolescent group and to determine if there was maturation in the learning disabled group tested in the earlier study.

Methods

SUBJECTS

Twenty-six Learning Disabled (LD) adolescents (24 boys, 2 girls) with reading problems ranging in age from 12 years, 9 months to 18 years, 4 months with a mean age of 15 years, 4 months (S.D. = 18.8 months) served as subjects. The adolescents in this group all had severe problems in reading and spelling. All of the students were enrolled in a high school program. Most were receiving some educational assistance at school. Most were receiving help at a Learning Centre associated with McGill University.

Reading difficulties were substantiated by scaled scores below 100 on the Kaufman Test of Educational Achievement (KTEA) Decoding subtest. The LD subjects' mean KTEA reading scaled score was 78.3 (S.D. = 11.1). Normal intelligence was substantiated on a prorated full scale WISC-R IQ of at least 85 (based on Vocabulary, Block Design, Coding, and Mazes). The mean prorated full scale IQ for the LD group was 99.2 (S.D. = 10.18).

The control group consisted of 21 matched normal learners (19 boys, 2 girls). Selection criteria included teacher designation as a normal learner, a prorated full scale WISC-R IQ of at least 85 and a scaled score of at least 100 on the Kaufman single word reading subtest. The control subjects ranged in age from 12 years, 4 months to 17 years, 10 months with a mean age of 14 years, 10 months (S.D. = 17.5). Mean full scale WISC-R IQ was 117 (S.D. = 12.6) and mean scaled score on the Kaufman single word reading test was 113 (S.D. = 5.8). None of the subjects in both groups had any noticeable articulation problems.

TEST PROCEDURE

Tests administered to both groups included the Pseudoword Repetition Test (PSWRT), the Kaufman Reading Decoding subtest, and the Test of Written Spelling.

The PSWRT was designed at the McGill Montreal Children's Hospital Learning Centre. It consists of 30 nonsense words, each of which was derived from a polysyllabic word by means of phoneme substitution that yielded phonetically plausible pseudowords (See Appendix 1). Subjects were told that the words were not real and that they were to repeat the word after they heard it. The stimulus words were presented only once. A response was scored as correct as long as all major phonetic components of the word could be discerned in the correct sequence. Substitution, omission, insertion and interchanging of phonemes in adjacent syllables (Metatheses) were coded as errors.

RESULTS

Mean performances of the LD and control groups on IQ and academic measures can be seen in Table 1. Although the LD group's mean IQ was within the normal range, this group performed less well than the nondisabled group in terms of IQ.

Table 1. Mean performance for LD and control groups on prorated IQ and academic achievement.

	Learning	Disabled		Controls			
	N	M	SD	N	M	SD	F (1, 45)
WISC -R[a]	26	99.2	10.2	21	117.0	12.6	28.0*
Reading[b] K-TEA)	26	78.3	11.1	21	113.0	5.8	168.8*
Spelling[c] (TOWS)	26	30.6	10.9	21	56.0	3.6	103.4*

* p < .001

a WISC -R   Wechsler Intelligence Scale for Children - Revised
b K - TEA   Kaufman Test of Educational Assessment
c TOWS   Test of Written Spelling

Correct responses on the PSWRT ranged from 12 to 26 out of 30 in the LD group (M = 18.1, S.D. = 3.6) and from 21 to 29 in the nondisabled control group (M = 25.8, S.D. = 2.3). (See Figure 1). None of the subjects were able to repeat all of the 30 words correctly. Scores were generally lower in the LD group. Twenty-one LD subjects (88%) performed less well than all of the controls. Analysis of covariance revealed that the group difference was significant even with adjustments for IQ. F(1,44) = 33.9, p < .0001. Forty-two of the subjects (89.3%) were properly classified by the PSWRT. Three of the 26 LD students and 2 of the normals were misclassified. (See Figure 2.)

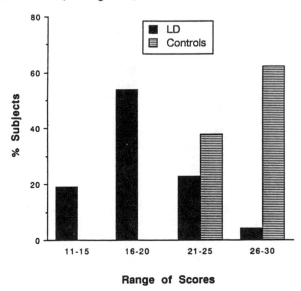

Figure 1. Distribution of scores on Pseudoword Repetition Test (percent subjects) for learning disabled and control groups.

An error analysis completed on 30 subjects (15 LD, 15 Normals) can be seen in Figure 3. Errors were categorized as Substitutions, Omissions, Insertions, or Metatheses. The percentage of errors was comparable for both groups in the Substitution, Omission and Insertion type of errors. Eleven percent of the errors made by the LD group made were Metatheses or order errors. No errors of this type were made by the control group.

In order to see if there was any maturation of phonological skills, as measured by the PSWRT, the scores of the adolescent group were compared to those of the younger group, aged 7 to 12 from the earlier study (See Figure 4). The Tukey procedure revealed a significant difference of p < .01 between the older and younger LD groups. The Scheffé, a more stringent measure, showed a significant difference of p < .05.

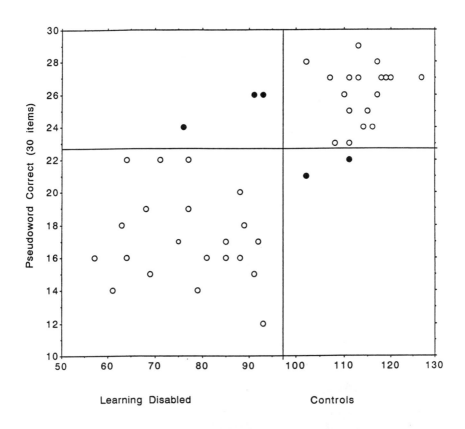

Figure 2. Distribution of scores on Pseudoword Repetition (total correct) in relation to single word reading (Standard Score).

The degree to which the various measures were intercorrelated is shown in Table 2. Performance on the PSWRT was closely associated with reading and spelling (p < .01). IQ was associated with reading but not as strongly as the PSWRT. Stepwise multiple regressions provided further confirmation of the predictive value of the PSWRT for reading ability and spelling ability. The PSWRT added significantly to IQ scores in predicting reading performance and spelling performance. Combined IQ and PSWRT scores accounted for 60% of the variance in the reading scores and 41% of the variance in the spelling scores.

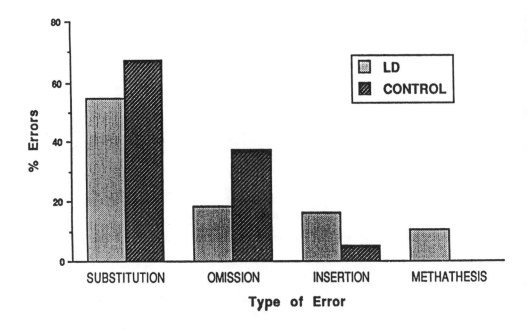

Figure 3. Pseudoword Repetition Errors (percentage) for learning disabled and control groups.

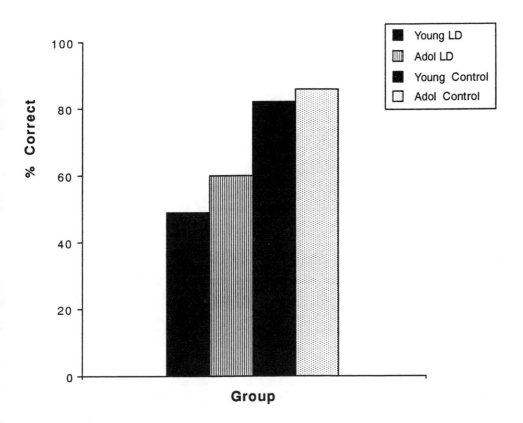

Figure 4. Distribution of scores on Pseudoword Repetition (percent correct) for learning disabled and control subjects of two age groups.

Table 2. Correlations among age, IQ, vocabulary, Pseudoword Repetition, reading and spelling.

	Age	IQ	Vocab.	Pseudoword Repetition	Reading SS	Spelling
Age	1.00					
IQ[a]	.08	1.00				
Vocabulary	-.02	.79**	1.00			
Pseudoword Repetition	-.35*	.60**	.59**	1.00		
Reading[b]	-.14	.65**	.68**	.74**	1.00	
Spelling[c]	.01	.57**	.64**	.61**	.91**	1.00

* $p < .05$; ** $p < .01$

a WISC - R Wechsler Intelligence Scale for Children - Revised
b K-TEA Kaufman Test of Educational Achievement
c TOWS Test of Written Spelling

Discussion

An earlier study of LD children aged 7 to 12 documented a close relationship between pseudoword repetition ability and reading and spelling skills, independent of IQ. Current results with LD adolescents support the findings in the earlier study. In the LD adolescent population an equally close correspondence between pseudoword repetition and reading and spelling abilities was found. Ceiling effects were not found in either the experimental or the control groups which would support the use of the PSWRT with a wide range of students.

Findings indicate that the LD adolescents had significantly less difficulty on the PSWRT than the younger LD group. To the extent that the PSWRT is measuring phonological processing, then one can say that phonological processing continues to improve or mature into adolescence, but is still a factor in the reading and spelling problems encountered by LD adolescents. These findings are not in keeping with those of Bruck (1992), who found no evidence of significant maturation in phonological awareness in a dyslexic population.

There are several possible explanations for the difficulty that LD students have in pseudoword repetition. One explanation is that some LD students have deficits in the perception of speech sounds. A number of studies have conceded the possibility that dyslexic children have difficulties at the level of speech perception. Brandt & Rosen (1980) investigated the discrimination and identification of stop consonants by dyslexic and normal readers. The dyslexics were not markedly impaired but were found to be inconsistent in their phonetic classification of auditory cues. Brady, Shankweiler and Mann (1983) found that good and poor readers performed equally well in a word repetition task when they were presented with words in a quiet environment. Poor readers made a greater number of errors than good readers when words were presented in noise. Snowling, Goulandris, Bowlby, & Howell (1986) found that noise masking did not adversely affect pseudoword repetition in this population.

The evidence is not conclusive. There are strands of evidence which point to phonemic deficits at the level of speech perception in dyslexic readers. However it would seem that difficulty in recognizing or discriminating speech sounds would have to be rather severe to account for the gross nature of the repetition errors committed by some of the disabled learners (e.g., substitutions of one phoneme for another, omission or transposition of phonemes or other changes in syllabic structure) and deficits in comprehension of spoken language would therefore be expected. Deficits of this nature were not readily apparent. (Taylor, Lean & Schwartz, 1989).

Another possibility is that the LD students have articulation difficulties. All of the LD students were interviewed by a speech pathologist and all of the scoring was done by a speech pathologist. None of the subjects showed evidence of any difficulty with articulation. More formal evidence in support of this observation is provided by Snowling's research (Snowling, 1981; Snowling et al., 1986). Snowling compared dyslexics to non-dyslexics on both word and nonword repetition tasks. In spite of the fact that word and nonword stimuli were comprised of similar phoneme sets, differences between groups were much more pronounced for nonwords than for words.

A further possibility is that difficulty in word repetition is a by-product of the more limited experience with print. When the older LD subjects were compared with younger normal subjects from the earlier study, the differences were found to be significant in favor of the younger normal group.

A more likely source of deficit in nonword repetition is an impairment in one or more of the processes by which phonological information is stored, manipulated or accessed from memory. Any of several types of impairment may be hypothesized -- inability or inefficiency in the formation of phonological codes, faster rates of memory decay, or impaired ability to program speech on the basis of coded information (Catts, 1986). Since both groups made addition, substitution and omission errors, the impairment may be more a matter of efficiency of processing than of qualitative differences. Brady, Mann, and Schmidt (1987) obtained a similar result in comparing errors of good and poor readers on a task requiring repetition of four item consonant-vowel syllables.

The finding of ordering errors or Metatheses in the adolescent group, but not in the normal controls, suggests that for some of the LD group, the difficulty is at least partially related to the temporal sequential demands of this task and would likely arise in the premotor or planning stage of speech production.

Whatever the nature of the deficient processes underlying poor repetition, there seems to be little doubt that these processes have implication for the development of reading and spelling skills. The PSWRT makes relatively minimal demands on memory, attention, or higher cognitive functions and identifies a unique source of variance in reading and spelling disabilities.

REFERENCES

Brady, S., Mann, V., & Schmidt, R. (1987). Errors in short-term memory for good and poor readers.
  Memory & Cognition, 15, 449-453.
Brady, S., Shankweiler, D., & Mann, V. (1983). Speech perception and memory coding in relation to
  reading ability. *Journal of Experimental Child Psychology, 35,* 345-367.
Brandt, J. & Rosen, J.J. (1980). Auditory phonemic perception in dyslexia: Categorical identification and
  discrimination of stop consonants. *Brain and Language, 9,* 324-327.
Bruck, M. (1992). Persistence of dyslexics' phonological awareness deficits. *Developmental
  Psychology,.28,* 874-886.
Catts, H. (1986). Speech production/phonological deficits in reading disordered children. *Journal of
  Learning Disabilities, 19 ,* 504-508.
Catts, H. (1989). Phonological processing deficits and reading disabilities. In A. Kamhi and H. Catts
  (Eds.), Reading disabilities: A developmental language perspective. (p. 101-132). Boston: Little
  Brown and Company.
Gathercole, S.E., Willis, C. S., Emslie, H., & Baddeley, A.D. (1992) Phonological memory and
  vocabulary development during the early school years: A longitudinal study. *Developmental
  Psychology, 28,* 887-898.
Hulme, C. & Snowling, M. (1992). Deficits in output phonology: an explanation of reading failure.
  Cognitive Neuropsychology, 9, 47-72
Snowling, M. (1981). Phonemic deficits in developmental dyslexia. *Psychological Research, 43,* 219-
  234.
Snowling, M. Goulandris, N., Bowlby, M., & Howell, P. (1986). Segmentation and speech perception in
  relation to reading skill: A Developmental analysis. *Journal of Experimental Child Psychology, 41,*
  489-507.
Taylor, G., Lean, D., & Schwartz, S. (1989). Pseudoword repetition ability in learning disabled children.
  Applied Psycholinguistics, 10, 203-219.

Appendix 1 : Pseudoword list (in order of presentation)

	Pseudoword	Corresponding real word[a]
1.	MESKITS	(Biscuits)
2.	TROPAPLY	(Probably)
3.	ERESHANT	(Elephant)
4.	FOLTANO	(Volcano)
5.	SKAPEDDI	(Spaghetti)
6.	SPAPISTICS	(Statistics)
7.	TEROSCOTE	(Telescope)
8.	IMBICHENT	(Indigent)
9.	KEBESTRIAN	(Pedestrian)
10.	KARPIGULAR	(Particular)
11.	ETOSPROSEE	(Apostrophe)
12.	ADNESTERIC	(Atmospheric)
13.	PANAMITY	(Calamity)
14.	CARIMATURE	(Caricature)
15.	PONVERLATION	(Conversation)
16.	GRISHANTHENUM	(Chrysanthemum)
17.	TORICHIPAL	(Dirigible)
18.	ZACRADERY	(Secretary)
19.	ARAMINAM	(Aluminum)
20.	PHIROTOFICAL	(Philosophical)
21.	DIDLIOKRAFY	(Bibliography)
22.	SARNATUTICAL	(Pharmaceutical)
23.	ONAMIFIDY	(Anonymity)
24.	GYSIOLOCHIPAL	(Physiological)
25.	DECONFILIATION	(Reconciliation)
26.	ILIODINTRATIC	(Idiosyncratic)
27.	TERSPECACITY	(Perspicacity)
28.	GONFLIDRATION	(Conflagration)
29.	NAGMIVISHENT	(Magnificent)
30.	GRETIMINARY	(Preliminary)

[a] Each pseudoword derived from the corresponding real word. Real word served as pronunciation guide for pseudoword.

PHONOLOGICAL DEFICITS AND THE DEVELOPMENT OF WORD RECOGNITION SKILLS IN DEVELOPMENTAL DYSLEXIA

CHARLES HULME
Department of Psychology
University of York
Heslington, U. K.YO1 5DD

MARGARET SNOWLING
Department of Psychology
University of Newcastle upon Tyne
Newcastle, U. K. NE1 7RU

ABSTRACT: In the present chapter we consider the development of word recognition skills in dyslexic children. Our particular focus is on the way in which phonological deficits impede the development of these skills. The data presented are drawn from a single case of a dyslexic boy, JM, whom we have studied longitudinally for some seven years. We will first consider current theories of the development of visual word recognition skills and their impairment in dyslexic children. We then go on to outline the nature of the phonological deficits seen in JM and present data bearing on how, in the face of these severe phonological deficits, he has managed to learn to read. We then present evidence indicating that JM possesses reasonably efficient recognition mechanisms for words in his sight vocabulary. We conclude by considering the implications of our studies for theories of reading development with a particular focus on the promise of connectionist models.

Dyslexia and Theories of Learning to Read

Theories of learning to read have postulated the development of two systems: a lexical system for the recognition of familiar words and a system of letter-sound rules that can be used to decode novel words (providing they possess regular spelling to sound correspondences). Another way of describing these systems is by reference to two strategies: a visual strategy for accessing a sight vocabulary and a phonological strategy for decoding unfamiliar words. It has often been suggested that the phonological strategy is extremely important to the child because it functions as a self-teaching device.

Recently a reconceptualization of the processes involved in word recognition skills and their development has come from connectionism (Seidenberg & McClelland, 1989; van Orden, Pennington & Stone, 1990). Seidenberg & McClelland (1989) developed a distributed developmental model of word recognition and naming designed to capture some of the processes involved in the acquisition of a sight vocabulary. In their model, an orthographic store coding the visual properties of words is connected, via a set of hidden units, to a phonological store coding their phonological properties. The connection weights between units in the two stores, via the hidden units, are set by training using the back propagation algorithm. As a result of such training the model comes to encode knowledge about the correspondences between English words and their pronunciations in the connection weights between the orthographic and phonological stores. This model then gives us a way of conceptualizing the growth of a sight vocabulary as a pattern of connection weights between two different classes of representation (orthographic and phonological). Such a model is a single, rather than a dual-route model, and generalization and regularity effects in word

R.M. Joshi and C.K. Leong (eds.), Reading Disabilities: Diagnosis and Component Processes, 225–236.
© 1993 Kluwer Academic Publishers. Printed in the Netherlands.

recognition emerge as natural by-products of a connectionist system with distributed, sub-symbolic, representations (see, van Orden, Pennington & Stone, 1990). The implications of a connectionist framework for studies of the development of word recognition skills in normal and dyslexic children are only just beginning to become clear, and we will return to them later.

Within the more traditional "dual-route" framework, research on developmental dyslexia has pointed to the prevalence of phonological reading deficits as indexed by poor non-word reading (see Rack, Snowling & Olson, 1992, for a review), and in some experiments, the absence of a regularity effect (e.g., Frith & Snowling, 1983). It has been argued that dyslexic children with deficient phonological reading strategies lack the vital 'self-teaching' mechanism that allows normal children to expand their word recognition skills. Nevertheless, although the acquisition of a visual lexical system is slow for such dyslexic children, considerable progress can be made in learning to read by relying on visual strategies and other intact mechanisms. Hence, dyslexic children may learn to read by gradually expanding their "sight vocabulary" or lexical knowledge of printed words (Snowling & Hulme, 1989; Funnell & Davidson, 1989).

The dominant theoretical approach to studies of reading development and its disorders, in the last decade and a half, has come from stage theories (Marsh, Friedman, Welch, & Desberg, 1981, Frith, 1985, Ehri, 1986, Morton, 1989). These developmental theories have been very closely allied to dual-route theories of adult reading, and have generally viewed the acquisition of visually-based strategies as preceding the development of phonological strategies. For example, according to Frith (1985), the child moves from an initial, logographic phase in which reading proceeds via partial visual cues to an alphabetic phase when letter-sound relationships can be used. Logographic and alphabetic skills are subsequently amalgamated to allow the child to become a fluent, automatic reader within the orthographic phase.

Within Frith's (1985) framework, dyslexics fail to make the transition to the alphabetic phase. Thus, their reading remains visually based and they are unable to deal with words they have not seen before. Development may proceed following "arrest" but it is assumed that it will be atypical. Seymour (1986) suggested that developmental difficulties within a system he described as the phonological processor (principally in the grapheme-phoneme translator) may force readers to continue to expand their lexical system along logographic lines rather than setting up the complex set of connections between letters and sounds, which characterizes the lexicon of the reader within the orthographic phase.

One central and distinctive feature of stage models is the assumption that there is a sequential dependence between stages. Hence, in order to become a proficient adult reader (and speller), the child must pass through the stages in a given order. In such stage models, it must be presumed that dyslexics who have difficulty with alphabetic reading, will fail to become proficient readers. One problem here, however, is the absence of a sufficiently well-specified theory of what constitutes evidence of efficient "adult-like" word recognition skill, or "orthographic" reading in Frith's terms. We will consider the viability of stage theories and the promise of connectionist models after having considered data bearing on how JM has managed to learn to read and the extent to which his word recognition system can be considered to function normally.

JM: Learning to Read without Phonology?

A BRIEF CASE HISTORY

JM was first seen when he was 8 years old. His WISC-R Full Scale I.Q. was 123 and he was reading and spelling two years below expectation. He had a history of articulatory speech difficulties and great difficulty with phonological reading strategies, being able to read words but totally unable to read non-words. He had difficulty with a range of phonological tasks, particularly those testing phonological awareness and output processing, and he had residual articulation problems (Snowling, Stackhouse, & Rack, 1986).

THE NATURE OF JM'S PHONOLOGICAL IMPAIRMENTS

JM has severe phonological difficulties. One focus of our studies has been to establish the nature of his phonological impairments. A series of studies has established that JM's phonological difficulties are not completely general: it seems his most prominent difficulties are with output phonology or speech production processes (Hulme & Snowling, 1992). One task that taps these difficulties is verbal repetition. We asked JM to repeat words (e.g., anemone, statistical) and non-words derived from them and pronounced analogously (adebole, spapistical). Even at the age of 13 years JM was significantly worse on this task than 10 year old reading-age matched control children. His difficulty here affected both word and non-word repetition. Another source of evidence for JM's difficulties with output phonological tasks comes from his immediate memory span performance. This has been consistently impaired (Snowling & Hulme, 1989; Hulme & Snowling, 1992).

To make a direct comparison between input and output processing we constructed an auditory discrimination and repetition test using identical materials (Hulme & Snowling, 1992). This employed a set of 40 non-words devised by Gathercole and Baddeley (1989). The input task consisted of an auditory discrimination task with 20 pairs of identical non-words (e.g., bannifer-bannifer) and 20 pairs that differed by a single phoneme (e.g., thickery-shickery). In the corresponding output task JM was simply asked to repeat the 40 non-words. The results were very clear. JM was nearly perfect on the input task and slightly better than the reading-age matched controls, but on the output (repetition) task he had great difficulty being significantly worse than reading-age controls. We also found that JM performed similarly to reading-age controls on another input task, auditory lexical decision, while he had much more difficulty repeating the words and non-words used in this task than did controls. Overall our results indicated that JM's phonological difficulties certainly affected speech production processes more severely than speech perception processes.

HOW HAS JM LEARNED TO READ IN THE FACE OF HIS PHONOLOGICAL IMPAIRMENTS?

Over the years we have studied him, JM has certainly made progress in learning to read, albeit slowly and laboriously. He has made roughly half the normal rate of progress in reading, while his spelling difficulties have been more obdurate. His progress in learning to read seems to have been achieved in the absence of any well developed phonological reading strategies. The most direct evidence for this comes from his great difficulty in dealing with non-words. When he was first assessed at age 8 years JM had been completely unable to pronounce any non-words. On two subsequent reassessments at age 12 and 13 years, he remained much worse than reading-age control children in dealing with non-words, and was completely unable to pronounce complex non-words containing clusters that lacked orthographic neighbors e.g., otbemp, ildpos (Snowling & Hulme, 1989; Hulme & Snowling, 1992), This great difficulty in reading non-words is evidence for JM's inability to make the transition from Frith's logographic to alphabetic stage of development.

We decided to use JM's limited ability to read nonwords as a way of exploring the strategies available to him to learn to recognize unfamiliar printed words (Hulme & Snowling, 1992). One possible, artifactual, source of difficulty for JM in pronouncing non-words arises from considering his speech difficulties. Non-words, as well as looking unfamiliar, by definition involve unfamiliar combinations of sounds. It could be, therefore, that JM's great difficulty in dealing with them arises from a problem in actually pronouncing them, as opposed to decoding them. To check on this we asked JM to read a set of pseudohomophones, non-words that are pronounced as words (e.g., nirce). JM pronounced pseudohomophones no better than other non-words of equal visual similarity to words, while reading-age matched controls pronounced the pseudohomophones much more easily than the control nonwords (cf., Pring & Snowling, 1986). We interpret this finding in normal children to indicate that non-words are not read simply by a process of left to right letter to sound conversion, but instead are decoded partly by accessing lexical knowledge. In JM's case however, his decoding skills are so seriously deficient he appears unable to make effective use of his lexical knowledge. In any event these results indicate that JM's non-word reading deficit was not attributable to any simple inability to pronounce unfamiliar items; his difficulty does seem to be one of decoding the items.

In a further study we looked at JM's ability to benefit from semantic context and the degree of visual similarity between words and the non-words presented for him to read. We believed from our previous studies that he would benefit from both of these since he has excellent semantic skills, and appeared to place reliance on a visual strategy in reading. In this study all the non-words were once again pseudohomophones. Half of the non-words differed from the word they had been derived from by a single grapheme (clown-klown) while half differed by two grapheme changes (clown-kloun). Half of the non-words were presented in isolation while half were preceded by a semantic prime (e.g., nail-scroo, cough-snease). The results of this study showed that JM was more sensitive to the visual similarity between the non-words and their base words than were controls. In addition, JM showed a much larger effect of semantic priming than the controls. It appears from these data that JM is highly dependent upon visual factors and semantic context when learning to decode novel words. In a sense we can consider this pattern as adaptive, since essentially JM is making use of his visual and semantic strengths to compensate for his phonological weakness (cf. Snowling, 1987).

ARE JM'S WORD RECOGNITION SKILLS NORMAL?

These studies seem to have established that JM has learned to read in an atypical way. An issue that naturally arises is whether, given such an atypical course of development, his word recognition system functions at all normally. It is perfectly possible, theoretically, to imagine that although he has been delayed in creating recognition devices for printed words, those devices he has developed function perfectly normally. An alternative is that JM's difficulties have not only compromised the rate at which he has learned to recognize words, but also resulted in incomplete or defective recognition devices. This is certainly a possibility that would gain credence from stage theories, and is consistent with clinical impressions that dyslexic children are inconsistent and error-prone in recognizing even simple words. We decided to examine these possibilities by looking directly at JM's recognition of words. We examined the speed and accuracy of his naming of words, presented on two separate occasions. Presenting the words twice allowed us to examine the consistency of his responses from one occasion to the next.

JM was asked to read 112 words divided equally into four classes which varied according to Frequency and Regularity (after Seymour 1986). The words in the different categories were matched according to word length (3 to 6 letters) and syllable structure (one or two syllables).

The words were presented on a Macintosh microcomputer. Pronunciation latencies were measured with a voice key which also terminated the display. JM and each control subject were presented with the entire set of 112 items twice, once during the morning session and once during the afternoon session of the same day.

Accuracy of Word Reading

Normal children read high-frequency words more accurately than low-frequency. On the low-frequency words the control children also found the regular words easier to read than the irregular. This regularity effect is not altogether straightforward to interpret: traditionally such effects have been attributed to the use of phonic decoding strategies in reading unfamiliar words. However, it is also possible that regular words are easier to read because lexical analogies can be made for regular words more readily than for irregular words.

Consistency of Word Reading

JM's performance on high-frequency words was generally similar to that of controls. However, his performance on low-frequency words differed from controls; his accuracy on low-frequency irregular words was within the normal range but his accuracy on low-frequency regular words was less good than that of the normal readers. In sum, while normal readers showed a regularity effect on low-frequency words, this was reduced in JM.

One of our central questions concerned the consistency of JM's responding between one trial and the next. To examine this, we calculated the number of times he read a word correctly on the first trial and incorrectly on the second, and the number of times he read a word incorrectly on the first trial and correctly on the second. Arguably, the latter type of "inconsistency" is less serious than the former as it may indicate an effect of learning between trials. In contrast, reading a word correctly on its first presentation and then incorrectly on a subsequent occasion indicates a failure to access a representation of a word that is known on the second trial. We also calculated the number of times words were consistently incorrect (an error was made on both trials).

Although JM was consistently incorrect to the same extent as controls he showed a greater tendency to read words first correctly and then incorrectly (C/I) than first incorrectly then correctly (I/C). It was argued above that the tendency to be correct first and then incorrect is a serious type of inconsistency, pointing to a failure to retrieve a familiar word. JM made more of these kinds of error than all but one control subject. In contrast, we argued that words which are initially read incorrectly and subsequently correctly may have been learned during the course of the experiment. JM showed less tendency to do this than all but one control, a different child to the one who had made a high proportion of correct/incorrect responses.

These results might be taken to suggest that JM's lexical processing is mildly inefficient because of his tendency to misread words which he knows. His tendency not to learn words between one trial and the next underlines his specific learning difficulty. This may plausibly be related to his deficient phonological reading strategies. Normal subjects could be observed to make unsuccessful attempts at decoding novel words on the first trial in this experiment, and then subsequently decode these same items on their second presentation. JM in contrast very rarely did this.

Speed Of Word Naming

We also examined the speed of the controls' and JM's word reading. Reaction time distributions, for correct responses, were plotted for JM and the group of Reading-Age matched controls, for the high- and low-frequency words separately. These distributions are shown in Figures 1 and 2.

As Figures 1 and 2 show, the majority of JM's responses were fast, occurring within the first 1000 milliseconds and the remainder within 1500 milliseconds. The data from the Reading-Age matched controls were very similar, a majority of responses occurring within 1000 milliseconds with perhaps relatively fewer at between 1000 and 1500 milliseconds. None of the normal control subjects demonstrated a pattern of performance which departed from this. In both figures JM shows a slightly elevated tail to his reaction time distributions, reflecting a slightly greater proportion of very slow responses in his case than the controls.

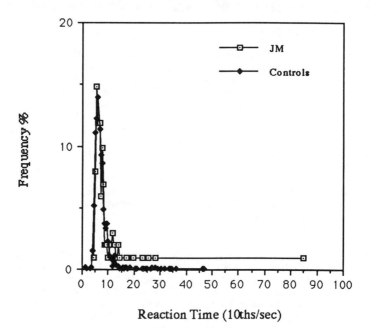

Figure 1. Reaction time distributions for high-frequency words for JM and controls.

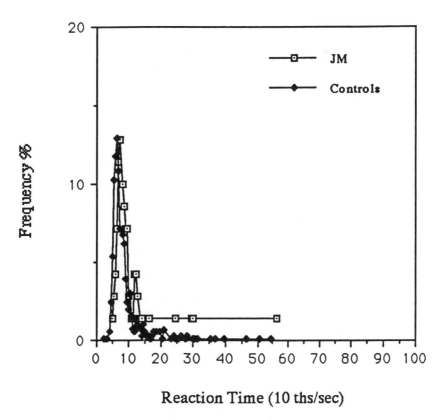

Figure 2. Reaction time distributions for low-frequency words for JM and controls.

These data again suggest that there may be some minimal inefficiency in JM's reading, as indicated by a small proportion of RTs which are rather longer than those found within the normal group.   However, overall his distribution of RTs looks remarkably normal and these data certainly do not point to any gross abnormalities in JM's word recognition system.

The data from these studies of word recognition in JM seem to be consistent with two major conclusions about the nature and development of his word recognition system.   In the first place we have incontrovertible evidence that JM has learned to read in the absence of any efficient phonological reading strategies.   In the absence of such strategies it appears that he placed greater than normal reliance on the use of semantic context and a visual strategy in reading. The second major finding is that the word recognition system that has developed in this atypical way seems far less aberrant than one might have expected it to.   JM names a large number of words in his sight vocabulary with reasonable speed, and although he shows some signs of being less consistent in naming words from one occasion to the next the degree of this inconsistency is small enough to make us circumspect in interpreting it.

Conclusions: The Development of word recognition skills in the absence of alphabetic strategies.

It appears that JM has completely failed to develop alphabetic competence; he cannot effectively apply letter-sound rules even of the most basic kind. The strong hypothesis following from Frith's (1985) model is that JM should fail to become an orthographic reader. This would mean that he would continue to read logographically utilizing partial cues. It would follow that his reading would be visually-based, inaccurate and prone to inconsistency.

The evidence presented here is equivocal with regard to this position. While there are some inefficiencies in JM's reading and he does make relatively more visual errors than normal controls, there is no evidence for gross abnormalities within his word-recognition 8system. If being an orthographic reader means having automatic access to word-recognition devices or logogens (cf. Morton, 1989), then JM has developed these for a large number of words within his sight vocabulary. Whether this constitutes having entered the 'orthographic phase' remains an open question awaiting further specification of what type of processing this would entail.

The relative adequacy of JM's word-recognition skills, in the presence of such severely deficient phonological reading strategies, remains somewhat surprising. The most straightforward interpretation of this finding is that nonlexical phonological strategies are irrelevant to creating new lexical recognition devices for words. Whilst the absence of effective phonological reading strategies may delay the acquisition of lexical recognition devices, it does not alter the nature or quality of such representations. In JM's case, the development of this system has been grossly delayed even if the outcome has been lexical representations that do not differ from those of normal readers. Thus, if the strict hypothesis of sequential dependence between stages in stage models of reading development is adhered to, JM's case refutes such models.

We will now go on to consider the results of this study within the context of current connectionist models. The view that letter-sound rules are irrelevant to the development of adequate word recognition skills would certainly find sympathy with proponents of "single-route" models (Glushko, 1979; Seidenberg and McClelland, 1989; van Orden et al., 1990). However, learning within such models would still demand a central role for phonology. In the Seidenberg & McClelland model, the effective word recognition system of the proficient reader consists of a network of connections between phonology and orthography. We have argued elsewhere that one criticism of this model is that it pays no attention to the evidence showing that an important predictor of the ease of learning to read is the adequacy of children's phonological skills (see, Goswami & Bryant, 1990, for a review). However, it is reasonable to suppose that the general approach to modeling word recognition embodied in the Seidenberg and McClelland model could be modified by incorporating a prestructured phonological store. In such a model it would be expected that the pre-existing structure of a phonological store would facilitate learning the mappings of orthographic onto phonological representations (see Hulme, Snowling, & Quinlan, 1991).

Following this logic, one might expect the development of mappings between orthography and phonology to be hindered in a child like JM who has phonological difficulties. The effect on development of a phonological impairment can be thought of in two different ways within a connectionist framework. The simplest view would be that the development of mappings between orthography and phonology is delayed. An alternative, more radical view, would be that the nature of the mappings created between phonology and orthography would be actually deviant or disordered in children with phonological difficulties. It is not at all certain whether rule-like behavior would emerge from such a network.

We favor the more radical alternative; that JM's lexical system has followed an aberrant course of development. In terms of a connectionist model we believe that JM's dyslexic difficulties can be thought of as resulting from deficiencies in phonological representations. We would suggest that from the outset of reading development, JM has lacked phonological representations at the sufficient level of specification to allow the creation of mappings between phonology and orthography. He has therefore been unable to capitalize on the alphabetic principle linking spelling patterns with sound. Consequences for his development have been an extreme delay in the acquisition of the word recognition system, the failure to abstract the statistical regularities of the language, and the failure to acquire letter-sound translation "rules". It is notable however, that his word recognition system is not grossly abnormal. It deals well with high- and low-frequency words that are in his sight vocabulary, having benefited from the frequent co-occurrence of their spoken and written forms. For these words the mappings between orthography and phonology are sufficiently well defined to allow consistent reading from one occasion to the next.

We see reading development as best conceptualized within a sub-symbolic framework. However, in considering the development of children's reading skills within such a framework we would argue that it is crucial to make a distinction between the growth and availability of knowledge and the use of strategies. It is the lack of a clear separation between these two concepts that has caused difficulties for stage models such as those of Marsh et al. (1981) and Frith (1985).

We would argue that reading development properly begins when the child has only a few sight words and these "inputs" are connected to an equally small set of pronunciations or "outputs". At this stage, no generalization is possible because of the limited knowledge the network has encoded. It cannot abstract regularities relating inputs to outputs because such regularities depend critically upon a sufficiently large and representative training corpus. Stage models have described this state of development as a "visual" or "logographic" stage.

As the child learns new words, the network begins to abstract statistical regularities relating inputs to outputs. This is when the abstraction of alphabetic rules first becomes possible and corresponds to the state in stage models when alphabetic strategies become available. Within a connectionist framework, this state could be equated with what Van Orden et al. (1990) refer to as the emergence of "strong rules". Essentially these emerge as a consequence of covariant learning between letters and their pronunciations in a variety of word contexts. For example, the consistent connections between particular letters (B) and particular sounds (/b/) would emerge relatively easily from such a system.

As development proceeds, the connections between inputs and outputs become richer. At this stage the network embodies knowledge which can make accessible the more complex, hierarchical grapheme-phoneme rules that in stage models are thought of as characterizing the competent reader. This state of the network corresponds to the "orthographic" stage of development in Frith's model. We wish to emphasize that in this reconceptualization of stage models, the different surface behaviors which have usually been considered as indicators of the emergence of different strategies, can be viewed as natural consequences of changes in the underlying knowledge base. The knowledge base however, is encoded by one and the same simple underlying network architecture.

An important feature of Frith's (1985) stage model is that it provides a clear way of describing disorders of literacy development in relation to patterns of normal development. We believe it is important to retain this feature of a developmental model and that this is possible within the sort of connectionist framework we have outlined. We have talked about JM and the implications of our framework for normal development.   We now need to consider its broader implications for studies of dyslexia.

A critical feature of connectionist models is the level of representation they embody. In JMs case we have focused upon difficulties at the level of phonological representations. We have argued that a connectionist framework allows us to consider disorders of development in two different ways. Mappings between phonology and orthography may simply be delayed in their development or more radically, may develop in aberrant ways. We have argued that in JMs case, development is best captured in terms of the development of an aberrant system. We would hypothesize that this is true for dyslexic children whose development is proceeding by the acquisition of a sight vocabulary in the absence of the development of alphabetic reading skills as indexed by, for example, poor non-word reading. These children have often been described as developmental phonological dyslexics (Seymour, 1986; Snowling, Stackhouse, & Rack, 1986). This is not the only pattern observed in dyslexic children however,

Another common pattern in dyslexic children is the relatively slow development of word recognition skills and relatively intact phonological reading strategies in comparison to children of the same reading age (see, for example, Johnston, Rugg, & Scott, 1987). These children can read non-words relatively well and have often been described as developmental surface dyslexics (Coltheart, Masterson, Byng, Prior, & Riddoch, 1983) or, more rarely, as developmental morphemic dyslexics (Seymour, 1986). The relatively intact pattern of these children's reading suggests that, within our connectionist framework, the mappings between phonology and orthography are developing normally, albeit slowly. Our hypothesis would be that such children display phonological deficits which are less severe than those found in "phonological" dyslexics such as JM. In such cases it may be that there is a lack of readiness within the phonological domain at the point when these children are presented with the task of learning to read.

The simple framework we have outlined makes it possible to unite observations of individual differences seen in dyslexic children. Our hypothesis is that differences in the severity and/or form of phonological impairment seen in different children may affect the development of a system of mappings between orthography and phonology in different ways (see also Snowling, Stackhouse, & Rack, 1986). Broadly, some children may simply show delays in the acquisition of the mappings between orthography and phonology whilst others in addition show the development of an aberrant system of mappings.   A further complication is that we have focused exclusively on the readiness or intactness of underlying phonological representations. While this is fitting in the light of the vast body of evidence relating dyslexia to underlying weaknesses in phonological skills, we have no doubt that the patterns of development observed could be modified in complex ways depending upon the intactness of the visual representational system. Thus dyslexic difficulties due solely to underlying visual deficiencies are possible, in principle (see, for example, Seymour's (1986) description of visual processor dyslexics), though we believe such cases are very rare. Far more common, we believe, are cases where there may be complex interactions between difficulties at the level of both visual and phonological representations (see, Goulandris & Snowling (1991) for the discussion of one possible case).

ACKNOWLEDGMENT

This research was supported by grant no. G8801538 from the Medical Research Council and grant no. SPG8920217 from the Tri-council initiative in Cognitive Science. We thank JM for his willing participation.

REFERENCES

Coltheart, M., Masterson, J., Byng, S., Prior, M., & Riddoch, J. (1983). Surface dyslexia. *Quarterly Journal of Experimental Psychology, 35A,* 469-496.

Ehri, L. (1986). Sources of difficulty in learning to spell and read. In M.L. Wolraich & D. Routh (eds.). *Advances in Developmental and Behavioral Pediatrics,* (vol. 7. pp. 121-195). Greenwich, CT: JAI Press.

Frith, U. (1985). Beneath the surface of developmental dyslexia. In Patterson, K.E., Marshall, J.C., & Coltheart, M. (Eds), *Surface Dyslexia.* (pp. 301-330). London: Routledge & Kegan Paul.

Frith, U. & Snowling, M. (1983). Reading for meaning and reading for sound in autistic and dyslexic children. *British Journal of Developmental Psychology, 1,* 329-42,

Funnell, E. & Davison, M (1989). Lexical capture: A developmental disorder of reading and spelling. *Quarterly Journal of Experimental Psychology, 41A,* 471-488.

Gathercole, S.E. & Baddeley, A.D. (1989). Evaluation of the role of phonological STM in the development of vocabulary in children: A longitudinal study. *Journal of Memory and Language, 28,* 200-213.

Glushko, R. (1979). The organization and activation of orthographic knowledge in reading aloud. *Journal of Experimental Psychology: Human Perception and Performance, 5,* 674-691.

Goswami, U. & Bryant, P.E. (1990). *Phonological skills and learning to read,* London; Lawrence Erlbaum.

Goulandris, A. & Snowling, M. (1991). Visual memory deficits: A plausible cause of developmental dyslexia? Evidence from a single case study. *Cognitive Neuropsychology, 8,* 127-154.

Hulme, C. & Snowling, M. (1992). Deficits in output phonology: an explanation of reading failure? *Cognitive Neuropsychology, 9,* 47-72

Hulme, C., Snowling, M., & Quinlan, P. (1991). Connectionism and learning to read: Steps towards a psychologically plausible model. *Reading and Writing: An Interdisciplinary Journal, 3,* 159-168.

Johnston, R.S., Rugg, M., & Scott, S. (1987). Phonological similarity effects, memory span and developmental reading disorders: The nature of the relationship. *British Journal of Psychology, 78,* 205-211.

Marsh, G., Friedman, M.P., Welch, V., & Desberg, P. (1981). A cognitive-developmental theory of reading acquisition. In T.G. Waller & G.E. MacKinnon (eds.), *Reading research: Advances in theory and practice,* (vol. 3, pp. 199-221). New York, Academic Press.

Morton J. (1989). An information-processing account of reading acquisition. In A. Galaburda (Ed.), *From reading to neurons.* (pp 43-66). Cambridge, Mass.: MIT Press.

Pring, I.S., & Snowling, M.J. (1986). Developmental changes in word recognition: An information processing account. *The Quarterly Journal of Experimental Psychology, 38A,* 395-418.

Rack, J., Snowling, M. & Olson, R. (1992). The nonword reading deficit in dyslexia: A review. *Reading Research Quarterly, 27,* 29-53.

Seidenberg, M. & McClelland, J. (1989). A distributed, developmental model of word recognition and naming. *Psychological Review, 96,* 523-568.

Seymour, P.H.K. (1986). *Cognitive analysis of dyslexia.* London: Routledge and Kegan Paul.

Snowling, M. J. (1987). *Dyslexia: A cognitive-developmental perspective.* Oxford: Basil Blackwell.

Snowling, M. & Hulme, C. (1989). A longitudinal case study of developmental phonological dyslexia. *Cognitive Neuropsychology, 6,* 379-401.

Snowling, M., Stackhouse, J., & Rack, J. (1986). Phonological dyslexia and dysgraphia: a developmental analysis. *Cognitive Neuropsychology, 3,* 309-339.

Van Orden, G., Pennington, B., & Stone, G. (1990). Word identification and the promise of subsymbolic psycholinguistics. *Psychological Review, 97,* 488-522.

PART III   READING/SPELLING STRATEGIES -- EDITORS' INTRODUCTION

Within our context of component processes of reading disabilities and reading acquisition, strategies can be taken to mean knowledge of procedures that can operate on orthographic, phonologic and syntactic-semantic information to enhance reading and/or spelling performance. The main questions raised by the authors in this Part III include: How do readers/spellers access lexical knowledge? Do poor readers/spellers compared with their controls use different strategies? Does phonological awareness, as discussed in the preceding Part II, play the same role in facilitating the reading of poor readers and emergent readers using the more transparent Danish, German, and modern Greek languages? Would "garden variety" poor readers of another relatively shallow language -- Dutch -- be characterized by poor decoding and language comprehending? Elbro, Näslund, Porpodas, van den Bos and Spelberg draw on their research programs to address aspects of these issues with their different linguistic groups. A fuller treatment of reading and writing disorders in different alphabetic orthographies (ranging from shallow to deep alphabets); the Japanese syllabary; and the Chinese morphemic system is provided by Aaron and Joshi (1989).

Elbro reports on the different reading strategies of his Danish developmental dyslexics compared with their reading-level matched controls and also a subsample of the dyslexics with contrast subgroups matched on word decoding and adjusted IQ, and on age and IQ. Elbro distinguishes between the ability and the tendency to use letter-level recoding strategy and suggests that a "slow and non-automatic" access to phonolgical representation may explain the tendency for the dyslexics towards letter-level recoding in reading. **Näslund** summarizes a developmental study with groups of second grade German children varying in intelligence levels to estimate the contribution of verbal ability, verbal memory and phonological awareness to reading performance. This latter component is shown to have a robust concurrent and long-term effect on reading over a wide range of intelligence (see also Siegel, Stanovich, this volume).

Within the broad framework of phonological processing, **Porpodas** shows in three experiments using spoken or written rhyming and non-rhyming Greek letter strings the inefficient storage and retrieval of the phonetic code by poor Greek readers compared with their controls. He thus adds to the general findings of the role of phonetic recoding and its effect on reading disabilities and acquisition, as first investigated by the Haskins and other groups. **Van den Bos and Spelberg** report on their detailed quantitative and qualitative analyses of reading and related language comprehension skills of nine-year-old special school (SPS) Dutch children and their chronological-age matched regular school (RES) peers. Van den Bos and Spelberg show that their SPS children perform lower in decoding and listening comprehension than their RES counterparts in accordance with the Simple View of reading (see Stanovich; Tunmer & Hoover, this volume); and reiterate the need for instruction in components of language comprehension.

Differences in information processing strategies and the effects of instruction on phonological processing in developmental dyslexics are the subjects of investigation of three sets of studies with children using the English language. **Aaron, Wleklinski and Wills** discuss individual differences in the organizing and processing of information and suggest that developmental

R.M. Joshi and C.K. Leong (eds.), Reading Disabilities: Diagnosis and Component Processes, 237–238.
© 1993 *Kluwer Academic Publishers. Printed in the Netherlands.*

dyslexics possibly depend overly on the "simultaneous strategy" and less so on the "sequential strategy" in processing the English orthography.

Specifically, **Felton** reports on a developmental study of the within-group relationship amongst kindergarten phonological processing variables and reading outcomes at the end of grades one and two. She finds great variability in phonological deficits in "at-risk" children with phonological recoding (focus on rapid, automatized naming) as the most predictive of subsequent reading outcomes (decoding, word identification and word attack subskills). Felton emphasizes the importance of direct instruction of the alphabetic code to assist children with different kinds and degrees of phonological processing deficits (see also, Adams, 1990). In a systematic training study using a multiple-baseline single subject design, **Uhry** investigates the spelling-reading connection in three fourth grade dyslexic children. In agreement with other studies (see, for example, Ehri & Robbins, 1992), she also shows the positive effect of phonetic spelling training on reading, but finds greater improvement in including phonemic segmentation tasks in the spelling training using the microcomputer.

The different studies in this Part III thus provide some answers to the challenge posed in Part I of differential diagnosis leading to differential and effective treatment.

REFERENCES

Aaron, P.G., & Joshi, R.M. (eds.). (1989). *Reading and writing disorders in different orthographic systems*. Dordrecht, The Netherlands: Kluwer Academic Publishers.

Adams, M.J. (1980). *Beginning to read: Thinking and learning about print*. Cambridge, MA: The MIT Press.

Ehri, L.C., & Robbins, C. (1992). Beginners need some decoding skill to read words by analogy. *Reading Research Quarterly*, 27, 12-26.

DYSLEXIC READING STRATEGIES AND LEXICAL ACCESS:
A Comparison and Validation of Reading Strategy Distributions in Dyslexic Adolescents and Younger, Normal Readers

CARSTEN ELBRO
Department of General and Applied Linguistics
University of Copenhagen
Njalsgade 86
DK-2300 Copenhagen S
Denmark

ABSTRACT: Research on subtypes of developmental dyslexia often assumes that dyslexics fall into discrete groups with different reading strategies and underlying deficits. A strong tendency towards a letter-by-letter recoding strategy in reading has traditionally been assumed to be a sign of poor skills in the visual modality. Dyslexics who read relatively few words 'immediately' have been considered to suffer from 'visual' or 'dyseidetic' dyslexia. The present study questioned these assumptions. In the first part individual reading strategies in 26 severely impaired developmental dyslexics were compared with strategies in 26 reading-level-matched younger, normal readers. Reading strategies were found to be distributed along a continuum in both groups, and no indications of subgroups were found. Half of the dyslexic subjects read by means of more whole-word oriented strategies than did any of the normal controls. In the second part of the study much of the variance in reading strategies in the dyslexic sample was found to be accounted for by differences in lexical access to whole word phonology. This finding was replicated in *a post hoc* analysis of the data from the Colorado twin study (Olson and colleagues). The results indicate that terms like 'visually' impaired or 'dyseidetic' used for letter-by-letter readers may be grossly misleading. Rather, dyslexics with a relatively small vocabulary of 'sight words' may have specific difficulties with retrieval of the sounds of words.

At the previous NATO institute in 1982 Robin Morris and Paul Satz listed a number of requirements for classification systems of dyslexia. One year earlier these authors had published a similar list of problems faced by current subtype research. Few of these problems, if any, seem to have been solved since then:

1) Only a few studies show concordance as to the number of subgroups and their characteristics. Various numbers of subgroups with varying characteristics have frequently been found even in studies which have used the same type of materials and methods.
2) Considering statistically based classifications in particular, the subgroups are seldom covering all the dyslexic subjects they were based on, i.e., there are a varying number of subjects who do not fit into any subgroup.
3) Few non-statistical classification studies have checked the extent to which subgroups are distinct and do not overlap with each other.

R.M. Joshi and C.K. Leong (eds.), Reading Disabilities: Diagnosis and Component Processes, 239–251.
© 1993 *Kluwer Academic Publishers. Printed in the Netherlands.*

A number of equally serious problems may be added:

4) No studies have provided clear evidence that the existence of subgroups is characteristic of dyslexic readers as opposed to normal readers, or at least that there is a greater variation in reading strategies among dyslexic readers than among normal readers (Bryant & Impey, 1986; Ellis, 1985; Wilding, 1989).
5) The most influential hypothesis of the causes of different subtypes has not been empirically verified. This hypothesis, which may be named 'general cognitive', holds that differences in reading and spelling strategies are caused by different patterns of weaknesses and strengths in general cognitive abilities such as auditory-verbal processing, visuo-spatial processing, and articulatory programming (Boder, 1973; Boder & Jarrico, 1982; Doehring, Trites, Patel, & Fiedorowicz, 1981; Johnson & Myklebust, 1964; Lyon, 1983). The subgroups defined by internal criteria, that is, patterns of reading skills and strategies, have not been externally validated (Doehring *et al*, 1981; Malatesha & Dougan, 1982; Olson, Kliegl, Davidson, & Foltz, 1985; van den Bos, 1984). And the subgroups defined by external criteria, or patterns of scores on so-called neuro-psychological tests, have not displayed predictable patterns of reading skills and strategies (Lundberg, 1985; Mattis, French, & Rapin, 1975).

A classification of subtypes of dyslexia needs to rest *both* on characteristics of reading behavior and on characteristics that are external to reading and spelling. Because if it does not, one cannot be certain about the causes of the observed reading difficulties.

On the one hand, a reader who makes many so-called 'visual paralexias', i.e., misreads letters and words for others with similar visual shapes, is not necessarily handicapped by poor visual perception or poor visual memory. Other impairments might also explain this problem in reading, such as a failure to separate certain speech sounds, or an impaired access to words in the mental lexicon (Katz, 1986).

On the other hand, one cannot conclude that a certain pattern of general cognitive abilities is the cause of reading difficulties. Poor visual perception is not necessarily the cause of certain reading difficulties just because a dyslexic reader scores below the expected grade level on a visual recognition test. A substantial number of normal readers also score at the same low level on visual tests.

The present study had two connected purposes: 1) to verify whether or not dyslexic readers use more diverse reading strategies than do normal readers, and eventually 2) to explain why.

Letter-By-Letter Reading

In answer to the first problem, i.e., the different number of subgroups, one may begin by limiting subgroups of interest to those based on differences in reading and spelling strategies. It is important for reading research to *explain differences in reading and spelling*, not to explain differences in general cognitive abilities.

There is ample evidence that some dyslexics use letter-by-letter recoding in reading more than others (Baron, 1979; Boder, 1973; Denckla, 1977; Mitterer, 1982; Olson et *al*, 1985; Seymour, 1986). In fact, this seems to be the most well-documented difference in reading strategies among dyslexics.

However, there is likely to be more than one dimension within the use of a letter-by-letter recoding strategy. As Olson and his co-workers have pointed out (1985), one should distinguish between the *ability* and the *tendency* to use a strategy. To be able to do something in reading does not necessarily imply that one uses this ability.

The second problem, the one concerning the imperfect 'coverage' of many classifications, may be tackled by giving up the idea of *discrete* subgroups - at least as an axiom underlying the research strategy. If differences in reading behavior are described along one or more continua (Stanovich, 1989), no reader will have to be excluded. With this solution, it is also possible to test the subgroup hypothesis directly by looking for signs of a bimodal distribution of subjects.

The continuum solution can also deal with the third problem, because if we give up the claim that exclusive dyslexic subgroups exist before we have identified them a possible overlap is no longer a problem.

Finally, by comparing the reading strategies of a group of disabled readers with the distribution of strategies in a reading-level-matched group of normal readers, we will be in a position to know whether or not disabled readers read by means of the same strategies as do normal readers. In particular, it is important to see whether some disabled readers deviate significantly from normal strategies. And in this way we may also be in a position to solve the fifth problem.

The first part of the study was thus aimed at strategy differences between dyslexic and normal readers. In this part we were looking at differences in *tendency* to use a letter-by-letter reading (see Elbro, 1990, 1991, for details).

Subjects

The study used a reading-level-match design including 26 older dyslexic subjects compared to 26 younger normal readers on the basis of reading level and age-adjusted intelligence (Table 1). The reading measure was a standard sentence comprehension test (Nielsen, Kreiner, Poulsen, & Søegård, 1986); and the intelligence test was Raven's progressive matrices. The dyslexic adolescents came from a special school near Copenhagen for dyslexics who have been unresponsive to remedial teaching in normal schools. Their reading disabilities were specific and were not explained by lack of reading instruction, poor intelligence, or grave neurological, sensory, or emotional disturbances (cf. Critchley, 1970). Reading age of each of the dyslexic adolescents was three years or more below chronological age. The normal controls were selected from public and private schools in the same area. Danish was the first language of all subjects.

Materials and Procedure

Seven measures of tendency to use letter-by-letter reading were constructed. These measures were all based on oral reading of isolated words and on a sentence comprehension test. The measures were:

1. *Regularity effect.* The impact of orthographic regularity on reading accuracy was measured by means of 20 pairs of words. A great effect of 'regularity' was considered an indication of a letter-by-letter recoding strategy. Each pair consisted of a conventionally

Table 1 Subjects in the reading-level-match design.

	N	Age	Sentence reading (correct)	Raven raw score	Raven percentile
Dyslexic teenagers	26	15.3 (0.11)	33.5 (8.5)	44.3 (6.3)	56 (24)
Normal readers grade 2 - 3	26	9.4 (0.8)	33.2 (8.2)	31.2 (6.4)	63 (20)

spelled word (e.g., *sail)* and a word with a phonologically unpredictable spelling [e.g., *pear* (fruit)]. The words were matched in pairs on frequency, number of letters, syllables, morphemes, word class, and, as far as possible, on concreteness.

2. *Ratio between accuracy in word reading and sentence reading speed* A reader using a letter-by-letter recoding strategy will be reading rather slowly. Thus, the reading of single words will be relatively accurate in comparison with a slow sentence reading.

3. *Percentage of words not read immediately.* Using a letter-level recoding strategy, a reader is unlikely to identify a word immediately (Boder, 1973; Boder & Jarrico, 1982). This measure comprised 148 real words, nonsense words being excluded. Words read within 0.8 sec. were considered read immediately.

4. *Percentage of letter-preserving errors.* A letter-by-letter reader will be expected to produce a high proportion of misreadings which are still in accordance with the phonemic principle in being letter-preserving (e.g., *life* -> "liffi", *pear* -> "peer").

5. *Nonsense words given in response to real words.* A reader using a letter-level recoding strategy will be likely to give some nonsense words in response to real words. Whole-word readers, on the other hand, are unlikely to respond with nonsense words at all.

6. *Frequency effect (small).* A reader who uses a letter-by-letter recoding strategy is likely to be less dependent on the frequency of words than a reader using a whole word strategy. This is so because a reader cannot recognize a word as a whole unless he or she has seen it before.

7. *Lexicality effect (small).* In order to use a recoding strategy, the reader must have the necessary skills. This means that a reader who is using a letter-by-letter recoding strategy must be relatively undisturbed by reading nonsense words compared to real words. The impact of nonsense words on accuracy was assessed by means of 20 nonsense words matched with 20 real words for length and consonant-vowel structure.

Subjects were tested individually in a quiet room at their own school. All subjects attempted to read 168 words aloud in the same order. Twenty real words were read first, then the 20 nonsense words, and finally the rest of the words. Before the nonsense words were read, the subjects were told that they were going to read some invented words which did not sound like real words. No time limits were imposed, but subjects were encouraged to make a guess at words they could not read or simply to continue to the next word. Responses were tape recorded for subsequent error analysis and measurement of latencies.

Quotients between log(odds) were calculated in order to score the impact of regularity, frequency, and lexicality on the accuracy of each reader (Allerup & Elbro, 1990; Elbro, 1990).

Results

The results of the 7 measures of reading strategies were subjected to a conventional non-parametric correlation analysis and an analysis of homogeneity (Rasch, 1968). Both analyses gave satisfactory indications of homogeneity. Consequently each subject could be assigned a strategy index which was the sum of measures on which he or she were judged to be a letter-by-letter reader. Criteria for letter-by-letter reading was, of course, the same for all subjects.

The strategy indices were internally validated by comparisons with spelling strategies. The correlations between reading index and the proportion of sound-preserving spelling errors was significant (r = 0.63, p < 0.01)[1].

The strategy distribution in the dyslexic and the normal readers is depicted in Figure 1. The essentially normal distribution of dyslexic subjects replicates the results of previous studies with fewer measures of recoding strategies (e.g., Olson *et al*, 1985). No tendency emerged towards bimodality. This is an important result, since it contradicts the widespread notion of distinct subgroups based on differences in the use of a letter-by-letter reading strategy.

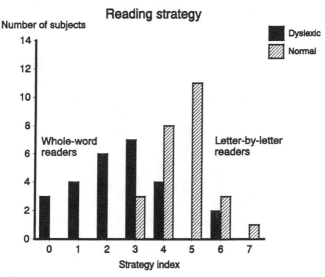

Figure 1. Distribution of dyslexic and normal readers on the whole-word (index 0) versus letter-by-letter recoding (index 7) dimension. Subject groups were matched on sentence reading comprehension.

It is also obvious from Figure 1 that dyslexics read by means of other strategies than do normal readers. Half the dyslexic subjects (with indices 0, 1, and 2) displayed a more whole-word oriented reading strategy than did any of the normal subjects. This finding, taken together with the fact that only one normal reader (with index 7) was not matched by any dyslexic subject, indicates that there are greater differences among the strategies of disabled readers than among r. rmal readers of the same reading ability.

The study was aimed at differences in decoding strategies mainly at the word level. Hence it may be argued that dyslexic and normal readers should have been matched for word decoding rather than sentence comprehension. In order to meet this requirement, subsamples consisting of 17 dyslexic and 17 normal readers were matched for word decoding and age-adjusted IQ. The decoding strategy distributions in these two groups did not differ much from the distributions in the larger groups (Figure 2).

Discussion

Before initiating a search for possible causes of differences in reading strategies, it should be established that there are in fact differences in reading strategies among dyslexics worth explaining. There would be no point in an explanation of differences that did not go beyond random variation.

Furthermore, the existence of subgroups should not be assumed beforehand, as is common in most statistical studies. There is no sound basis on which subgroup research can continue without first establishing that dyslexics read by significantly different strategies.

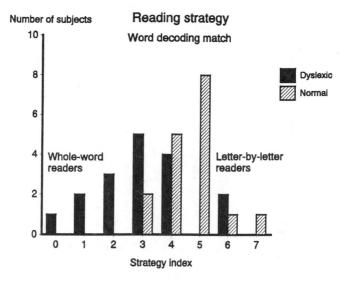

Figure 2. Distribution of dyslexic and normal readers on the whole-word (index 0) versus letter-by-letter recoding (index 7) dimension. Subject groups (N = 17 x 2) were matched on word decoding.

The dissociation between ability and tendency to use a letter-by-letter recoding strategy means that there are at least two types of variation to be explained at the grapheme-phoneme level of reading rather than just one: The first difference is in the *ability* to use a letter-level recoding strategy; the second difference is in the *tendency* to use a letter-level recoding strategy, which is also a question of an external validation of the whole-word versus speller dichotomy that is so widely used in diagnosis of dyslexia.

There is ample evidence that much of the variance in phonological coding *ability* is explained by phonological abilities with spoken language, e.g., abilities in phonological segmentation of spoken words. But there is no empirically verified explanation of why some dyslexics *tend* to use a letter-by-letter reading strategy to a greater extent than others. Of course differences in teaching methods play a role, but the question remains to be answered whether there are all individual causes as well.

Lexical Access To Whole-Word Phonology

If a reader is going to have success with a letter-by-letter recoding strategy, it is essential that phonological representations of possible words are easily and automatically accessed in the mental lexicon. If possible words do not appear by themselves from the lexicon as the reader spells out the letters of the word, he or she will have to spell the whole word, and even then not be sure of accessing a word which matches the resulting sound string. Hence, a slow and non-automatic lexical search would be a severe handicap in reading, and in theory it may explain the particular strategies of dyslexics who have a strong inclination towards letter-level recoding.

A number of studies have found indications that dyslexic readers as a group have some difficulties in naming tasks (Denckla & Rudel, 1976; Katz, 1986; Snowling, Wagtendonk, & Stafford, 1988; Wolf, 1984, 1986; Wolf & Goodglass, 1986). However, no study has been concerned with the possible connection between naming ability and reading strategies in the phonemic dimension. If letter-by-letter reading dyslexics are slower at picture-naming than whole-word dyslexics, but just as fast on a test of automatized naming; it may be considered an indication of difficulties in lexical access. The following part of the study was concerned with this possibility.

Subjects

The subjects were the same as in the previous part for reading strategies with the exception of three dyslexics who had left school and could not be reached, and one normal reader who was in the hospital. A second control group of 13 normal readers were added, matching the dyslexic subjects in age and IQ.

Materials and procedure

In order to obtain separate measures of lexical access and articulatory fluency, two naming tests were constructed: a picture-naming test, and a naming test with geometrical figures.

The picture-naming test consisted of 45 pictures from a children's picture card game pasted in groups of three on pieces of cardboard. Subjects were tested individually and instructed to name the pictures as fast and accurately as possible. When a subject had finished, he or she was asked to point out pictures of objects he or she had misnamed or failed to name at all during the test. The boards with nine pictures on each were used for this purpose.

The automatized naming task consisted of simple geometrical forms which were to be named along either one, two, or three dimensions: 1) form, 2) form and color, and 3) form, color, and number. Each of the three series of figures contained 15 items.

Results

Naming latencies were measured per picture triad from tape recordings by means of an electronic stop watch. In order to determine the range of answers which could be considered correct, a number of fluent adult speakers were asked to name the pictures. Their answers were then taken as the choices for correct answers.

Results showed marked differences among the dyslexic subjects. Mean naming time for the 45 pictures ranged from 46.6 sec. to 121.8 sec. with a mean of 74.7 sec. Furthermore, picture-naming times correlated significantly with reading strategy (the letter-by-letter reading index) ($r = 0.58$, $p < 0.01$). Automatized naming did not correlate with reading strategy.

In order to compare dyslexics who have different reading strategies with each other and with the normal controls, the dyslexic subjects were split into two groups: a group of whole-word readers (strategy index 0-3), and another group of letter-by-letter readers (index 4-7). Important differences became apparent when the results of the two naming tests were compared. Most of the visible differences in Figure 3 were statistically significant. The performance of the letter-by-letter reading dyslexics was remarkable in particular because it was the only group to use significantly longer naming times in the picture naming test than in the test of automatized naming. To test the differences between the two dyslexic groups, an ANOVA was performed with naming latencies as dependent variable and 2 subject groups and 2 naming tasks as independent factors. The interaction between subject groups and tasks was highly significant ($F(1,41) = 12.26$, $p < 0.005$).

The significant cross-over effects of the two naming tasks indicate that the long picture-naming times in the letter-by-letter group should probably not be attributed to factors associated with articulation. Instead, difficulties in access to whole-word phonology should be considered. None of the subjects seemed to speculate about the contents of the pictures, but some of them took a long time to find the names of the objects. Hence, the results supported the hypothesis that differences in ease of lexical access may explain some of the individual differences in the *tendency* to use letter-by-letter reading.

Comparison with Data from the Colorado Twin Study

The above findings were supported by a re-analysis of the data from the Colorado twin study (Olson, Wise, Conners, Rack, & Fulker, 1989). A partial result from a timed word-recognition test was used as a measure of reading style: subjects read words orally from a list of 183 words until they missed 10 of the last 20 words attempted. Since the test was timed, they could miss words in two ways: either by misreading them or by taking more than 2 seconds to read them correctly. The number of words read correctly (of the last 10) in more

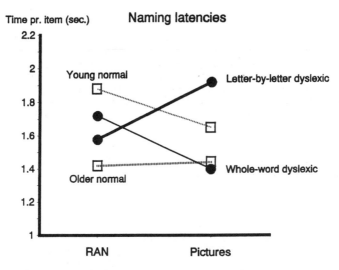

Figure 3. Picture—naming time compared to speed in rapid automatized naming.

than 2 seconds was then used as a measure of reading strategy. Readers with a high tendency to use letter-by-letter reading with difficult words were supposed to score high on this measure, whereas whole-word readers were expected to score low.

In order to obtain a group of subjects similar to the one for the Danish study, the 59 subjects with a ratio between reading age (on the PIAT word recognition test) and chronological age below 0.62 were selected. This cut-off point corresponded roughly to the average ratio (0.65) of the total sample of the 172 disabled readers and was selected on the basis of a dip in the reading ability distribution. The mean age of the 59 subjects was 16:0 years, WISC verbal IQ was 92.6, and performance IQ was 103.2 on average.

There was a moderate correlation between the number of slowly read words and picture-naming time (product-moment r= 0.35, $p < 0.01$). This indicates that the subjects who were slow at picture-naming also tended to be slow but accurate readers. The correlation increased slightly when differences in age and general coding speed (measured by the WISC coding task) were accounted for (partial correlation r = 0.39, $p < 0.005$). Differences in rapid automatized naming speed did not explain the correlation.

The significant correlation points in the same direction as the results of the Danish study: a connection exists between reading strategy and lexical access speed in the most severely dyslexic adolescents. And this connection seems to be specific for language tasks, since it is independent of non-linguistic coding tasks such as the WISC coding task.

It should be noted, however, that the correlation was found in the lower third of the Colorado sample that corresponded roughly to the subjects in the Danish study as regards reading ability. There was no significant correlation between reading strategy and naming speed in the total group representing the about 10 percent poorest readers.

Discussion

A look at the scores of the dyslexic adolescents taken as *one group* shows parallels with a number of results from previous research. As in other studies (e.g., Katz & Shankweiler 1985; Snowling et al., 1988) the dyslexics did not take longer time to name pictures than normal readers of the same age, but they tended to make more errors although the difference was not statistically significant. And, in line with the prediction study by Wolf and colleagues (Wolf, 1984; 1986; Wolf & Goodglass, 1986), the dyslexic subjects in the present study were slower at the automatized naming test when compared to normal readers of the same age.

More clear-cut findings appeared, however, when the data from the dyslexic adolescents were analyzed in the light of their reading strategies. The letter-by-letter recoding dyslexics were outperformed in naming ability not only by the normal readers of the same age, but also by much younger readers of similar reading ability.

General Discussion

The most striking finding was that dyslexic adolescents traditionally termed 'visually' impaired or 'dyseidetic' because of relatively poor whole-word reading seems to be impaired by slow lexical access to whole-word phonology. Judged from scores in the visually oriented Raven test, no signs of visual impairments were found in these slow but accurate readers (Elbro, 1990). Thus, if remediation is aimed at improving the visual skills of such dyslexics, much time and energy may be wasted. However, before this conclusion could be reached, a number of important distinctions would need to be made.

First of all, it is necessary to establish an internally valid measure of the aspects of reading one wants to explain. Then, instead of assuming a bimodal or any other distribution of scores on the measure chosen, the experimental design should allow one to look at the actual distribution.

Next, the 'general cognitive' hypothesis should not be taken for granted. There is no solid empirical basis under the axiom that differences in reading and spelling strategies are caused by different patterns of general cognitive strengths and weaknesses.

Finally, a possible external validation of the reading measure should be considered in the light of the particular population in which it was found.

The fact that a significant correlation between reading strategy and lexical access was only found among the most impaired readers in the Colorado sample and not at all in the normal readers supports the notion that ease of lexical access does not determine the reading difficulties *per se* but is of importance for the degree to which the dyslexic reader may compensate for his/her primary, phonological coding deficits.

Hence, dyslexic adolescents who continue to use primarily a letter-by-letter reading strategy may be impeded in two ways: at first they probably have primary phonological difficulties which arrest their reading development in the logographic phase (cf. Frith, 1985); and later they are not able to compensate for their difficulties to the same extent as other poor readers because they are impeded by slow lexical access.

Nevertheless, the possibility exists that slow lexical access also obstructs the development of skills in using orthographic conventions at levels above using single letters spelling patterns. A reader with slow access to the phonological representations of words may not be in a position to recognize orthographic patterns with predictable pronunciation because he or she is slow at associating between words on higher levels. However, the design of the present study did not allow for a test of this obstruction hypothesis against the compensation hypothesis just mentioned. This is so because the variation in reading abilities was relatively small and because the reading tests were not aimed at an assessment of the use of higher-level orthographic conventions.

ACKNOWLEDGMENTS

This study was supported by grants from The University of Copenhagen, The Danish Research Council for the Humanities (15-7123), and Martin Levy's Memorial Legacy. The author would like to thank many people for comments and support, but Ingvar Lundberg, University of Umea, Sweden, deserves special mention for his valuable guidance throughout the study. The author is grateful to Richard Olson and John Rack, University of Colorado, Boulder, for access to and help with the analysis of the data from the Colorado twin study.

NOTE

1. Where nothing else is mentioned, non-parametric statistical tests were used with data in limited intervals such as accuracy scores. The Mann-Whitney U-test was used in comparisons of means, and the Spearman rank test was used for calculations of correlations.

REFERENCES

Allerup, P. & Elbro, C. (1990). Comparing differences. The use of log odds in calculation of individual differences in scores in two related tests. Paper presented at The Ninth Symposium on Computational Statistics, Dubrovnik, Yugoslavia, 1990.

Baron, J. (1979). Orthographic and word-specific mechanisms in children's reading of words. *Child Development, 50,* 60-72.

Boder, E. (1973). Developmental dyslexia: A diagnostic approach based on three atypical reading-spelling patterns. *Developmental Medicine and Child Neurology, 15,* 663-687.

Boder, E. & Jarrico, S. (1982). *The Boder Test of Reading Spelling Patterns: A Diagnostic Screening Test for Subtypes of Reading Disability.* New York: Grune & Stratton.

Bryant, P. & Impey, L. (1986). The similarities between normal readers and developmental and acquired dyslexics. *Cognition, 24,* 121-137.

Critchley, M. (1970). *The dyslexic child.* London: Heinemann.

Denckla, M. B. (1977). Minimal brain dysfunction and dyslexia: Beyond diagnosis by exclusion. In M. I. Blau, I. Rapin & M. Kinsbourne (Eds.), *Topics in child neurology.* (pp. 243-261) New York: Spectrum.

Denckla, M. B. & Rudel, R. G. (1976). Naming of object-drawings by dyslexic and other learning disabled children. *Brain and Language, 3, 1-15.*

Doehring, D. G., Trites, R. L., Patel, P. G. & Fiedorowicz, C. A. (1981). *Reading disabilities: The interaction of reading, language, and neuropsychological deficits.* New York: Academic Press.

Elbro, C. (1990). *Differences in dyslexia A study of reading strategies and deficits in a linguistic perspective.* Copenhagen: Munksgaard. (Doctoral Dissertation, Copenhagen University).

Elbro, C. (1991). Dyslexics and normal beginning readers read by different strategies: A comparison of strategy distributions in dyslexic and normal readers. *International Journal of Applied Linguistics, 1*, 19-37.

Ellis, A. W. (1985). The cognitive neuropsychology of developmental (and acquired) dyslexia: A critical survey. *Cognitive Neuropsychology, 4*, 169-205.

Frith, U. (1985). Beneath the surface of developmental dyslexia. In K. E. Patterson, J.C. Marshall, & M. Coltheart (Eds.), *Surface dyslexia: Neuropsychological and cognitive studies in phonological reading*. (pp. 301-330) London: Lawrence Erlbaum.

Johnson, D. & Myklebust, H. R. (1964). *Learning disabilities. Educational principles and practices*. New York: Grune & Stratton.

Katz, R. B. (1986). Phonological deficiencies in children with reading disability: Evidence from an object-naming task. *Cognition, 22*, 225-257.

Katz, R. B. & Shankweiler, D. (1985). Repetitive naming and the detection of word retrieval deficits in the beginning reader. *Cortex, 21*, 617-625.

Lundberg, I. (1985). Longitudinal studies of reading and reading difficulties in Sweden. In G. E. MacKinnon & T. G. Waller (Eds.), *Reading research: Advances in theory and practice. Vol. 4*. (pp. 65-105) N.Y.: Academic Press.

Lyon, G. R. (1983). Learning disabled readers: Identification of subgroups. In H. R. Myklebust (Ed.), *Progress in learning disabilities. Vol. V*. (pp. 103-133). N.Y.: Grune & Stratton.

Malatesha, R. N. & Dougan, D. R. (1982). Clinical subtypes of developmental dyslexia: Resolution of an irresolute problem. In R. N. Malatesha & P. G. Aaron (Eds.), *Reading disorders. Varieties and treatments*. (pp. 69-92.) New York: Academic Press.

Mattis, S., French, J. H. & Rapin, I. (1975). Dyslexia in children and young adults: Three independent neuropsychological syndromes. *Developmental Medicine and Child Neurology, 17*, 150-163.

Mitterer, J. O. (1982). There are at least two kinds of poor readers: Whole-word poor readers and recoding poor readers. *Canadian Journal of Psychology, 36*, 445-461.

Morris, R. & Satz, P. (1984). Classification issues in subtype research: An application of some methods and concepts. In R. N. Malatesha & H. A. Whitaker (Eds.), *Dyslexia: A global issue*. (pp. 59-82) The Hague: Martinus Nijhoff Publishers.

Nielsen, J. C., Kreiner, S., Poulsen, K. & Søegård, A. (1986). *Sætningslæseprøverne SL60 & SL40. SL-håndbog*. Copenhagen: Dansk Psykologisk Forlag.

Olson, R. K, Kliegl, R., Davidson, B. J. & Foltz, G. (1985). Individual and developmental differences in reading disability. In G. E. MacKinnon & T. G. Waller (Eds.), *Reading research: Advances in theory and practice, Vol. 4*. (pp. 1-64). New York: Academic Press.

Olson, R., Wise, B., Conners, F., Rack, J., & Fulker, D. (1989). Specific deficits in component reading and language skills: Genetic and environmental influences. *Journal of Learning Disabilities, 22*, 339-348.

Rasch, G. (1968). *Probabilistic models for some intelligence and attainment tests*. Chicago: Chicago University Press.

Seymour, P. H. K. (1986). *Cognitive analysis of dyslexia*. London: Routledge & Kegan Paul.

Snowling, M., Wagtendonk, B., & Stafford, C. (1988) Object-naming deficits in developmental dyslexia. *Journal of Research in Reading, 11*, 67-85.

Stanovich, K. E. (1989). Various varying views on variation. *Journal of Learning Disabilities, 22*, 366-369.

van den Bos, K. P. (1984). Letter processing in dyslexia subgroups. *Annals of Dyslexia, 34*, 179-193.

Wilding, J. (1989). Developmental dyslexics do not fit in boxes: Evidence from case studies. *European Journal of Cognitive Psychology, 1*, 105-127.

Wolf, M. (1984). Naming, reading, and the dyslexias: A longitudinal overview. *Annals of Dyslexia, 34*, 87-115.

Wolf, M. (1986). Rapid alternating stimulus naming in the developmental dyslexias. *Brain and Language*, 27, 360-379.

Wolf, M. & Goodglass, H. (1986). Dyslexia, dysnomia, and lexical retrieval: A longitudinal investigation. *Brain and Language*, 28, 154-168.

THE SPELLING-READING CONNECTION AND DYSLEXIA: CAN SPELLING BE USED TO TEACH THE ALPHABETIC STRATEGY?

JOANNA K. UHRY
Teachers College, Columbia University
Box 223
New York, New York 10027
USA

ABSTRACT: Dyslexic children are believed to have difficulty in decoding because they are deficient in phonological skills. Their reading is apt to rely on memorized words rather than on the alphabetic strategy in which unknown words can be sounded out and blended. While the literature suggests that spelling promotes alphabetic decoding in normal young readers because it increases phoneme segmentation skills, there is little systematic attempt to examine the effects of spelling instruction as a method of teaching this strategy to dyslexic children, nor have researchers who have looked at the spelling-reading connection examined the kinesthetic effect of handwritten spellings. The present study explores the effects of spelling instruction on three dyslexic fourth graders using a multiple-baseline single subject design. Results indicate that specific words were successfully memorized using a variety of methods (i.e., analytic reading, spelling with naming letters while copying words by hand, spelling with phoneme segmentation on the computer and by hand). Generalization of patterns to nonsense words was relatively poor, but showed dramatic improvement when spelling training included a phonemic segmentation component using the computer.

There is recent interest in the connections between spelling and reading in young children (e.g., Bissex, 1980; Graves & Stuart, 1985). A number of studies show strong positive correlations between kindergarten spelling and later reading (e.g., Mann, Tobin, & Wilson, 1987; Morris & Perney, 1984), and even a causal relationship between spelling instruction and reading acquisition (Ehri & Wilce, 1987), which Ehri attributes to shared reliance on phonological awareness in both spelling and reading.

Extensive reviews of the literature suggest differences between dyslexic and normal readers in regard to phonological development (e.g., Snowling, 1987; Stanovich, 1982). Frith (1985) presents a model of reading acquisition in which dyslexics fail at the transition to the alphabetical strategy, or left-to-right, letter-by-letter sounding out and blending strategy. Frith's notion that dyslexics compensate by using other ways to read is supported by evidence that older deficient readers are less skilled at phonological tasks (Bradley & Bryant, 1978), and less skilled at using grapheme-phoneme conversion to read nonsense words (Snowling, 1980) when compared to younger, normal children matched for reading level.

Frith (1985) also theorizes that when children learn the alphabetic strategy, they learn it first for spelling, while continuing to read using a "logographic" strategy for memorizing a few words in context. Bradley and Bryant's (1979) work supports this difference in strategy use between spelling and reading, and suggests that the difference is particularly marked in poor readers. If spelling instruction has a positive effect on normal beginning readers

R.M. Joshi and C.K. Leong (eds.), Reading Disabilities: Diagnosis and Component Processes, 253–266.
© 1993 *Kluwer Academic Publishers. Printed in the Netherlands.*

because it promotes phonological awareness and phonemic segmentation skills, then it is a logical method for teaching phonologically deficient dyslexics.

The literature on using segmenting and spelling to facilitate reading suggests positive results for young children who are at risk for reading failure. In tandem with a three year correlational study of the relationship between early phonological skills and later reading, Bradley and Bryant (1983) trained preschool subjects who were particularly weak at sound categorization. With scores at least two standard deviations below peers, they certainly were at risk for reading failure. After two years of training in categorizing spoken words by rhyme and alliteration, the two experimental groups scored higher than untrained controls, and higher than controls trained in categorizing by concepts. One of these experimental groups was also trained in representing sounds with plastic letters and only this group was actually statistically superior to controls. While we know that trained subjects' scores were higher on word lists and timed passages, we do not know what strategy was used by these remediated readers. The group trained in both sounds and letters was statistically higher in spelling than the three other groups. This advantage in spelling suggests the possibility of an alphabetic strategy, but data were not collected to provide insight into strategy use (e.g., nonsense word reading or error analysis).

Ehri and Wilce (1987) trained kindergarten children who were not at risk for dyslexia but were not yet readers. They taught these children to spell by teaching them to listen for sounds in words and then to represent these sounds with lettered tiles. After about a month of spelling instruction, they found trained subjects to be significantly better at learning to read words with these letters over several trials, compared to controls who were trained in letter sounds alone. They were also superior at segmenting and spelling. However, error analysis did not provide evidence of blending, and Ehri attributed successful reading to another kind of phonetic strategy, which she calls a "phonetic cue" strategy. This involves making associations between a few letters and their sounds in spoken words, such as the *j--l* in *jail*. In Ehri's view, spelling and reading share common skills in letter-sound associations and phoneme segmentation, but not in blending. Because training lasted only a month, it is not clear what the long term effects of spelling training might have been in regard to phonetic reading.

Hoping to clarify this point, Uhry and Shepherd (1990) worked for the better part of a school year with bright first graders who were heterogeneous in regard to reading skills. They were trained to segment short-vowel words using small blocks to represent sounds, and to spell on the computer in an analog of Ehri and Wilce's (1987) lettered tiles. Trained subjects were superior to controls after six and a half months of training in regard to several reading-related measures. In contrast with Ehri and Wilce's findings, training did give these first graders an advantage over controls in blending; they were superior in oral blending and in reading phonetically regular nonsense words (Uhry, 1991).

While training in our study was expected to facilitate the reading of nonsense words with short vowels (e.g., *eldop*), trained subjects also had the advantage in reading nonsense words in which clusters of letters functioned as units (e.g., *conration*). This implies some sort of analogy strategy, which traditionally has been considered as a stage beyond alphabetic decoding (Frith, 1985; Marsh, Desberg, & Cooper, 1977). Once the letter-by-letter strategy is in place, Frith believes that children are ready to recognize whole units of letters through analogies to familiar words. The view that this is too complex a strategy for beginners has been challenged by Goswami (1986) who found very young children able to read by analogy. Ehri and Robbins (1992) found that beginning readers with some ability in alphabetic decoding were better able to read by analogy than those without it. Griffith (1991) has used multiple regression to explore the relationship between phonemic awareness and word-specific information, and suggests that the former contributes to memory for units of letters. This supports Frith's notion that aspects of earlier strategies are incorporated into later ones. That is, processing each individual letter helps children recognize units of letters. Thus, the alphabetic strategy would be a necessary condition for sounding out individual letters and blending them, but also for recognizing letters in units and reading them through analogy to known words. If dyslexics struggle with alphabetic reading, then they must also struggle with analogy reading.

During our training study (Uhry & Shepherd, 1990), case histories were collected to see if children at-risk for dyslexia would be able to internalize either the alphabetic or analogy strategies. There were several children in each group who were at-risk for reading failure because of poor phonological and prereading skills. They were distributed evenly across the two treatment groups and observed carefully (Uhry, 1990). Observations focused on strategy acquisition. While the lowest experimental subject scored two standard deviations below the mean for her group in regard to nonsense word reading at posttest, she scored just above the mean for controls. That is, with training her score resembled normal readers' scores, even though she was eventually diagnosed as dyslexic. Despite average scores, error analysis suggested that she was struggling with the alphabetic strategy at posttest. While she decoded short nonsense words quite well, half of her errors in longer words involved using only some of the letters and guessing look-alike real words. This is a strategy considered characteristic of older dyslexic readers (Treiman & Hirsh-Pasek, 1985). The question raised here was whether this dyslexic subject was becoming qualitatively different from normal readers or simply developing along a normal route but more slowly. We wondered whether she would have mastered the alphabetic strategy eventually had training continued.

Several important questions remain unanswered by these studies in terms of the effects of spelling training on dyslexic children. The Bradley and Bryant (1983) study suggests an advantage for trained subjects who were at risk for reading problems, but the reading measures were not sensitive to posttest strategies. Ehri and Wilce (1987) did not follow their preschool children through beginning reading instruction and did not include children at risk for reading failure. The Uhry and Shepherd study (1990) indicated a dramatic advantage in nonsense word reading for trained subjects, but anecdotal notes on the dyslexic subject are merely speculative.

There is another point to consider in thinking about the use of spelling to teach dyslexics to read, and this is the kinesthetic experience of handwritten spellings. None of these three spelling-to-read studies explored the effects of handwritten spellings; all involved selecting rather than generating letters. The Bradley and Bryant (1983) study ignored a large body of literature, reviewed by Hulme (1981), suggesting that children with reading problems often respond well to multisensory techniques such as tracing letters while saying letter names. Bradley's (1981) earlier work had indicated that handwritten spellings were effective in teaching poor readers to spell. She used a technique called "Simultaneous Oral Spelling," or "SOS," an Orton-Gillingham multisensory technique designed to teach irregular spellings (Gillingham & Stillman, 1956). Hulme and Bradley (1984) used SOS to suggest that handwritten spellings provided an advantage over selecting letters for both young normal readers and older poor readers in regard to effects on spelling ability. Cunningham and Stanovich (1990) replicated this study with first graders, but added a computer condition.

Results indicate, again, that handwritten spellings were more effective than selecting letters on tiles or on a computer keyboard. This effect held for spelling, as in the prior studies, and for reading as well.

In general, however, the focus of the SOS studies was on spelling-to-spell, rather than on the effect of spelling training on reading. One important difference between these studies, and the spelling-to-read studies mentioned earlier, is that training included copying while naming letters, but did not include listening for the sounds in the words. This SOS technique used in the spelling-to-spell studies was developed to teach irregular words. It involves saying the letter name aloud, but does not include segmenting the spoken word into phonemes. In the three spelling-to-read studies (Bradley and Bryant, 1983; Ehri & Wilce, 1987; Uhry & Shepherd, 1990), subjects analyzed spoken words and then spelled sounds with letters. Thus, there is a substantial difference in treatment between the spelling-to-read and spelling-to-spell studies. Hulme's (1981) review of the literature concludes that tracing letters improves visual recognition, and possibly, naming visual stimuli. It may be that handwritten SOS spelling is an effective strategy for spelling irregular words, but not necessarily the best way to teach the alphabetic principle.

The version of SOS used in the spelling-to-spell studies by Bradley (1981) and by Cunningham and Stanovich (1990), which will be called "SOS-1" here, is not the only format for this technique. A second version for phonetically regular words is described in a teacher's guide for multisensory Orton-Gillingham training by Cox (1980). This second version, which will be called "SOS-2" here, involves listening for sounds in spoken words without written models. This is a more logical version to use in order to teach the mapping of spoken sounds onto printed letters, and it resembles the treatments in the spelling-to-read studies much more closely than does SOS-1, the version for irregular words. It seems to be the more sensible choice for teaching the alphabetic strategy to children with dyslexia, but comparison of the two SOS's has not been carried out.

The Present Study

Two questions are raised in the present study. First, can instruction in either copied spellings (SOS-1) or phonetic spellings (SOS-2) be used to facilitate nonsense word reading in children with dyslexia? And second, do these children need to spell by hand in order to facilitate reading phonetically regular words, or is computer spelling an effective technique? A single subject design was used with multiple baselines across three dyslexic fourth graders. This design works well in examining instructional methods (Guralnick, 1978), while allowing for a particularly high degree of control in regard to subject description (Edgar & Billingsley, 1974). It combines aspects of group studies and case histories, the two methods traditionally used with dyslexics according to Snowling (1987).

Baseline treatment (A) involved introduction of a weekly letter-sound pattern with new words practiced to mastery. This method was chosen for baseline treatment because it represented the phonics-based remedial reading treatment which had resulted in memorized word stores for the subjects. The three experimental treatments used various spelling instructional methods to encourage nonsense word reading as well. The first experimental spelling treatment (B) involved SOS-1 in which words were copied with each letter named as it was written. The second (C) involved SOS-2 with listening, segmenting, and typing words on a computer keyboard prior to unscrambling the words in computer spelling games. The third (D) was designed to tease apart components of (C) by asking subjects to listen and segment, but to spell by hand rather than on the computer.

Method

SUBJECTS

The three dyslexic subjects were upper middle class students in a regular school. Scores on the Wechsler Intelligence Scales for Children (WISC-R) ranged from the bright average to superior range. The girl and two boys had histories which included deficits in oral reading and phonological skills in the presence of above-average listening comprehension and mathematics skills. All were reading at least a standard deviation below their IQ-matched classmates on the Gates-MacGinitie Reading Tests; they read at approximately a mid-third grade level, close to two grade levels below the class mean which was at the late-fifth grade level early in the fall of their fourth grade school year.

The three dyslexics were able to sound out and blend phonetically regular short and long vowel words, but not words with vowel digraphs or *r*-controlled vowels. They could blend three sounds on the Roswell-Chall Auditory Blending Test, although Subject 1 had only learned to blend a few months before the study began. While subjects could blend, they did not tend to use this skill spontaneously, often guessing another word with letters in common. All were poor at nonsense word reading.

PROCEDURES

Training involved learning a new vowel digraph or *r*-controlled vowel (e.g., *au* or *ar*) pattern each week for the duration of the twenty week study. During the first (pretest) of four fifteen minute weekly sessions, a new sound was taught using a key word card (Cox, 1971) with picture and letters (e.g., a saucer and *au*). Next, target words were selected for each subject; words which they understood orally, but could not yet read were chosen from lists of words with the target pattern (Bowen, 1972). Treatment for the experiment's baseline condition (A) and three experimental conditions (B), (C), and (D) involved different methods of teaching these ten new words during the two 15 minute instructional sessions. During the fourth session, subjects were individually posttested on their words.

Experimental Treatments

During baseline treatment (A) the ten target words were read to mastery with the researcher modeling a sounding out and blending strategy for unknown words. During experimental treatment (B) the words were taught using the handwritten SOS-1 technique for irregular words which is described by Bradley (1981). The subject and the researcher read the word together, and then the subject copied the word three times, naming each letter as it was written. If a word was misspelled, the researcher said the letters with the subject until it was correctly written. Experimental treatment (C) involved SOS-2 and differed from (B) in several respects. Computer spelling games were substituted for handwritten spellings. First, subjects listened as the examiner said the word aloud, segmented the word into sounds, and then typed the word into the computer. If there were errors, the researcher modeled segmenting until the subject could write the word correctly. Next, games provided practice writing these words; *Magic Spells* (Learning Company, 1984) provided an unscrambling format, and *Spellicopter* (Designware, 1983), an unscrambling format with a timed video game chase format. Both games provided immediate feedback for misspellings with that portion of the game recycled until a word was correctly spelled. Unlike subjects in the Cunningham and Stanovich computer study (1990), these fourth graders had prior experience writing on the computer and were familiar with the keyboard. Experimental treatment (D) combined listening and segmenting with handwritten spellings in an attempt to separate out the elements of (B) and (C). The researcher said the word aloud, and the subject repeated it, segmented it, and then wrote it. Again, if there were errors, the researcher modeled segmenting until the subject wrote the word correctly.

Posttest Instruments

At the end of each week, subjects were tested on their own ten words using three different formats. The first, Words-In-Lists, involved reading the ten words mixed in a list of look-alike words. The second, Words-In-Text, consisted of short reading passages incorporating the words of all three subjects, but scored on each subject's own ten words. The third test, Nonsense Words, involved changing each subject's ten words into rhyming nonsense analogs. In all cases the score was an error count for the ten words.

Results

Means and standard deviations for each subject on each test during each treatment phase are provided in Table 1. Scores were graphed for weekly posttests. See Figure 1 for Words-In-Lists results, Figure 2 for Words-In-Text, and Figure 3 for Nonsense Words.

Graphed results indicate patterns which are consistent across subjects. The figures demonstrate a slightly fluctuating pattern of scores throughout baseline (A) for all three subjects with subject 1 somewhat steadier than the others. Note that subjects 2 and 3 had marked increases in errors during week 3 when they were tested on the day of a school party, a phenomenon which was controlled through scheduling later on in the study. Other than this one notable fluctuation, there was only mild variation from week to week during both phonetic reading instruction in baseline (A) and handwritten copied spellings in experimental treatment (B) without any marked change at the onset of treatment (B). Subjects 1 and 2 maintained error score levels without a marked slope throughout these first two phases, but the slightly downward slope for Subject 3 may indicate gradual, mild improvement.

In comparing the three tests during baseline (A) and treatment (B), the error rate appears to be higher for Nonsense Words than for the two tests using real words. That is, there were very few errors on measures of real word reading, but all three subjects misread roughly half the list of nonsense words each week during these two phases.

Subjects were not returned to baseline after treatment (B) because there seemed to be no appreciable difference between these first two treatments. However, with the advent of segmented computer spellings in treatment (C) there was a marked change in performance. The graph in Figure 3 indicates a sharp drop in the error rate for all three subjects on Nonsense Word reading. In other words, while subjects successfully memorized most real words in all three conditions, the reading of nonsense words improved dramatically with sounding out and playing games on the computer (C).

The strength of the computer spelling game treatment (C) was verified by returning subjects to baseline treatment (A). For all subjects there was an immediate increase in error level.

Table 1. Mean Scores and Standard Deviations (in Parentheses) for Errors on Weekly Reading Tests by Phase and Subtest for Each Subject

	(A) Read: Baseline	(B) Spell: Copy-Name by Hand (SOS-1)	(C) Spell: Segment on Computer (SOS-2)	(A) Read: Baseline	(D) Spell: Segment by Hand
Words-in-Lists					
Subject 1	1.4 (0.55)	1.7 (0.58)	0.3 (0.50)	2.0 (1.00)	1.4 (0.55)
Subject 2	2.3 (1.63)	1.0 (0.00)	0.3 (0.58)	1.3 (0.58)	1.3 (0.50)
Subject 3	2.4 (1.40)	1.8 (1.17)	0.3 (0.58)	2.0 (1.00)	1.0 (0.00)
Words-in-Text					
Subject 1	1.6 (0.55)	1.0 (0.00)	1.0 (0.82)	2.0 (1.00)	0.8 (0.84)
Subject 2	1.5 (1.38)	1.0 (0.82)	0.0 (0.00)	1.7 (1.15)	1.0 (0.82)
Subject 3	1.1 (1.46)	0.8 (0.75)	0.7 (0.58)	1.0 (1.00)	1.0 (0.00)
Nonsense Words					
Subject 1	5.8 (0.84)	5.0 (0.00)	1.0 (0.00)	4.3 (0.58)	2.2 (0.45)
Subject 2	6.0 (0.89)	5.8 (0.50)	0.7 (0.58)	3.3 (0.58)	2.3 (0.50)
Subject 3	6.0 (1.00)	4.7 (1.00)	0.7 (0.58)	2.7 (0.58)	1.0 (0.00)

Because there was a difference in both instructional method (copying and naming vs. segmenting) and kinesthetic experience (handwriting vs. computer), a third condition was introduced following this return to baseline. Experimental treatment (D) combined handwriting with sounding out and spelling. The graphs in Figures 1-2 suggest, as in other conditions, that most real words were mastered by posttest. The graph in Figure 3 suggests that nonsense word reading improved somewhat in this condition, but not so dramatically as in treatment (C). In fact, it is difficult to tell visually whether this improvement was part of an overall trend or is specifically associated with treatment (D). Gains here could be attributed either to overall treatment effects or to effects of sounding out, the element distinguishing (B) and (D).

Errors on nonsense word reading were analyzed in order to provide insight into the strategies these subjects were using to decode unknown words. There were so few errors during successful treatment (C) that it did not seem reasonable to attempt to compare error types across treatments. Classification of all nonsense word errors for the three subjects combined is presented in Table 2. There were three main categories, with letter-sound errors accounting for 49 percent, guesses from partial cues accounting for 28 percent, and lack of systematic left-to-right reading accounting for 23 percent. When these three categories were broken down into subcategories, real-word guesses of target and non-target words combined accounted for only 12 percent of the total errors.

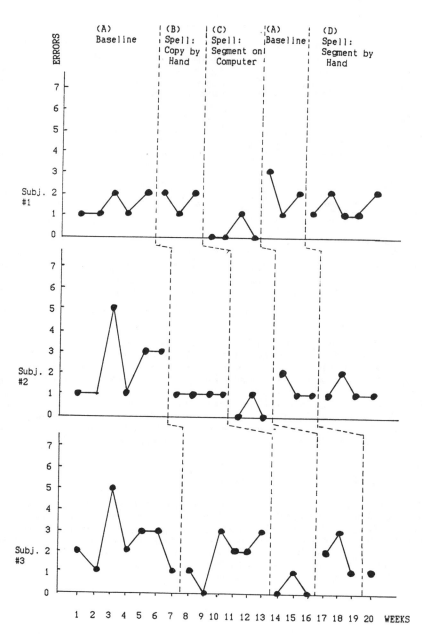

Figure 1. Errors on Words-in-Lists for each subject during each of the treatment phases with a possible range of 0-10.

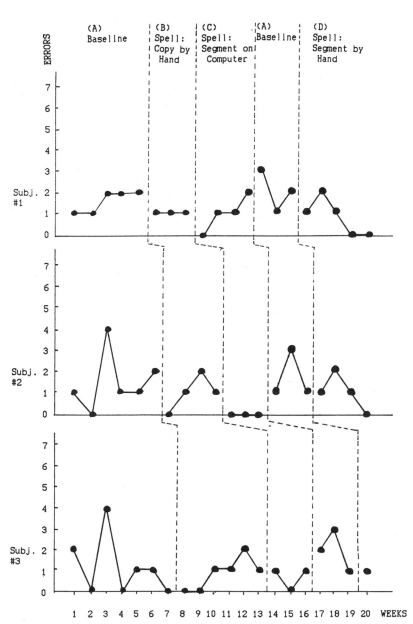

Figure 2. Errors on Words-in-Text for each subject during each of the treatment phases with a possible range of 0-10.

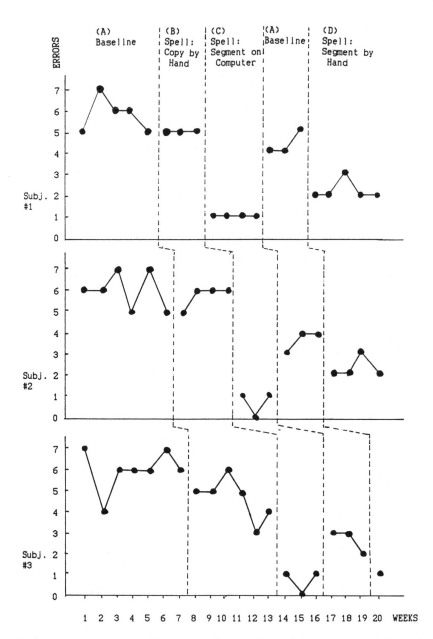

Figure 3. Errors on Nonsense Words for each subject during each of the treatment phases with a possible range of 0-10.

Table 2. Number of Errors and Percentage of Errors for 3 Categories and 12 Subcategories of Error Types on Nonsense Word Reading for the 3 Subjects Combined

	Number of Errors	Percentage of Errors
Letter-sound errors in systematic phonetic reading	104	49
Vowel errors on current target pattern	37	16
Short-short vowel substitutions	16	7
Short-long and long-short vowel substitutions	19	8
Other vowel errors	3	1
Consonant substitutions	18	8
Consonant vowel transpositions In consonant blends	21	9
Guesses from partial cues	65	28
Real word guesses - target words	11	5
Real word guesses - non target words	16	7
Partial analogies to target words	38	16
Lack of systematic phonetic reading	55	23
Omissions	8	3
Insertions	10	4
Accent or syllable break	9	4
Multiple errors combining any of above	28	12

Overall, experimental results suggest a clear and dramatic advantage for the computer condition with SOS-2 sound training (C). Results were less marked but positive, nevertheless, for the handwriting condition with sound training (D). Segmenting and phonetic spelling training appeared to facilitate the alphabetic reading strategy for these three dyslexic fourth graders, with a slight advantage for the computer over handwritten spellings.

Discussion

Results are generally consistent with prior studies (Bradley & Bryant, 1983; Ehri & Wilce, 1987; Uhry & Shepherd, 1990) in which phonetic spelling training had a positive effect on reading skills. There were no marked treatment differences here in real word learning, with subjects close to ceiling during all four treatment conditions. It is not surprising that these fourth graders were able to learn to read close to 10 new words a week when provided with a variety of phonetic instructional approaches. This is consistent with literature suggesting that dyslexic children can memorize specific words (Boder, 1973). The important issue here was the use of phonetic spelling to facilitate nonsense word reading. As in the Uhry and Shepherd study, the result which was most dramatic involved improvement in nonsense word reading associated with phonetic spelling on the computer.

Results here were not consistent with spelling-to-spell studies, which suggested the advantage of handwritten spellings (Bradley, 1981; Cunningham & Stanovich, 1990; Hulme & Bradley, 1984). Surprisingly, the most dramatic technique in the present study involved the computer. A number of factors may be involved here. First of all, keep in mind that Bradley (1981) and Cunningham and Stanovich (1990) taught children specific irregular words whereas the goal here was to teach transfer of complex but regular vowel patterns from multisyllable real words to nonsense words. As Hulme (1981) points out, combining tracing or copying letters with saying letter names strengthens visual recognition. This most likely explains why it helps children to learn specific irregular spellings. The task in the present study, however, was application of the alphabetic principle in decoding phonetically regular new words. Keep in mind that computer training here involved listening, segmenting, and then spelling. Segmenting and phonetic spelling appear to facilitate increased skill at manipulating the phonological properties of words here as well as in the earlier spelling-to-read studies. Of the two handwritten spelling treatments here, the second (D) was the more effective, and this also involved segmenting and phonetic spelling. The powerful effect here seems to be listening and segmenting, in combination with visual representations of sounds.

This does not resolve the computer vs. handwriting question because the computer typing phase still needs to be teased apart from the computer game phase. However, results do seem contradictory to Cunningham and Stanovich (1990) in that the effects of treatment in the present study were not tied primarily to kinesthetic elements. It may be that this is a more important point in regard to memorized spellings than to alphabetic reading strategies. In other words, alphabetic reading may share common elements with alphabetic spelling (Ehri & Wilce, 1987), but not with memory for specific irregular spellings.

An important underlying issue here is that of strategy use. We know that these dyslexic subjects struggled to read nonsense words prior to computer treatment and were successful afterwards, but what kind of errors did they make when they misread nonsense words? Based on Treiman and Hirsh-Pasek's (1985) finding that poor readers' nonsense word errors tended to involve real word guesses, one would expect to find a large percentage of real-word-guess errors. Surprisingly, this did not appear to be the case. There were a few (e.g., "video" for *vidow*, "tool" for *toal*), but even when two types (i.e., target and non-target words) of real-word-guesses were combined, they made up only 12 percent of the total errors (see Table 2). About half of all errors represented a fairly systematic attempt to work through new words, moving letter-by-letter and from left to right, with misreading of just one letter or unit of letters. Vowels were particularly troublesome, and about half of the vowel errors involved misreading the current week's vowel pattern (e.g., *foast* as "fost"). In other words, the new pattern had not been thoroughly learned, suggesting that automaticity was an issue. Letter-sound patterns represent one of Ehri and Wilce's (1987) common elements of reading and spelling, and phonetic spelling treatment (SOS-2) appears to have helped here through explicit instruction in these patterns.

Ehri and Wilce's (1987) other element common to reading and spelling is an understanding of the alphabetic system, or awareness that a sequence of sounds is mapped onto a sequence of printed letters. The other half of the nonsense word errors here can be attributed to two different types of failure in systematic, left-to-right reading. Twenty-eight percent involved some form of guessing from partial cues. An example of this is the reading of *founge* as "finger". Another type of real-word-guess constituted a subset of errors in which the real word was one of that week's target words (e.g., *scrooner* as "schooner"). Keep in mind that the Nonsense Word test was administered directly after the two real word tests.

We may have the "orthographic priming" effect that Treiman and Hirsh-Pasek (1985) achieved in dyslexic readers by presenting a real word just before a rhyming nonsense word. Another group of errors appeared to involve blending initial consonants or consonant clusters onto known endings, which was exactly the strategy it was hoped subjects would adopt. However, errors suggest incomplete processing of letter cues. The nonsense word seemed to be based on a target word by analogy, but matched with the wrong analogy word. For example, at one point subject 3 learned the words *brigadier* and *Algiers*. At the week's end he misread the nonsense word *pligadier* as "palgier."

The remaining 23 percent of errors involved failure to stick with a left-to-right, letter-by-letter strategy. There were omissions and insertions. Vowels were scrambled with consonants in consonant blends (e.g., *plinnow* as "pilnow"). There were also misreadings with multiple error patterns, where the subject simply appeared overwhelmed by the length and complexity of a word.

Keep in mind that the subjects made these error types throughout the study, and that all error types decreased markedly following phonetic spelling training on the computer. The errors seem to represent a jumble of stages with reversion to earlier strategies when dealing with particularly complex words. By contrast, we can assume that near mastery of nonsense word lists during successful treatment phases represented successful integration of alphabetic and analogy reading. A group comparison study with consistent training in one phonetic spelling method over a period of time would be the necessary next step in order to see how thoroughly these strategies could become incorporated into the repertoires of dyslexic readers.

The particular contribution of the present study is the finding that phonetic spelling training had a facilitative effect on the ability of dyslexic children to generalize knowledge of specific words and on their ability to use systematic alphabetic and analogy strategies in reading nonsense words. It is very encouraging to find that these fourth graders, who were quite deficient in reading nonsense words at pretest, and who struggled with nonsense words on weekly tests, made such dramatic gains in ability to process all available letter cues and to make analogies to target words.

REFERENCES

Bissex, G. L. (1980). *GNYS AT WRK: A child learns to write and read.* Cambridge, MA: Harvard University Press.
Boder, E. (1973). Developmental dyslexia: A diagnostic approach based on three atypical reading-spelling patterns. *Developmental Medicine and Child Neurology, 15,* 663-87.
Bowen, C. C. (1972). *Angling for words.* Novato, CA: Academic Therapy Press.
Bradley, L. (1981). The organization of motor patterns for spelling: An effective remedial strategy for backward readers. *Developmental Medicine and Child Neurology, 23,* 83-91.
Bradley, L., & Bryant, P. E. (1978). Difficulties in auditory organization as a possible cause of reading backwardness. *Nature, 271,* 746-7.
Bradley, L., & Bryant, P. E. (1979). Independence of reading and spelling in backward and normal readers. *Developmental Medicine and Child Neurology, 21,* 504-514.
Bradley, L. & Bryant, P. E. (1983). Categorizing sounds and learning to read - a causal connection. *Nature, 301,* 419-421.
Cox, A. (1971). *Initial reading deck.* Cambridge, MA: Educators Publishing Service.
Cox, A. (1980). *Structures and techniques: Multisensory teaching of basic language skills.* Cambridge, MA: Educators Publishing Service.
Cunningham, A., & Stanovich, K. (1990). Early spelling acquisition: Writing beats the computer. *Journal of Educational Psychology, 82,* 159-162.

Edgar, E., & Billingsley, F. (1974). Believability when N = 1. *Psychological Record, 24*, 147-160.

Ehri, L. C. (1987). Learning to read and spell words. *Journal of Reading Behavior, 19*, 5-31.

Ehri, L. C. (1989). Movement into word reading and spelling: How spelling contributes to reading. In J. M. Mason (Ed.), *Reading and writing connections* (pp. 65-81). Boston: Allyn and Bacon.

Ehri, L. C., & Robbins, C. (1992). Beginners need some decoding skill to read words by analogy. *Reading Research Quarterly, 27*, 12-26.

Ehri, L. C., & Wilce, L. S. (1987). Does learning to spell help beginners learn to read words? *Reading Research Quarterly, 20*, 163-179.

Frith, U. (1985). Beneath the surface of developmental dyslexia. In K. Patterson, J. Marshall, & M. Coltheart (Eds.), Surface dyslexia: Neuropsychological and cognitive studies of phonological reading. (pp. 301-330) London: Erlbaum.

Gillingham, A.M., & Stillman, B. U. (1956). *Remedial training for children with specific disability in reading, spelling, and penmanship*. New York: Sackett & Wilhelms.

Goswami, U. (1986). Children's use of analogy in learning to read: A developmental study. *Journal of Experimental Child Psychology, 42*, 73-83.

Graves, D., & Stuart, V. (1985). *Write from the start*. Portsmouth, NH: Heineman Educational Books.

Griffith, P. L. (1991). Phonemic awareness helps first graders invent spellings and third graders remember correct spellings. *Journal of Reading Behavior, 23*, 215-233.

Guralnick, M. J. (1978). The application of single-subject research designs to the field of learning disabilities. *Journal of Learning Disabilities, 11*, 415-421.

Hulme, C. (1981). *Reading retardation and multisensory teaching*. London: Routledge & Kegan Paul.

Hulme, C. & Bradley, L. (1984). An experimental study of multisensory teaching with normal and retarded readers. In R. Malatesha & H. Whitaker (Eds.), *Dyslexia: A global issue* (pp. 431-443). The Hague: Martinus Nijhoff.

Mann, V. A., Tobin, P., & Wilson, R. (1987). Measuring phonological awareness through the invented spellings of kindergarten children. *Merrill-Palmer Quarterly, 33*, 365-391.

Marsh, G., Desberg, P., & Cooper, J. (1977). Developmental changes in reading strategies. *Journal of Reading Behavior, 9*, 391-394.

Morris, D. & Perney, J. (1984). Developmental spelling as a predictor of first-grade reading achievement. *The Elementary School Journal, 84*, 441-457.

Snowling, M. J. (1980). The development of grapheme-phoneme correspondence in normal and dyslexic readers. *Journal of Experimental Child Psychology, 29*, 294-305.

Snowling, M. J. (1987). *Dyslexia*. Oxford: Basil Blackwell, Ltd.

Stanovich, K. E. (1982). Individual differences in the cognitive processes of reading: 1. Word decoding. *Journal of Learning Disabilities, 15*, 485-493.

Treiman, R. & Hirsh-Pasek, K. (1985). Are there qualitative differences between dyslexics and normal readers? *Memory and Cognition, 13*, 357-64.

Uhry, J. K. (1990). The effect of spelling instruction on the acquisition of beginning reading strategies. *Dissertation Abstracts International, 50*, (University Microfilms No. 9033917).

Uhry, J. K. (1991). *The effect of segmentation training on blending in beginning readers*. Paper presented at the annual meeting of the American Educational Research Association. (Eric Document Reproduction Service No. ED332 154).

Uhry, J. K. & Shepherd, M. J. (1990). *The effect of spelling instruction on beginning reading strategies*. Paper presented at the annual meeting of the American Educational Research Association. (Eric Document Reproduction Service No. ED331 020).

IMPACT OF INSTRUCTION ON WORD IDENTIFICATION SKILLS IN CHILDREN WITH PHONOLOGICAL PROCESSING PROBLEMS

REBECCA H. FELTON
Section of Neuropsychology
Bowman Gray School of Medicine
Winston-Salem, N. C. 27157-1043
U. S. A.

ABSTRACT: Children were identified in kindergarten as at risk for reading disability based on poor performance on measures of phonological processing (phonological analysis and phonological recoding). At-risk students were taught in grades one and two using either a Code approach (structured phonics) or a Context approach to reading instruction. A third group of at-risk students was designated as a passive control group. At the end of grades one and two, children in the Code group earned higher scores on word identification and significantly higher scores on nonword reading than children in either the Context or Control groups. Classification of children as having general phonological analysis or recoding problems indicated that problems in phonological analysis were the most common. A smaller group of subjects had problems only in phonological recoding. In addition, a small group of children had problems in both analysis and recoding. Although the majority of children in each of the treatment groups showed general deficits in phonological analysis, only phonological recoding measures were significantly correlated with reading outcome. It was concluded that direct instruction in the alphabetic code can have a positive impact on the development of nonword reading skills in children with differing types and degrees of phonological processing deficits.

Numerous investigations have established that there is a strong relationship between phonological processing abilities and skill in reading. In a recent review of these studies, Wagner and Torgesen (1987) conclude that there is strong support for a causal relationship between phonological awareness and reading and indication of a causal role for other types of phonological processes in learning to read. In their view, a major research question is the relationship between specific types of phonological processing and specific aspects of reading. Stanovich (1988) has proposed that phonological processing difficulties constitute the core set of cognitive deficits in individuals with dyslexia as well as in the majority of other poor readers. Although it is unclear whether phonological processes are prerequisites or facilitators of beginning reading skill (Williams 1986), it is clear that such processes play an important role particularly in the development of phonological coding (decoding) skills. There is also abundant evidence (see Rack, Snowling, & Olson 1992, for a review) that failure to appreciate fully the alphabetic code is a major and persisting deficit in the majority of poor readers.

Given the strength of the relationship between phonological processing skills and reading, it is encouraging that numerous investigations have demonstrated that the acquisition of beginning reading skills can be facilitated by training in phonological analysis (Ball & Blachman, 1991; Bradley & Bryant, 1983; Lie, 1991; Olofsson & Lundberg, 1985) as well as

R.M. Joshi and C.K. Leong (eds.), Reading Disabilities: Diagnosis and Component Processes, 267–278.
© 1993 Kluwer Academic Publishers. Printed in the Netherlands.

by direct code approaches to reading instruction (Brown & Felton, 1990; Enfield & Greene, 1981; Williams, 1980). Because the majority of these studies have involved heterogeneous groups in which most of the children possess intact phonological processing skills, questions remain concerning the impact of instruction on children with significant deficits in phonological processing. To address this issue, Brown and Felton (1990) identified a group of kindergarten children as at risk for reading disabilities and assigned them to one of two contrasting reading instructional programs for first and second grades. Initial results of this investigation indicated that the direct code (structured phonics) approach was most successful with the at-risk children.

Although these findings indicated that direct instruction in the alphabetic code resulted in better overall reading scores for at-risk children, the relationship between specific phonological processing problems and the degree to which children developed phonological coding skills in reading remained unresolved. Since the kindergarten battery used to select at-risk children in the Brown and Felton study (1990) contained many measures of phonological processing, we were able to select groups of children for study who demonstrated different types and degrees of problems in phonological processing. In addition, we were able to add a group of children who demonstrated similar levels of phonological processing problems in kindergarten but who were not placed in either of the research instructional groups.

In this paper, we present the results of the investigation of the impact of instruction on the development of word identification skills in children who entered first grade with a range of phonological processing deficits. Of particular interest is the relationship between the type and extent of phonological processing problems and the word identification skills attained by these students during first and second grades.

Method

SUBJECTS AND PROCEDURES

Subjects (n=81) were drawn from a large sample of public school children (N=991) who were screened for risk of reading disability in the spring of their kindergarten year, using teacher ratings and the Otis-Lennon Mental Abilities Test (Otis & Lennon, 1968). Children rated by teachers as being above average to superior in predicted potential for success in reading, or who had an IQ of below 80 on the Otis-Lennon were not studied further. The remaining children were tested individually with a battery of measures including, but not limited to, tests of phonological awareness and recoding (rapid naming). To be considered at risk, students had to score one or more standard deviations below the group mean or below the 17th percentile for the sample on at least three of the research measures.

These procedures (described more fully in Felton & Brown, 1990 and Brown & Felton, 1990) resulted in a final sample of 81 at-risk subjects. Forty-eight of these students (divided into six groups of eight children) were placed into regular first grade classrooms, and were randomly assigned to one of two treatment conditions (i.e., instructional methods). Twenty-four students were assigned to the Direct Code method and were taught with a code-emphasis approach to reading which stressed sound-symbol relationships as the primary tool for word identification. Another twenty-four students were assigned to the Context method and were taught with a meaning-emphasis approach to reading which stressed context and picture clues as major tools, for word identification. Each group of eight at-risk students in the treatment conditions was taught by a research teacher who provided all of their reading instruction (in the regular classroom) during first and second grade. The remaining 33 at-risk students were designated as passive controls and were assigned to regular first and second grade classes taught by school system personnel who also used the Context approach to reading instruction. Thus, the major difference between the Context and Control group was the extra amount of instructional time the research teachers were able to provide to their students.

At the end of the second grade, 19 students remained in the Direct Code treatment group, 23 students remained in the Context treatment group, and 29 students remained in the Passive Control group. Examination of scores on the kindergarten tests indicated that the passive control subjects were, as a group, impaired on fewer measures of phonological processing than the treatment groups. Therefore, children (N = 23) from the passive control conditions were matched to children in the Context and Code treatment conditions on a measure of extent of phonological processing problems. "Extent" was defined as the number of kindergarten tests of phonological processing on which the student met the study criteria for at risk. This procedure resulted in subjects (Direct Code = 19; Context = 23; Passive Control = 23) within each condition whose scores on this variable ranged from 2 to 12 (Mean = 5.6 for each group).

To evaluate the nature of the phonological processing problems of children within each treatment group, the research tests were divided into those measuring (1) phonological awareness and (2) phonological recoding. The tests used to measure these constructs are described below. Since our previous analyses (Felton & Brown, 1990) had shown that phonological analysis tests were uncorrelated with phonological recoding tests in this sample, we developed a set of criteria for classifying each subject as having deficits primarily in phonological analysis or in recoding skills. These criteria were, by necessity, arbitrary but represent what we consider to be a conservative approach to classification. To be classified as having a deficit in phonological analysis, the child had to fall below the 17th percentile for the total reference sample on at least three of the 5 measures of phonological analysis. Likewise, to be classified as having a recoding problem, the child had to score below the 17th percentile on at least 4 of the 6 phonological recoding measures. Children could, of course, qualify for both the phonological analysis and recoding classifications or for neither of these.
At the end of first and second grades, each child was administered tests (described below) designed to measure progress in word identification skills.

RESEARCH INSTRUMENTS

Kindergarten Screening Measures

1. *Otis-Lennon Mental Ability Test - Primary 1*, Level 2 (Otis & Lennon, 1968).
2. *Metropolitan Readiness Test* - Level *11, Form P* (Nurss & McGauvran, 1976). The following component scores comprising the Prereading Skills composite were used in this analysis: Auditory discrimination of initial sounds and sound-symbol associations; Visual discrimination of visual symbols and separation of visual patterns from context; and Language cognitive concepts, grammatical structures of standard English, and listening skills.

Kindergarten Measures of Phonological Processing

Phonological Awareness

1. *Initial Consonant Not Same* (Stanovich, Cunningham, & Cramer, 1984). The child listens to four words spoken by the examiner and chooses the word that does NOT begin with the same sound as the first word in the list (10 items).

2. *Final Consonant Different* (Stanovich et al., 1984). The child listens to four words spoken by the examiner and chooses the word that has a different ending sound from the others (10 items).

3. *Rhyme.* The child names as many words as she can that rhyme with the word spoken by the examiner (10 items).

4. *Lindamood Auditory Conceptualization Test* (Lindamood & Lindamood, 1979). The child manipulates different colored blocks to indicate conceptualization of the speech sound patterns presented by the examiner (28 items with possible converted scores ranging from 0-100).

5. *Syllable Counting Test* (Mann & Liberman, 1982). In our abbreviated version, the examiner pronounces 1, 2, or 3 syllable words and the child uses a wooden dowel to tap out the number of syllables heard (22 items; score is number of errors).

Phonological Recoding

1. *Rapid Automatized Naming Test* (Denckla & Rudel, 1976). The child is asked to name, as rapidly as possible, items (colors, numbers, objects, letters) presented visually on a chart (score is number of seconds required to name each set of stimuli).

2. *Rapid Alternating Stimuli Test* (Wolf, 1984). The child is asked to name, as rapidly as possible, items presented visually on a chart. The two sets (RAS-A) task consists of 5 letters and 5 numbers in a fixed A-B-A-B pattern. The three sets (RAS-B) task consists of 5 letter, 5 numbers, and 5 colors, repeated in a fixed A-B-C-A-B-C pattern.

Reading Outcome Measures

1. *Decoding Skills Test* (Richardson & DiBenedetto, 1985). The DST is a criterion referenced test developed as a research tool for use in studies of dyslexia. For this study, we report Subtest II (Phonic Patterns) which requires untimed reading of graded lists of phonetically regular real words and analogous nonsense words. Raw scores are generated for four types of words: monosyllabic real words, polysyllabic real words, monosyllabic nonsense words, and polysyllabic nonsense words. The DST was given at the end of second grade only.

2. *Woodcock Reading Mastery Test - Form* A (Woodcock, 1973). The Word Identification and Word Attack subtests of the WRM, a norm referenced test, were administered. Word Identification requires reading a list of sight words graded in difficulty and Word Attack requires reading a list of nonsense words. The WRM test was given at the end of first and second grades.

Results

Subject Characteristics

A general linear model procedure comparing means for the three treatment groups (Code, Context, and Control) showed no significant differences between groups in age, Otis-Lennon IQ, race, sex or prereading skills composite score on the Metropolitan Readiness Test (see Table 1). Males outnumbered females 16 to 7 in the Context group, 11 to 8 in the Code group, and 15 to 8 in the Control group. The ratio of white to non-white students was 13 to 10, 11 to 8, and 15 to 8 for the Context, Code, and Control groups, respectively.

Performance on Phonological Processing Measures at Kindergarten

Descriptive statistics for the kindergarten phonological processing variables are shown in Table 2. Although the groups did not differ on most variables, there were significant differences between groups on the Lindamood, Rhyme, and RAN-number tasks. The Code and Control groups scored significantly higher than the Context group on the Lindamood. Children in the Context group scored significantly higher than the Code group on the Rhyming task. Scores of children in the Control group were significantly higher (i.e., slower naming) than those in the Context group on rapid automatized naming of numbers. Thus, while the three groups varied somewhat in their performance on individual tests, there is no evidence of an overall advantage of any group on phonological analysis or phonological recoding measures. This outcome is not surprising since the groups were matched on severity level (i.e., number of phonological processing variables that subjects were impaired on).

Table 1. Subject characteristics by treatment group.

	Context	Code	Control
	M (SD) range	M (SD) range	M (SD) range
Age at initial screening	6.2 (.50) 5.6 - 7.3	6.0 (.35) 5.6 - 6.8	6.3 (.43) 5.6 - 7.4
Otis-Lennon IQ	96.7 (7.8) 86 - 110	99.0 (8.7) 86 - 117	97.1 (12.3) 82 - 123
MRT-Prereading[a] skills composite	46.2 (10.3) 22 - 61	47.2 (9.6) 29 - 61	47.9 (9.4) 32 - 62

[a] MRT = Metropolitan Readiness Test

Table 2. Phonological processing scores by treatment group.

	Context	Code	Control
	M (SD) range	M (SD) range	M (SD) range
Phonological Analysis			
Rhyming	6.3 (6.6) 0 - 20	3.0 (3.4) 0 - 9	4.3 (5.1) 0 - 20
Syllable Counting[a]	6.8 (2.7) 2 - 11	6.9 (2.9) 1 - 11	6.3 (3.9) 0 - 18
Initial Consonant Not Same	5.1 (2.2) 1 - 10	5.3 (2.6) 0 - 9	5.3 (2.8) 0 - 9
Final Consonant Different	3.7 (2.2) 0 - 8	3.4 (2.2) 0 - 9	3.5 (2.2) 0 - 9
Lindamood	20.7 (11.8)* 0 - 37	30.3 (15.0)* 3 - 63	31.7 (17.6)* 0 - 58
Phonological Recoding			
RAN - colors[b]	71.5 (16.9) 42 - 100	71.8 (12.5) 45 - 99	77.4 (22.2) 51 - 160
RAN - Objects[b]	103.1 (27.9) 74 - 196	97.8 (29.7) 56 - 163	106.3 (27.5) 61 - 181
RAN - numbers[b]	70.3 (22.3)* 36 - 121	75.6 (19.9) 44 - 113	85.0 (25.6)* 41 - 122
RAN - letters[b]	86.3 (40.2) 42 - 241	89.7 (32.4) 44 - 160	84.0 (26.0) 54 - 160

* p < 0.05

[a] Error scores

[b] Scores represent time in seconds. Thus, higher scores indicate slower naming.

An examination of the data in Table 2 indicates that, within each group, there is a wide range of scores on each of the phonological processing variables. Even though all of the subjects were originally classified at risk based on the criteria described in the methodssection, there are clearly children in each treatment group whose performance was well within normal limits on some of the measures. In order to examine the nature of the subject's phonological processing problems, children were classified as having general deficits in phonological analysis, phonological recoding, or both. The results of this classification are presented in Table 3.

As these data indicate, more than half of the children within each treatment group met the criteria for deficits in phonological analysis or recoding. Of the children with deficits, the majority had problems with phonological analysis. Of the three treatment groups, the Code group had the largest number of children with some type of phonological processing problems. A minority of children in each treatment group had deficits in both analysis and recoding. Interestingly, a number of children in each group did not meet the criteria for deficits of either type. The percentage of children in this category was the highest for the Control group. It is important to note that failure to meet the criteria for a general deficit in a category does not mean that the subjects did not have deficits. They simply did not have enough deficits in either the analysis or the recoding domain to meet our arbitrary criteria.

Performance on Reading Outcome Measures

Using a general linear models procedure, we evaluated whether or not there were significant differences between group means on several measures of reading ability at the end of first and second grades. To account for the multiple group comparisons, the significance level was set at $p<.02$.

Table 3. Types of phonological processing deficits by treatment groups

	Context		Code		Control	
	N	(%)	N	(%)	N	(%)
Phonological Analysis Deficits	9	(39)	8	(42)	5	(22)
Phonological Recoding Deficits	1	(4)	5	(26)	5	(22)
Analysis and Recoding Deficits	4	(18)	1	(6)	3	(13)
	14	(61)	14	(74)	13	(57)
Criteria for Deficits Not Met	9	(39)	5	(26)	10	(43)

End of First Grade

At the end of first grade, there were significant group differences between groups on the word attack subtest of the Woodcock Reading Mastery Test (WRM) with the Code groups earning higher scores than either the Context or the Control groups. There were no significant differences between groups on the word identification subtest. These scores are summarized in Table 4.

Since the WRM is a norm referenced test, one method of analysis is to compare individual subject's scores to test norms. While we recognize that the grade equivalents on nationally normed tests may be somewhat inflated, they do offer one means of comparison. On the WRM, students are considered to be reading words (word identification) at an end of first grade level (G.E. 1.8-1.9) if they earn raw scores ≥ 33. Using this criterion, 11 (48%) of the Context, 7 (37%) of the Code, and 12 (52%) of the Control subjects could be considered to be on grade level in their ability to read sight words. In view of these percentages, it is interesting to note that, although the overall means were not different for the groups, subjects in the Context and Control groups had a more restricted range of scores than in the Code group. This is accounted for by the fact that one child in the Code group earned a very high score on word identification and the fact that no child in the Code group earned a score below 11. In contrast, there was one child in each of the Context and Control groups whose word identification scores were extremely low and there were no children whose scores were above 66.

Of major interest for this study is the distribution of scores on the word attack subtest. On the WRM, students are considered to be at an end of first grade level on word attack skills if they earn a raw score between 11 to 15 (out of a possible 50 items). Using this criterion, 3 (13%) of the Context, 11 (58 %) of the Code, and only 1 (4%) of the Control subjects could be considered to be on grade level in reading nonwords. While the majority of Code group children had developed nonword reading skills, most of the Control and Context group children had not.

End of Second Grade

Although, there were no statistically significant group differences on WRM word identification scores at the end of the second grade, the Code group earned the highest scores and both treatment groups scored higher than the Control group. Using the criterion of end of second grade level performance on the WRM norms (scores >75), 10 (43%) of the Context, 8 (42%) of the Code, and 6 (26 %) of the Control group were reading words on grade level.

On the WRM word attack subtest, the pattern was similar to that for the first graders, with the Code group scoring higher that both the Context and Control groups. However, only the difference between the Code and Control group scores reached statistical significance. Based on WRM norms, 8 (35 %) of the Context, 9 (47%) of the code, and 4 (17%) of the Control group subjects were reading nonwords at a level commensurate with their peers.

To further evaluate nonword reading skills, the Decoding Skills Test (DST) was given to the second graders. On this test, the real words are phonetically regular and the nonwords are analogous to the real words. On all of the DST subtests, the Code group earned higher scores than the Context or the Control groups. These differences were statistically significant for all of the comparisons between the Code and Control groups. The differences between Code and Context groups approached statistical significance for the monosyllabic nonwords and the polysyllabic real words (p<.05 and .03 respectively) and reached significance on the polysyllabic nonwords (p<.01).

Table 4. First and second grade reading scores by treatment group.

	Context	Code	Control
	M (SD) range	M (SD) range	M (SD) range
First grade			
WRM/word identification	32.9 (15.8) 4 - 66	36.4 (26.6) 11 - 94	34.0 (16.9) 1 - 65
WRM/word attack[*]	5.3 (5.1) 0 - 16	14.6 (12.1) 1 - 42	3.0 (4.0) 0 - 12
Second grade			
WRM/word identification	64.6 (23.3) 28 - 100	76.6 (22.6) 32 - 116	60.8 (23.0) 6 - 95
WRM/word attack[*]	16.9 (11.4) 0 - 43	22.1 (15.4) 2 - 47	9.5 (9.8) 0 - 36
DST-monosyllabic real words[*]	15.9 (8.3) 2 - 29	20.6 (7.2) 6 - 30	12.7 (8.6) 0 - 28
DST-monosyllabic nonwords[*]	11.8 (8.3) 0 - 27	16.8 (8.6) 0 - 29	7.9 (7.3) 0 - 20
DST-polysyllabic real words[*]	11.6 (9.9) 0 - 29	17.7 (9.2) 2 - 30	9.6 (7.3) 0 - 22
DST-polysyllabic nonwords[*]	6.5 (8.4) 0 - 26	12.6 (9.5) 0 - 28	3.1 (5.2) 0 - 17

Note: All scores are raw scores.   [*]p < .02 for one or more group comparisons.

RELATIONSHIPS BETWEEN PHONOLOGICAL PROCESSING SKILLS AND READING

An earlier analysis (Felton & Brown, 1990) of the relationship between phonological processing in kindergarten and reading at the end of first grade for the entire (n=81) group of children identified as at risk indicated that, with IQ controlled for, there were no significant correlations between measures of phonological awareness and reading (either word identification or word attack). There were significant, although moderate, correlations between phonological recoding measures and word identification but not word attack skills. In this study, we have analyzed the relationships between phonological processing and reading *within* treatment groups which were matched on a number of variables (including IQ and number of at risk indicators).

For each group of subjects, correlation coefficients were calculated between all of the kindergarten measures of phonological analysis and recoding and the end of second grade word identification and word attack scores. In two major respects, the results are quite similar to those obtained in our earlier analysis of the entire group. Using the p<.02 significance level, none of the phonological measures were correlated with word attack scores. In addition, within each group, only phonological recoding measures were significantly correlated with word identification scores. Even though the groups were matched on the number of risk indicators, we also calculated the correlation between this variable and reading. This variable, which may be considered a measure of the severity of the phonological processing deficits, was not correlated with reading outcome in either the Context or the Control groups. However, severity level was positively correlated with both word identification (p<.0008) and with word attack (p<.001) in the Code group.

Discussion

The purpose of the study was to investigate the impact of instruction on the development of word identification skills in children with varying types and degrees of phonological processing problems. Analysis of the nature and extent of phonological processing problems in these at-risk children indicates that the majority have problems primarily in the phonological analysis domain. However, a group of students has problems primarily in the area of phonological recoding with relatively intact analysis skills. In addition, a smaller group of students has deficits in both the phonological analysis and recoding domains.

Regardless of the nature or extent of the phonological processing problems, the direct code method of instruction resulted in significantly better nonword reading scores. In addition, children taught with a direct code approach were also superior to children in the other conditions on measures of word identification. Although the group differences on word identification did not reach statistical significance, they indicate that the Code group subjects were developing sight word skills as well as decoding skills. This finding is particularly interesting given that the direct code instruction placed very little emphasis on sight word vocabulary during the first and second grades. In contrast, the context instruction placed a great deal of emphasis on the development of sight word vocabulary and relatively less on decoding skills. It must be noted, however, that the context curriculum contained all of the same decoding skills as the code approach so children in this condition were directly taught decoding skills. The difference was in the emphasis placed upon decoding, the method in which these skills were taught, and the type of reading materials used (controlled versus noncontrolled vocabularies).

In addition to the superiority of the code approach, it is also clear that the children in the Context groups benefited from the additional instructional time they received. Children in the Control groups, who were taught with the same materials as the Context treatment group, made much less progress in word identification and word attack skills. The contrast between the treatment groups and the Control group in nonword reading skills is particularly interesting given the fact that a higher percentage of children in the Code and Context groups had general phonological processing problems than in the Control group.

Investigation of the relationship (within groups) between kindergarten phonological processing variables and reading at the end of second grade indicated that only phonological recoding variables were significantly correlated with reading and only with word identification scores. This finding is consistent with the results of our earlier analysis of the at-risk sample as an entire group and supports our contention (Felton & Wood, 1989) that difficulties in phonological recoding may significantly impair the development of fluent word recognition skills. Because of our interest in the impact of the *extent* of phonological processing problems on reading, we also evaluated the relationship between the number of phonological measures on which a child did poorly in kindergarten and reading outcome. By definition, the children with the highest scores on the "extent" variable were children who had problems in both phonological analysis and recoding. Interestingly, this variable was correlated with reading (word identification and word attack) only in the Code group. One interpretation of this finding is that direct code instruction effectively taught most of the children so that only the most severe and pervasive impairments impacted the reading development of children in this group. In this context, it should be noted that the child with the lowest scores on word attack in the Code group was also the child with the most severe and pervasive phonological deficits.

In conclusion, these results support the finding of great variability in the phonological processing deficits of phonological dyslexics reported by Snowling, Stackhouse, and Rack (1986). Snowling and her colleagues proposed that the extent and severity of phonological processing deficits will "partly dictate the course of literacy development" (p. 333) but suggested that the possible impact of remedial intervention not be discounted. This study provides evidence that early intervention with direct code instruction can have a significant impact on the development of reading skills in children with clear phonological analysis and recoding deficits. These results also indicate that children with particularly severe and pervasive deficits may require more intensive or longer periods of instruction in order to fully acquire fluent word identification skills.

NOTE: This research was supported by PHS Grant HD21887 to Bowman Gray School of Medicine and by PHS Grant NSI9413 to UNC-Greensboro, Subcontract to Bowman Gray School of Medicine.

REFERENCES

Ball, E.W., & Blachman, B.A. (1991). Does phoneme awareness training in kindergarten make a difference in early word recognition and developmental spelling? *Reading Research Quarterly, 26*, 49-66.
Bradley, L., & Bryant, P.E. (1983). Categorizing sounds and learning to read -- A causal connection. *Nature, 301*, 419-421.
Brown, I.S., & Felton, R.H. (1990). Effects of instruction on beginning reading skills in children at risk for reading disability. *Reading and Writing: An Interdisciplinary Journal, 2*, 223-241.
Denckla, M.B., & Rudel, R.G. (1976). Naming of object drawings by dyslexic and other learning disabled children. *Brain and Language, 3*, 1-16.

Enfield, M.L., & Greene, V.E. (1981). There is a skeleton in every closet. *Bulletin of the Orton Society,* *31,* 189-198.

Felton, R.H., & Brown, I.S. (1990). Phonological processes as predictors of specific reading skills in children at-risk for reading failure. *Reading and Writing: An Interdisciplinary Journal, 2,* 39-59.

Felton, R.H., & Wood, F.B. (1989). Cognitive deficits in reading disability and attention deficit disorder. *Journal of Learning Disabilities, 22,* 3-13.

Lie, A. (1991). Effects of a training program for stimulating skills in word analysis in first-grade children. *Reading Research Quarterly, 26,* 234-250.

Lindamood, C.H., & Lindamood, P.C. (1979). *Lindamood Auditory Conceptualization Test.* Allen, TX.: DLM.

Mann, V.A., & Liberman, I.Y. (1982). Phonological awareness and verbal short-term memory: Can they presage early reading problems? *Haskins Laboratories Status Report on Speech Research, SR-70,* 221-237.

Nurss, J.R., & McGauvran, M.E. (1976). *Metropolitan Readiness Test.* New York: Harcourt Brace Jovanovich.

Olofsson, A., & Lundberg, I. (1985). Evaluation of long-term effects of phonemic awareness training in kindergarten: Illustrations of some methodological problems in evaluation research. *Scandinavian Journal of Psychology, 26,.*21-34.

Otis, A.S., & Lennon, R.T. (1968). *Otis-Lennon Mental Ability Test.* New York: Harcourt Brace Jovanovich.

Rack, J.P., Snowling, M.J., & Olson, R.K. (1992). The nonword reading deficit in developmental dyslexia: A review. *Reading Research Quarterly. 27,* 29-53.

Richardson, E., & DiBenedetto, B., (1985). *Decoding Skills Test.* Parkton, MD: York Press, Inc.

Snowling, M., Stackhouse, J., & Rack, J. (1986). Phonological dyslexia and dysgraphia - a developmental analysis. *Cognitive Neuropsychology, 3,* 309-339.

Stanovich, K.E. (1988). The right and wrong places to look for the cognitive locus of reading disability. *Annals of Dyslexia, 38,* 154-177.

Stanovich, K.E., Cunningham, A.E., & Cramer, B.B. (1984). Assessing phonological awareness in kindergarten children: Issues of task comparability. *Journal of Experimental Child Psychology, 38,* 175-190.

Wagner, R.K., & Torgesen, J.K. (1987). The nature of phonological processing and its causal role in the acquisition of reading skills. *Psychological Bulletin, 101,* 192-212.

Williams, J.P. (1980). Teaching decoding with an emphasis on phoneme analysis and phoneme blending. *Journal of Educational Psychology, 72,* 1-15.

Williams, J.P. (1986). The role of phonemic analysis in reading. In J.K. Torgesen & B.Y. L. Wong (eds.), *Psychological and educational perspectives on learning disabilities.* (pp. 399-416) New York: Academic Press, Inc.,

Wolf, M. (1984). Naming, reading, and the dyslexias: A longitudinal overview. *Annals of Dyslexia, 34,* 34-115.

Woodcock, R.W. (1973). *Woodcock Reading Mastery Tests.* Circle Pines, MN. :.American Guidance Service, Inc.

PREDICTING READING ACQUISITION IN HIGH AND LOW IQ GROUPS

JAN CAROL NÄSLUND
The University of New Mexico
College of Education
Albuquerque, New Mexico 87131
U.S.A.

ABSTRACT: A developmental study completed in Germany provided the data to compare groups of children varying in second grade reading performance and IQ on language related skills in kindergarten and in second grade. This population is suited for such a developmental study, given the lack of preschool literacy knowledge in comparison to other populations. Children were first tested in phonological awareness, verbal memory, and verbal ability at age 6, before formal literacy training, and once again in second grade, when reading performance and IQ were tested. Multivariate analyses indicated interaction effects for reading performance and IQ for the memory span tests (two time points) and for the verbal ability tests (at both time points). Reading performance for children in the lower IQ range varied with verbal ability and verbal memory. Children in the higher IQ range did not differ in these two measures in relation to reading performance. The phonological awareness measures (at both time points) indicated a main effect for reading performance, but not for IQ, and no significant interaction. Phonological awareness varied with reading performance in both IQ groups. This study suggests the robustness of phonological awareness in its long term and concurrent relationship to reading performance over a wider range of general IQ levels, in comparison to other variables believed to significantly influence reading. It also suggests that there may be divergence in the importance of certain predictor and covariate factors in emergent reading among different populations of children.

Traditionally, specific reading deficits are identified by lower than expected reading ability in comparison with performance or verbal IQ. When individuals demonstrate poor reading comprehension despite average to above average IQ or verbal comprehension, this usually signals some specific linguistic deficit. If reading performance is not "up to par" with other cognitive skills, it is likely that some particular processing problems are present which affect reading skills to the exclusion of other academic skills (such as arithmetic) (see Siegel and Linder, 1984). One obvious problem with defining specific reading deficits in this way is that for those with lower performance or verbal IQ, specific causes of reading problems may or may not be due to the same factors as those with a high-IQ/Reading discrepancy. This particular bias in defining specific reading disabilities precludes consideration of an alternate hypothesis: that reading difficulties in individuals of both low and high general ability (as measured by verbal or performance IQ) may stem from some of the same sources of cognitive processing.

Hoover and Gough (1990) propose that poor reading comprehension performance of individuals who otherwise have adequate verbal comprehension stems from specific problems in decoding text. These decoding specific problems are believed to arise from a deficit in

R.M. Joshi and C.K. Leong (eds.), Reading Disabilities: Diagnosis and Component Processes, 279–293.
© 1993 *Kluwer Academic Publishers. Printed in the Netherlands.*

phonological awareness, and the inability to phonologically recode text in order to efficiently hold the information in working memory. If individual words are not decoded properly, this obviously limits comprehension of text. Overwhelming evidence exists in the literature supporting metalinguistic awareness as a pivotal factor in acquiring decoding skill. This evidence has led to the assumption that metalinguistic awareness deficits are directly linked to reading specific problems.

Perception and phonological recoding of units of speech are believed to influence the accuracy of storing and processing information drawn from spoken and written communication, and are also believed to be pivotal in beginning reading acquisition. Good readers apparently use phonological recoding spontaneously to decode words and store information in working memory during reading. Poorer readers apparently make less use of this process than better readers (Brady, Mann, & Schmidt, 1987: Brady, Shankweiler, & Mann, 1983; Mann, Liberman, & Shankweiler, 1980).

Phonological awareness has been shown to be a strong predictor of reading performance in children in comparison to verbal and performance IQ (Bryant, Bradley, MacLean, & Crossland, 1989; Stanovich, Cunningham, and Feeman, 1984). Analyses in these studies pertained to younger children in general, not accounting for possible differences among children with varying performance IQ levels. In order to test whether IQ/Reading discrepancies are valid indicators of specific reading problems, it should be determined if factors which have been shown to correlate and affect reading performance in general differentially relate to reading performance of individuals with lower and higher performance IQ. Previous research has pointed to a variety of linguistic factors interacting with and influencing reading acquisition, such as verbal memory span, verbal comprehension and grammatical sensitivity, vocabulary, and phonological processing abilities (Näslund & Schneider, 1991; Schneider & Näslund, 1992; Siegel & Ryan, 1988). In this study, the extent of influence of verbal ability, verbal memory, and phonological awareness on second grade reading performance in various populations of readers is compared in order to determine which of these are a pivotal factors in predicting reading performance for both lower and high IQ groups.

A Developmental Study

Children in Bavaria, Germany rarely learn to read or write before entering first grade, although being read to is an important part of preschool Kindergarten programs, which children attend from about the age of three or four until about the age of six (given the availability of much sought after Kindergarten spots). Most children are first faced with the task of synthesizing and analyzing speech--two necessary skills for "breaking the code" in learning to read--some time after they enter first grade, after much of their linguistic development is in place.

This situation in the Bavarian Kindergartens provided the opportunity to measure preliterate Verbal Ability, Verbal Memory, and Phonological Awareness without the confound of wide variation in reading ability. The children in this study were first tested in these three skills and letter knowledge in the third year of Kindergarten (average age 6.1 years). Letter knowledge was very low at this Kindergarten testing time (mean, 5.8 letters; median, three letters; and mode, one letter), a right-tailed distribution which is representative of typical Bavarian populations. At the beginning of second grade the same children were assessed in word decoding and reading comprehension, and as well retested in Verbal Ability,

Verbal Memory, and Phonological Awareness. These linguistic skills were compared among groups of children differing in second grade IQ and reading performance.

The comparisons made among these measures are intended to demonstrate whether patterns of relationships among these variables (as measured in Kindergarten and second grade) in relation to reading performance differ among children who vary in performance IQ. These variables may be more or less proximally (or distally) related to reading performance among children if IQ/Reading discrepancies indicated real differences in cognitive processing directly associated with reading. For example, assuming that phonological awareness is developmentally associated with reading specific problems, one would expect this factor measured in Kindergarten and second grade to differentiate reading performance among children with higher and lower performance IQ equivalently. On the other hand, if verbal ability is a more distal factor, associated with a wider variety of academic abilities in addition to reading (i.e., problem solving in general), one might expect the influence of this factor at both testing times to be stronger for lower IQ levels and less influential among higher IQ populations, reflecting a correlation between verbal and performance IQ. Verbal ability might not be expected to differentiate better and poorer readers among higher IQ children, but might be expected to correlate with reading performance among lower IQ children.

The pattern of results for memory span are more difficult to predict. On the one hand, given an expected influence of phonological recoding in working memory during reading, verbal memory span may be expected to differentiate reading performance among higher (and lower) IQ children. On the other hand, higher IQ children may use a variety of heuristics for performance of memory tasks (i.e. rehearsal) that might compensate for lower phonological recoding in working memory, and therefore a direct relationship of verbal memory span and phonological recoding in reading processes may not be as strong among higher IQ children in comparison to lower IQ children.

Methods

A group of 87 children participating in the Munich Study of Longitudinal Genesis of Individual Competencies (LOGIC, see Weinert & Schneider, 1989, 1992) was divided into comparison groups according to performance on the Columbia Mental Maturity Scale (CMMS, Burgemeister, Blum, & Lorge, 1972), a Reading Comprehension Test developed by the author for this and a larger scale study in the Bavarian region, and a Word Decoding task. There was a total of 170 in the original sample, however a significant proportion of these children were either not promoted to Kindergarten, discontinued participation, or missed sessions at one of the measurement times used in this study. Stanovich (1989) has indicated that many studies addressing specific reading problems, as opposed to poor reading due to lower general cognitive aptitude do not provide equivalent comparison groups. In this study, therefore, we define our group with specific reading problems as those children who are above average on the CMMS (an IQ equivalent score of 110 and above, which for this particular sample was the mean and median), and perform in the lower 50th percentile in both Reading Comprehension and Word Decoding (L-READ). The performance of this group is compared with children who have CMMS scores above 110 (H-CMMS) and performance in Reading Comprehension and Word Decoding above the 50th percentile (H-READ), children CMMS scores below 110 (L-CMMS) and both Reading Comprehension and Word Decoding performance in the lower 50th percentile (L-READ), and finally, children with CMMS scores below 110 (L-CMMS) and reading skill performance above the 50th percentile (H-READ).

Measures administered in kindergarten (average age, 6 years 1 month) were: 1) Verbal Ability: the Verbal Section of the German form of the WISC (Hannover-WISC; Eggert, 1978); 2) Verbal Memory: a German version of Daneman and Blennerhassett's (1984) Sentence Memory Test, which differed from the original study in that children were asked to repeat in entirety increasingly larger sets of syntactically and semantically correct, but unrelated sentences (total sentences correctly recalled are reported); and 3) Phonological Awareness: a German version of Bradley and Bryant's (1985) Phonological Oddity Task, where children choose from sets of four words each which word does not share a first or end sound from sets of four words. Ceiling effects in the middle-sound oddity task, in comparison to well-distributed scores in the first and end-sound tasks prompted the decision not to include the middle-sound task in the composite score. In second grade, children were administered: 1) Verbal Ability: The Verbal Comprehension, Vocabulary, and General Knowledge inventories from the Verbal Section of the German form of the WISC for early grade school (Tewes, 1985), 2) Verbal Memory: repeat of the Sentence Memory Test, and 3) Phonological Awareness: a test of Recognition and Manipulation of Phonological Change, where children indicate which sounds differed between similar pseudowords, and themselves alter the pronunciation of pseudowords according to directions to replace sounds, or to switch two sounds within a pseudoword. Phonological Awareness tasks administered at both times include some amount of phonological recoding in working memory. This component is present in many tasks used to measure Phonological Awareness.

The Reading Comprehension test consisted of two parts. The first part consisted of cloze-format items testing word usage within the context of individual sentences. The second part of the test consisted of reading five short stories and two or three cloze-format comprehension questions following each story. These items required deducing answers from the text.

A word decoding speed task was derived, in part, from Rott and Zielinski's (1986) test of word decoding speed. All thirty words were one-syllable. Words from Rott and Zielinski's (1986) list that were not found in lists provided by the official Bavarian Education Commission for use in reading instruction were not used in our study. These were presented in a fixed-random order on a black computer screen. Letters were white and about four inches high. The words were in upper and lower case, as found in normal German text. Children were given practice reading words aloud as quickly as possible before timed measurements were taken. Reading time was measured from the time the word appeared on the screen until the experimenter pressed a designated computer key just after the child finished pronouncing each word. Pilot testing indicated that children often extended the sound of the first phonemes while decoding the rest of the word (for example, "brrrrr...aun"). Therefore, word decoding could not be accurately detected by taking measurements at the beginning of children's utterances. Given that interest was in word decoding speed, actual pronunciation time was measured. One may be able to infer that very fast word decoding speed indicates fast word recognition, and slower speeds indicate that children are taking longer to recognize words.

As indicated in this and other studies of German children (Wimmer, Hartl, & Moser, 1990) German second graders make very few errors in decoding words in comparison to English and American children. German orthography is transparent in comparison to English, and this may account for the low error rate. In a current study, Näslund, Schneider, Lenz, Doll, and Trolldenier have collected data from first and second graders in the region of Northern Bavaria on decoding words and non-words presented as lists. First graders make a large percentage of errors, but second graders' error rates are very low on word reading, and the correlation of errors in decoding word strings with reading comprehension is not significant. The study reported in this chapter made use of reading four-letter words presented singly. Given that speed was the major concern, conditions were designed to minimize errors. More errors may have been made if words were longer, and in addition, if lists of words were to be read as quickly as possible. Therefore, error rate was excluded in the analyses, as it was not a significant factor among these German second graders on this particular task.

Means and standard deviations for all measures and numbers of subjects for each comparison group are shown in Table 1. It should be noted, that raw scores are reported for each of the Verbal Ability tests. Scores vary given that only the three age-corrected parallel sections (verbal comprehension, general knowledge and vocabulary) used in both Kindergarten and in the second grade were included in the analyses, and scoring for these sections differ in the two tests. These scores cannot be used to indicate improvement over the two year period, but are used to assess relative influence at both time points.

Newman-Keuls tests were conducted for the CMMS/READ comparison groups in order to determine equivalency of the two CMMS groups and the two READ groups with respect to the criterion measures used to define those groups. Results indicate that the two L-CMMS did not significantly differ in performance on the CMMS (p>0.05), as was also true for the H-CMMS groups, regardless of READ performance. The two L-READ groups did not significantly differ in Reading Comprehension or Word Decoding, as was also true for the H-READ groups, regardless of CMMS performance. All other comparisons demonstrated significant differences (at the p<0.05 alpha level). Both H-CMMS groups differed significantly in CMMS compared to L-CMMS groups regardless of Reading Comprehension and Word Decoding scores, and both H-READ groups differed significantly from L-READ groups in READ measures regardless of CMMS scores. After determining this group equivalence, Verbal Ability, Phonological Awareness, and Verbal Memory in Kindergarten and second grade were assessed in relation to CMMS and READ via MANOVA. The variances for all measures were equivalent across CMMS comparison groups, as determined by F-tests for homogeneity of variance. Therefore, results are not likely to reflect ceiling or floor effects across comparison groups.

Results and Discussion

A MANOVA was performed with all variables (from Kindergarten and Second Grade) in order to determine the main effects and interactions of CMMS and READ for the IQ/READ comparison groups. Results showed a main effect for CMMS ($F_{6,50}$=4.55, p<0.001), a main effect for READ ($F_{6,50}$=4.73, p<0.001), and an interaction of CMMS and READ ($F_{6,50}$=3.90, p=0.003). In order to determine if the same interaction effect is found at each of the time periods, separate MANOVAs were performed for the Kindergarten and second grade measures. For the model including Kindergarten Verbal Memory, Verbal Ability, and Phonological Awareness, there was a significant main effect for CMMS ($F_{3,56}$=4.11, p<0.01), a main effect for READ ($F_{3,56}$=4.28, p=0.009), and an interaction for CMMS and READ ($F_{3,56}$=3.21, p=0.03). For the model with the second grade measures, there was a significant main effect for CMMS ($F_{3,55}$=7.58, p=0.0002), a main effect for READ ($F_{3,55}$=9.76, p<0.0001), and a significant interaction between CMMS and READ ($F_{3,55}$=6.83, p=0.0005).

Table 1. Means and standard deviations (in parentheses) for CMMS/READ groups.

READ GROUPS	L-READ		H-READ	
CMMS GROUPS	L-CMMS	H-CMMS	L-CMMS	H-CMMS
Cases	N=20	N=11	N=12	N=19
CMMS	98.35 (8.83)	116.55 (5.50)	104.46 (3.53)	122.20 (10.76)
Reading Comprehension	15.30 (5.29)	13.45 (5.37)	27.23 (1.79)	26.70 (2.00)
Decoding Speed (in seconds)	2.27 (0.47)	2.60 (0.57)	1.42 (0.20)	1.39 (0.23)
Kindergarten Measures				
Phon. Awareness	8.60 (3.08)	8.64 (3.26)	13.33 (2.27)	13.25 (3.54)
Verbal Ability (total sentences)	44.70 (9.18)	50.36 (5.80)	52.54 (5.52)	53.55 (6.32)
Memory Span	11.00 (4.91)	16.18 (4.31)	20.00 (5.85)	16.60 (7.83)
Second Grade Measures				
Phon. Awareness	16.40 (3.53)	15.10 (4.46)	18.62 (3.55)	20.00 (2.75)
Verbal Ability	15.55 (6.64)	21.45 (7.50)	25.42 (4.96)	22.58 (7.32)
Memory Span (total sentences)	15.75 (4.04)	24.73 (6.13)	28.54 (5.62)	25.25 (8.83)

A MANOVA was performed for a model testing the main effects and possible interaction of CMMS and READ for the Phonological Awareness measured at both testing times. Figures 1 & 2 show the separate results for Phonological Awareness measures in Kindergarten and in second grade. (In these, and all subsequent Figures, values are plotted in converted z-scores for comparison purposes.) However, the MANOVA model includes measures from both testing times. No main effect was found for CMMS ($F_{2,54}=0.05$, p=0.95), a main effect was found for READ ($F_{2,54}=20.08$, p<0.0001) and no significant interaction was found ($F_{2,54}=0.81$, p=0.45). A Repeated Measures analysis was also performed with the same pattern of between-subject results as the MANOVA (F-test at p<0.0001 level for READ, p=0.97 for CMMS, and p=0.36 for the interaction). This analysis was performed to test the possible effect of non-independence, given the expected covariance of phonological processing measures at both testing times, even though the inventories were not the same. None of the within-subject interactions in the Repeated Measures analysis were significant. These results suggest that Phonological Awareness as measured in kindergarten, before most children learn about letters and their sounds, and phonological recoding in working memory, as measured in second grade after reading acquisition is underway, vary at a significant level with reading performance for children with a broad range of performance IQ.

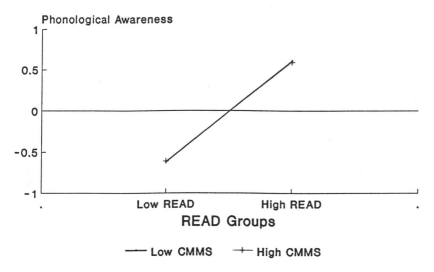

Figure 1. Kindergarten phonological awareness in CMMS/READ groups.

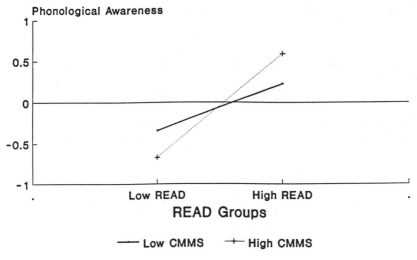

Figure 2. Second-grade phonological awareness in CMMS/READ groups.

Figures 3 and 4 present the performance of CMMS/READ groups on the Verbal Ability measures for each testing time. A repeated measures test was performed in order to test the main and interaction effects of CMMS and READ for Verbal Ability over both testing times. Although the two Verbal Ability measures used different scaling, the repeated measures analysis was used given that the tests were representing the same latent variable, and are considered age-corrected parallel version of the same subscales. The within subject test of the main effect of Verbal Ability was significant ($F_{1,58}=18.99$, $p<0.0001$). This result likely reflects differences in scaling used at the two testing times rather than within subject differences in Verbal Ability test performance. There were no significant interaction effects for Verbal Ability and CMMS, Verbal Ability and READ, or Verbal Ability, Read, and CMMS. This indicates that relationships among CMMS, READ and the Verbal Ability Tests are similar across testing times. The between subjects effects analysis indicated a significant main effect for CMMS ($F_{1,58}=6.06$, $p=0.017$), a main effect for READ ($F_{1,58}=9.72$, $p=0.003$) and a significant interaction effect for CMMS and READ ($F_{1,58}=4.56$, $p=0.037$). This interaction suggests that Verbal Ability covaries with reading performance among those with performance IQ scores in the medium to low range. However, among higher performance IQ children, higher Verbal Ability appeared to have little significance in predicting reading performance of children with poor phonological awareness skills.

Verbal Ability
Kindergarten

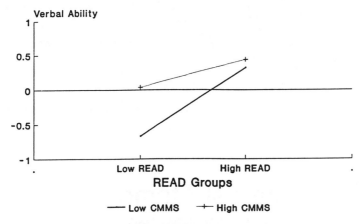

Figure 3. Kindergarten verbal ability in CMMS/READ groups.

Verbal Ability
Second Grade

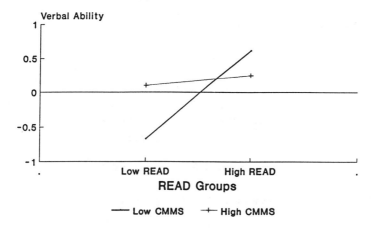

Figure 4. Second grade verbal ability in CMMS/READ groups.

Given the evidence for phonological recoding processes in verbal working memory during reading in previous research, the results of Repeated Measures for Verbal Memory in this study would be expected to replicate the results found for Phonological Awareness. Figures 5 and 6 indicate that this is not the case. The Repeated Measures results instead reflect the same interaction pattern as found in Verbal Ability. Between-subject results showed a main effect for CMMS ($F_{1,59}$=15.14, p=0.0003), main effect for READ ($F_{1,59}$=23.88, p<0.0001), and a significant interaction of CMMS and READ ($F_{1,59}$=14.06, p=0.0004). The within-subject results did not indicate a significant effect of testing time on Verbal Memory ($F_{1,59}$=1.19, p=0.28). None of the within-subject interactions reached significance. This suggests that the relationship of Verbal Memory to other variables was likely stable across testing times. Verbal memory span covaried with READ in the lower performance IQ range, but did not significantly vary among higher performance IQ children who varied in READ.

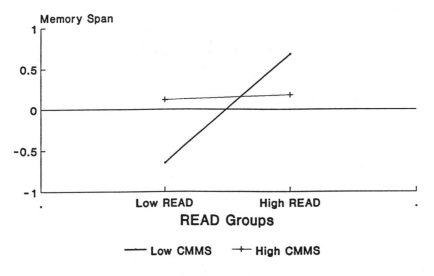

Figure 5. Kindergarten verbal memory in CMMS/READ groups.

Verbal Memory
Second Grade

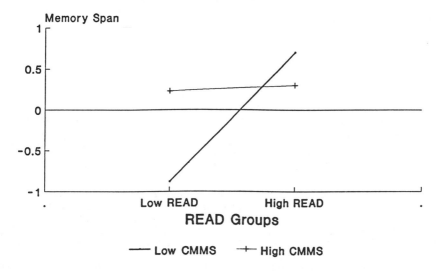

Figure 6. Second grade verbal memory in CMMS/READ groups.

For the second Verbal Ability and Memory Span tasks in both Kindergarten and second grade, the better readers among the L-CMMS group performed somewhat better than the H-CMMS children as a group. Perhaps not too much should be made of these tendencies, given that differences did not reach statistical significance (using Newman-Keuls contrasts among all CMMS/READ groups). The probability that this tendency reflects testing error is low considering the consistency of pattern of results for two testing times, two years apart for the same children. One possible explanation for part of these results is that perhaps Verbal Ability and Verbal Memory are not robust in predicting reading behavior among children with a High-IQ/Reading performance discrepancy. These two measures do vary with reading performance of children in the lower to average IQ ranges. The interaction effects, and tendency for higher Verbal Ability and Memory Span for lower/average IQ children who are also good readers may suggest some compensatory behavior regarding reading tasks. In the case of Memory Span interactions, some high IQ children may actually attend to exact wording in sentences less than children with average to below average IQ. This possibility needs to be investigated.

There may be some precedence for such findings in German samples. For example, memory for definitions, events, names, or tasks to be performed are strong priorities in German schools, and this may be reflected in educational practices. Some research has shown that German children are more strategic in their metacognition skills than American children (Schneider, Borkowski, Kurtz, & Kerwin, 1986), and this also may factor in their performance on Verbal Memory tasks, and possibly in their Verbal Ability performance. Attributions of academic performance are also different among German children than (for example) American children. German children tend to attribute good performance less to effort (which is the American tendency) and more to ability. Further investigation of this topic might reveal less effort and more reliance on ability in some experimental tasks among higher IQ children, and more reliance on effort among lower/average IQ children.

General Discussion

Using a strict criterion for defining an IQ/Reading Performance discrepancy, differences for our predictor measures were found among children defined by low and high achievement in reading comprehension. Results in preschool as well as second grade revealed that our H-CMMS poor readers, when judged on Phonological Awareness, performed similarly to the L-CMMS poor readers. It was also found that Verbal Memory and Verbal Ability in Kindergarten and second grade did not differ among H-CMMS poorer and better readers. However, these measures did differ among L-CMMS poorer and better readers.

It was surprising that Verbal Memory and Phonological Awareness did not covary in these analyses for the H-CMMS groups, given that one might predict performance on verbal memory measures by phonological processing ability (see Brady, Mann, & Schmidt, 1987; Brady, Shankweiler, & Mann, 1983; Mann, Liberman, & Shankweiler, 1980). It would seem that interactions among multiple linguistic skills in predicting reading performance (Näslund, 1990) may be evident in children with average and below average general cognitive ability, given that performance in some linguistic skills may reflect performance in cognitive skills in general. In contrast, children demonstrating a High-IQ/Reading discrepancy appear deficient in specific skills pertaining to phonological processing.

Previous research has demonstrated mixed results when employing relatively low criterion to define IQ-reading performance discrepancies (85 and higher on tests of nonverbal and verbal IQ; see Stanovich, 1989, 1991). These low criteria may not allow assessment of reading specific problems, given that scores on psycholinguistic predictive measures may still reflect general ability (as indicated by IQ). Stanovich's (1991) definition of reading disability separates it from other types of general learning disabilities. It is represented by a continuous distribution of performances with an arbitrary criterion of IQ/Reading discrepancy for what we have come to know as "dyslexia". This study has provided some evidence for this definition by revealing differences among groups of high and low performance IQ readers.

Bowers, Steffy, and Tate (1988) and Stanovich (1991) have suggested using verbal comprehension measures instead of performance IQ scores in developing criteria for deciding specific reading disability. After controlling for nonverbal IQ, Bowers et al. (1988) found that verbal memory span was still a significant predictor of decoding performance. However, memory span was no longer a significant predictor when they further controlled for verbal IQ. In addition, rapid naming of digits, a measure of phonological processing in lexical access, significantly predicted decoding skill after controlling for both nonverbal and verbal IQ. They refer to these results in defending the use of verbal IQ rather than performance IQ in determining aptitude/reading discrepancies. Stanovich (1991) has supported this as well, suggesting that the discrepancy of concern is not with general ability and reading, but with verbal comprehension and decoding. This argument follows the suggestion by Gough and Tunmer (1986), that if an individual is capable of comprehending verbally transmitted text, then decoding abilities alone should account for a significant proportion of observed reading problems.

These results led Bowers et al. (1988) to be concerned that in using performance IQ/reading discrepancies, there may be an over-representation of children with lower verbal IQ in the High-IQ/poor reader groups. However, this was not the case in the sample described here. The concern expressed by Bowers et al. (1988) may pertain more to setting a low IQ criterion for defining IQ/Reading discrepancy, and therefore increasing the probability that children with lower Verbal IQ would be included in IQ/Reading discrepancy groups. With regard to our kindergarten predictors and second grade measures, the H-CMMS/poorer-READ group did not tend to score significantly lower on the Verbal Ability measure than the H-CMMS/high-READ group. The H-CMMS groups performed similarly on both Verbal Ability measures, regardless of reading performance.

There is much criticism concerning the use of IQ criterions for judging the degree of an individual's specific reading disability (Bowers et al., 1988; Christensen, 1992; Siegel, 1989; Stanovich, 1991, 1992). Without developing this argument fully, and therefore not drawing the reader through the full circularity of such argumentation, attention to such discrepancies does aid to understanding specific deficits within experimental settings, so long as experimenters carefully consider what skills their performance IQ measures are tapping. Performance on the CMMS requires a child to make judgments about relationships among sets of objects, and use strategies to decide which object does not correspond to the rules governing the relationships among these. These tasks likely reflect the type of thinking required in making inferences in comprehension of speech or text, without the specific influence of vocabulary or other learned language skills. In addition, the reciprocal influence between psycholinguistic competencies and performance on verbal comprehension tests is still an open research question. Stanovich (1992) cautions us in assuming causal relations among psycholinguistic and other cognitive processes, given our lack of certainty of how phonological processing differences arise. (To be more specific, those not explained by abnormalities of development or injury to the brain.) This caution should also extend to assuming independence in development of verbal ability and speech perception and production.

The CMMS was not considered in this study as a definitive measure of nonverbal IQ, but instead a performance measure reflecting the analytical and discrimination skills which normally correspond to school performance. A score of over 110 on the CMMS was used to denote a high degree of performance in discrimination, analytical thinking, and understanding about relationships among entities. When above average performance of these skills does not correspond to word decoding and reading comprehension, one might be justified in suspecting that reading specific factors are involved. Adopting a high criterion for performance IQ in our discrepancy classifications revealed much the same results as found by Bowers et al. (1988) regarding the failure of sentence memory span to significantly predict performance for children with specific reading problems, and the robustness of phonological processing in reading in comparison to verbal ability and memory.

NOTE

This work was carried out while the author was at the Max-Planck-Institute for Psychological Research in Munich, Germany with the support of the Alexander von Humboldt Foundation.

REFERENCES

Bowers, P.; Steffy, R., & Tate, E. (1988). Comparison of the effects of IQ control methods on memory and naming speed predictors of reading disability. *Reading Research Quarterly, 23,* 304-319.
Bradley, L. & Bryant, P. (1985). *Rhyme and reason in reading and spelling.* Ann Arbor, MI; University of Michigan Press.
Brady, S., Mann, V., & Schmidt, R. (1987). Errors in short-term memory for good and poor readers. *Memory and Cognition, 15,* 444-453.
Brady, S., Shankweiler, D., & Mann, V. (1983). Speech perception and memory coding in relation to reading ability. *Journal of Experimental Psychology, 35,* 345-367.
Bryant, P., Bradley, L., MacLean, M., & Crossland, J. (1989). Nursery rhymes, phonological skills, and reading. *Journal of Experimental Child Psychology, 33,* 386-404.
Burgemeister, B., Blum, L., & Lorge, J. (1972). *Columbia Mental Maturity Scale.* New York: Harcourt Brace Jovanovich.
Christensen, C. A. (1992). Discrepancy definitions of reading disability: Has the quest led us astray? A response to Stanovich. Commentary: *Reading Research Quarter;y, 27,* 276-278.
Eggert, D. (1978). *Hannover Wechsler Intelligenztest für das Vorschulalter (HAWIVA).* Berlin; Huber.
Daneman, M., & Blennerhassett, A. (1984). How to assess the listening comprehension skills of prereaders. *Journal of Educational Psychology, 76,* 1372-1381.
Gough, P. B., & and Tunmer, W. E. (1986). Decoding, reading, and reading disability. *Remedial and Special Education, 7,* 6-10.
Hoover, W., & Gough, P. B. (1990). The simple view of reading. *Reading and Writing: An Interdisciplinary Journal, 2,* 127-160.
Mann, V., Liberman, I. Y., & Shankweiler, D. (1980). Children's memory for sentences and word strings in relation to reading ability. *Memory and Cognition, 8,* 329-335.
Näslund, J.C. (1990). The interrelationships among preschool predictors of reading acquisition for german children. *Reading and Writing: An Interdisciplinary Journal, 2,* 327-360.
Näslund, J.C., & Schneider, W. (1991). Longitudinal effects of verbal ability, memory capacity, and phonological awareness on reading performance. *The European Journal of Psychology of Education, 6,* 375-392.
Rott, C., & Zielinski, W. (1986). Entwicklung der lesefertigkeit in der grundschule. *Zeitschrift für Entwicklungspsycholoie und Pädagogische Psychologie, 18,* 165-175.
Schneider, W., Borkowski, J.G., Kurtz B. E., & Kerwin, K. (1986). Metamemory and motivation: A comparison of strategy use and performance in German and American children. *Journal of Cross-Cultural Psychology, 17,* 315-336.
Schneider, W., & Näslund, J. C. (1992). Cognitive prerequisites of reading and spelling: A longitudinal approach. In A. Demetriou, M. Shayer, and A. Efklides (Eds.), *Neo-Piagetian theories of cognitive development: Implications and applications for education* (pp.256-274). London: Routledge.
Siegel, L. S. (1989). IQ is irrelevant to the definition of learning disabilities. *Journal of Learning Disabilities, 22,* 469-478.

Siegel, L. S., & Linder, B. A. (1984). Short-term Memory processes in children with reading and arithmetic learning disabilities. *Developmental Psychology, 20*, 200-207.

Siegel, L. S. & Ryan, E. B. (1988). Development of grammatical-sensitivity, phonological awareness, and short-term memory skills in normally achieving and learning disabled children. *Developmental Psychology, 24*, 28-37.

Stanovich, K. E. (1989). Various varying views on variation. *Journal of Learning Disabilities, 22*, 366-369.

Stanovich, K. E. (1991). Discrepancy definitions of reading disability: Has intelligence led us astray? *Reading Research Quarterly, 26*, 7-29.

Stanovich, K. E. (1992). Response to Christensen. Commentary: *Reading Research Quarterly, 27*, 279-280.

Stanovich, K. E., Cunningham, A. E., & Feeman, D. J. (1984). Intelligence, cognitive skills, and early reading progress. *Reading Research Quarterly, 19*, 278-303.

Tewes, U. (1985). *Hamburg Wechsler Intelligenztest für Kinder (HAWIK-R)*. Berne, Switzerland; Huber.

Weinert, F. E. & Schneider, W. (1989). *The Munich longitudinal study on the genesis of individual competencies (LOGIC). Report No. 5: Results of wave three*. Munich, Fed. Rep of Germany: Max-Planck-Institute for Psychological Research.

Weinert, F. E., & Schneider, W. (1992). *The Munich longitudinal study on the genesis of individual competencies (LOGIC). Report No. 7: Results of wave five*. Munich, Fed. Rep of Germany: Max-Planck-Institute for Psychological Research.

Wimmer, H., Hartl, M., & Moser, E. (1990). Passen "englische" Modelle des Schriftspracherwerbs auf "deutsche" Kinder? Zweifel an der Bedeutsamkeit der logographische Stufe. (Do "English" models of reading acquisition apply to German children? Doubts concerning the significance of the logographic stage.) *Zeitschrift für Entwicklungspsychologie und pädagogische Psychologie, 22*, 136-154.

PHONETIC SHORT-TERM MEMORY REPRESENTATION IN CHILDREN'S READING OF GREEK

COSTAS D. PORPODAS
Section of Psychology, Department of Education
University of Patras,
261 10 Patras,
GREECE.

ABSTRACT: The objective of this study was to test the role of phonetic STM representation in reading, in a replication study where young Greek children, who were either good or poor readers, were involved. Given that STM is one of the cognitive prerequisites of reading and that phonetic coding is well involved in STM storage during reading, the aim of the present investigation was to see whether the good readers could be distinguished from the poor readers on the basis of their reliance on phonetic coding when the Greek spelling system was employed. Three experiments were conducted involving the STM storage and recall of rhyming and nonrhyming letter and word strings, presented orally and/or visually to good and poor young readers of Greek. The results showed that, overall and irrespective of the way of stimuli presentation, the good readers were more affected by the phonetic confusability factor than the poor readers. Those results were interpreted on the basis of the inefficient phonetic representation hypothesis which implicates the way in which letter-sound correspondence rules are established.

Introduction

The objective of this paper was to present some empirical data on the role of phonetic short-term memory representation in reading of Greek by Greek school children who were either good or poor readers. Since the relationship between phonetic representation in short-term memory and reading ability has been extensively investigated in other languages (and mainly in English), the contribution of this study is limited to the testing of those issues on the Greek language.

There were two main reasons of undertaking the research reported in this paper. The first reason was to replicate some of the relevant studies, reported in the literature, in order to see the degree of applicability of the existing theories on this issue when the Greek spelling system is employed. The second reason was to acquire some evidence on the issue in question from the Greek language. The findings could enable us to draw some inferences on the problem of predicting reading achievement on the basis of phonological memory deficits as well as on the question of implications for reading acquisition.

Since this study involved the use of the Greek language by native readers, it is thought to be necessary, prior to the presentation of the theoretical framework of the issue under investigation, to present some basic information on the nature of the Greek spelling system.

R.M. Joshi and C.K. Leong (eds.), Reading Disabilities: Diagnosis and Component Processes, 295–306.
© 1993 *Kluwer Academic Publishers. Printed in the Netherlands.*

The Greek Spelling System

The Greek writing system was the first system to which the alphabetic principle was applied when it was discovered around the 10th century B.C. According to that principle, different written characters represented different consonant and vowel sounds of the spoken language (Gelb, 1963). Since that time, the spoken form of the Greek language (as it is the case in many other languages) has undergone various evolutionary and developmental changes while the written form has remained essentially unchanged. As a result, Greek is written now not in the way it is pronounced, but as it was pronounced almost twenty-five centuries ago (Triantaphyllidis, 1913).

A closer examination of the Greek language over its long history of almost 3000 years, shows that in comparison to some other Indo-European languages (e.g., the Germanic and Romancic languages), the Greek language has undergone, on the whole, only moderate changes. In the spoken form, despite the changes that have occurred through the centuries, there are some aspects that have remained almost unchanged. Among those aspects that have remained constant are the pronunciation of many words, many grammatical forms, various elements used in the construction of new words, and a great number of morphemes and elements of syntax (Tombaidis, 1987). In its written form the Greek language has remained virtually unchanged through the centuries. The changes that have occurred through its history were minor and without any significance to its spelling nature. More specifically, among the changes worth mentioning are the introduction of the left to right direction of writing (since in antiquity the written Greek language was first written from right to left and then in a ploughlike direction) and the use of lower case letters.

As a result of the difference in the developmental changes between the spoken and the written forms of the Greek language through the centuries, modern Greek spelling is not entirely phonetic, and a number of inconsistencies could be observed. Some of those inconsistencies are (cf. Triantaphyllidis, 1913; Tombaidis, 1987; Zakestidou & Maniou Vakali, 1987):

(a). Different letters or letter combinations are used for the same phoneme. For example:

* The phoneme [i] is written with the letters: η, ι, υ, ει, οι, υι.
  (e.g. : συνειρμικός, οικιστής, υιικός)
* The phoneme [o] is written with the letters: o, ω.
  (e.g.: όμως, ώμος)
* The phoneme [e] is written with the letter - ε - and the letter combination - αι -
  (e.g.: φαίνεται).
* The phoneme [u] is written with the letter combination- ου –.
  (e.g.: ουρανού).
* The phoneme [s] is written with the letters : σ, ς, σσ.
  (e.g.: σύσσωμος).

(b) Some letters in different contexts represent different phonemes. For example:

* The letter υ is pronounced as:

                    -ι- (e.g.,: κύβος),
                    -φ- (e.g.,: ευχαριστώ),
                    -β- (e.g.,: αύριο),
                    or it is silent (e.g.: εύφορος).

* The letter -τ- is pronounced as:

t - (e.g.: κάτω),
or as - d -   (e.g.: πέντε).

(c). In some cases, some letters are not pronounced and they are almost voiceless. For example:

* The letter -υ- (e.g.: Εὔβοια).
* The double consonants : λλ, κκ, ββ, etc.
  (e.g.: κάλλος, λάχχος, Σάββατο).
* The letter -π- in the consonant cluster -μπτ– (e.g.: πέμπτη, etc.).

All those inconsistencies that are encountered in modern Greek occur because through that long period from antiquity up to the present day, the pronunciation of some phonemes has changed while the letters which represent them remained the same. Thus, modern Greek spelling has lost some of its phonetic characteristics and it could be regarded as a system of "historic orthography" that normally reflects the etymology of words rather than their phonetic condition.

Phonological Representation in Reading

The involvement of short-term memory (STM) in language processing has been an interesting issue in current psychological theory and research. More specifically, the involvement of STM is regarded as essential to spoken language perception and comprehension since it is thought that the language perceiver needs to hold information about shorter segments (e.g., words) of longer segments (e.g., sentences). However, it is well documented that the language perceiver does not remember the speaker's utterance word-by-word but recalls it in the form of a paraphrase (Liberman, A., Mattingly, & Turvey, 1972). That paraphrase is based on a temporary storage system in a form of a phonetic representation, or in a form of an abstract representation of the articulatory gestures which constitute the utterance. This view is supported by the work on the working memory framework (cf. Baddeley & Hitch, 1974), according to which one component of the working memory, that is the articulatory loop, comprises a phonological store and an articulatory rehearsal process, where phonological representations are registered and held by a rehearsal process. Further support for the concept of phonological representation has been given by experimental findings, according to which phonological representation mediated not only comprehension of language but also recall of strings of letters or words (Baddeley, 1978; Conrad, 1964; Levy, 1977; Liberman I., Shankweiler, Liberman, A., Fowler, & Fischer, 1977).

Although it is well supported that phonological representation is decisively involved in all normal language processing (Mann, 1984), the involvement of phonological representation in the reading process has been an issue with great theoretical interest for the researcher and practical implications for the classroom teacher. The idea for the involvement of phonological representation in reading has its origin in the nature of the reading process. "If reading is rightly conceived of as an alternative means of perception of language, then we may expect it to share many processes in common with the perception of speech. Reading involves interpretation of symbols that stand as surrogates for speech segments. Thus the reader's task is literally to convert print to speech, whether overtly or (more usually in the case of the experienced reader) into some covert form. Although we do not rule out the possibility that read words can be held temporarily in some visual form, it seems reasonable to suppose that in reading, no less than in perception of speech by ear, the perceiver makes use of a phonetic representation in order to comprehend the message" (Liberman & Shankweiler, 1979, pp. 114-115). In addition, as Mann (1984, p. 2) points out "...even readers of Chinese logography, an orthography in which access to the lexicon is necessarily nonphonetic, appear to make use of phonetic representation when their task involves recovering the meaning of written sentences and not simply words alone." Furthermore, if we restrict our inquiry on the reading of an alphabetic language, we can assume that "...there is an additional reason for supporting that the reader derives a phonetic representation from print. The (written) symbols are a cipher on the phonemes of the language. Thus a reader who uses the alphabet analytically, necessarily derives a phonetic representation" (Liberman & Shankweiler, 1979, p. 115).

Given, therefore, that STM is one of the cognitive prerequisites of reading and that phonetic coding is well involved in STM storage during the reading process, it could be assumed that good readers could be distinguished from poor readers on the basis of their reliance on phonetic coding. The experimental findings in support of this hypothesis have shown that poor readers tended to be deficient in ordered recall of strings of namable objects, letters and words, irrespective of the manner (visual or oral) of presentation. Similarly poor readers tended to fail in recalling the words of spoken sentences as accurately as good readers (Katz, Shankweiler, & Liberman, I., 1981; Liberman I., & Shankweiler, 1985; Liberman I., Mann, Shankweiler, & Werfelman, 1982; Mann, 1984; Mann, & Liberman, I.. 1984; Mann & Liberman, I., & Shankweiler, 1984; Torgesen & Houck, 1980; Wagner & Torgesen, 1987). Although the precise nature of the relation between phonological representation and the reading process and its development is not known, there are findings to suggest that the contribution of phonological representation is critical at the time when the child is learning and applying simple letter-sound correspondences (Gathercole & Baddeley, 1989).

In order to test the involvement of phonological representation in reading of the Greek language we conducted three experiments involving young children who were native speakers and readers of the Greek language.

Experiment 1

The objective of this experiment was to examine the involvement of phonetic representation in STM storage of written letter strings. The design of this experiment was based on the experimental procedure followed by Conrad's (1964) study with adults as subjects and Liberman et. al.'s (1977) study with children as subjects. The hypothesis under investigation was that the subjects who were largely relying on phonetic representation of letter names when retaining letters in STM, would face more difficulties and would make more confusion errors with rhyming letter names than with nonrhyming ones.

The subjects involved in this study were school children of Primary 2 grade, from schools of the Patras area, Greece. They had been selected in such a way as to form two groups matched in terms of chronological age and intelligence but differentiated in terms of reading ability level. The first group included *good readers* (n=18; mean C.A. = 7.8 yrs; mean I.Q. = 118.5) and the second group *poor readers* (n=18; Mean C.A. = 7.7 yrs; mean I.Q. = 116) The subjects' placement in each of the two groups was based on their performance in a screening word reading test.

The stimuli used were 16 strings of five uppercase consonants of the Greek alphabet. Eight of those strings consisted of letters the names of which were phonetically confusable (that is, they were rhyming names as in the letter string M, N, X Π, Ξ), whereas the other half of the letter strings consisted of phonetically nonconfusable letters (that is nonrhyming names as in the letter string B, K, T, Λ, Δ). The task required the subjects to recall on paper the *visually presented* (for 4-5 sec) letter string. Recall was tested under two conditions: immediately following the presentation and after a 30-sec delay. During the delay interval there was a discussion as an intervening task in order to prevent rehearsal.

The subjects' performance was scored with and without regard for serial position. In Figure 1, the data are presented in terms of errors over all serial positions in the letter string. The data show first that the good readers made significantly fewer errors (p<.05) than the poor readers both in immediate and delayed recall for every type of letter strings (rhyming and nonrhyming), except from the nonrhyming condition in the delayed recall, where the difference did not reach the level of significance. Secondly, the effect of phonetic confusability was greater in the good than the poor readers but it was significant (at p<.05 level) only for the good readers' performance in the immediate recall condition. Thirdly, the subjects of both groups made significantly more errors (p<.05) in the delayed than in the immediate recall. These results might be taken to imply that the good readers rely to a great extent on phonetic coding during processing and storage of linguistic information. This is supported by the absence of a large difference between the two groups in the delayed recall condition where rehearsal had been prevented. It could be assumed, therefore, that the good readers' better performance is likely due to the more efficient employment of phonetic coding.

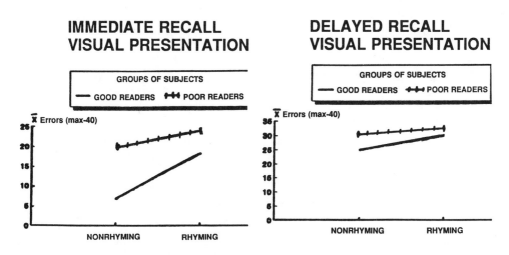

Figure 1. Mean error scores of good and poor readers on immediate and delayed recall of letter strings in nonrhyming and rhyming conditions in visual presentation (Exp. 1).

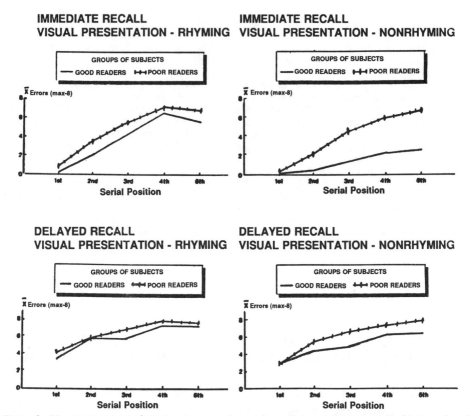

Figure 2. Mean error scores of good and poor readers on immediate and delayed recall of letter strings in rhyming and nonrhyming conditions as a function of serial position in visual presentation (Exp. 1)

Fig. 2 presents the data as a function of serial position of letters. From the top two graphs it is apparent that while the poor readers have had an almost similar performance in two letter strings conditions, the good readers' performance was differentiated in the nonrhyming condition, mainly in the immediate recall.

In summary, the good readers seem to be penalized by the presence of phonetic confusability in the letter strings. This may mean that they rely heavily on a phonetic code in STM. However this does not mean that the poor readers do not recode phonetically at all, but simply that they are likely to rely to a lesser degree on phonetic coding and that they may use, in parallel, other information as well. One way to clarify the nature of that coding difference in STM, between the two groups of readers, is to repeat the same experiment by employing auditory stimuli. This was done in the next experiment.

Experiment 2

The rationale of this experiment was the following. Since in the case of auditorily presented materials phonetic coding cannot be avoided, then it is likely that in auditory presentation all subjects may be "forced" to code the incoming speech signal phonetically. If, therefore, the poor readers' difficulty was specific to recoding the visually presented script, then the *auditory presentation* would be expected to give different results, and more specifically, to present the same difficulty to both good and poor readers. But if the poor readers' difficulty was mainly a problem of phonetic coding in STM, then the effect of letter confusability would be different in the two groups of subjects irrespective of the written or auditory way of stimuli presentation.

The subjects employed, the material used and the procedure followed in this experiment were the same to those of the 1st Experiment, except that the stimuli presentation was auditory. The results of this experiment presented in Fig. 3, show the errors over all serial position in the letter strings, whereas the results presented in Fig. 4 show the errors as a function of serial positions of letters. From these results it is clear, first, that the good readers made much fewer errors (p<.05) than the poor readers in both immediate and delayed recall for every type of letter strings. Secondly, the effect of phonetic confusability was evident in the performance of both groups of subjects but it was significant (at p<.05 level) only in the good readers' performance in the immediate recall condition. This could be interpreted as indicating that the poor readers' problem relying on the weaker employment of phonetic coding. Thirdly, the subjects of both groups made more errors in the delayed than in the immediate recall condition, but there was not a group by letter string interaction in the delayed recall condition. The overall picture of the results of Figure 4 was almost similar to that of the results of Figure 2 of the previous experiment.

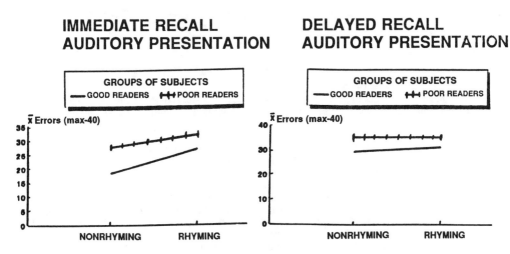

Figure 3 Mean error scores of good and poor readers on immediate and delayed recall of letter strings in rhyming and nonrhyming conditions in auditory presentation (Exp. 2).

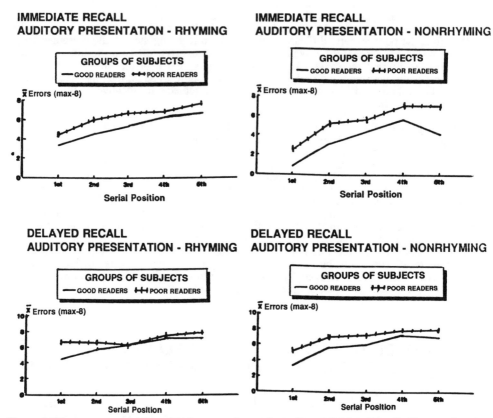

Figure 4. Mean error scores of good and poor readers on immediate and delayed recall of letter strings in rhyming and nonrhyming conditions as a function of serial position in auditory presentation (Exp. 2).

In conclusion, the results of the two experiments seem to indicate that, irrespective of the way of presentation (visual or auditory) of the linguistic stimuli, the good readers are likely to be more affected than the poor readers by the letter confusability factor. However, when the presentation was auditory (and especially in delayed recall) the confusability factor effect was not so different in the two groups of subjects. This may well mean that the poor readers' essential difficulty was in recoding the visually, rather than the auditorily, presented linguistic stimuli. The most probable explanation, of such findings is that the subjects of the two groups are likely to use differently the phonetic representation (especially of the visually presented information) in STM, and that in particular the poor readers seem to use inefficiently the phonetic representation. In order to test these conclusions with more ecologically valid reading materials, we conducted the next experiment.

Experiment 3

The objective of this Experiment was to test the role of phonetic coding in STM when words are used as stimuli. The experimental paradigm used was similar to that used by Mann et. al., (1980). Within that framework the aim was to test the influence of phonetic confusability on the subjects' ability to repeat 16 strings (one at a time) of 4 spoken words each. Thus, the testing material consisted of 8 phonetically confusable word strings which were matched to 8 phonetically nonconfusable word strings. The subjects employed were the same who had participated in the two previous experiments.

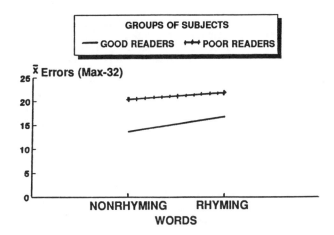

Figure 5. Mean error scores of good and poor readers on recall of word strings in nonrhyming and rhyming conditions (Exp. 3).

The results of this experiment are shown in Figure 5. From these results it is evident, first, that the good readers made significantly few errors (p<.05) than the poor readers, and, secondly, that the good readers were more penalized than the poor readers in recalling the phonetically confusable words.

The conclusion that could be drawn from the results of this experiment is more or less in line with the main conclusion that was drawn from the two previous experiments. The good readers, overall, seem to be more efficient than the poor readers in processing and storing linguistic information in STM. More specifically, since the good readers seemed to be more affected by the phonetic confusability factor, it is likely that their reading efficiency might be associated with their better employment of phonetic coding for linguistic information in

STM. In addition, it was also evident that the good readers were less penalized (in comparison to poor readers) when the linguistic stimuli changed from letter strings to meaningful words. So as the stimuli became more meaningful the qualitative differentiation between the good and poor readers became less evident. Whether it means that the semantic aspect of the stimuli minimizes the subjects' reliance on phonetic coding and, therefore, that the poor readers' problem relies mainly on decoding the less meaningful material is not quite clear from the present study.

Discussion

From the results of the three experiments it is clear that the Greek children who are good readers tend to be more successful than the poor readers in recalling strings of written or spoken linguistic stimuli. In view of these findings the question that arises is why the good and poor readers differ in their reliance on phonetic representation in reading. The possibility of a difference in the general cognitive ability and a deficiency of the poor readers should be excluded, since the two reading groups were matched for intelligence. The explanation therefore should be sought in other grounds.

One way to explain these results would be to assume that the poor readers either do not employ at all a phonetic representation in reading (and therefore rely on other kinds of representation in order to process reading) or that the phonetic representation that they try to employ is less effective. The best way to consider the possibility of the non-employment of a phonetic representation would be a qualitative error analysis (which is not included in the present paper). However, the poor readers were not totally erroneous in their performance, but they simply made more errors than the good readers. They seem, therefore, to employ a phonetic representation in their reading process which, however, is less well formed or less lasting than that of the good readers (Mann, 1984; Wolford & Fowler, 1984).

If this explanation is accepted, then the question arises as to the reasons of the poor readers' alleged less effective phonetic representation. In view, on the one hand, of Rabbit's (1968) findings that the stressing of speech perception by a background noise had some inordinate effects on STM, and, on the other hand, of Brady et. al.'s, (1983) findings that the poor readers made 35% more errors in identifying spoken words partially masked by noise (which errors could not be attributed neither to basic vocabulary deficiencies nor to general auditory perception), it seems probable that the less effective phonetic representation is likely to be linked to some kind of deficient speech encoding. This hypothesis was not directly examined in the present study. However, we need to consider, first, that the learning of the spoken language (i.e., the ability to perceive and produce speech) precedes the learning of the written language, secondly, that a relationship has been found to exist between the children's level of phonetic STM representation at the kindergarten and their reading ability in the first grade (Porpodas, 1991); thirdly, that the difficulty with phonetic representation at the pre-school level has been shown to be an antecedent of reading failure at the primary school level (Mann, 1984); and, fourthly, that there is evidence of the relationship between memory and success in reading and of poor readers' inefficiency in repeating nonwords (Snowling, 1981). Taken together, all these findings suggest that the degree of effectiveness of phonetic representation is likely to be related to spoken language processing.

However, the way in which speech encoding is likely to be related to the reading process is not easily specified, because the nature of this relationship seems to be a complex one. Nevertheless, it seems likely that the contribution of phonological encoding to reading development takes place when the relationship between letter groups and sounds are being acquired. Research findings by Gathercole & Baddeley (1989) indicate that phonological memory may be particularly important in establishing simple letter-sound correspondence rules, possibly in much the same way as in learning the sounds of new words (Gathercole & Baddeley, 1990, p. 358).

In conclusion, on the basis of the results of the present study, it seems that irrespective of the nature of the spelling system involved, there seems to be a clear relationship between the phonological encoding in STM and the development of the reading skill in children. If this is so, then there might be some important educational implications starting from the training of the beginner readers in phonological memory, involving the methodological procedure in teaching learning to read and even including the possibility of predicting reading failure on the basis of phonological STM level.

ACKNOWLEDGMENTS: The assistance given by the teacher G. Koustourakis in the running of the experiments as well as the kind understanding by the teachers and pupils of the schools involved in this study (from the area of Patras, Greece) is greatly acknowledged.

REFERENCES

Baddeley, A.D. (1978). The trouble with levels: A reexamination of Craik & Lockhart's framework for memory research. *Psychological Review, 85*, 138-152.
Baddeley, A.D. & Hitch, G.J. (1974). Working memory. In G. Bower (Ed.), *The Psychology of learning and motivation.* (Vol. 8., pp. 47-90). New York: Academic Press.
Brady, S., Shankweiler, D., & Mann, V. (1983). Speech perception and memory coding in relation to reading ability. *Journal of Experimental Child Psychology, 35*, 345-367.
Conrad, R. (1964). Acoustic confusion in immediate memory. *British Journal of Psychology, 55*, 75-84.
Gathercole, S.E., & Baddeley, A.D. (1989). Evaluation of the role of phonological STM in the development of vocabulary in children: A longitudinal study. *Journal of Memory and Language, 28*, 200-213.
Gathercole, S.E. & Baddeley, A.D. (1990). Phonological memory deficits in language disordered children: Is there a casual connection? *Journal of Memory and Language, 29*, 336-360.
Gelb, I.J. (1963). *A study of writing.* Chicago: University of Chicago Press.
Katz, R., Shankweiler, D., & Liberman, I.Y. (1981). Memory for item order and phonetic coding in the beginning reader. *Journal of Experimental Child Psychology, 32*, 474-484.
Levy, B.A. (1977). Reading: Speech and meaning processes. *Journal of Verbal Learning and Verbal Behavior, 16*, 623-638.
Liberman, A.M., Mattingly, I.G., & Turvey, M.T., (1972). Language codes and memory codes. In A.W. Melton & E. Martin (Eds.). Coding processes in human memory (pp. 307-334). Washington, D.C.: Winston.
Liberman, I.Y., Mann, V., Shankweiler, D., & Werfelman, M. (1982). Children's memory for recurring linguistic and nonlinguistic material in relation to reading ability. *Cortex, 18*, 367-375.
Liberman, I.Y. & Shankweiler, D. (1979). Speech, the alphabet, and teaching to read. In L. Resnick & P. Weaver (Eds.), *Theory and practice of early reading* (Vol. 2, pp. 109-132). Hillsdale, N.J.: Erlbaum.
Liberman, I.Y. & Shankweiler, D.P. (1985). Phonology and the problems of learning to read and write. *Remedial and Special Education 6*, 8-17.
Liberman, I.Y., Shankweiler, D., Liberman, A.M., Fowler, C. & Fischer, F. (1977). Phonetic segmentation and recoding in the beginning reader. In A.S. Reber & D.L. Scarborough (Eds). *Toward a psychology of reading* (pp. 207-225). Hillsdale NJ.: Erlbaum.
Mann, V.A. (1984). Reading skill and language skill. *Developmental Review, 4*, 1-15.

Mann, V., & Liberman, I.Y. (1984). Phonological awareness and verbal short-term memory: Can they presage early reading success? *Journal of Learning Disabilities, 17*, 592-599.

Mann, V., Liberman, I.Y., & Shankweiler, D. (1980). Children's memory for sentences and word strings in relation to reading ability. *Memory & Cognition, 8*, 329-335.

Porpodas, C.D. (1991). Linguistic awareness, verbal short-term memory and learning to read Greek. Paper presented at the 4th EARLI Conference, Torcu, Finland.

Rabbit, P.M.A. (1968). Channel-capacity, intelligibility and immediate memory. *Quarterly Journal of Experimental Psychology, 20*, 241-248.

Snowling, M.J. (1981). Phonemic deficits in developmental dyslexia. *Psychological Research, 43*, 219-234.

Tombaidis, D., (1987). *Concise history of the Greek language.* Athens: OEDB (in Greek).

Torgesen, J.K., & Houck, D.G. (1980). Processing deficiencies of learning disabled children who perform poorly on the digit-span test. *Journal of Educational Psychology, 72*, 141-160.

Triantaphyllidis, M. (1913). *Our Orthography.* Athens: Estia (in Greek).

Wagner, R.K., & Torgesen, J.K. (1987). The nature of phonological processing and its casual role in the acquisition of reading skills. *Psychological Bulletin, 101*, 192-212.

Wolford, G., & Fowler, C.A. (1984). Differential use of partial information by good and poor readers. *Developmental Review. 4*, 16-35.

Zakestidou, S. & Maniou-Vakali, M. (1987). Orthographic problem in grades 1 and 2 of the high school. *Nea Paideia, 42*, 80-93 & *43*, 98-110, (in Greek).

DEVELOPMENTAL DYSLEXIA AS A COGNITIVE STYLE

P. G. AARON   MARTIN WLEKLINSKI   and   CORA WILLS
Department of Educational and School Psychology
Indiana State University
Terra Haute, Indiana 47809
U. S. A.

ABSTRACT: In this chapter, the following cognitive skills are examined as potential contributors to developmental dyslexia: visual memory for orthography, visual memory for non-verbal materials, and processing skills of phonological and semantic features of the written word. Available evidence suggests that developmental dyslexia is the result of the utilization of an uncommon information processing strategy. No solid evidence emerged in the present studies to link dyslexia to weak visual memory or deficient semantic skills. It is suggested that it may be advantageous to view developmental dyslexia as the manifestation of a unique cognitive style rather than as a defect.

Visual Memory for Orthography and Reading Disabilities

The importance of phonology in the acquisition of word-recognition skills is well documented. There is convincing evidence to show that deficits in phonological skills impede the process of learning to read and that creating an awareness about phonology facilitates reading acquisition in children. Because poor word recognition ability is an important feature of developmental dyslexia, a weakness in phonological skill is thought to be causally associated with dyslexia.

It has, however, been reported that whereas phonological skill is necessary for the acquisition of word-recognition skill, it may not be a sufficient condition. This conclusion is based on the observation that some children, in spite of having adequate phonological skill, are poor in word recognition. It is thought that word-recognition deficit in these children is due to an inability to form adequate visual/orthographic representations of the printed words (Reitsma, 1983). This form of reasoning naturally leads to the expectation that deficits associated with the visual processing of the written word could also play a role in reading disabilities. If visual processing deficit can, by itself, lead to word recognition problems, the result would be a form of developmental reading disability, which is quite distinct from phonological dyslexia. The notion that there are subtypes of developmental dyslexia is not new. Attributing reading disability to weak visual and auditory memories, Johnson and Myklebust (1967) identified two forms of developmental reading disorders, *visual dyslexia* and *auditory dyslexia*. In a broad sense, Boder's (1973) *dysphonetic dyslexia* and d*yseidetic dyslexia* are comparable to these two subtypes respectively. More recently, in a longitudinal study of 190 dyslexic children, Gjessing & Karlsen (1989) identified children who committed reversal errors in reading and misspelled "irregular" words phonetically as "visual dyslexics". The possibility that there are two distinct types of developmental dyslexia is not a trivial question because these two subtypes of dyslexia may respond differently to different kinds of remedial efforts and, therefore, mandates a differential diagnosis. Such a differential treatment has, indeed, been advocated by Johnson (1978).

R.M. Joshi and C.K. Leong (eds.), Reading Disabilities: Diagnosis and Component Processes, 307–317.
© 1993 *Kluwer Academic Publishers. Printed in the Netherlands.*

Traditionally, visual perceptual factors were implicated in explaining "visual dyslexia". It has, however, been suggested recently that "visual dyslexia" may be caused by a difficulty specifically in forming visual-orthographic representation of words. For instance, in a case study of a college student with developmental dyslexia, Goulandris and Snowling (1991) concluded that the subject's reading and spelling difficulties were accompanied by visual-memory deficits which prevented her from establishing orthographic representations. In a study of college students, Stanovich and West (1989) also report that there are individual differences in reading and spelling that are caused by variation in orthographic processing skills.

Not withstanding the intuitive appeal of such a classification of dyslexia, little convincing evidence is available to support the view that subtypes of developmental dyslexia exist. It was pointed out by Guthrie as early as 1978 that there is little evidence for the existence of subgroups of poor readers. This situation has remained essentially unchanged till the present. In addition to the paucity of convincing evidence, the concept of " visual dyslexia" is further weakened by the possibility that an inability to form proper orthographic representations may be the result of insufficient reading experience. For instance, in their study of college students, Stanovich and West (1989) concluded that the development of orthographic memory is environmentally determined. Based on their studies of children, Olson, Wise, Conners, Rack, and Fulker (1989) also noted that orthographic processing skill is largely non-heritable. It is to be remembered that, by definition, a reading disorder that is environmental in origin is not considered developmental dyslexia.

The status of orthographic memory as an independent factor in reading is also not clear. For instance, it is not certain if orthographic representations can be formed and sustained without phonological support. This is evident from the fact that *orthography* itself is defined as "the graphemic patterns of written language and their mapping onto phonology, morphology, and meaning" (Henderson, 1984). Thus, the inability to process orthographic information may involve semantic as well as phonological skills, in addition to visual memory. As Ehri (1987) points out, visual image for a spelling pattern can become amalgamated with phonological and semantic features of the word. If this is the case, it is only natural to expect poor phonological and semantic skills also to affect orthographic skill. This leaves the role of "visual memory" in word recognition an open issue.

Investigators have, nevertheless, proposed some putative features that may qualify as visual components of orthographic skill. For instance, Berninger (1990) has identified spatial redundancy and sequential redundancy of graphemes in words as visual components of orthographic memory. In addition to these, she considers multi-letter units such as rimes, bigrams, trigrams, and four-letter sequences (e.g., ed, ing, tion) and word patterns (e.g., rag, bag, tag) also as visual orthographic units. Having these visual patterns in memory may facilitate skilled reading; but does it follow that not being able to retain these features in memory hinders acquisition of word recognition skills? The question then is, "Is there a visual memory for spelling patterns of the written word that is independent of the word's phonological and semantic features?" If so, " is it possible that the reading disability of some dyslexic individuals can originate from visual memory deficits associated with orthography?" The present report discusses the extent of contribution of visual memory, phonology, and semantic features of orthography to visual word recognition.

PART I: STUDY 1.

Procedure

The aim of this study was to determine the relative contributions of visual memory for spelling pattern, phonology, and semantics to word recognition.

A series of four word-recognition tasks was administered to 128 children from grades 2 through 5. Each task consisted of 12 target words and 12 pairs of test words. The child was asked to read the 12 target words silently and then select from the 12 pairs of test words, the one he/she had seen before. The target stimuli in task 1 consisted of nonwords and the test words were homophonic pairs (e. g., *dore - doar, dore*). It is assumed that this task cannot be performed successfully by relying on meaning because they are nonwords; the target "word" cannot be correctly identified by relying on phonology because the test words are pairs of homophones; successful performance, therefore, depends almost entirely on visual memory for the target "word". Stimuli in task 2 were "grammar" words and the test words were pairs of verbs such as *has* and *let*. This task can be performed successfully by utilizing phonology and visual memory for words, but not by relying on word meaning. Task 3 consisted of content words and their homophones (e.g., *sea - see, sea*). This task can be successfully carried out by utilizing the visual-orthographic and semantic features of the word but not by relying on phonological features of the words. The target words in task 4 consisted of content words; the test words were non-homophonic content words (e. g., *cat - dog, cat*). In contrast to the first three tasks, the fourth task can be carried out by relying on visual memory for words, phonology, or meaning as well as any combination of the three. Performance on task 4 was taken as a measure of word recognition skill of the child obtained under optimal conditions and, therefore, was used as the dependent variable.

These tasks were administered individually in a predetermined, randomized order. Each child was given descriptions of the tasks and sample tasks were presented.

Results

The data were analyzed in order to determine the degree of variance each one of the variables (viz., visual memory for orthography, phonology, and semantics) contributes to word recognition. A step-wise regression analysis was carried out with performance on task 4 as the dependent variable. Regression analysis showed that phonological feature of the word made the greatest contribution to word recognition with a multiple R of .23. The change it made in the prediction of word recognition skill was significant at the .01 level. Word-meaning was the next highest contributor; the change in predicting word recognition was significant ($F_{(2,122)} = 2.8$, P, <.043). Visual memory made little or no contribution and the change it made in predicting word recognition was not significant ($F_{(3,123)}=.01$, $p.<.99$). Even though phonology emerged as the major contributor to word recognition, it accounted only for a small amount of variance. This may be due to the small number of words used in each test (12 words) which did not differentiate the subjects well. It is recommended that researchers who use word lists have at least 20 items in each word list.

Discussion

The following conclusions are drawn from these data. Amongst the three variables examined, visual memory for words accounts for the least amount of variance seen in word

recognition skill. Phonology accounts for the greatest amount of variance; word meaning comes next to phonology. At the 2nd grade level, as compared to higher grades, word meaning played a relatively unimportant role. Word recognition at the 2nd grade level was barely above chance when it is dependent upon visual memory alone. This may be interpreted to mean that developmental dyslexia seen in children of this age cannot be confidently attributed to deficits in orthographic visual memory. This indicates that a subtype of dyslexia referred to as "visual dyslexia" cannot be reliably identified at this level.

It is possible that some children in grades 3 and above are deficient in visual memory for words which makes them poor readers. In order to answer this question, another analysis of the data was carried out.

PART I: STUDY 2.

Procedure

Children in grades 3 and 4 from the above study, who performed at or below chance level (i. e., a score of 6 or lower) on task 1 (visual memory for orthography) but had a score above group mean on task 2 (phonology) were identified. Similarly, children who obtained a score of 6 or lower on task 2 (phonology), but a higher than mean score on task 1 (visual memory) were also identified. Subsequently, their performances on a reading test, a language test, and a cognitive ability test were examined. Using these criteria, we identified 7 children as having poor visual memory but adequate phonological skill and 2 children as having poor phonological skill but adequate visual memory. The small number is due to the fact that many children with low word recognition scores performed poorly on both visual memory and phonology tasks. The reading and language scores of these children were obtained by noting their performance on the *Indiana Statewide Testing for Educational Progress* (ISTEP) test. This is a standardized instrument which is administered to all children in elementary and junior high schools on a statewide basis. A measure of the cognitive skills of these children was assessed by the *Cognitive Skills Test* which provides a cognitive skills index (CSI). It is a group-administered test with four subtests: sequences, analogies, memory and verbal reasoning. The Cognitive Skills Test is primarily nonverbal even though the memory and verbal reasoning subtests in grades 3 and above require some reading. The CSI is often regarded as equivalent to an IQ score.

Results

Data presented in Table 1 show that children with poor visual memory for words are poor readers. However, they are also poor in language and tend to have a below-average IQ (CSI index). Because of the low IQ scores, these children cannot be considered dyslexic. Their poor reading appears to be one aspect of their low level cognitive skills and cannot be attributed solely to poor visual memory. The two children with adequate visual memory but poor phonological skills are deficient in reading skills. Their spoken language skill, however, appears to be normal and so are their CSI scores. These two children conform to the definition of developmental dyslexia.

In conclusion, poor visual memory for orthography is associated with poor reading skills, but poor visual memory appears to be part of an overall cognitive deficit.

Table 1. Performance of children with low visual-memory/normal phonology scores and that of children with low phonology/normal visual-memory scores.

Children with Low Visual Memory for Words

Student Number	Scores on				Reading			
	Task 1	Task 2	Task 3	Task 4	Vocab.	Comp.	Lang.	CSI (IQ)
1.	6.0	9.0	9.0	11.0	45%	28%	40%	83
2.	5.0	9.0	9.0	9.0	40%	28%	14%	89
3.	4.0	10.0	6.0	11.0	15%	10%	27%	87
4.	5.0	9.0	4.0	8.0	26%	20%	11%	80
5.	5.0	10.0	7.0	8.0	10%	40%	36%	82
6.	7.0	11.0	12.0	10.0	18%	49%	46%	91
7.	5.0	9.0	11.0	8.0	46%	28%	39%	...

Children with Low Phonology Scores

Student Number	Scores on				Reading			
	Task 1	Task 2	Task 3	Task 4	Vocab.	Comp.	Lang.	CSI (IQ)
1.	11.0	5.0	9.0	11.0	33%	56%	55%	117
2.	8.0	6.0	9.0	9.0	42%	37%	53%	105

Nonverbal Visual Memory, Phonology, Semantic Skills, and Dyslexia

It is sometimes proposed that dyslexia in some children is caused by low-level impairments in the transient visual system (Lovegrove, Martin, & Slaghuis, 1986). A recent article in *New York Times* (Sept. 15, 1991) linked developmental dyslexia to sluggishness of the physiological processing of the visual system. Because such a physiology-based visual defect is likely to affect verbal and nonverbal tasks equally badly, a comparison of dyslexic children's performance on non-verbal visual tasks and verbal visual tasks can be used to investigate the possibility that a sluggish visual system underlies dyslexia. If some children are found to be deficient in both these tasks, it will implicate visual processes in the etiology

of developmental dyslexia. If dyslexic children perform as well as normal readers on the nonverbal visual task, but poorly on the verbal-visual task, then dyslexia can be traced to difficulty in the processing of some non-visual feature associated with the written language. Indeed, Vellutino (1979) reports that dyslexic children do not differ from normal readers in recalling letters of the Hebrew language, a script with which both groups of children studied by him were unfamiliar. A conceptual clarification is relevant at this point. That is, a distinction should be maintained between sensory deficits that lead to reading disability and cognitive deficits that result in reading disability. Such a distinction would place reading difficulties that arise from sensory processing defects such as scoptopic sensitivity and problems traceable to the parvo and magno visual systems in one category and developmental dyslexia in yet another category.

Except for some isolated reports, the existence of dyslexic children (i.e., poor readers with average or higher IQ) who are weak in visual memory skills but are endowed with normal phonological skills is not well documented. As noted earlier, in the present study, children with weak visual skills have global cognitive deficits in addition to visual memory deficits. An additional investigation was, therefore, undertaken to see if, among a small group of dyslexic children, there might be some whose poor reading performance could be attributed exclusively to weak visual memory.

PART II: STUDY 1.

Procedure

The same 124 children used in earlier studies were administered five different tasks. Task 1 required each child to name the color of 20 patches as quickly as possible. Task 2 and 3 required the child to read aloud two lists of 20 high-frequency grammar words and 20 content words as quickly as possible. The words in these two lists were matched for frequency and syllable length and words within each list were printed in different colors. Tasks 4 and 5 were modified versions of the Stroop test. In this task, the child was presented with the same lists of grammar and contents words, but was instructed to tell the name of the color the words were printed in. Before administering tasks 4 and 5, children were administered a trial task. All these tasks were administered individually. Reaction time (RT) was the dependent variable. This large group of children was used to collect normative data against which the performances of dyslexic children were compared. It was hypothesized that if some defective visual process is the underlying factor in some cases of dyslexia, these dyslexic children would be as slow in naming colors as they are in pronouncing words. If they are relatively slower in pronouncing words as compared to naming colors, then some property of the written language is responsible for word recognition difficulties experienced by these children. The Stroop task was utilized to determine the extent to which phonological and semantic features of the word interfere with color naming. The degree of interference is usually interpreted as a measure of automaticity with which words are processed; larger the interference, greater is the automaticity of word processing. The two lists of words used in this study differ from each other in meaning and not in phonology. Any difference obtained in the amount of interference when naming the color of the words in these two lists would be an indicator of the differences in the degree of automaticity with which the phonological and semantic features of these words are processed.

Results

The performance of the normative group on the five tasks is shown in Table 2. Data obtained from the normative group reveal some interesting information.

1. The time taken to name nonverbal visual information (color patches) is more or less constant across the four age levels. In grades 3, 4, and 5 the RT for color patch naming is somewhat higher than RT for word reading. This may be because uttering names of colors takes slightly more time than uttering function and content words.

2. There is a significant difference in the RT in word reading between the second grade and the upper grades. This may indicate that by the time they are in the third grade, most children have mastered word pronouncing skills.

3. At all levels, reading grammar words takes significantly longer time than reading content words, ($t = 7.88, p,<.001$).

4. At all levels, naming the color of both grammar words and content words takes longer time than word reading. This shows that word recognition has become a somewhat automatic process even in elementary grades.

5. No significant difference exists in the amount of interference obtained in naming the color of content words and function words ($t = .39, p,<.70$).

Table 2. Performance of the normative group on the five tasks relating to the Stroop test.

		Reading time in Sec.			Naming time in Sec.	
Grade	No.	content word list	grammar word list	color patches	color of content words	color of grammar words
2	31	16.45	22.48	18.04	32.66	31.37
3	27	11.70	13.73	15.74	22.14	23.20
4	34	11.55	14.65	15.61	24.08	24.21
5	32	12.49	14.83	15.95	21.97	21.40
Total 1:124						
Mean		13.03	16.42	16.31	25.13	24.95
SD		5.58	8.43	4.19	7.84	7.27

From this group of 124 children, and from cases referred to our Psychology Clinic, we were able to identify 8 children who showed a marked discrepancy between their reading scores (from the ISTEP test or Woodcock Reading Mastery Tests) and their IQ (CSI, or WISC-R) scores. Performance of these children in the five tasks is shown in Table 3.

Table 3. Performance of dyslexic children on the Stroop-related tasks.

Student No.	Grade	Reading achieve- ment	IQ	Reading time (Sec.)		Color naming time (Sec.)		
				content words	grammar words	color patches	content words	grammar words
1.	2	29%	106	22.82	30.45	21.35	31.28	27.55
2.	2	29%	104	13.25	35.11	16.31	39.03	37.48
3.	2	37%	105	15.94	17.92	12.80	29.78	30.62
4.	2	26%	98	43.67	55.48	16.76	37.75	28.24
5.	2	26%	99	27.66	46.66	18.01	36.79	27.63
6.	2	51%	112	18.96	17.73	20.33	42.97	30.96
7.	2	28%	109	33.45	32.96	25.04	43.52	38.92
8.	3	45%	106	11.02	23.05	18.76	23.05	21.59
Mean				23.34	32.42	18.66	35.52	30.37

The same procedure, but lists containing low-frequency words were used to assess the processing skills of six dyslexic college students. The data regarding their performance along with scores obtained from 14 normal mature readers are shown in Table 4.

The following conclusions can be drawn from the data presented in Tables 3 and 4.

1. Dyslexic children are much slower than children from second grade in pronouncing content words as well as grammar words ($t = 2.20$, $p<.03$; $t = 2.24$, $p<.03$, respectively.). Dyslexic college students are also slower than other college students in reading and more so in reading grammar words.

2. Dyslexic children do not differ from the normative group of second graders in naming the colors of patches ($t = .38$, $p<.70$). There is also no significant differences between these two groups in RT when they named the colors in which the content and grammar words are printed ($t = .91$, $p<.36$; $t = .33$, $p< .74$, respectively). It may, therefore, be concluded that these dyslexic children do not show deficits in the visual processing of nonverbal information. Dyslexic children are slow in processing only verbal stimuli. Even

though dyslexic college students are somewhat slower than controls in naming colors, the difference is not very striking.

Table 4. Performance of Six Dyslexic College Students on the Stroop Tasks.

Student No.	Age	Reading achievement (WRMT) W.A*	W.I*	IQ (WAIS, FSIQ)	Reading time (Sec.) content words	grammar words	Color naming time (Sec.) color patches	content words	grammar words
1.	21	14.0	9.8	90	10.0	15.1	10.0	19.0	16.2
2.	21	5.9	9.0	101	9.0	10.0	11.0	10.0	10.0
3.	33	9.7	12.0	98	9.4	9.9	13.0	17.8	12.4
4.	22	8.0	11.0	111	13.0	11.0	14.0	20.0	19.0
5.	25	3.7	8.7	93	9.5	10.2	10.3	20.1	16.7
6.	30	16.9	7.8	109	20.2	20.5	8.9	14.2	11.3
Mean					11.9	16.8	11.2	16.9	14.3

Normative data obtained from 14 college students

| | | | | | 8.5 | 8.6 | 5.3 | 12.2 | 11.5 |

* Word Attack and Word Identification subtests of Woodcock Reading Mastery Tests (Grade Equivalent).

3. A Within group comparison shows that dyslexic children process grammar words at a significantly slower rate than content words ($t = 2.95$, $p<.02$). Even though a similar difference is seen in normal readers in grade 2, it tends to diminish as children grow older and disappears at the college level. In contrast, this difference persists in dyslexic subjects regardless of age.

4. For the total group of 124 children from whom normative data were collected, no significant difference in the Stroop interference effect is seen between the color naming of content and grammar words ($p = .39$, $p,<.70$). Even second grade children from the normative group did not show a difference in the Stroop interference effect ($t = .91$, $p<.36$). In contrast, dyslexic subjects show greater interference effect when they named the colors of content words than when they named the colors of grammar words, the difference being

statistically significant ($t = 3.18$, $p<.01$). A similar but less striking difference is seen in the performance of dyslexic college students. These findings are interpreted to mean that dyslexic subjects are more skilled in processing words for meaning than for phonology. Because grammar words are not nearly as "automatically" processed as content words, recognition of grammar words becomes a relatively more capacity-demanding task. This may explain why grammar-word-reading takes much time for dyslexic subjects, regardless of age.

5. Because content words and grammar words used in this study differ primarily in their meaning, it is concluded that dyslexic children process words for meaning more readily than for pronunciation.

Conclusion

The studies described in this chapter indicate that, compared to phonologic and semantic features, visual memory plays a relatively minor role in word recognition. Investigations described here also suggest that dyslexic subjects can process nonverbal visual information as well as normal readers do. It appears, therefore, that some non-visual feature associated with the written language is responsible for the slow word-recognition of dyslexic readers. In addition, the Stroop interference study indicates that dyslexic children are more "automatized" for the processing of content words than grammar words. All these data link developmental dyslexia to a weakness in the processing of phonology rather than any deficit associated with the processing of cognitive aspects associated with the visual features of the written language.

Even though the number of dyslexic children studied is very limited, data presented in Table 2 suggest that dyslexic children have average or above-average memory for pure visual information. As a matter of fact, an earlier study by one of the authors (Aaron, Bommarito, & Baker, 1984), found that, in a long-term memory task, dyslexic college students recognized more photographs of human faces correctly than normally-reading college students did.

Interestingly, an analogy could be drawn between the two processing systems discussed in the present paper, (viz., phonology and visual memory) and the "sequential" and "simultaneous" information-processing strategies. Some investigators (e.g., Aaron, 1978; Kershner, 1977) have considered developmental dyslexia as a result of an imbalance in these information processing strategies. Witelson (1977) linked developmental dyslexia to an imbalance in the processing strategies of the two cerebral hemispheres. Geschwind (1982), after noting that dyslexic individuals can possess superior skills and talents in certain areas, described dyslexia as a "pathology of superiority". In view of the fact that dyslexia is defined in terms of average or superior intelligence, and the fact that in a society that is devoid of written language, dyslexia could not exist, a case can be made for considering developmental dyslexia as a *cognitive style* and investigating it from the perspective of a "difference model" rather than a "deficit model". Cognitive style has been defined as "consistent individual differences in the ways of organizing and processing information" (Messic, 1976, p.5). One of the nearly 20 or so cognitive styles is successive-simultaneous processing of information. Developmental dyslexia can be viewed as a tendency to depend excessively on the simultaneous strategy for processing orthography and to under-utilize the sequential processing strategy.

REFERENCES

Aaron, P.G. (1978). Dyslexia, an imbalance in cerebral information processing strategies. *Perceptual and Motor Skills, 47*, 699-706.

Aaron, P.G., Bommarito, T., & Baker, C. (1984). The three phases of developmental dyslexia. In R. N. Malatesha & H.A. Whitaker (Eds.) *Dyslexia: A global issue.* (pp. 1-44). The Hague, Netherlands: Martinus Nijhoff.

Berninger, V.W. (1990). Multiple orthographic codes: Key to alternate instructional methodologies for developing orthographic phonologic-connections underlying word identification. *School Psychology Review, 19*, 581-533.

Boder, E. (1973). A diagnostic approach based on three atypical reading-spelling patterns. *Developmental Medicine and Child Neurology, 15*, 663-687.

Ehri, L.C. (1987). Learning to read and spell words. *Journal of Reading Behavior, 19*, 5-31.

Geschwind, N. (1982). Why Orton was right. *Annals of Dyslexia, 32*, 13-30.

Gjessing, H.J., & Karlsen, B. (1989). *A longitudinal study of Dyslexia.* N.Y.: Springer-Verlag.

Goulandris, N., & Snowling, M., (1991). Visual memory deficits: A plausible cause of developmental dyslexia? Evidence from a single case study. *Cognitive Neuropsychology, 2.* 127-134.

Guthrie, J.T. (1978). Principles of instruction: A critique of Johnson's "Remedial approaches to dyslexia". In A.L. Benton, & D. Pearl (Eds.), Dyslexia: *An appraisal of current knowledge* (pp. 423-433). N.Y.: Oxford University Press.

Henderson, L., (1984). Introduction. In L. Henderson (Ed.). *Orthographies and reading.* (pp. 1-9). Hillsdale, NJ.: Lawrence Erlbaum.

Johnson, D., (1978). Remedial approaches to dyslexia In A. L. Benton, & D. Pearl, (Eds.). *Dyslexia: An appraisal of current knowledge,* (pp. 397-421). N.Y.: Grune and Stratton.

Johnson, D., & Myklebust, H. (1967). *Learning disabilities,* N.Y.: Grune and Stratton.

Kershner, J.R. (1977). Cerebral dominance in disabled readers, good readers, and gifted children: Search for a valid model. *Child Development, 48,* 61-76.

Lovegrove, W., Martin, F., & Slaghuis, W. (1986). A theoretical and experimental case for a visual deficit in specific reading disability. *Cognitive Neuropsychology, 3,* 225-267.

Messic, S. (1976). *Individuality in learning,* San Francisco, CA.: Jossey Bass.

Olson, R., Wise, B., Conners, F., Rack, J., & Fulker, D. (1989). Specific deficits in component reading and language skills: Genetic and environmental influences. *Journal of Learning Disabilities. 22,* 339-348.

Reitsma, P. (1983). Printed word learning in beginning readers. *Journal of Experimental Child Psychology, 36,* 321-329.

Stanovich, K.E., & West, R.F. (1989). Exposure to print and orthographic processing. *Reading Research Quarterly, 24,* 402-433.

Vellutino F.R. (1979). *Dyslexia: Theory and research.* Cambridge, MA: The MIT Press.

Witelson, S. (1977). Developmental dyslexia: Two right hemispheres and none left? *Science, 195,* 309-311.

READING COMPREHENSION AND RELATED SKILLS IN NINE-YEAR-OLD NORMAL AND POOR READERS

KEES P. VAN DEN BOS   HENK C. L. SPELBERG
Vakgroep Orthopedagogiek,
Rijksuniversiteit Groningen
Grote Rozenstraat 38, 9712 TJ Groningen
The Netherlands

ABSTRACT: This research investigates the general level of forced-choice and free-recall reading comprehension test performance, and related language comprehension skills, in groups of 9-year-old children from regular elementary schools and from special schools for learning disabilities. Language comprehension variables consist of scores on a vocabulary test, listening comprehension versions of the reading comprehension tests, and a working-memory listening span test. The special school population scores lower than the regular elementary school population on all of these variables. A comparison of scores on the language comprehension variables between (poor) reading skill-matched subsamples of the two populations does not show significant differences. Other comparisons are between the results of regression analyses on data of the two original samples of children and the matched subsample. The majority of the analyses shows parallel predictive regression patterns. The following conclusions are drawn: first, poor reading comprehension seems restricted by a lower degree of skill on the same variables that explain the full ability range of the normal population. Second, the majority of poor readers in the special and regular elementary schools needs extra instructional attention in the component of linguistic comprehension.

Introduction

If students in the early grades of Dutch regular elementary schools (RES) show severe achievement problems in the absence of primary emotional disorders or cultural disadvantage, and if their IQ does not warrant the classification of '(mildly) mentally retarded' (for whom there are also special schools), referral to a special school (SPS) for 'learning disabilities (LD) and educational problems' often follows.

With regard to the achievement problems of this group of children, the area of reading - especially *decoding* difficulties - has received much attention from Dutch researchers in the past two decades. However, less attention has been given to their skill in the other major component of reading, viz., *reading comprehension*, and to the relationship between this skill and underlying linguistic and functional memory processes.

A likely reason for this relative 'neglect' stems from the assumptions that (1) adequate decoding ability is *the* technical prerequisite for reading comprehension, (2) that decoding is the central issue in *beginning* reading (Perfetti, 1984), and (3) that reading-disabled children in special schools have 'normal' intelligence, which is usually defined as a Full Scale IQ of 85 or higher. The child's normal intelligence is then thought of as a guarantee for normal thinking and comprehension development. Thus, if the decoding disability could be remediated, reading comprehension should develop normally.

R.M. Joshi and C.K. Leong (eds.), Reading Disabilities: Diagnosis and Component Processes, 319–334.
© 1993 *Kluwer Academic Publishers. Printed in the Netherlands.*

Although we do not want to dispute the importance of decoding for reading there are good reasons for studying reading comprehension and its constituent factors in young learning disabled children. The main arguments are that even with normal IQ's some individuals may have comprehension problems which *cannot* be explained from decoding difficulties and which will *not* automatically disappear as a result from decoding training. Secondly, for almost all reading-disabled children there seems to be the risk of a developmental stagnation of reading comprehension skills which is due to less successful experience with printed materials. The stagnation will have negative consequences for vocabulary, syntactic and inferential abilities which are normally developed through the processing of propositions in written text. These problems, in turn, will prevent the child from acquiring the 'formal style' of language (Calfee, 1982b) that characterizes language in books, and which is functional in literate school discourse (Frederiksen, 1979; Van den Bos, 1985; 1989). Before considering early preventive or compensatory programs we need more direct data on young children's reading comprehension abilities.

The present study was designed to explore the level of reading comprehension performance and its underlying or related skills in 9-year-old children from special schools (SPS) for LD and compared them with 9-year-old third-graders from regular elementary schools (RES). We expected to find a significantly lower level of reading comprehension test performance in the former group of children. This prediction was based on (a) the generally reported positive correlation between scores on reading comprehension and decoding tests, and (b) the finding that random samples of children from special schools for LD always show significantly lower decoding performance than random samples of age matched children in regular elementary schools (Van den Bos, 1990).

However, this prediction only tells us about reading comprehension tests performance as partially determined by the variable of decoding, and does not inform us about the contribution of other variables that constitute more *directly* the reading *comprehension* process itself. In the next section of this chapter we will describe a model that contains some of these hypothetical variables. The question is whether these variables have different 'values' or 'impact' for children from special schools (SPS) and their counterparts from regular elementary schools (RES). We are not only interested in *quantitative* but also in *qualitative* group differences. Quantitative differences are defined as group differences in scores on variables, such as predictor variables and criterion variables. Qualitative differences are defined as differences in the predictive structure of the variables that underlie the criterion. If no differences of predictive or explanatory patterns of reading comprehension skill are found between the normal population (RES) and the learning disabled population (SPS) the view of decoding ability as a continuum (Perfetti, 1985) could be extended to 'reading comprehension as a continuum'. In the total population, reading comprehension differences would be more a matter of *degree* rather than *kind* (Perfetti, 1985).

A second research question concerns the following: In the previous paragraphs SPS and RES-children were distinguished, but it is not unlikely that also in the RES-population a (relatively small) group of poor readers exists. However, these children were not - or will not be - referred to a special school. Perhaps they lack additional school problems that may characterize referred LD children. We are not interested, however, in these possible additional referral factors. Instead, our research question is, whether there are any reading related differences between the population of SPS children with poor reading skills and the - probably small - subgroup of RES children with the *same* poor reading skills. Absence of reading related cognitive differences between the two (sub)populations would mean that, as far as reading is concerned, the distinction between schooltypes is not relevant, and similar remedial strategies and 'normalized' curriculum applications (Reid, 1988) would seem to be a logical choice.

Reading Model

Our assessment battery was based on Calfee's (1982a) model and associated assessment system (IRAS: the Interactive Reading Assessment System; Calfee & Calfee, 1981). Reading as a skill is seen as the interactive product of separable components, which can be measured independently: decoding, word definition, parsing of sentences, and comprehension of small and large passage structures. Calfee's IRAS allows assessment of comprehension through the reading as well as the listening 'mode'.

In line with the recent 'simple model' of reading (Gough & Tunmer, 1986), Calfee's components can be 'regrouped' into a reading comprehension model with two main components (viz., decoding and linguistic comprehension) where word definition and sentence and passage comprehension - provided that they are measured in the *listening* mode - can be treated as underlying variables of linguistic comprehension.

The idea of separability of decoding and linguistic comprehension will be further dealt with in the next section. In the subsequent section, the concept of working-memory (which is not included in Calfee's model) will be discussed.

SEPARABILITY OF DECODING AND LINGUISTIC COMPREHENSION

There are two assumptions to consider. The first assumption is that the processes of decoding and linguistic comprehension are different by their very nature. Decoding can be seen as a process based on rules, i.e., letter/orthographic pattern - sound correspondence rules (Gough & Tunmer, 1986). Linguistic comprehension, however, is a meaning-based process on the level of words, sentences and discourse (Gough & Tunmer, 1986; Perfetti, 1984).

The second assumption is that in processes of a very different psychological nature, there is separability or independence (Calfee, 1982a) at the level of individual skills. In other words, any combination of skill levels of the two processes is possible. For example, in some individuals a high decoding skill can co-occur with low linguistic comprehension, or vice versa. Despite this independence, there is a general trend of a positive correlations between decoding, linguistic comprehension and reading comprehension skills. This, however, can easily be explained by the way in which reading comprehension is measured, namely by means of a reading task in which both decoding and linguistic comprehension are necessary components.

Since our aim in this study was to assess and predict the 'comprehension component' of reading comprehension as 'pure' as possible, the question has to be considered as to what estimation procedures would be adequate. Whereas in several previous studies on reading comprehension the problem of a reading comprehension test score 'contaminated' by decoding is either not mentioned at all (see, e.g., Berger, 1978) or 'quasi-solved' (Oakhill, Yuill, & Parkin, 1986; Smiley, Oakley, Worthen, Campione & Brown, 1977), we think that 'purer' measurements are appropriate.

Purer tests of these processes, therefore, should not allow a decoding bias when measuring linguistic comprehension, and not a meaning bias when measuring decoding. Eliminating a meaning bias in decoding is usually done by using so-called context-free decoding tests or even nonsense word tests in order to avoid meaning contributions to the decoding of the single words. It is also possible to statistically solve this measurement problem. In the present study we will use a context-free decoding test, and handle the possible meaning bias by statistically partialling out vocabulary test contributions to decoding test scores. Furthermore, we planned to partial out scores on this 'new' variable from reading comprehension test scores in order to make these scores relatively 'decoding-free' and more purely reflecting comprehension.

READING COMPREHENSION AND WORKING-MEMORY

The concept of working-memory plays an important role in various reading theories, and it refers to capacity as well as to functional aspects of comprehension of sentences (Daneman & Carpenter, 1980; Perfetti, 1985). Empirical support for the relationship between working-memory and reading (and listening) comprehension can be derived from Daneman & Carpenter (1980). They report moderate to high correlations in samples of *adults* between scores on the listening and reading versions of a working-memory test and scores on reading and listening comprehension tests. Other studies, however, in which working-memory contributions were investigated with *children* have not always produced consistent results. Oakhill et al. (1986) report a study with 7- to 8-year-old skilled and less skilled comprehenders on a reading task. All children had normal word recognition skills. In a particular experiment, a working-memory test was administered to the two groups, but no differences in memory performance were found. According to Oakhill et al. (1986), this result suggests that impairment in comprehension does not stem from a defective working-memory. The validity of this conclusion can be questioned, however. The task used by Oakhill et al. (1986) was, in fact, a serial recall task with *lists* of four words or pictures. This is a rather different operationalization of working-memory compared to the one in Daneman & Carpenter (1980). Moreover, the task seems to be rather far removed from memory for connected discourse at the level of *sentences,* and this is the level at which 'local processing operations', that is, propositional encoding and integration (Perfetti, 1985), occur during comprehension.

It seemed appropriate, then, to determine how scores on Daneman & Carpenter's (1980) test are related to reading and listening comprehension in the present study's samples of young children at different reading skill levels.

Method

THE VARIABLES AND THEIR OPERATIONALIZATIONS

The reading model specifies the following variables: decoding, reading and listening comprehension, word definition, parsing of sentences, and working-memory. In the Interactive Reading Assessment System (IRAS; see Calfee & Calfee, 1981) the variable 'parsing of sentences' is measured by a sentence reading test. However, the scoring system of the subtest taps only "oral reading fluency..." (Calfee & Calfee, 1981; p. 9). We thought this operationalization is too far removed from comprehension, and did not include the test in our battery.

We will now discuss the operationalizations of the other variables.

Decoding

As stated before, decoding is defined as a rule-based and not so much a meaning-based process. Pure measurement of decoding should, therefore, not contain a meaning bias. In this study, a context-free decoding test is used, but since the words are still meaningful vocabulary-test scores will be partialled out from the decoding test scores. The context-free decoding test is a

Dutch standardized test (Brus & Voeten, 1973; b-form) in which the child is presented with a card with 116 meaningful words that must be read aloud. The test's duration is one minute and the child's score is the number of words correctly read. In the remainder of this paper the variable of decoding will be also referred to as **DEC**. The vocabulary test is the WISC-R subtest vocabulary (**VOC**). The decoding test score from which vocabulary will be partialled out, will be referred to as **DECvoc**.

Reading comprehension

This variable is operationalized by two tests: Reading comprehension-forced choice (**fc**), and Reading comprehension-free recall (**fr**). Reading comprehension (**RC**) test scores from which **DECvoc** will be partialled out will be called **RCdecvoc**.

The first reading comprehension test is a Dutch standardized test for mid-3rd grade children (CITO, 1981; form M3). The child silently reads three narrative and three expository passages of varying lengths (91-475 words) and marks his or her answer to 25 forced-choice questions with four response alternatives each. Four scores are computed

RC-fc	the total score for all 25 items;
RC-lit	the score on 11 questions that ask for literal information in the text;
RC-inf	the score on seven inferential questions, that is, questions about information that is not explicitly stated in the text;
RC-sum	the score on seven 'main idea' or 'summary' questions.

The second reading comprehension test is based on the passage comprehension part for grade 3 children of a translated version (Van Eldik & Risselada, 1988) of Calfee & Calfee's (1981) Interactive Reading Assessment System (IRAS). The test consists of two sets of two passages. Within each of the two sets, one is a narrative passage and the other an expository one. The passages' lengths vary from 110 to 147 words. In our test version the child reads one of the narrative passages and one of the expository passages, and listens to the other passages, or vice versa. After reading or listening the child is asked to retell (free recall) the passage. Responses to a passage are scored *per* element in a six-element structure (Calfee & Calfee, 1981; Hoover, Calfee & Mace-Matluck, 1984; Van Eldik & Risselada, 1988). Two points are given for correctly recalled elements, one point for briefly recalled elements and no points for incorrect responses or failure to mention. The next step is a probe procedure in which standard questions are asked about elements that were either omitted or incompletely or incorrectly recalled. Although we also administered and scored this procedure, we will only refer to the free-recall scoring in the present paper. Finally, it should be mentioned that children who scored lower than 20 words on the decoding test, were not given the reading version of the test, but listened to all four passages.

The foregoing makes clear that the children did not read the same passages that they listened to, or vice versa, and not all children 'processed' the same texts within the reading or listening conditions. In order to obtain a comparable score for each child, scores per passage were transformed into z-scores, after which the z-scores were summed. In order to avoid negative numbers in these sum-scores, a linear transformation was applied with a mean of 10 and a standard deviation of 3. The scores of the RES-population were the frame of reference for transformations of scores of the SPS children. Resulting scores from the free-recall reading comprehension test will be referred to as **RC-fr**.

Listening comprehension

The first listening comprehension (LC) test was based on a standardized test of reading comprehension (forced choice) for end grade-3 children (CITO, 1981; form E3). This test was shortened and adapted to the listening situation. A narrative text (241 words) and an expository text (193 words) are both followed by eight multiple choice questions with three response alternatives each. Four scores are computed:

LC-fc	(Listening comprehension - forced choice): the total score on all 16 items;
LC-lit	the score on 9 questions that ask for literal information in the text;
LC-inf	the score on 4 inferential questions;
LC-sum	the score on 3 summary questions.

The second listening comprehension test was based on the IRAS-version (Calfee & Calfee, 1981) which was discussed in the previous section. The resulting score for listening comprehension (which was computed in a similar way as the score RC-fr) will be referred to as LC-fr (listening comprehension - free recall).

Word definition

This comprehension element was assessed by the subtest Vocabulary (VOC) from the Dutch standardized version of the WISC-R test. Along with the vocabulary test, we also decided to include the WISC-R Similarities (SIM) and Information (INFO) subtests in the battery. From the scores on these three subtests each child's Verbal IQ (VIQ) was estimated by means of a regression equation which was computed from data of the appropriate age level in the norm population. The variable VIQ was included in our study because we were interested in determining whether Verbal IQ would add significantly to the explained variance of reading comprehension, compared to Vocabulary alone.

Working memory (listening span)

The listening span test is an auditory working-memory test based on Daneman & Carpenter's (1980) reading and listening span tests. The test contains five difficulty levels numbered two through six, which are presented to the child in that order. Each level consists of three sets of concrete sentences with an average length of ten words. At levels two to six the sets contain two, three, four, five and six sentences respectively. Half of the sentences in the test are 'true' and half are 'false'. The true-false order is randomized but approximately balanced within sets. The child listens to the tape-recorded sentences and is required to say 'yes' when a sentence is true, or 'no' when a sentence is false, immediately after each sentence. The end of a set is marked by a tone and upon hearing this tone the child must reproduce the final words of all of the sentences of that set. According to Daneman & Carpenter's (1980) scoring system, a level is given one credit if two or three of its sets are reproduced correctly and half a point for only one correct set. If the subject fails to recall correctly three or two sets at a particular level, the test is stopped in Daneman & Carpenter's procedure. The resulting score is called LS.

PLAN OF ANALYSES

The first main research question is whether differences in SPS- end RES children's reading comprehension performance are only *quantitative* or *qualitative as well*. The question of quantitative differences will be addressed by applying MANOVA's with Schooltypes as an independent variable. The question of qualitative differences is addressed in the following way: Are the SPS sample's scores on reading comprehension explained by different comprehension component contributions than in the RES sample? In other words: Are there different predictor profiles? Stepwise multiple regression analyses will be employed, with the variables RC-fc and RC-fr as criterion variables and various combinations of the other variables as predictors.

The second question concerns whether or not there are differences in the variables underlying reading comprehension between SPS-and RES-children of the *same* age and the *same* level of reading comprehension performance. Applications of MANOVA's with repeated measures (pairwise matched subjects are involved) seem to be the appropriate statistical technique for answering the question.

SUBJECTS AND GENERAL PROCEDURE

The series of tests was administered to 129 3rd graders (61 girls, 68 boys) sampled from eight randomly chosen regular elementary schools (RES) in the town of Groningen, and 81 children (22 girls, 59 boys) from seven special schools (SPS) for learning disabilities. Actually, this SPS-sample included the whole 9-year-old population of special school-referred LD children in the town of Groningen. The SPS children had the same mean chronological age (M = 8.9 years; SD = 3.6 months) as the children from the RES-group (M = 8.9 years; SD = 3.6 months). Tests were individually administered, except for the standardized forced-choice reading comprehension test, which was administered in groups.

Many teachers expressed the opinion that students with very low decoding performance would get too frustrated when they would be presented with texts in reading comprehension tests. Somewhat arbitrarily, we decided to require a minimum of 20 correctly read words per minute in order to participate in the reading comprehension tests. Under this criterion none of the RES students, but 50% of the SPS students were dropped from participation in the reading comprehension tests. However, all other tests were administered as described above.

Results

Table 1 presents test score means and standard deviations for RES and SPS students. Most of the RES means are based on the original 129 individuals (some children were ill at some test administrations). The data of the SPS sample are presented for two groups: the group of SPS students (n = 41) with a decoding score of 20 or higher, and therefore were administered the reading comprehension tests, and the group of SPS students (n = 40) who had decoding score below 20, and who were not administered the reading comprehension tests.

The remainder of this report will be restricted to comparisons and analyses of data from the RES sample and the SPS sample with 'adequate' decoding scores (n = 41).

A comparison between the RES sample and the SPS group (n = 41) with decoding scores of 20 or higher showed significant differences on the variables **DEC, RC-fc, RC-fr, LC-fc, LC-fr, VIQ, VOC**, and **LS**, as indicated by a MANOVA, $F(8,153) = 13.70$, $p < .0001$, and by F-values in univariate statistical tests, which were all significant (p-values $< .025$). The scores on question types (**lit, inf**, and **sum**) in the forced-choice reading comprehension (**RC-fc**) and listening comprehension (**LC-fc**) tests were compared by means of t-tests. Differences were significant (t-values higher than 3.09) except for means on **lit** and **inf** questions in the LC-fc test, which did not differ significantly (t-values .38 and 1.83, $p < .05$, respectively).

Table 1. Means and standard deviations for test results in all RES children (n=129), SPS children (n=41) who had a decoding test score of at least 20 points, and 'very poor decoding' (VPD) SPS children (n=40) who had a decoding test score below 20 points. Note: numbers in brackets represent maximally obtainable scores.

		Group	
variable	RES (n=129)	SPS (n=41)	SPS-VPD (n=40)
DEC	52.92 (12.81)	35.78 (11.66)	10.63 (4.78)
Reading comprehension			
fc [25]	17.31 (4.96)	8.85 (4.09)	
lit [11]	8.12 (2.35)	4.39 (2.40)	
inf [7]	4.81 (1.58)	2.15 (1.56)	
sum [7]	4.38 (1.72)	2.32 (1.44)	
RC-fr	10.00 (3.00)	7.59 (3.90)	
Listening comprehension			
fc [16]	12.58 (2.51)	11.66 (2.21)	10.37 (3.00)
lit [9]	6.87 (1.68)	6.76 (1.61)	6.20 (1.68)
inf [4]	3.33 (.82)	3.05 (.92)	2.60 (1.39)
sum [3]	2.39 (.81)	1.85 (.69)	1.57 (.68)
LC-fr	10.00 (3.00)	7.89 (3.29)	6.80 (3.19)
WISC-R			
VOC	9.73 (2.48)	7.32 (2.56)	6.67 (2.60)
INFO	9.93 (2.76)	7.38 (2.74)	6.88 (2.79)
SIM	10.17 (2.77)	7.32 (2.59)	6.95 (3.26)
VIQ	99.81 (11.35)	86.40 (10.86)	83.76 (12.45)
LS	.68 (.53)	.39 (.46)	.11 (.24)

DEC = decoding	RC-fc = Reading comprehension - forced choice
fc = forced choice	RC-fr = Reading comprehension - free recall
lit = literal information	LC-fc = Listening comprehension - forced choice
inf. = inferential questions	LC-fr = Listening comprehension - free recall
sum = summary questions	LS = Listening span

We will now address the question whether the reading related variables (**VOC, VIQ, LC-fc, LC-fr,** and **LS**) predict reading comprehension in the two groups of children in a similar way.

Table 2 presents the correlations between all variables. It is evident from this table that the RES group's variable list is longer than for the SPS group. In the section of variables it was stated that Vocabulary would be partialled out from Decoding, and the resulting variable from Reading Comprehension. Of course, this only makes sense if the correlations between the variables are substantial. Table 2 makes clear that this partialling out procedure was meaningful for the variables **DEC** and **RC-fc** in the RES group only.

Table 2. Intercorrelations of all variables for RES (n=129) and SPS (n=41) subjects.

Regular Elementary School Subjects

		1	2	3	4	5	6	7	8	9
1	DEC									
2	DECvoc	.94								
3	RC-fc	.40	.22							
4	RCdecvoc-fc	.20	-.00	.97						
5	RC-fr	.03	-.12	.50	.54					
6	LC-fc	.06	-.10	.50	.53	.47				
7	LC-fr	.04	-.11	.42	.46	.64	.54			
8	VOC	.35	-.00	.55	.57	.41	.47	.42		
9	VIQ	.42	.13	.62	.60	.41	.48	.47	.86	
10	LS	.40	.28	.32	.27	.17	.25	.30	.40	.43

Special School Subjects

		1	3	5	6	7	8	9
1	DEC							
3	RC-fc	.04						
5	RC-fr	-.26	.52					
6	LC-fc	.18	.40	.43				
7	LC-fr	.13	.39	.76	.59			
8	VOC	.12	.52	.47	.41	.47		
9	VIQ	.08	.52	.38	.40	.48	.84	
10	LS	.36	.48	.24	.26	.26	.31	.34

DEC = Decoding; DECvoc = Decoding with vocabulary partialled out; RC = Reading comprehension; fc = forced choice; fr = free recall; RCdecvoc = Reading comprehension with DECvoc partialled out; LC = Listening comprehension; VOC = WISC - R Vocabulary; VIQ = WISC -R Verbal; LS = Listening Span.

Next, a series of stepwise regression analyses was performed on reading comprehension test data for RES and SPS samples separately. Table 3 summarizes the results for the RES group's data. The first analysis used the variable **RCdecvoc** (see Table 2) as criterion, and the variables **LC-fc, LC-fr, VOC, VIQ,** and **LS** as predictors. The predictor explaining most of the variance was **VIQ. LC-fc** significantly increased the explained variance with another eight percent. The other variables did not contribute significantly.

Table 2 shows that **VIQ** was highly correlated with **VOC**. In order to see whether **VOC** would be sufficient, the regression analysis was repeated with **VIQ** left out as a predictor. Compared to the previous analysis, this resulted in only a small decrease of explained variance: in this analysis **VOC** and **LC-fc** explain 41% of the variance, whereas in the previous analysis **VIQ** and **LC-fc** explained 44% of the variance.

A third regression analysis had **RC-fc** as criterion, and to the previous list of predictors **DEC** was added. Again, **VOC** and **LC-fc** together shared the largest part of explained variance, but, not unexpectedly, **DEC** added significant independent variance.

The fourth regression analysis used the free-recall reading comprehension test (**RC-fr**) as criterion variable, and the variables **LC-fc, LC-fr, VOC**, and **LS** as predictors. The variable **LC-fr** was the best predictor, with 41% of variance explained. The variable **VOC** contributed another three percent to the explained variance. The other predictors did not contribute significantly.

The next series of stepwise regression analyses was conducted on the SPS children's reading comprehension data. The results are summarized in Table 4. The first analysis used **RC-fc** as criterion, and the variables **LC-fc, LC-fr, VOC**, and **LS** as predictors. Results in Table 4 indicate that **VOC** is the best predictor followed by **LS**.

The second analysis used **RC-fr** as criterion and the variables **LC-fc, LC-fr, VOC**, and **LS** as predictors. The results in Table 4 indicate that **LC-fr** is the best predictor, and **VOC** is the next best one.

Finally, we consider the question of whether there are differences in comprehension variables for poor reading SPS subjects who have the same age and reading skill as subjects from the RES sample. Using Spelberg's (1983) multiple matching program, twenty pairs of children were formed, one member from the RES population and one member from the SPS population. These pairs were matched on **DEC, RC-fc** and **RC-fr** scores. The RES members' means and standard deviations on these variables were 37.75 (9.57), 10.80 (3.91), and 8.64 (2.82), respectively, and the SPS members' means and standard deviations were 36.80 (9.93), 10.65 (3.72), and 8.85 (3.69), respectively. Table 5 displays the matched pairs' means and standard deviations on the comprehension variables.

A repeated measures MANOVA indicated no significant Schooltype differences on these variables, $F (5,15) = 1.01$, $p = .46$. Thus, there do not seem to be relevant cognitive differences with respect to comprehension components between SPS and RES children of the *same* reading levels.

In order to determine what the predictor structures would be in this matched-pairs group ($n = 40$), stepwise regression analyses were performed on the variables **RC-fc** and **RC-fr**, with the predictors **LC-fc, LC-fr, VOC**, and **LS**. Similar to the previous results of the total RES sample (see Table 3; analyses 3 and 4) **LC-fc, LC-fr**, and **VOC** were significant predictors. These findings are summarized in Table 6.

Table 3. Significant predictors according to stepwise regression analyses in reading comprehension measures for Regular Elementary School (RES) subjects.

Regular Elementary School Subjects

Analysis 1
Criterion : RC decvoc-fc
Predictor variables: LC-fc, LC-fr, VOC, VIQ, and LS
Result:

Var	R	R^2	F-change	Signif
VIQ	.60	.36	71.13	.0000
LC-fc	.66	.44	16.61	.0001

Analysis 2
Criterion: RCdecvoc-fc
Predictor variables: LC-fc, LC-fr, VOC, and LS
Result:

Var	R	R^2	F-change	Signif
VOC	.57	.32	60.01	.0000
LC-fc	.64	.41	19.05	.0001

Analysis 3
Criterion: RC-fc
Predictor variables: DEC, LC-fc, LC-fr, VOC, and LS
Result:

Var	R	R^2	F-change	Signif
VOC	.55	.30	55.39	.0000
LC-fc	.62	.38	14.39	.0002
DEC	.67	.45	15.27	.0002

Analysis 4
Criterion: RC-fr
Predictor variables: LC-fc, LC-fr, VOC, and LS
Result:

Var	R	R^2	F-change	Signif
LC-fr	.64	.41	85.26	.0000
VOC	.66	.44	5.37	.0221

RCdecvoc-fc = Reading comprehension --forced choice with decoding-vocabulary partialled out;
LC-fc = Listening comprehension - forced choice; LC-fr = Listening comprehension - free recall
VOC = vocabulary; VIQ = Verbal IQ; LS = listening span; RC-fc = Reading comprehension - forced
choice; RC-fr = Reading comprehension - free recall

Table 4. Significant predictors according to stepwise regression analyses in reading comprehension measures for Special School (SPS) subjects.

	Special School Subjects				

Analysis 1
Criterion: Reading Comprehension -- forced choice (RC-fc)
Predictor variables: LC-fc, LC-fr, VOC, and LS
Result:

Var	R	R^2	F-change	Signif	
VOC	.52	.27	14.27	.0005	
LS	.63	.40	7.92	.0078	

Analysis 2
Criterion: Reading Comprehension -- free recall (RC-fr)
Predictor variables: LC-fc, LC-fr, VOC, and LS
Result:

Var	R	R^2	F-change	Signif	
LC-fr	.75	.57	44.78	.0000	
VOC	.79	.62	4.57	.0400	

LC-fc = Listening Comprehension - forced choice; LC - fr = Listening Comprehension - free recall;
VOC = Vocabualry; LS = Listening Span

Table 5. Means and standard deviations of reading related variables in reading-matched Regular School (RES) and Special School (SPS) Subgroups.

	matched pairs	
variables	RES (n = 20)	SPS (n = 20)
Listening Comprehension -- forced choice (LC-fc)	11.90 (2.61)	12.25 (2.00)
Listening Comprehension -- free recall (LC-fr)	9.10 (3.50)	9.14 (2.97)
Vocabulary (VOC)	8.15 (2.25)	8.15 (2.32)
Verbal IQ (VIQ)	91.15 (9.65)	89.85 (9.80)
Listening Span	.30 (.37)	.43 (.41)

Table 6. Significant predictors according to stepwise regression analyses in reading comprehension measures for reading-matched Regular School (RES) and Special School (SPS) subjects

matched pairs				

Analysis 1
Criterion: Reading Comprehension -- forced choice (RC-fc)
Predictor variables: LC-fc, LC-fr, VOC, and LS
Result:

Var	R	R^2	F-change	Signif
LC-fc	.49	.24	11.81	.0014
VOC	.56	.31	4.05	.0514

Analysis 2
Criterion: Reading Comprehension - free (RC-fr)
Predictor variables: LC-fc, LC-fr, VOC, and LS
Result:

var	R	Rsq	F-change	Signif
LC-fr	.70	.49	37.11	.0000

LC-fc = Listening Comprehension - forced choice; LC - fr = Listening Comprehension - free recall;
VOC = Vocabulary; LS = Listening Span

Discussion

This study's focus is on the performance level on reading comprehension tests in 9-yr-old SPS and RES children, and on their performance on tests of comprehension components which predict reading comprehension, such as word definition (vocabulary), listening comprehension of passages, and working-memory (listening span) for words in auditorily presented sentences.

From the SPS group's significantly lower performance on the reading comprehension test and the majority of comprehension component tests, it can be concluded that the SPS group's reading skills (decoding and comprehension) are at risk in a fairly general sense. This does not only hold for the SPS group to whom the reading comprehension tests were administered. The other half of the SPS children did not participate in the reading comprehension tests (due to very poor decoding skills), but their performance on the comprehension component tests was so poor (see the data in Table 1) that one would expect an even larger reading comprehension difference with RES children than for their SPS counterparts who have problems in decoding but who are relatively better in it.

A small subsample from the RES group could be matched on (poor) reading skills with SPS children. How do these matched groups compare on comprehension component tests? The results suggest that the distinction between the schooltypes seems not relevant, as the groups show identical performance on the comprehension related variables.

The SPS children and the matched poor RES readers, as well as the group of very poor decoding SPS children, showed one positive exception to the generally poor performance on the comprehension component tests. The exception was the relatively good performance on the category of literal questions in the listening comprehension test (**LC-fc**). At first sight, this finding does not seem compatible with the SPS groups' poor performance (which also characterized the RES subgroup of poor readers) on the listening span (**LS**) test. Both tasks seem to require memory storage and retrieval of literal information at the level of words. However, a difference between the two tasks might be the extent to which they require a *'decontextualized' phonological memory*. The ability to memorize 'last words' from isolated sentences (listening span test) is probably dependent on phonological memory skills, and these skills are not well developed in many poor readers (Torgesen, Rashotte & Greenstein, 1988). In auditorily presented texts, however, literal information is much more embedded in meaningful semantic structures, and these basic forms seem to be represented by poor readers as well. This is not to say, however, that the more sophisticated forms of verbal processing (such as inferencing and summarizing) are also at the level of populations with normal verbal skills.

Group differences in the degree of skill (quantitative differences) were central in the discussion so far, but what about 'qualitative' differences? In other words, were there different profiles of predictors of reading comprehension between RES and SPS (n = 41 subgroup) samples? Regression analyses on **RC-fr** scores yielded similar results for the two groups. For both groups **LC-fr** was the best predictor, followed by **VOC** (see analysis 4 in Table 3 and analysis 2 in Table 4). The variable working memory (listening span) was not a significant predictor for either of the two samples.

Somewhat different regression structures were found for the variable **RC-fc**. In the RES and SPS samples **VOC** was the 'first' predictor, but the samples differed in other predictors that were significant. In the RES group, **RC-fc** was predicted by **LC-fc** and **DEC** (see analysis 3, Table 3), whereas in the SPS group the second significant predictor was formed by working memory (**LS**) (see analysis 1, Table 4). This finding can be interpreted as follows. It is likely that in the SPS group the combination of poor decoding skills, poor vocabulary and poor functional working memory processes (Perfetti, 1985) 'frustrate' the meaning context *in the reading situation* so much that even 'literal' questions (which do not pose a problem in the listening situation) cannot be answered at the level of normal readers anymore. Apparently, such a 'degraded' (Stanovich, 1986) reading process is better predicted (as well as restricted!) by lower-order processes, such as the phonological processes in the listening span test.

However, this explanation has been constructed after a result that was *not* replicated in another analysis, that is, in the analysis on data of matched poor readers from the SPS and RES samples. Here (see analysis 1, Table 6), the variables **LC-fc** and **VOC** were significant predictors, and this finding is analogous to the finding in the original RES sample. Therefore, poor readers' reading comprehension is predicted by the same comprehension factors that predict the score-distribution of the normal population.

Compared with the RES sample, the SPS group's mean scores were significantly lower on listening comprehension and vocabulary, and so were their decoding scores. This total pattern resembles more the *'garden variety'* (Gough & Tunmer, 1986) poor reading, which is characterized by poor decoding and poor language comprehension skills, than *'dyslexic'* reading (poor decoding and adequate comprehension) or *'hyperlexic'* reading (adequate decoding, poor language comprehension). Note similar diagnostic categories in Aaron (1991) and Van den Bos (1991). Instead of the terms 'garden variety' and 'hyperlexic reading' Aaron (1991) used the terms General Cognitive Deficit (GCD) and Nonspecific Reading Disability (NSRD), respectively, whereas Van den Bos (1991) used the terms General Reading/Language Delay and Specific Language Comprehension Delay, respectively.

In order to see whether actual assignment of *individual* performance to these categories would lead to similar conclusions as were drawn from the group data, 'poor' performance on the decoding and listening tests was defined as a score below one standard deviation from the RES sample's mean score, and 'adequate' was defined as a score within or above one standard deviation from the RES sample's mean score.

Employing combined standard 'listening' scores, and applying the 'norms' of adequate and poor decoding and listening to the RES and SPS subjects, we found respective prevalences of 72% and 11% 'normal' reading *component* profiles, 5% and 44% 'garden variety' (general reading/language delay) profiles, 11% and 40% 'dyslexic' profiles, and 12% and 5% 'hyperlexic' (specific language comprehension delay) profiles. Especially the observed prevalence rate of 'only' 44% 'garden variety' profiles in the SPS group somewhat mitigates the previous suggestion on the basis of comparisons of SPS and RES groups means, that the SPS group would show an 'overall' comprehension deficit. Nevertheless, it is evident that the majority of SPS children and a not unimportant number of poor reading RES children need extra instructional attention in language comprehension skills.

ACKNOWLEDGMENTS

The first author would like to thank the Netherlands Organization for Scientific Research (NWO) and the Centre National de la Recherche Scientifique (CNRS) for sponsoring his visit to the NATO ASI at Chateau de Bonas (Grant No. F 59-311). At the ASI a first draft of this chapter was extensively discussed with Linda Siegel, and we thank her for her thorough comments.

REFERENCES

Aaron, P.G. (1991). Can reading disabilities be diagnosed without using intelligence tests? *Journal of Learning Disabilities, 24*, 178-186.
Berger, N. (1978). Why can't John read? Perhaps he's not a good listener. *Journal of Learning Disabilities, 11*, 633-638.
Brus, B.Th., & Voeten, M.J.M. (1973). *Een minuut-test*. Vorm B. Nijmegen: Berkhout.
Calfee, R.C. (1982a). Cognitive models of reading: Implications for assessment and treatment of reading disability. In R.N. Malatesha & P.G. Aaron (Eds.), *Reading disorders* (pp. 151-176). New York: Academic Press.
Calfee, R.C. (1982b). Literacy and illiteracy: Teaching the nonreader to survive in the modern world. *Annals of Dyslexia, 32*, 71-91.
Calfee, R.C., & Calfee, K.H. (1981). *Interactive reading assessment system (IRAS)*. Stanford, CA.: Stanford University and Palo Alto Unified School District.
CITO-group (1981). *Toets voor begrijpend lezen*, leerjaar 3, 4 en 5 basisonderwijs. Arnhem: Centraal Instituut voor Toetsontwikkeling (National Institute for Test Development).
Daneman, M., & Carpenter, P. (1980). Individual differences in working memory and reading. *Journal of Verbal Learning and Verbal Behavior, 19*, 450-466.
Frederiksen, C.H. (1979). Discourse comprehension and early reading. In L.B. Resnick & P. Weaver (Eds.), *Theory and practice of early reading* (Vol. 1, pp. 155-186). Hillsdale, N.J.: Lawrence Erlbaum Associates.
Gough, P.B. & Tunmer, W.E. (1986). Decoding, reading, and reading disability. *Remedial and Special Education, 7*, 6-10.

Hoover, W.A., Calfee, R.C., & Mace-Matluck, B.J. (1984). *Teaching reading to bilingual children study.* Vol. 5: Reading growth. Austin, Texas: Southwest Educational Development Laboratory.

Oakhill, J., Yuill, N., & Parkin, A. (1986). On the nature of the difference between skilled and less-skilled comprehenders. *Journal of Research in Reading, 9,* 80-91.

Perfetti, C.A. (1984). Reading acquisition and beyond: decoding includes cognition. *American Journal of Education, 93,* 40-61.

Perfetti, C.A. (1985). *Reading ability.* New York: Oxford University Press.

Reid, D.K. (Ed.), (1988). *Teaching the learning disabled.* Boston: Allyn and Bacon, Inc.

Smiley, S., Oakley, D., Worthen, D., Campione, J., & Brown, A. (1977). Recall of thematically relevant material by adolescent good and poor readers as a function of written versus oral presentation. *Journal of Educational Psychology, 69,* 381-387.

Spelberg, H.C.L. (1983). *Computerprogram Match.* Technical Report, nr. BIVO-83-002-RP. Groningen: University of Groningen, Department of Special Education.

Stanovich, K.E. (1986). Matthew effects in reading: Some consequences of individual differences in the acquisition of literacy. *Reading Research Quarterly, 21,* 360-406.

Torgesen, J.K., Rashotte, C.A., & Greenstein, J. (1988). Language comprehension in learning disabled children who perform poorly on memory span tests. *Journal of Educational Psychology, 80,* 480-487.

Van den Bos, K.P. (1985). Learning to read and learning to think. In W.A. van de Grind & K.J.P. van Wouwe (Eds.), *Teaching thinking* (pp. 23-26). Leiden: Forum Humanum Netherlands.

Van den Bos, K.P. (1989). Relationship between cognitive development, decoding skill, and reading comprehension in learning disabled Dutch children. In P.G. Aaron & R.M. Joshi (Eds.), *Reading and writing disorders in different orthographic systems* (pp. 75-86). Dordrecht: Kluwer Academic Publishers.

Van den Bos, K.P. (1990). Individual differences in reading comprehension. In P. Reitsma & L. Verhoeven (Eds.), *Acquisition of reading in Dutch* (pp. 91-104). Dordrecht: Foris Publications.

Van den Bos, K.P. (1991). De definiëring van dyslexia volgens een eenvoudig leesmodel. In K.P. van den Bos & H. Nakken (Eds.), *Dyslexie '91* (pp. 23-41). Lisse: Swets & Zeitlinger.

Van Eldik, M.C.M., & Risselada, G. (1988). *De ontwikkeling van de leescomponententest.* Unpublished M.A. thesis. Groningen: University of Groningen.

Author Index

A

Aaron, P. G., 4, 8, 10, 13, 19, 20, 41, 46, 48, 92, 93, 237, 316, 332
Aaronson, D., 86
Abbott, R., 33, 35, 36, 37, 38, 39, 40, 49, 50, 87
Ackerman, R. T., 6
Adams, M. J., 6, 97, 98, 185, 238
Afflerbach, P., 66
Ahrens, M., 20, 22
Albrow, K. H., 99
Alegria, J., 147, 160, 179, 180, 187
Allerup, P., 243
Alsdorf, B., 35
Aman, M., 8, 17
Anderson, J. R., 117
Anderson, R. C., 64
Angle, H. V., 86
Applebee, A. N., 3
Aram, D. M., 75, 92, 93
Arnold, L. E., 80

B

Backman, J., 4, 14, 79136
Backman, L., 117
Baddeley, A. D., 13, 17, 94, 98, 227, 304
Baker, C., 316
Baker, L. A., 6
Baldwin, R. S., 72, 74, 75, 76
Ball, E. W., 6, 9, 146, 269
Balthazar, M., 151
Barneby, N. S., 80
Barnett, D. W., 88, 90
Baron, J., 6, 9, 240
Barron, R. W., 110, 118
Beaumont, J. G., 86
Beck, I. 6, 9, 150, 162
Beck, L. J., 105, 106, 108
Beech, J. R., 13, 15, 94
Beery, K., 35
Bell, L., 6, 150, 162
Belton-Kocher, E., 88, 90

Bentler, P. M., 38, 39
Bereiter, C., 119
Beresford, R., 201
Berger, M., 113, 114
Berger, N., 321
Bergman, A., 79
Berninger, V. W., 33, 35, 36, 37, 38, 39, 40, 49, 50, 87, 308
Bertelson, P., 147, 180, 187
Berti, F. B., 79
Bever, T. G., 106, 108
Bierwisch, M., 116
Billingsley, F., 256
Binet, A., 2, 116, 119
Birnbaum, R., 16
Bisanz, G. L., 152
Bishop, D. V. M., 179, 180
Bisiachi, P. S., 181
Bissex, G. L., 253
Blachman, B. A., 6, 9, 146
Bloom, A., 12, 79
Boden, M. A., 119
Boder, E., 10, 240, 242, 263, 307
Bohannon , J., 163
Bohn, L., 106
Boksebeld, L. M., 112
Bommarito, T., 316
Boring, E. G., 73
Borkowski, J. C., 290
Bowen, C. C., 257
Bower, P. M., 79
Bowers, P., 15, 18, 291
Bowey, J. A., 163, 164
Bowlby, M., 155, 219
Bradford, A., 201
Bradley, L., 6, 9, 13, 143, 144, 148, 152, 153, 155, 160, 163, 164, 165, 253, 254, 255, 256, 257, 263, 269, 208, 284
Brady, S., 6, 15, 17, 113, 148, 155, 162, 185, 219, 282, 304
Bragg, R., 38